The Public Health

Provided with the compliments of

Lundbeck

The Public Health Impact of Mental Disorder

Edited by

David Goldberg & Digby Tantam
Department of Psychiatry, University of Manchester

 Hogrefe & Huber Publishers
Toronto • Lewiston, NY • Bern • Göttingen • Stuttgart

Library of Congress Cataloging-in-Publication Data

The Public health impact of mental disorder / D. P. Goldberg, D. J. Tantam (editors).
p. cm.
Based on lectures delivered at the Fifth European Symposium on Social Psychiatry, held in Manchester in April 1989.
Includes bibliographical references.

1. Community psychiatry—Congresses. 2. Social psychiatry—Congresses. 3. Public health—Congresses. I. Goldberg, David P. II. Tantum, D. J. (Digby J.). 1948–   .
III. European Symposium on Social Psychiatry (5th : 1989 : Manchester, England)
[DNLM: 1. Community Psychiatry—congresses. 2. Mental Disorders—congresses. 3. Public Health—congresses. WM 30.6 P976 1989]

RC455.P83   1990   362.2'0422—dc20   90-4355 CIP

Canadian Cataloguing in Publication Data

Main entry under title:
The Public health impact of mental disorder
Papers based on presentations to the Fifth European Symposium on Social Psychiatry, held in Manchester, England, in April 1989.
Includes bibliographical references.

1. Social psychiatry—Congresses. 2. Mental health planning—Congresses. 3. Psychiatric epidemiology—Congresses. 4. Public health—Congresses. I. Goldberg, David P.
II. Tantam, Digby. III. European Symposium on Social Psychiatry (5th : 1989 : Manchester, England).

RA790.A2P82   1990   362.2   C90-093822-6

P. O. Box 51
Lewiston, NY 14092

12–14 Bruce Park Ave.
Toronto, Ontario M4P 2S3

ISBN 3-456-81901-3
ISBN 0-920887-65-1
Hogrefe & Huber Publishers • Toronto • Lewiston, NY • Bern • Göttingen • Stuttgart

Printed in Germany on acid-free paper

Table of Contents

Section IV
Prevention and Early Detection

Section V
The Organization of Services

Preface

Norman Sartorius*

An examination of the public health impact of mental illness at the end of the 20th century is necessary and timely. At least 300 million people in the world suffer from mental disorders, marring their lives and disabling them in the performance of their roles as parents, workers, spouses, neighbors, friends, or colleagues. Treatment of these disorders has made major strides forward; prevention for many of them—particularly for those related to an organic damage of the central nervous system—is now possible. And there is evidence that much can be done without waiting for the time when highly qualified personnel will be in place in all parts of the world. It is thus possible to act effectively now—and such action is justified and urgent if there is evidence that mental disorders and their control are of major importance to public health. This book marshals such evidence and is a call for urgent action to prevent mental illness or help those affected by it to live a life of quality.

In opening this array of evidence I shall attempt to draw some of the contours that mark the background of this effort. In so doing, I shall first refer to some of the developments affecting the practice of medicine over the past few decades; then examine the notion of mental health; and end with an attempt to show that there are areas in which mental health programs can be useful to public health.

With respect to diseases, humanity has never been in a better position than today. Life expectancy has been extended tremendously; pain can be effectively controlled; many communicable diseases can be treated with medicaments that remove the causal agents; many noncommunicable diseases— e.g. cardiovascular disorders, diabetes and diseases of the liver and kidney—can be offered treatment that prolongs life and improves its quality. Possibilities for diagnostic exploration have also increased immensely, and modern technological developments from fields as different as space travel and antarctic biology are continuously finding their application in health services.

Much has been achieved already—but not enough and not nearly as much as today's knowledge would warrant. There are three developments that are having an important impact in this respect. The first of these is the constant growth of strength in humanity's quest for equity; the second, the growth of disunity in mental health professions; and the third, the decline of public health doctrines as tenets for health care provision.

Poverty, prejudice, global or regional political interests, outdated cultural norms and habits, malevolent leaders and ignorance all conspire against an equitable distribution of knowledge and of resources necessary to vanquish disease. This has always been so: and throughout history there appeared social reformers proposing various measures to diminish inequity between the people in health services and other matters. The 20th century and particularly the latter half thereof has added a new dimension to these proposals: In addition to removing inequity between individuals and social groups within a country, there are now suggestions on how to remove inequity between countries or even continents.

This wish has become universal and has led to major conscious efforts to provide adequate health care even in poor countries, and even before general socioeconomic development makes all countries equal or similar in terms of services offered to their inhabitants. More so, the 1960s and 1970s in fact proposed that removing disease or attenuating its conse-

---

*   M.D., M.A., D.P.M., Ph.D., FRC. Psych., Director, Division of Mental Health, World Health Organization, Geneva, Switzerland.

quences can be a powerful contribution to economic development and social progress.

The provision of adequate health care to billions of people without money, trained staff, and in the presence of illiteracy, prejudice, and general misery is a challenge that humanity has not faced in the past.

In a first effort to respond to this challenge, medical practices of the richest countries were taken as a model and good-quality services were made available. For obvious reasons those covered mainly urban areas and reached a small proportion of the population. Nevertheless, it seemed that this was the right way, and that given a little more time and some additional resources, it would be possible to extend coverage, maintaining quality and using the same structure as in the well-organized towns of relatively rich countries. Soon it became obvious, however, that this was not happening: Mortality and morbidity rates for large portions of the population remained unchanged, and legislation about health care, where introduced, remained a pious wish. The cost of services that could provide care outside major towns grew exponentially with every hour of distance from the capital. Staff trained at a high cost remained in urban areas and devoted themselves solely to the provision of high-quality service to the richest part of the population. Traditional healers, often employing harmful techniques, continued to be the main source of (often inadequate) care in rural areas. In developing countries, classical public health notions did not seem to provide an adequate basis for action, particularly when it became obvious that general socioeconomic development can make a major contribution to disease control, and that, once this has occurred, high levels of investment into the health sector have no further impact on health indices. On the contrary, they seemed to be accompanied by a growing dissatisfaction of people with health care.

A change of strategy was, therefore, obviously necessary. It was embodied in the development of the concept of primary health care characterized by an active involvement of a variety of social sectors and by the con-

centration of resources on certain health problems to the exclusion of all others. Strategically, primary health care was clearly superior to previous proposals*. The way to its full success, however, was barred by two main obstacles: first, by the fact that most medical technology was not prepared for use in areas in which primary health care could have been most useful; and second, by the paradoxical necessity of matching increasing simplicity at the periphery with increasing complexity of management and sophistication of technological development at the center. Other obstacles were soon identified, for example, the unresolved ethical issues arising around the need to neglect certain patients' problems in order to be able to provide care to the majority; and the lack of acceptance of primary-care services by all those who could afford other types of services—also including, unfortunately, the community leaders.

For these and other reasons, primary health care in many countries became equated with second-rate care, reserved for the poor people; it lost its halo of efficiency and usefulness, and it no longer appeared sufficiently attractive for inclusion into the political platforms proposed to the population. Various attempts have been made to salvage the concept, for example, the invention of specialized primary care and the significant investment into research to develop techniques usable in primary-care conditions; but the battle has not been won. It is obvious that the primary-care strategy was an enormous step forward, but it is also obvious that the search for equity in health care—ensuring optimal care for the impecunious in the rich countries and the disadvantaged majorities in the poor countries—must continue. This search will continue to mark all health care and political reality: It will continue to be of particular importance in the care of those who lack advocates and require the full appreciation of humanitarian principles for their care—as do the mentally ill.

Never before have there been so many health professionals in the world, nor have there ever been as many members of other professions participating in the provision of

* Sartorius, N. (1988). Mental health in primary health care. *International Journal of Mental Health*, 17(3), 5–12.

health care. There has never been so much knowledge nor so many techniques that are necessary and useful in practicing medicine. Specialization of a significant number of medical practitioners is thus both desirable and inevitable. Similarly, it is to be expected that health-care institutions will multiply and specialize, and that the production of apparatus and medical supplies in general will require a narrow focus to achieve excellence.

But there are also negative and disagreeable consequences of this process. The first of them is that the distance between specialties grows, while the willingness of specialists to listen to each other diminishes. This leads to duplication of research and to inappropriate and increasingly expensive care.

Second, the distance between groups and institutions mainly responsible for service and groups dealing with research and training is also increasing. There is no sense of unity of purpose, and—much worse than that—there is disdain, disregard, accusation, and hatred, all too often highly visible and detrimental to the public image of both types of institutions.

Third, there is a major and increasing gap between the capital cities and the periphery. The previous relationship in which a single institution of excellence usually located in the capital of the country could impose a view about treatment or any other matter to the country as a whole is gone. Central direction has been replaced by negotiation, overall standards by averages of smaller groups. While useful in some respects, decentralization of authority and rejection of guidelines have also had negative consequences, for example, in monitoring trends in the prevalence of a disease or rapid introduction (or withdrawal) of a method of treatment.

Created many centuries ago, public health doctrines have been reformulated in a comprehensive and explicit way only relatively recently. The advice and prescriptions of many religions, which today could be seen as an expression of exquisite concern of the spiritual leaders for the health of the believers, have probably often been introduced into religious texts for a variety of nonhealth reasons. The prohibition of pork by religions originating in arid areas was interpreted for a considerable time as a measure against trichinosis. Yet the complexity of the causal chain for trichinosis was hardly common knowledge some 5000 years ago, and it is much more probable that raising pigs (rather than eating pork) was prohibited because of the extravagant quantity of water a pig needs to survive in a hot climate. Similarly, other measures that now appear as if they had been undertaken to protect the population from a disease were often the expression of political or economic needs that had little or nothing to do with improving the health of the masses. Only in the past few centuries has a reasonably well-composed set of doctrines been formulated with the explicit purpose of preventing certain diseases, prolonging life, extending working capacity, and reducing cost of care. In most of these doctrines, measures with immediate benefit for many citizens were seen as having priority over measures (regardless of the violations of human rights) that helped a single individual. Extension of life had priority over the avoidance of suffering or disfiguration that was necessary to achieve it. Prolongation of working capacity was seen as more important than improving the quality of people's lives. Prevention of disease and death was seen as a primary task for the State and for the services, and not as a responsibility of an individual; and changes of the environment were seen as preferable to requesting behavior changes from the individual.

Now, the pendulum seems to be swinging away from these public health principles, toward "individual" principles: The protection of the human rights of a few is often seen as more important than the health of the majority; prevention of disfiguration is more important than saving lives, so that doctors will not insist on, say, a life-saving but severely disfiguring operation. The quality of life is gradually becoming more important than its mere extension, and in many countries health services are delegating the responsibility for prevention of diseases to the individual.

In many countries, the departure from public health principles is accompanied by a significant decrease of interest and of funding for prevention and other primary public health activities as well as by a decline in the excellence of schools of public health. A new model that would harmoniously incorporate both individual and public health needs is yet to be formulated, important as it might be.

In planning action, it is easier to deal with conflict than with confusion. Confusion and vagueness about the concept of mental health have, for a long time, been a powerful reason for the low position given to mental health programs and for the difficulty of mobilizing all those concerned with supporting an overall program of strategy and useful action.

There are at least four pitfalls on the way to a definition of mental health:

- The first of these is to believe that mental health—or somatic health—can exist on its own. Health is indivisible. It involves and is apparent in mental, physical, and social functioning, which are interdependent. In English the word "health" has its root in the word "hâl," the whole, the integral existence of a human being, with a mental life. The words "mental life" in this definition refer to the fact that humans are thinking beings; that inner experience linked to interpersonal relationships—in other words mental life—makes them human, aware, conscious, alive. Mental life is not a state of being permanently carefree and joyful, blissful and elated; it has pleasant and unpleasant contents, includes worries and optimism, plans and regrets. It is a characteristic feature of human existence and cannot exist on its own in the same way that an individual cannot lead a human existence without it.

- Another pitfall, related to the first, is the belief that mental and physical disorders exist on their own. Mental disturbances can accompany, follow, cause, or precede physical disorder and vice versa. The words "physical disorder" and "mental disorder" do not mean that the malfunction is limited to an organ or function; rather, they indicate the predominance of signs of involvement of an organ or organic system. Both—physical and mental disorders—affect the health state of the individual, a health state in which various diseases and impairments occur.

- A third pitfall is the belief that health and illness are mutually exclusive. They are mutually exclusive only if health is defined in a restrictive way as the absence of disease. But health can also be defined as a state of balance between the self, others, and the environment. Such a state of balance can incorporate impairment: Health and disease or impairment in this definition are orthogonal to each other, rather than opposite. Health is always present, regardless of the presence of disease—as the skies are present in spite of the clouds on the horizon.

- A fourth pitfall lies in the belief that mental illness, folly or madness, and badness are sufficiently similar to forego a serious attempt to define and delineate them. Some individuals may be labelled with more than one of these terms. Some mad people are also mentally ill, and some of the latter may be evil. But the occasional co-occurrence of these characteristics in no way justifies using them as if they were synonymous. Mental illness, madness, and badness are not only different in meaning, they belong to different spheres of discourse. Mental illness is a term that belongs to the universe of concepts linked to medicine, health care, psychiatry, treatment; madness has to do with the perception of the usual and the unusual, with perceived norms of behavior; and badness with accepted ethics of society, morals, deontology, and so forth. It is of cardinal importance to keep these terms separate. If mentally ill people are seen as ill (rather than as mad or bad), it is easier to seek ways of providing them with appropriate health or other services; the mad, the unusual, and extraordinary can then be better understood; and the bad ones can be dealt with more easily, in socially appropriate ways.

Seen in this light, mental health programs must be sharply different from clinical psychiatry. Psychiatry deals with the prevention, diagnosis, and treatment of a mental disorder. It does so predominantly in a clinical setting, working with individual patients and their immediate surroundings, for example, their families. Mental health programs, on the other hand, are concerned with the ways and means of reducing psychiatric disorders in the population. Furthermore, and perhaps more importantly, mental health policies and programs must ensure that mental health sciences contribute to the control of other diseases and to the harmonious development of humans in their rapidly changing societies. Mental health programs thus have a vastly different set of responsibilities and interests, and must involve a variety of other social sectors, such as education, welfare, and justice, in implementing their tasks.

So defined, mental health programs can be useful in the process of medical practice and in socioeconomic development in general, in at least four ways:

- First, they can help in improving the treatment of mental illness and psychological distress in general health care facilities. As much as 20% of all contacts with general health care services occur primarily because of a psychological disorder. Most of these problems remain unrecognized; they are often handled inappropriately, causing unnecessary cost and suffering. Relatively brief training can change this situation dramatically. Such training can also improve the skills of medical practitioners in dealing with psychological problems arising in association with somatic disorders and thus significantly enhance their effectiveness.

- Second, mental health programs could be helpful in returning the soul to medicine. They could advocate and provide the necessary skills to diminish the current trend of dehumanization of medicine.

  Investment into health care has grown constantly in many countries, particularly in developed ones. It has reached worrying proportions, taking up to 10% of the gross national product. Machines, ranging from electronic pulse measurement to nuclear magnetic resonance apparatus, are making their appearance even in the poorest countries. Training in the minutiae of immunology, neurogenetics, and many other highly sophisticated topics attracts most medical students and usually results in reducing the time and interest for interpersonal interaction and attention to the crucial role that human contacts can play in health care.

  In spite of the high and constantly growing cost of medical care, the population's satisfaction with treatment and services received is decreasing. Nor are personnel in health services satisfied with their roles and professional work. There is a continuous flux of doctors, nurses, and others from clinical work toward laboratories, lucrative "office" forms of medicine, jobs in education, and part-time occupations.

  Certain forms of work, of course, are particularly stressful. For understandable reasons, these include geriatrics, terminal-illness and burn-injury wards. Psychological disorders (as well as turnover) of staff in such units are high, but similar phenomena also appear in other wards. The complaints of staff usually center on the fragmentation of their role in relation to the patient. Other reported reasons for dissatisfaction invoke conditions of work, though these probably reflect the basic lack of the feeling of purpose, of being useful.

  In all three situations—improving the relations between doctors and patients, preventing "burn-out" phenomena and dissatisfaction of health staff, and counteracting overreliance on machines and excessive cost increase—mental health programs have specific advice and skills to offer. Unfortunately they are rarely consulted, and when consulted, they are sometimes reluctant to offer advice.

- Third, mental health programs have developed methods that should be used in medical practice outside psychiatry. These include methods to measure quality of life and its changes under the influence of treat- ment; methods to assess lifestyles and behavior likely to play a causative role in the occurrence of diseases; methods to assess satisfaction of the population and health care providers with a particular service or treatment regimen; methods that can be used in changing health-damaging behavioral patterns; and many others. In this area, mental health programs can also serve as bridges between medicine and the behavioral sciences, bridges that can help both of these vast groups of disciplines to better utilize the fund of knowledge they have accumulated.

- Finally, mental health programs can help in thinking about ways in which health can be understood and promoted, about ways in which it can be placed higher on the scale of values of individuals and societies. This is absolutely essential and a main factor in ensuring that people will undertake measures that will prevent disease; that they acquire strength to cope with it if it occurs in themselves or in their family; that they actively participate in decisions about developments that will respect human principles; and that they understand that health is a dimension of human existence and not a commodity that can be purchased, sold, or industrially produced.

However, none of these tasks can be successfully attempted if mental health programs do not find a way of involving other disciplines and sectors in their actions, and if the leaders of these programs do not accept public health principles as the framework for their effort. This book may help to convince them that mental health programs are basically and intrinsically an integral and useful part of societies' effort to reduce disease and enhance the quality of life of their populations—of societies' efforts to promote public health.

Section I

The Public Health Approach to Mental Disorder

The chapters in this book are all based on lectures delivered to the Fifth European Symposium on Social Psychiatry, which was held in Manchester, United Kingdom, in April, 1989. The chairman of the AEP Section Committee on Social Psychiatry and Epidemiology was Professor Heinz Hafner of Mannheim, Germany, and the meeting took place under his chairmanship. The theme of the conference was directly relevant to the aims and activities of the WHO program in mental health, which made it possible to propose this book for the joint aegis of the Association of European Psychiatrists and the World Health Organization.

We have chosen papers to ensure that the whole range of the public health approach can be illustrated. The two chapters in this section are based on the opening plenary session, where a psychiatrist and an expert in public health each reviewed the field from his own standpoint.

In a thoughtful opening chapter, Assen Jablensky sees the major achievement of social psychiatry as being its success in putting mental health care into the orbit of public health. However, public health is itself seen as being in a state of crisis, since a longer life-span means more survive for chronic disease; public health action which works in the West is not always appropriate for the developing world; a global ecological crisis could bring new major health hazards; and the AIDS epidemic indicates a fundamental conflict between public health imperatives and human rights. To this list might be added the increasing numbers of refugees in every part of the world who may be at particular risk of ill-health, including psychological ill-health, and whose concentration and numbers in

camps or other temporary situations makes extraordinary demands on services; and the disruption of extended family networks brought about not only by these gross social upheavals, but more insidiously and even more thoroughly by urbanization.

Jablensky sees the crisis in public health as being inextricably related to problems in social psychiatry. He discerns two major shortcomings that have contributed to our present problems. First, there has been an expansionist attitude, exemplified both in overarching claims to be able to resolve major social problems using psychiatric concepts and techniques, and in the selective presentation of epidemiological data to suggest massive unmet need for mental illness services; and second, there has been a lack of demonstrable success in preventing mental illness. Part of the explanation for the latter deficiency is seen to be the relative underdevelopment of the methodology for evaluating the effects of intervention—a point to which we return in our introduction to Section V. Jablensky identifies our modest progress in understanding the social matrix in which mental illness occurs as being an important contributory factor to the gap which yawns between our claims and our achievements.

Writing from the standpoint of an expert in community medicine, Walter Holland defines public health as a practical specialty concerned with the application of population-based research findings in an attempt to cure or prevent disease and to allocate resources appropriately. He criticises the efforts of psychiatrists to contribute to the field on the grounds that the validity of our diagnoses is questionable and risk factors have not been unequivocally determined, so that a large part of the variance of the cause of mental disorders is unknown.

These are harsh criticisms. It is true that the validity of psychiatric diagnoses needs further improvement; but the problems are being addressed (Robins et al., 1989; Grayson et al., 1990). It is not really clear that they are all that different from those confronting investigators 25 years ago in elucidating the causes of coronary heart disease, where risk factors had also not been determined, and where a great deal of the variance of cause was unknown—except, that is, in the amount of resource that society has been prepared to devote to researching the problems of mental disorders compared to heart disease. In our view, the problems are inherently soluble.

We are pleased to include four chapters in this volume that address risk factors in mental disorder, but agree that much remains to be done. We also agree that further work must be done in identifying "at risk" groups, although we heard at the Symposium about work by Cox and his colleagues in preventing episodes of puerperal depression (Holden, Sagovsky & Cox, 1989), and are aware of work on preventing episodes of relapse in schizophrenics which exemplify the sort of work that should be done (Herz et al., 1988).

Holland concludes that it is for psychiatrists interested in research to come up with better models of how to prevent disease and its progression, and he advises us to use epidemiological designs that enable testable hypotheses to be examined. We suspect that this advice is easier to give than to act upon. Most research teams that undertake major surveys have the wit to include measurement of possible aetiological variables; but there are problems about including variables which take a long time to assess in a large-scale survey. Examples of this would be the time necessary to assess life events using the *Life Events and Difficulties Schedule* (LEDS), or to measure Expressed Emotion. Both of these instruments have now been used in numerous research designs, but neither can be included in large scale surveys.

Despite his earlier reservations, Jablensky concludes his chapter by stating his own faith in a future preventive orientation, but correctly notes that the extent to which preventive schemes will come about will depend upon the priorities which such activities are accorded by society.

Jablensky's and Holland's conclusions, taken together, present a formidable challenge to psychiatry: not only must we increase our public health contribution, but it must be shown to be effective in order for that greater priority is given to the next generation of preventative treatments and research strategies.

Section II of the book is devoted to papers concerning mental disorders in primary care and general medical settings. Many of the speakers at the Symposium referred to the "Goldberg-Huxley Model" when discussing this topic, so we have taken the opportunity of describing the model in our introduction to this section. This model is often used to buttress the expansionist claims referred to by Jablensky. It is perhaps important to re-iterate that the model was not originally proposed with this end in mind; rather, its purpose was to strengthen the case for better recognition and treatment of common psychological disorders by family doctors. The main service implications were not a vast expansion of the mental illness services, but the provision of better training courses for family doctors as well as better coordination between family doctors and specialist nurses and social workers. However, Jablensky is correct in asserting that data from the model have often been used in a way that was not intended at the time the model was proposed.

Section III concerns the public health approach as it applies to specific conditions. We have not included schizophrenia here—although we recognize its great public health importance—since we have included a major contribution on schizophrenia in a later section illustrating tertiary prevention. We have therefore written a somewhat longer introductory section ourselves about schizophrenia. Inevitably, we were not able to cover the entire range of mental disorders, but we believe that we have been able to include those conditions which are of major public health importance. In view of the enormous public health importance of AIDS, we have taken the unusual step of including two chapters, one dealing with basic epidemiology and probing the relationship to drug dependency, the other dealing with psychological and social aspects of AIDS.

Section IV deals with prevention and contains four chapters dealing with attempts to focus more closely on possible aetiological factors in mental disorder as well as two chapters on secondary prevention in the form of case ascertainment by GPs. The last chapter in this section illustrates tertiary prevention and describes the Finnish National Schizophrenia Project.

Finally, Section V deals with the organisation and evaluation of services and includes contributions about community services for acute psychiatry, a system of support groups for relatives of patients with schizophrenia, service use by old people, the relationship between primary care and mental illness services, and a general review of planning and evaluation.

References

Grayson, D., Bridges, K., Cook, D., & Goldberg, D. P. (in press). The validity of diagnostic systems for common mental disorders: A comparison between the ID-Catego and DSM-3 systems. *Psychological Medicine, 20*.

Herz, M.I., Glazer, W.M., Mostert, M., & Hafez, H. (1988). *Intermittent medication in schizophrenia.* Paper for the 141st Annual Meeting of the American Psychiatric Association, Montreal, May 10th.

Holden, J. M., Sagovsky, R., & Cox, J. L. (1989). Counselling in general practice settings: A controlled study of health visitor intervention in the treatment of past-natal depression. *British Medical Journal, 298*, 223–226.

Robins, L., & Barrett, J. (1989). *The validity of psychiatric diagnosis.* New York: Raven Press.

Chapter 1
Public Health Aspects of Social Psychiatry

Assen Jablensky

In a recent paper, Sartorius (1988) predicted the imminent collective demise of social, epidemiological, biological and dynamic psychiatry, arguing that the different "special" versions of the subject have outlived their usefulness and must now "be handled in the broader context of efforts to promote public health." Yet the very fact that this forecast, ominous as it is for the future of a score of journals, academic chairs, international associations and symposia, appeared in the concluding chapter of a newly published *Handbook of Social Psychiatry* makes one wonder if the health of the discipline is indeed in such a peril. Publishers of handbooks count on a sufficiently long half-life of demand for their product, and the marketplace usually is a dependable indicator of the trends and undercurrents that determine the future of a scientific discipline.

If a new handbook can be regarded as an updated map of a scientific field, a glance at the chapter titles of the above-mentioned one (which range from psychiatric disorders in primary care to the social psychiatry of later life or the biological sequelae of adverse experiences) should lead to the conclusion that, if anything, the concerns of social psychiatry in the late 1980s are broader and more diverse than in the 1950s or 1960s. However, it is precisely this diversity that betrays an identity crisis and a change of direction.

It can be argued that both social psychiatry and public health are experiencing a crisis (in the sense of approaching a turning point rather than a "moment of danger and suspense," as the *Concise Oxford Dictionary* defines the second meaning of the word). The process could already be sensed in the 1970s but it gathered momentum in the 1980s, acquiring also some of the features of a millennial "Zeitgeist." Undoubtedly, the World Health Organization's crusade for "Health for All by the Year 2000" is both a reflection of, and a contributing factor to, the emerging changes in the theory and practice of public health and, by implication, of social psychiatry.

The Relationship Between Public Health and Social Psychiatry

Public health and social psychiatry are terms that are often taken for granted, and their contents are rarely defined. However, if we claim that they both are undergoing change and wish to examine their mutual relationship in the process of change, some anchoring definitions are required.

The "classic" definition of public health describes the subject as

> the science and art of preventing disease, prolonging life and promoting physical health and efficiency through organised community efforts for the sanitation of the environment, the control of community infections, the education of the individual in principles of personal hygiene, the organization of medical and nursing service for the early diagnosing and preventive treatment of disease, and the development of the social machinery which will ensure to every individual in the community a standard of living adequate for the maintenance of health (Winslow, 1951).

As pointed out by Ryle (1948), public health placed the emphasis on the environment, while its sister discipline of social medicine derives

> its inspiration more from the field of clinical experience and . . . places the emphasis on man, and endeavours to study him in and in relation to his environment.

Social psychiatry, according to the fifth edition of the *Psychiatric Dictionary* (Campbell, 1981) is characterised by the stress laid on the environmental influences and the impact of the social group on the individual ... not only with regard to aetiology, but also for purposes of treatment and, more important, in preventive work.

As early as 1943, the Royal College of Physicians adopted the view that the relationship between psychiatry and social medicine was like "the inside and outside of the same glove" (Interim Report of the Committee on Psychological Medicine, 1943). Social psychiatry, therefore, evolved within the broad context of social medicine, and from the beginning, the epidemiological approach to mental health problems has constituted its strongest nexus to public health. The general paradigm has its roots in the thought and deed of Rudolf Virchow who sought to reform medicine on the basis of four principles (Eisenberg, 1984):

1) the health of the people is a matter of direct social concern;

2) social and economic conditions have an important effect on health and disease, and these relations must be the subject of scientific investigation;

3) the measures taken to promote health and to contain disease must be social as well as medical; and

4) "medical statistics will be our standard of measurement."

Symptoms of Crisis: Public Health

In the post-World War II period, which saw the rise of public health to a factor in international relations (the World Health Organization was founded in 1948), the disciplines forming its superstructure rested on the foundation of a clear and coherent doctrine. The basic tenets of the doctrine were as follows:

1) All disease could be explained in terms of the epidemiological model of interactions among "agent," "host" and "environment." Logical analysis proceeding from the Koch-Henle postulates (modified by Yerushalmi & Palmer, 1959, and by Lilienfeld, 1959, to fit noncommunicable diseases) provided the guidelines for search of aetiologies and, hence, for prevention: (i) the characteristic

suspected to be a causal factor must be found more frequently in persons with the disease than in persons without; (ii) persons with the characteristic should develop the disease more frequently than those not having it; (iii) the specificity of the relationship between the characteristic and the disease should be established; (iv) the incidence of the disease should increase in proportion to the duration and intensity of the suspected factor; (v) the distribution of the suspected factor in the population should parallel that of the disease; (vi) a spectrum of illness should be related to the exposure to the suspected factor; (vii) reduction or removal of the factor should reduce or eliminate the disease; and (viii) populations exposed to the factor should develop the disease more commonly than those not exposed.

2) Prevention of disease should take precedence, in a rational society, over a purely curative orientation of the health services. The maxim "an ounce of prevention is worth a pound of treatment" was reflected, in post-World War II policies of many countries, in a relative separation of preventive and curative medicine (the former being a government's concern and the latter being based on insurance or private schemes).

3) The eradication of "pests," such as communicable diseases, poor environmental sanitation or malnutrition, was seen as the ultimate goal of the public health approach. Following the abortive attempt at a global elimination of malaria, this principle was triumphantly vindicated by the eradication of smallpox; a replication is now being sought in the WHO plan for a global extinction of poliomyelitis.

4) Statistics, measurement and evaluation, i.e. the methodological apparatus of epidemiology, provide the scientific basis of public health. Considerable advances have been made in this area, and the techniques of epidemiological analysis are at present markedly superior to those available only two or three decades ago.

5) Social policies, supported by government action and appropriate legislation, represent a principal tool of prevention.

6) A liberal social philosophy, integrating an egalitarian ethics and a belief in the importance of enlightened public attitudes, has always been the background to public health action.

The public health approach, incorporating the principles outlined above, has been highly successful in achieving several major objectives. In the industrially developed countries, communicable diseases have been brought under control, due to improved living conditions, environmental sanitation and immunisation. Infant mortality has been reduced to levels which until recently were considered unattainable; concomitantly, life expectancy has risen and, in some communities, it may be approaching the "natural" biological life span. The analysis of this trend has nurtured optimistic predictions about a "compression of morbidity and mortality" into a relatively short terminal period of synchronised, multiple organ and system failure, leaving a significantly enlarged segment of the life cycle free of chronic disease and disability.

One of the great discoveries of the public health approach has been the identification of risk factors for chronic noncommunicable diseases and the development of strategies for their control, exemplified by the methodology and design of the *multiple risk factor intervention trial* (MRFIT). The practical application of this strategy has been associated with spectacular reductions in mortality from cardiovascular and cerebrovascular disease and, possibly, with a drop in their incidence (Stamler). It should be noted, however, that such reductions have occurred in a fortunate conjunction with an unprecedented economic growth and improvement in standards of living for a large proportion of the population in the North-West corner of the globe. Even the most advanced statistical methods would be of no avail in disentangling completely the effects of specific public health policies and programmes from those of improved living conditions as regards the end result.

What, then, are the symptoms of crisis?

1) In the industrialised world the synergism between better living conditions on one hand, and disease control or death-delaying technologies on the other, has "added years to life" without a concomitant reduction of chronic disability and without means of curbing the incidence of diseases with an onset late in life, such as dementia, osteoporosis and diabetes. Gruenberg's "failures of success" have exposed the limits of the "classic" public health doctrine with its priority on disease control at the expense of disability reduction.

2) The "Western" algorithm of public health action has proved inefficient or even inapplicable in large portions of the Third World, where survival and health hinge on harsh economic realities and the cultural scale of values may be of a substantially different order from that shared by governments and health agencies in the affluent parts of the world.

3) The prospect of a global ecological crisis suggests as a possibility a qualitative shift in morbidity, with physicochemical mutagenesis, urban stress and a new wave of infectious diseases becoming major health hazards, superimposed on those already prevalent.

4) This, in turn, may result in an extremely complex pattern of morbidity for which our present doctrine of prevention and containment would be unsuitable.

5) The AIDS pandemic has highlighted yet another zone of conflict: that between public health imperatives and fundamental human rights.

The point of psychiatrists' excursion into the territory of contemporary public health is to take bearings that would enable them to better orientate their own professional activities within the larger social matrix. If the conclusion is that public health is in a state of flux, possibly leading to a "paradigm shift," then the question should be asked whether comparable developments are occurring in psychiatry—especially at its interface with society.

Symptoms of Crisis: Social Psychiatry

The "ideology" of social psychiatry has been shaped, by and large, by influences stemming from outside the mainstream of clinical and academic psychiatry. The principal milestones have been:

1) the mental hygiene movement (initiated by Beers, 1908), which was highly influential, particularly in the US, throughout the 1930s and 1940s;

2) the research carried out by the "ecological school" in psychiatric epidemiology (Faris & Dunham, 1939), which was the first demonstration of a significant association between measures of mental morbidity and a range of community-related variables;

3) the World War II experience in the management of stress-related conditions "in the situation where stress was occurring and involving feelings of responsibility to others close to the individual and using their support in treatment" (Lemkau, 1982);

4) the post-war research in the sociology of mental health, including investigations into social stratification and psychiatric morbidity (Hollingshead & Redlich, 1958) and the Manhattan study (Srole et al., 1962);

5) the development of therapeutic communities (Maxwell Jones, 1968).

It should be noted that, although social psychiatry emerged internationally with an Anglo-Saxon slant, similar developments had taken place earlier in Germany (Simon, 1927) and in the USSR (the first "psychiatric dispensary" opened its doors in Moscow in 1934, and the term "social psychiatry" had been used by Korsakov).

In analogy to the public health doctrine, the ideology of social psychiatry (in Parsons' sense of an interpretative scheme justifying action) can be summarised in several statements:

- Mental health problems can be understood, and are amenable to intervention, within a public health framework ("mental illnesses and disorders, at least at the present state of knowledge, require the broad view of aetiology historically espoused by public health"; Lemkau, 1982).

- A significant portion of mental morbidity in the community is preventable through socially organised effort aimed at eliminating or reducing pathogens (such as psychoso-

cial stress) or risk factors (such as maternal deprivation in early childhood; Bowlby, 1951). Where primary prevention cannot be achieved, the burden of illness can still be alleviated by secondary prevention (containment of symptoms) and tertiary prevention (reduction of disability).

- Psychiatric epidemiology, and especially the community survey method (Jablensky, 1986), provides a scientific basis for the strategy of intervention, with its emphasis on "denominator" data, measurement, standardization and statistical analysis. Goldberger's discovery of the aetiology of pellagra through epidemiological research and reasoning (Goldberger, 1926) is often quoted as a paradigmatic example, and the development of psychiatric case registers illustrates the link community-epidemiology-mental health service provision, which is essential to the theory and practice of social psychiatry.

- Social psychiatry endorses, explicitly or implicitly, the "promotion of mental health," in addition to the prevention of mental morbidity, as one of its major goals. This is consonant with the definition of health in the WHO Constitution as "a state of complete physical, mental and social well-being and not merely the absence of disease or infirmity" (WHO, 1986).

Based on such principles, social psychiatry has never been an "institution" or a "speciality," but rather a movement and a perspective. Its achievements fall into four broad domains:

1) Advocacy of the rights of the mentally ill, countering the stigma attached to mental illness, and asserting the legitimacy of mental health as a public health concern.

2) The study of the epidemiology of mental disorders, with special emphasis on their social causes and pathoplastic effects (examples include research on schizophrenia, depression, psychosocial aspects of physical disease, psychiatric sequelae of public health measures such as elective sterilization for family planning purposes, urban ecology and mental health, bereavement).

3) Promotion of social treatments and methods of management, such as social skills

training, crisis intervention, counselling, therapeutic communities).

4) Furthering of the methodology of research and communication in the mental health field, especially as concerns the development and promotion of a "common language" (the classification of mental disorders and psychosocial problems in ICD-10; the standardization of diagnostic guidelines and criteria; and the designing of research instruments). Contrary to the popular view that psychiatry is dealing with intangible entities and "soft" data, it is precisely the mental disorders chapter of ICD that contains a glossary (8th and 9th revisions) and detailed clinical diagnostic guidelines (10th revision).

Based on such broad principles, social psychiatry should be seen as an ideology (in the sense of a shared system of beliefs), or as a particular set of attitudes toward the practice of psychiatry, rather than as a special discipline. For several decades, it has provided a strong impetus to mental health programmes throughout the world.

What achievements can be put to the credit of social psychiatry? Perhaps first and foremost is its success in placing psychiatric research and mental health care into the orbit of public health, and its advocacy of the rights of psychiatric patients and their families.

Secondly, through its alliance with epidemiology, social psychiatry has stimulated and guided research into the incidence, prevalence and causes of mental disorders, the determinants of their course and outcome, and the functioning of mental health services. Although at the present time we tend to focus increasingly on the genetic basis and biological mechanisms of the major mental disorders, our knowledge about the nature of schizophrenia, depression, the mental morbidity associated with aging and the psychosocial accompaniments of physical disease would be grossly incomplete and of little relevance if we are unable to integrate it into an epidemiological and social matrix.

Thirdly, social psychiatry has been instrumental in the development of a "common language" for the mental health disciplines, which includes the successive revisions of the International Classification of Diseases and

its glossary of mental disorders to which a set of diagnostic guidelines and criteria has been added in the latest, 10th revision. Since communication in the mental health field would be difficult without measurement and standardization, the development of instruments has been part and parcel of the efforts to promote a "common language."

Fourthly, social psychiatry has been a driving force in the development of new treatments and methods of management of mental disorders, ranging from crisis intervention, counselling and social skills training to therapeutic communities.

However, the positive contributions of social psychiatry should not conceal its shortcomings in meeting its proclaimed goals, or certain counterproductive aspects of its ideology.

As any doctrine of practical action based on an ideology, social psychiatry, too, has been subject of critique from both "left" and "right." The critique from the "left" has been part of the general argument of the antipsychiatry movement. In particular, social psychiatry has been faulted with:

- inability to free itself of the "medical model" (adherence to a conventional notion of disease, diagnosis and classification);

- emphasis on the adjustment of the psychosocial functioning of the individual to the norms of society rather than on the promotion of radical changes in the socioeconomic conditions that cause mental ill-health.

On the other hand, the critique from the "right" has portrayed social psychiatry (and psychiatry in general) as an intrusive form of social control violating the rights of individuals to personal autonomy. As is often the case, "left" and "right" tend to converge, once their arguments are pushed to extremes; the recent troubles in which psychiatric case registers have found themselves in some countries seem to be the result of such a convergence of different political interests.

If we adopt a more neutral "centrist" point of view, we can still identify several shortcomings and errors of judgement which have prepared the ground for the present crisis:

(1) A significant error lies in what might be termed the expansionist attitude in social

psychiatry, manifesting itself in: (i) aspirations of social engineering (i.e. attempts to resolve major social problems or to design new societal structures using the concepts and techniques of psychiatry); and (ii) a selective collection or interpretation of epidemiological data in a way supporting the notion of a massive, unmet psychiatric need in the society.

The first Director-General of the World Health Organization, the psychiatrist George Brock Chisholm, was one of the initiators of the first post-war International Congress on Mental Health (London, 1948), which had as its main theme "Mental Health and World Citizenship." To quote Chisholm (1949):

> Our civilization, like a great ship, driven by the enormous power of its scientific development, is rushing on into treacherous and unreliably charted seas . . .

In Chisholm's opinion, psychiatrists and sociologists were the experts to whom the guidance of the ship ought to be entrusted, because their professional training enabled them to understand "the need of interhuman relations on a world scale."

A similar error has been the overuse of the "numerical argument" to advocate an expansion of the mental health services. While there is no doubt that the incidence and prevalence of some conditions, such as dementia, are increasing, the projected growth in the rates of other conditions is less certain—and for some disorders (including schizophrenia) may need to be revised downwards. It is a sobering fact that, while social psychiatry has in the past aspired to a scientific leadership of enlightened social policies, truly major decisions and reforms, such as the deinstitutionalisation of mental health care in a number of countries have been based on moral, political and economic considerations, and not on scientific evidence.

(2) Another shortcoming of social psychiatry is the lack of demonstrable success of the psychosocial approach in the area of prevention. Primary prevention is at present feasible in a number of conditions associated with significant mental impairment and disability, ranging from rubella encephalopathy, congenital hypothyroidism and phenylketonuria to Down syndrome and brain damage from subclinical lead intoxication. Advances in molec-

ular genetics suggest new prospects of primary prevention of severe disorders that first become manifest in adulthood or in advanced age: the identification of a polymorphic DNA marker linked to the gene responsible for Huntington's disease may be followed by similar discoveries in Alzheimer's disease, schizophrenia and some of the affective psychoses. These developments, which may ultimately result in techniques for prenatal diagnosis, have taken place outside the ambit of social psychiatry.

As regards the domain proper of social psychiatry, i.e. prevention by behavioural and social means, the evidence for a significant impact of techniques such as crisis intervention, counselling, social skills training and the non-institutional management of chronic psychotic illness is still weak. Part of the explanation may lie in the relative underdevelopment of the methodology of evaluation of the effects of interventions.

Generally, the schism between social and biological psychiatry—between the clinical and behavioural sciences on one hand and the neurosciences on the other—has reinforced the tendency for these different approaches to evolve into separate, special disciplines, each speaking its own language. The unfortunate result is a fragmentation of what ought to be an integrated (albeit multifaceted) strategy of mental health research and prevention.

Perception of Crisis: Psychiatric Futurology

The difficulties social psychiatry is experiencing today should be seen in the broader context of an identity crisis that seems to affect the discipline of psychiatry as a whole. Evidence for this can be derived from a number of critical publications by prominent members of the profession which have appeared in the past decade and contain searching analyses of its present state as well as a variety of visions of its future. The concerns expressed in this literature appear to be related to four major themes.

1) *The concepts of mental health and illness.* The dilemma "brain diseases or problems of living" continues to be central to social psy-

chiatry. However, in a provocative paper, significantly entitled "Mindlessness and Brainlessness in Psychiatry," Eisenberg (1986) sees a fresh solution in a kind of a complementarity principle: "Exclusively biological and psychological theories in psychiatry stand in relation to one another much as wave and particle theory do in subatomic physics." Whatever new advances may be forthcoming in our understanding of the biological basis of the mind, the theory and practice of psychiatry will continue "drawing on knowledge of the ecological matrix in which mental illness is embedded" (Shepherd, 1988).

2) *The territorial imperative.* The possibility of a future redefinition of the domain of psychiatry, up to its complete dissolution into neurology, dealing with the organic syndromes and many of the conditions classified today as functional psychoses, and psychology, dealing with the behavioural disorders, has been raised by Torrey (1974). From the standpoint of an opposing ideology, a similar concern has been expressed by Lehmann (1986): "Is psychiatry in the process of selling its birthright for a mess of technological hardware, molecular biology and highly reliable diagnostic algorithms of questionable validity?" Lehmann nevertheless expects that psychiatry will retain its identity vis-à-vis neurology and the behavioural sciences and, as a minimum, will deal with five groups of problems and tasks: the management of emergencies and acute psychiatric conditions; drug therapy of mental disorders; the treatment of patients who do not respond; clinical research; and teaching. In a response to Torrey, a "laissez-faire" future for psychiatry has been suggested by Brown (1976): "the question of who will deal with the most pervasive although relatively minor, of our mental health problems will be decided in the marketplace."

3) *The relationship to medicine.* The ideology of social psychiatry has been criticised for its departure from medical thinking: "We became the first medical specialty without ties to any organ or organ system . . . One by-product of our nearly exclusive reliance on psychosocial explanatory theories was

that we rid ourselves of problems that did not fit into our newly found identity. We abandoned the epileptics, the demented, the developmentally disabled and the retarded and asked the police to take care of the alcoholics, the substance abusers, and the delinquents . . ." (Detre, 1987).

4) *The place of psychiatry in the social matrix.* In a paper published in 1971, Shepherd (1971) made a prediction about the state of the discipline in 1984. In an Orwellian vein, he feared that "the expanding role of the psychiatrist has far outstripped the gains in established knowledge." Quoting Grotjahn's maxim "Culture interposes itself between man and nature," Shepherd noted that "in some measure this maxim affects every branch of modern medicine but in none is it more relevant than to psychiatry, which is so closely embedded in the social matrix in which the subject is practised." The increasing gap between the expanding ambitions of social psychiatry in the 1960s and the early 1970s, and the modest progress in the scientific understanding of the social matrix has undoubtedly contributed to the present crisis; Shepherd's prediction has, by and large, been fulfilled. Yet another aspect of the relationship between psychiatry and society has been highlighted by Blakemore (1981): "Psychiatry must be sensitive to its unique role as an arbiter of personal responsibility and as an organ of social and political judgement. It must not allow society to shrug off on to medicine the essential ethical judgements about the definitions of the boundaries of normality."

Crisis as a Change of Direction, Content and Paradigm

The overview presented above of the ways psychiatrists perceive their own discipline and project its future is indeed indicative of a conceptual change within the field. It is unlikely that another "psychiatric revolution" will be soon at the doorstep; gradual shifts in emphasis, novel attempts at conceptualizing the nature of mental health and illness (overcoming the biosocial schism), and an increasing involvement of psychiatrists in new areas of application of knowledge present a more credible scenario of the change of paradigm which is already occurring. Whether the term "social psychiatry" will survive in the process is irrelevant; the continuing social embeddedness of the theory and practice of psychiatry is hardly in doubt.

In the view of the present writer, there are several foci around which the new concerns of social psychiatry are becoming organised.

1) *Mental morbidity in primary care.* Mental disorders, and in particular those classified as neurotic, constitute a large proportion of the total volume of morbidity and psychosocial problems presenting at the primary care level in different cultures. Anxiety and depression, with an associated variety of somatic symptoms, are the most common manifestations; co- morbidity, in particular the association of neurotic disorders and physical illness, is extremely common. Neurotic symptoms are usually intertwined with psychosocial problems, and constraints of time, skills and access to specialist services necessitate approaches to the diagnosis, classification and management of neurotic disorders which are different from those employed in psychiatric outpatient and inpatient settings.

2) *Containment of psychiatric disability.* No less than one-fifth of all disability is caused by psychiatric illness, and it is unlikely that much progress will be made in the foreseeable future in the reduction of the impairments leading to disability. Current psychopharmacological research will soon result in more effective and safer means of controlling the "positive" symptoms of severe psychotic illness, but our understanding of the neurobiological mechanisms underlying the "negative" disorders is rudimentary. There is much promise in clinical and behavioural research aimed at the elimination or modification of environments known to be harmful and to aggravate impairments and disabilities, as well as in efforts to improve the coping resources of individuals with mental disorders.

3) *Social issues in applied neuroscience.* Techniques that at present are experimental and confined to the laboratories will even-

tually be available for clinical or public health applications. The mapping of the entire human genome is now a feasible proposition, and a range of linkage markers and DNA probes for the direct identification of genes associated with the susceptibility to major mental disorders will spill out into clinical and social psychiatry, posing new psychosocial and ethical problems: the right to knowledge about genetic risk as determined by recombinant DNA diagnosis; the methodology of interpretation of such information; the question of access to molecular diagnosis of mental disorders with an onset late in life (who should have the test, who should have access to the results?). These are challenges that will require new professional skills.

4) *New prospects of prevention.* A nontrivial part of the aggregate mental morbidity is at present preventable by means that are available and can be applied on a population scale at an affordable cost. Immunisation against neurotropic infections, prenatal and obstetric care, good nutrition, prevention of accidents and responsible parenthood (including attention to the cognitive needs of infants and children) can reduce the incidence of CNS damage, which provides the ground for a variety of specific disorders. The integration of knowledge resulting from clinical and epidemiological research into the provision of care for people suffering from affective and schizophrenic illnesses can limit the prevalence of severe impairments and disabilities. Finally, appropriate modifications in community organization can provide a variety of social niches for people with residual impairments, without allowing such impairments to result in a severe handicap.

Epidemiology and social psychiatry, serving as the coordinating framework and the research basis for such a preventive reorientation of mental health programmes, have produced—on a modest scale so far—evidence that prevention in the mental health field can be a realistic objective. The extent to which the potential of prevention will be exploited depends not so much on social psychiatry or public health, but on the feasibility of an enlightened approach to society's priorities.

References

Beers, C. W. (1908). *A mind that found itself.* New York: Longmans Green.

Blakemore, C (1981). The future of psychiatry in science and society. *Psychological Medicine, 11*, 27–37.

Bowlby, J. (1951). *Maternal care and mental health.* Geneva: World Health Organization.

Brown, B. S. (1976). The life of psychiatry. *American Journal of Psychiatry, 133*, 489–495.

Campbell, R. J. (1981). *Psychiatric Dictionary* (5th ed.). Oxford: Oxford University Press.

Chisholm, G. B. (1949). Social responsibility. *Science, 109*, 27–43.

Detre, T. (1987). The future of psychiatry. *American Journal of Psychiatry, 144*, 621–625.

Eisenberg, L. (1984). Rudolf Ludwig Karl Virchow, where are you now that we need you? *American Journal of Medicine, 77*, 524–532.

Eisenberg, L. (1986). Mindlessness and brainlessness in psychiatry. *British Journal Psychiatry*, 497–508.

Faris, R. E., & Dunham, H. W. (1939). *Mental disorders in urban areas: An ecological study of schizophrenia and other psychoses.* Chicago: University of Chicago Press.

Goldberger, J. (1964). In M. Terris (Ed.), *Goldberger on Pellagra.* Baton Rouge: Louisiana State University Press.

Gruenberg, E. M. (1977). The failures of success. *Millbank Memorial Fund Quarterly, 55*, 3–24.

Hollingshead, A. B., & Redlich, F. C. (1958). *Social class and mental illness.* New York: John Wiley.

Jablensky, A. (1986). Epidemiologic surveys of mental health of geographically defined populations in Europe. In M. M. Weissman, J. K. Myers, & C. E. Ross (Eds.), *Community surveys of psychiatric disorders* (pp 257– 313). New Brunswick: Rutgers University Press.

Jones, M. (1968). *Social psychiatry in practice: The idea of the therapeutic community.* Harmondsworth: Penguin Books.

Lehmann, H. E. (1986). The future of psychiatry: progress-mutation or self destruct? *Canadian Journal of Psychiatry, 31*, 362–367.

Lemkau, P. V. (1982). The historical background. In M. O. Wagenfeld, P. V. Lemkau, & B. Justice (Eds.), *Public mental health: Perspectives and prospects* (pp. 16–29). Beverly Hills: Sage.

Lilienfeld, A. M. (1959). On the methodology of investigations of etiologic factors in chronic diseases—some comments. *Journal of Chronic Disease, 10*, 41–46.

Ryle, J. A. (1948). *Changing disciplines.* Oxford: Oxford University Press.

Sartorius, N. (1988) Future directions: a global view. In A. S. Henderson, & G. D. Burrows (Eds.), *Handbook of social psychiatry* (pp. 341–346.). Amsterdam: Elsevier.

Shepherd, M. (1971). A critical appraisal of contemporary psychiatry. *Comprehensive Psychiatry, 12*, 302–320.

Shepherd, M. (1988). The Maudsley Lecture 1987: Changing disciplines in psychiatry. *British Journal of Psychiatry, 153*, 493–504.

Simon, H. (1927). Aktivere Krankenbehandlung in der Irrenanstalt. *Allg. Zschr. Psychiat, 87*, 97–145.

Srole, L., Langner, T. S., Michael, S. T., Opler, M. K., & Rennie, T. (1962). *Mental health in the metropolis.* New York: McGraw-Hill.

Torrey, E. F. (1974). *The death of psychiatry.* Radnor, Pennsylvania: Chilton Book Company.

Winslow, R. (1979) quoted after Hobson, W. (Ed.). *The theory and practice of public health* (5th ed.) (xi–xiii). New York: Oxford University Press.

Yerushalmi, J., & Palmer, C. E. (1959). On the methodology of investigations of aetiologic factors in chronic diseases. *Journal of Chronic Disease, 10*, 27–40.

Chapter 2

Public Health Concerns: How Can Social Psychiatry Help?

Walter Holland & Beverley Fitzsimons

In this chapter we discuss the interaction between public health and social psychiatry in the identification of the causes and spread of mental illness, the development of preventive strategies for mental illness, the appropriate treatment and provision of optimal care, and the issues that are likely to be at the forefront of the discussions about the future of the treatment of the mentally ill.

The changing pattern of disease in recent years with increased attention on the burden of mental illness on society, has brought epidemiology, public health and health services research to the forefront of health care and the planning of health services. Epidemiology is the study of the causes and distribution of disease, in populations rather than individuals, and as such is concerned with the prevalence of various mental disorders in defined populations. Since health is influenced to some extent by the availability and usage of health services, epidemiology is also concerned with the measurement of need, demand for and use of health care. It is the basic science of public health, a specialty which covers the organisation of health care systems and medical aspects of the administration of health services. Public Health is a practical specialty concerned with the application of population based research findings in an attempt to cure or prevent disease, and to allocate resources appropriately.

Health services research involves the accumulation of knowledge and the development of techniques relevant to the administration of health services and, as a result, the adaptation of health care to needs. In the past, the overwhelming emphasis in epidemiology was on the conquest of infectious or communicable disease, and the major concern was the improvement of basic environmental factors such as sanitation, housing and working conditions. However, the limitations of clinical or curing medicine are now emerging. In developed countries interest is now increasing in the major chronic diseases, man made environmental hazards such as pollution and in the planning and delivery of health services both in hospitals and in the community. Thus, it is vital to ensure that attention continues to focus on the mentally ill at a time when neglect of environmental factors could have an adverse effect.

The emphasis of health care is turning toward prevention and palliation of many incurable conditions, and toward the care of vulnerable groups such as the elderly and mentally handicapped or ill. In addition, health services almost everywhere are faced with increasing financial restraints, with inflated costs in the health care sector and the introduction of expensive new technology. Providers of health care must decide rationally how limited resources should be divided and good health care planned.

Public health has been defined in numerous ways. One of the earliest definitions comes from C. E. A. Winslow as quoted in Hanlin and Picket (1984):

> Public health is the science and the art of 1—preventing disease, 2—prolonging life, and 3—organised community efforts for the sanitation of the environment, the control of communicable infections, the education of the individual in personal hygiene, the organisation of medical and nursing services for early diagnosis and preventive treatment of disease and the development of the social machinery to ensure everyone a standard of living adequate for the maintenance of health, so organising these benefits as to enable every citizen to realise his birthright of health and longevity.

It has also been conceived by Ellencweig and Yoshbe (1984) that the goal of public health is the protection of the community against the hazards engendered by "group life."

Public Health Concerns and Social Psychiatry

Identifying Causes of Ill Health

In order to improve the mental health of the public, an understanding of the causes of mental illness is needed, appropriate strategies for prevention need to be devised to prevent the occurrence of such illness, and appropriate treatment developed to ameliorate its progression.

A variety of strategies can be used to identify the causes of disease and therefore of mental ill health. Essentially the epidemiologist tries to compare the frequency of a condition in different groups of individuals in order to provide hypotheses which enable further investigations to be mounted. The aim of these investigations is to determine the reasons for the differences in frequency of conditions under study in different populations and thus to enable appropriate health care strategies to be developed.

Early studies of mental disorders showed wide variations in prevalence of many disorders due to varying criteria used in diagnoses. Now some arbitrary but consistent guidelines have been drawn up and inter country comparisons are now possible.

The limitations of epidemiology in psychiatric care are dependent on the degree of understanding of the aetiology of psychiatric disorders. One of the major problems in the study of mental disorders is that the validity of diagnoses is questionable. Risk factors have not been unequivocally determined and a large part of the variance in mental disorder is still unaccounted for. Diagnostic methods have evolved from diagnoses made by clinicians to a method of scoring in which scores were calculated according to the presence or absence of certain symptoms. More recently there has been a return to clinical standardised techniques, rather than a reliance on symptoms and signs alone.

Thus, social psychiatrists have a vital task to perform—that of providing unequivocal definitions of conditions in order that accurate studies of prevalence and aetiology can be carried out. Risk factors need more stringent examination, and psychiatric epidemiologists must use both disciplines to try to identify reasons for the wide variation. In the 1970s and 1980s more information regarding psychiatric disorders has become available. There is increased diagnostic precision which has meant it is easier to conduct epidemiological surveys. Epidemiological designs which yield testable hypotheses are needed. Studies have not developed beyond the standard age/sex/social class studies associated with mental illness, and do not elaborate on the mechanism by which these factors operate. There is a vital need to integrate psychiatric and epidemiological research—this will ensure appropriate comparison groups are chosen for study and that findings are more applied and are of more use to the mentally ill and their carers.

The difficulties that the investigator faces in developing approaches to research into mental health are partly due to the wide variation in the definitions used. For appropriate comparisons to be made between different populations a tool which enables the measurement of the same thing in different groups is required. As summarised by Goldberg and Tantam recently, the differences in frequency of mental disorders in different populations are extremely wide. Now that diagnostic precision has improved, it is likely that these difference are real and not due to measurement errors (Goldberg & Tantam, 1990). However, these studies rarely lead to new hypotheses as to how mental illness can be prevented and thus the study of mental illness is not significantly further forward.

A major difficulty facing physicians in all disciplines is that of assessing the most appropriate form of treatment with inadequate knowledge of the social and physical environment from which the patient came. It is widely acknowledged that environmental factors can be important influences on psychiatric disorders. So methods normally used for establishing the aetiology of infectious disease have also been used (with certain limitations) in the investigation of mental illness: for example, in identifying social and environmental factors which are important in the aetiology of depressive illness. Epidemiologists can study incidence of mental disorders in relation to changing environmental factors. Epidemiological study can help assess risk factors for particular conditions and try to pick up clues about their origin and mode of spread. (See, for example, the chapters by Brown and Kreitman in this volume.)

Once the aetiology has been investigated methods of control or prevention can be hypothesised and tested. Basically the description of the condition is the first step, where the incidence or prevalence of the condition is compared in different sub groups of the populations. Rates of onset are observed in groups with differing circumstances, be they personal or environmental. In this way data on the risk of onset can be gathered and the risks compared between different groups.

Methods of Identifying Psychiatric Problems

Interest in possible causes of certain disorders is often stimulated by anecdotal evidence from a clinician, or from routinely collected vital statistics. Observational evidence is circumstantial and inconclusive but can provide hints as to causation or association.

Tracing the direction of cause and effect is more difficult. It is rare that one factor alone is responsible for the onset of a particular condition. Multiple causation is more likely. Epidemiologists must take care—many disorders are the result of the accumulation of a number of factors whose interaction have been established using complex statistical techniques.

When likely causal agents are identified there are a number of ways to try to pin down causation such as case control studies, cohort studies and so on. Correlation does not necessarily indicate causation. If two factors are always found together one could cause the other, but equally they could both be caused by some third factor not considered in the analysis. The direction of causation may be difficult to establish—in a depressed alcoholic patient does the alcoholism cause the depression or vice versa?

Sometimes the field trial is the only way to identify causation. In a trial the epidemiologist has a much greater degree of control over the conditions of the various groups. The subject plays no part in selection to a particular experimental condition so eliminates an important source of possible bias.

Thus, psychiatrists have an important role in the identification of likely causal factors for mental illness.

Of course there have been other less conventional methods for the study of mental illness, the use of animal behaviour and the interpretation of anecdotal historical information. These often merely give hints for epidemiologists of important factors that will require more rigorous epidemiological testing. A method which is, however, increasing in importance is the use of genetic technology to identify genetically determined disorders. However, the late onset of some genetic disorders limits their value.

The confidence with which one can draw conclusions from any of these methods depends on the rigour with which they were applied and the consistency of the existing evidence with the findings. The use of vital statistics in the assessment of mental disorders can be problematic since the most reliable statistics routinely collected are mortality data, and mental disorders are rarely the direct cause of mortality. Suicide rates have been used as a proxy. Black (1988) described the case of schizophrenia which is not, in itself, fatal but is associated with increased mortality. An SMR of 2.53 was found in one study covering the 10 years after discharge, with suicide being the commonest cause.

Morbidity data are poor in quality and accuracy. Hospital admission data are of no use in the analysis of mental illness since the spectrum of mental illness is so wide that many cases of mental disorders do not result in hospitalization. In addition, changing political policy toward the care of the mentally ill and changing diagnostic practices can distort the figures.

Thus, the development of any accurate data set to identify cases of mental illness would make study much more accurate.

Prevention

Primary Prevention

Social change and psychiatric treatment can prevent some mental disorders but only if applied correctly to high risk groups such as the biologically vulnerable, or the socially disadvantaged. Public health measures to reduce biological risk factors for psychoses are important especially in developing countries where there is increased risk of brain injury, perinatal injury, infections, and so on.

Immunization programmes are vital in primary prevention. Perhaps one of the clearest examples of the success of prevention of mental illness comes from the campaign against measles and rubella and the consequent reduction in the incidence of Congenital Rubella Syndrome outlined by Gruenberg (1986). These studies are, however, fairly limited. They can only prevent a small proportion of mental illness. They do not satisfy the needs for undertaking studies on wider population groups having better hypotheses to explain the differences that exist between groups as outlined.

Health education is also important in the control of mental disorders. Examples include nutritional education concerning the use of iodine supplements in the prevention of mental handicap and the prevention and control through education and treatment of hypertension which is associated with multi-infarct dementia.

Research into the long term use of drugs is also necessary. Side effects should be monitored as should the psychiatric effects of drug withdrawal.

Public health is important in identifying "at risk" groups so that any action can be targeted for best effect and economy of action. For example counselling can be carried out after life events such as bereavement, unemployment, diagnosis of cancer, heart attack, or for high risk individuals such as people who have been abused or have been involved in family breakdown. The counselling role may be especially important in children as if untreated they are likely to reproduce the same circumstances in their own families in later life.

Secondary Prevention

Secondary prevention, for example, screening in primary care, has been suggested but there are grave doubts as to its usefulness. It is possible that targeting susceptible individuals for counselling may be effective. An example of this was recently described by Sharp (1989) in a study of emotional disorders in pregnancy and the puerperium. Since the months surrounding childbirth carry the highest lifetime risk for women of developing mental illness it follows that the high level of contact with primary care practitioners during pregnancy and the postnatal period provide an ideal opportunity for prevention. The study showed that one in four women living in relative socio-economic deprivation have psychiatric symptoms during pregnancy. The study identified five independent variables which exerted an independent effect on the likelihood of having psychiatric problems (financial problems, a past psychiatric history, poor social support, a poor marital relationship, and worry about the labour and delivery). It would seem likely that individuals with a number of these characteristics could be monitored more carefully in primary care in an effort to prevent problems.

Treatment

As the human lifespan increases the age structure of the population changes with a greater proportion of the population over the age of 75. Thus, there are more people entering the time of highest risk for organic brain disorders, and the prevalence of dementias is increasing in developed countries. This has implications for treatment, and psychiatrists must develop new methods of treatment if this development is to be controlled.

In the developing countries improvements in obstetric care should lead to a reduction in the prevalence of disorders associated with brain injury.

Optimal Health Care Provision

A public health problem with specific implications for mental health is the provision of optimal health services. A wide variety of models of psychiatric service provision exists, but trends in forms of care in use at any time are partly dependent on politics. Numerous studies have clearly demonstrated the effect of institutional care on progression and degeneration of individuals and on disease. However, present models of care do not appear to offer solutions either. Although some studies have shown improvement in mental illness in relation to treatment with ECT, drugs, etc., and it can be shown that progression of disease may be retarded by appropriate care facilities. None of the methods at present used for prevention has been able to prevent the development of mental illness or been able to show clearly beneficial effects, other than vaccinating against brain syndromes.

Psychiatry is crucial in the assessment of the effects of institutionalisation, and associated with it stigmatization and social disadvantage. The change toward community care must also be evaluated. The problem is that patients live in a more "normal" environment but there is a risk of neglect of treatment and greater risk of breakdown in carer due to insufficient support systems. Psychiatrists can assess the appropriateness of different types of care (for example, in families, alone, residential care for groups of people with similar conditions, institutional care), and other sorts of provision such as the use of sheltered employment. It is important that patients are treated with appropriate forms of care, with each form—be it long-stay institutional care or informal care within the family—and the appropriateness of the care is based on a properly resourced service. The patient himself is rarely consulted in the diagnosis routine which can lead to there being dissatisfaction with treatment. This has important public health consequences with psychiatrists in a crucial position to communicate with the patient and minimize dissatisfaction.

In England, the data point to an increase in readmissions for dementias but a fairly constant rate of first admission. This suggests that policy is tending toward an increase in the use of short stays (DHSS 1985). Public health research can help in this sort of policy-making.

There has been a change in the type of mental health care provision with a large reduction in the number of psychiatric long stay beds. Previously institutionalised patients have been placed in community care. The various forms of care must be evaluated and appropriate care for the varying severity of illness and dependence must be provided. Public health researchers can with psychiatrists help decide optimum care provision by undertaking properly designed and executed randomised controlled trials, which also include measures of long-term costs and effectiveness.

Future Concerns—Conclusion

AIDS is of major importance for future public health with specific implications for social psychiatry with the expected increase in cases and the associated problem of premature dementia (see chapters by Jepsen and Hjorther; and by King in this volume). Epidemiologists can work toward identifying the aetiology of the disease, but the current public health task is in the prevention of its transmission which is taking the form of health education regarding sexual behaviour and drug use. Decisions about appropriate forms of care for sufferers must also be made.

Thus, the public health practitioner and the psychiatrist are in the same quandary. They do not have the appropriate knowledge available to actually prevent the progression of mental disease or its occurrence. It is therefore up to psychiatrists interested in research to come up with better models of how to prevent disease and its progression than at present.

Social psychiatrists can help in the solution of public health problems by identifying accurately the aetiology and the causes of disorders; by defining the best methods of treatment and rehabilitation so that public health practitioners can act on the fullest information. The major problem at the moment is relatively few effective preventive strategies (the classical example being rubella) have been identified. It is remarkable that mental illness which is at the root of so much chronic ill health in our community has shown so few advances in strategies for prevention. Even in the 1980s information on mental disorders is largely confined to descriptive studies of prevalence and incidence, and treatment generally consists of drug regimes to ameliorate symptoms. We now know how we can reduce the burden of cancer of the lung. We know how to reduce the burden of chronic bronchitis or of coronary heart disease. It is however difficult to know how we can reduce the burden of mental illness and this surely is one of the greatest challenges that faces us at this time.

References

Batchelor, I. (1984). *Policies for a crisis? Some aspects of DHSS policy for the care of the elderly.* Nuffield Hospitals Provincial Trust.

Black, D. W. (1988). Mortality in schizophrenia. The Iowa record linkage study. *Psychosomatics, 29,* 55–60.

Department of Health and Social Security, (1985). *In-patient statistics from the Mental Health Enquiry for England 1982.* HMSO: London.

Ellencweig, A. & Yoshbe, R. B. (1984). Definition of Public Health. *Public Health Review, 12,* 65–78.

Giel, R. (1983). Mental health problems in the community: A discussion of their assessment. *World Health Statistics Quarterly 36,* 233–235.

Goldberg, D., & Tantam, D. (in press). The public health impact of mental disorders. In W. W. Holland, E. G. Knox, & R. Detels (Eds.), *The Oxford textbook of public health: Chapter 16* (Vol. 3) (2nd ed.). Oxford: Oxford University Press.

Gruenberg, E. M. (Ed.) (1986). *Vaccinating against brain syndromes: The campaign against measles and rubella.* New York: Oxford University Press.

Hanlin, G., & Picket, J. (1984). *Public health administration and practice.* St. Louis: Mosby.

Reid, D. D. (1960). *Epidemiological methods in the study of mental disorders.* Geneva: World Health Organisation.

Sharp, D. (1989). Emotional disorders and the puerperium: A longitudinal prospective study in primary care. In *United Medical and Dental Schools, Social Medicine and Health Services Research Unit and Division of Community Health Progress Report April 1st 1985—March 31st 1989.* London: UMDS.

Weissman, M. M. (1987). Advances in psychiatric epidemiology: Rates and risks for major depression. *American Journal of Public Health, 77,* 445–449.

Section II

Public Health Implications of the "Goldberg-Huxley Model"

*I*t has been known for many years that mental illnesses encountered in community surveys are less severe than those in persons admitted to psychiatric hospitals. In the main, the former comprise depressive illnesses and anxiety-related disorders, while the latter contain a substantial proportion of more severe illnesses, such as organic mental disorders, schizophrenia and bipolar affective disorders. It has also long been known that the majority of mental illnesses found on community surveys have not been seen by the mental illness services. It is clear that there is a filtering process at work between the community and the wards of the psychiatric hospital, which is selectively permeable to those with more severe disorders.

In many countries of the world, most patients are referred to the mental illness services by other professionals, so that one can postulate a filter between the community and the referring professional, as well as between that professional and the mental illness service. Goldberg and Huxley (1979) proposed five levels at which survey data could be considered, each one corresponding to a stage on the pathway to psychiatric care. They postulated four filters between these five levels; these are shown below.

The centre-piece of the model is of course the second and third filters, which occur in the primary-care physician's office. The model serves to relate morbidity in this setting to events in the community on the one hand, and in the mental illness services on the other. The original data reported from Manchester indicated that these filters were responsible for holding back most of the illnesses seen on community surveys, so that events in the primary-care physician's office are of crucial public health importance.

Two other research groups reported rates of morbidity at all five levels during the Manchester Symposium, and these are shown on the next page—together with the original data from Goldberg and Huxley.

It should be noted that whereas the data from Manchester and Groningen relate to annual period prevalence, the data from Verona relate to weekly period prevalence. It should be emphasised that the first "filter" (i.e. that between levels 1 and 2) is less permeable than the figures for Manchester and Groningen suggest, since although many psychologically disordered patients consult their doctors during the year, the consultations may be for other reasons. Also, many depressed patients do not mention their depressive symptoms,

Level:	Filter:	Description of filter:
1.	Community (total psychiatric morbidity in random samples)	
	1st filter	Illness behaviour
2.	Primary care (total psychiatric morbidity among attenders)	
	2nd filter	Ability to detect disorder
3.	Primary care ("conspicuous," or identified morbidity)	
	3rd filter	Willingness to refer
4.	Mental illness services (total psychiatric morbidity)	
	4th filter	Factors determining admission to hospital
5.	Mental illness services (admissions to hospital)	

Level:		Greater[1] Manchester (annual)	Groningen[2] (annual)	Verona[3] (weekly)
1:	Community	250	303	227
2:	Primary care (total)	230	224	34
3:	Primary care (conspicuous)	140	94	23
4:	Psychiatrists	17	34	4
5:	Psychiatrists (in-patients)	6	10	0.7

Sources of data:
[1]Goldberg and Huxley, 1980
[2]Giel, Koeter and Ormel (this volume, Chapter 3)
[3]Tansella and Williams, 1989

but confine their complaints to the doctor to the associated somatic symptoms.

There are two important public health implications of the rates shown in this table. Despite the fact that mental illness services are treating the most severe cases, the majority of disordered patients are seen in primary-care settings. However, many of these disorders will not be detected by the clinician seeing them. Providing that it can be shown that detection of such disorders actually helps the patient, training general practitioners and internists and surgeons in the detection and management of the common forms of mental disorder becomes an important public health task.

Since a substantial proportion of the more severe forms of mental disorder will in fact be referred to specialist mental illness services, the second implication is that it is of great public health importance to organise such services so that they are most cost effective, and so that chronic disability from severe mental disorder is minimised. It is quite wrong to think of "mental disorder" as a homogeneous entity, so that all resources are funnelled into primary care; the spontaneous remission rate of disorders seen in general medical settings is high, and those referred to levels four and five of the model are much more likely to have special treatment needs. However, the figures do argue for better coordination of services between primary care and specialised services.

It is clear that the Goldberg/Huxley model represents an oversimplified picture of the

pathway to psychiatric care, since in some countries patients may refer themselves directly to mental health professionals, while others will be referred by longer, less direct pathways—perhaps even involving multiple carers. This problem has been addressed by the World Health Organisation's "Pathways to Care" study, in which it has been shown that in at least five countries about two-thirds of patients seen by mental health professionals *do* follow this simple pathway, while most of the remainder are referred via clinics to general medical clinics in hospital.

The chapters that follow deal with three major areas. In Chapter 3, Robert Giel and his colleagues review the recent literature on the first three filters and conclude that, although there are difficulties in doing much to modify the first filter, much can be done to improve detection at the second filter.

In Chapter 4, Jose Vázquez-Barquero reviews mental health in primary-care settings, paying especial attention to his own surveys that have been carried out at both the community (Level 1) and in primary-care clinics (Level 2). He is able to show that gender, age and physical illness exert a marked effect on psychiatric morbidity, and he confirms that in the primary-care clinic psychological needs tend to be expressed in an idiom of bodily complaint. This chapter goes on to consider the great variation that exists between individual general practitioners in their ability to detect psychiatric disorder, and confirms that a substantial proportion of cases are not detected. The greater tendency for doctors to prescribe psychotropics to women could not be explained by higher rates of psychiatric disorder among women, although there is a greater likelihood of such a prescription as the score on a psychiatric screening questionnaire increases. The chapter ends with a plea for the development of new training strategies to improve the way in which mental disorders are managed in primary-care settings.

Antonio Lobo, in the last chapter of this section, deals with mental health in general medical clinics. Such clinics, taken together with primary-care clinics, account for a very high proportion (in Manchester, over 95%!) of those who are eventually seen by the mental illness service at level 4. Recent surveys have shown that at least 25% of those admitted to medical wards have a significant degree of psychiatric disorder, and that these disorders frequently go unrecognised by the medical staff. Lobo shows that the severity of psychiatric disorder is related to the severity of hormonal disorder among patients with endocrine disease; however, among medical outpatients it has been shown that those who are psychiatrically disordered are less likely to have an organic cause for their presenting symptoms. Thus, psychiatric disorder can both co-vary with the severity of physical disease processes as well as serve as a cause of somatic symptoms that are not organically determined. Lobo also shows that psychiatric disorder is most prevalent just after admission to hospital, and that a substantial proportion of these remit without treatment by the time of discharge. It seems likely that attentive and supportive care from the medical team is associated with a decrease in morbidity over time.

The public health implications of this work are less clear than they might be, since there are not yet many reported studies showing an improved outlook with early detection and treatment of psychiatric disorders seen in this setting. However, Hans Ormel and his colleagues (Chapter 14) report an uncontrolled study which suggests that there are advantages in detecting depressive disorders, and he reviews other studies with similar findings. If such studies are confirmed, there would appear to be scope for secondary prevention of disorders accompanying somatic complaints in general medical settings.

References

Goldberg, D. P., & Huxley, P. (1980). *Mental illness in the community: The pathway to psychiatric care.* London: Tavistock.

Tansella, M., & Williams, P. (1989). The spectrum of psychiatric morbidity in a defined geographical area. *Psychological Medicine, 19,* 765–770.

Chapter 3

Detection and Referral of Primary-Care Patients with Mental Health Problems: The Second and Third Filter

R. Giel, M. W. J. Koeter & J. Ormel

Goldberg and Huxley's (1980) model describing the "pathway" to specialist mental health care is limited to medical services with regard to its levels of morbidity and its filters. This renders figures regarding morbidity quite incomparable between countries, because of their differing health services structures. In the Netherlands, for example, municipal health services that are not included in primary care can, outside office hours, bypass the general practitioner and refer patients directly to the specialist mental health services. This implies that the permeability of the second and third filters (GP recognition and the decision to refer) is determined not only by the decision behaviour of the general practitioner. In addition, psychologists nowadays participate in the primary-care network, either privately or as members of a primary-care team, and therefore they may have an influence on morbidity at levels two and three and on permeability of filters two and three—which remains unidentified if their contacts with patients are not counted in the registration of morbidity. Clearly, studying permeability of the filters provides information that derives its meaning from the context of the health services infrastructure, and that cannot easily be generalized to other sociocultural situations.

In this paper we pick up cues that might be important in manipulating the filters, particularly the second and third. We do this first by reviewing the international literature since Goldberg and Huxley's (1980) pioneering work, and second by looking at a Dutch study (Ormel et al., 1989; Wilmink, 1989).

First, however, we would like to begin by presenting the model of the "pathway to specialist mental health care" completed for the Netherlands, as an orientation for the relative permeability of the successive filters.

The model completed for the Netherlands is shown below.

Levels 1 to 3 concern morbidity estimated with the *General Health Questionnaire* (ratings of 5 or more) for the general population aged 18–65 years, based on a community survey by Hodiamont (1986) and on a survey of general practices (Wilmink, 1989). Levels 4 and 5 are continuously being studied with the help of our psychiatric case register in the north of the country (Brook et al., 1985). The latter covers all ages in the catchment area and all mental health services, i.e. including institutions for the mentally retarded and psychogeriatric patients.

The impermeability of the third filter, which is not only determined by the indecision of the GP to refer, but is also dependent

LEVEL 1	Psychiatric morbidity in the community	303 per 1000
	FILTER 1: The decision to consult	
LEVEL 2	Total primary-care morbidity	224 per 1000
	FILTER 2: GP recognition	
LEVEL 3	Conspicuous primary-care morbidity	94 per 1000
	FILTER 3: The decision to refer	
LEVEL 4	All patients in mental health services	34 per 1000
	FILTER 4: The decision to admit	
LEVEL 5	Psychiatric inpatients	10 per 1000

on restraint exercised by the police, the municipal health services or the various social services, is evident. Less than 11% of morbidity in the community reaches the specialist mental health services annually. Even the GP offers a significant barrier with regard to his recognition of cases. He recognizes about 42% of those exhibiting illness behaviour in the form of a GHQ-rating above the cut-off score of 4/5.

Obviously, filters 2 and 3 are of prime importance in the whole filtering process, in which the role of the GP is central. But what cues are operative in getting a patient through filters 2 and 3? Before we address this question, let us briefly review what is known about the selective action of the first filter.

First Filter: Illness or Help-Seeking Behaviour

Very little research on psychiatric morbidity in the community and its relation to help-seeking behaviour exists in the literature. Furthermore, the incomparability of the few studies is demonstrated by the Epidemiologic Catchment Area investigation (Shapiro et al., 1984), not only because it employed different instruments and concentrated on DIS/DSM-III and not on GHQ cases, but also because of the—for the European observer—anomalous health services infrastructure. Many patients with emotional problems (except for the elderly; German et al., 1987) bypass primary care entirely, seeking help directly in the mental health specialty sector. In the three sites, New Haven, St. Louis and Baltimore, the 6 months prevalence rate ran from 191 to 240 per 1000 of the population aged 18 years or more. Help-seeking behaviour was determined retrospectively over the 6 months preceding the interview. About two-thirds of the total samples had done so for any health reason, including mental health visits. Of respondents with recent DIS/DSM-III disorders from 15.6 to 19.8% had made mental health visits, divided into 7.1–8.5% who went to a primary-care facility and 9.3–12.4% who went directly to the mental health specialty sector. This suggests a relatively impermeable first filter (one in 5 to 6 got through), and compared to

the situation in the Netherlands a rather similar third filter (one in 10 got through).

In general, but differing somewhat from one ECA site to another, both filters appeared less permeable for men, people aged 18–24 years and 65 years or more, as well as for people with substance abuse or dependence. The investigators concluded that help-seeking behaviour is quite low, particularly in people with cognitive disorders and substance abuse or dependence. Other cues to the permeability of the first filter were not presented.

In order to study the relationship between psychiatric morbidity and general practitioner consultation as well as some factors that might influence or modify this relationship, Williams et al. (1986) conducted a secondary analysis of data collected during their West London survey of the effects of exposure to aircraft noise. Of the men in the sample aged 16 years or more, 20.9% were GHQ positive (5+), and of the women 25.3%. During the 2 weeks prior to the investigation, about one-fourth had consulted their practitioner for "self" (23.7% of the GHQ positive men and 28.3% of the GHQ positive women). There was no evidence that sex selectively altered the permeability for minor psychiatric disorder of the first filter; the excess of female consultation could be accounted for by the female excess in morbidity in the population. An impression also commented upon by Blacker et al. (1987) concerning depression, who stated that young, working-class women are responsible for the lion's share of the community's depression; and that single, unemployed people living on their own overuse GP services.

For men in the Williams et al. study, employment status had an additive effect on the probability of consulting, because those not employed were more likely to consult, irrespective of their GHQ status. For men belonging to socio-economic groups 5 and 6, the presence of minor psychiatric disorder reduced the probability of their consulting the general practitioner. Williams and his co-workers assumed this relative impermeability of the first filter to be the result of sex- and social-class-related attitudes toward emotional problems and their management: they could reflect the people's notion that such problems are not appropriate matters to consult a doctor on.

Self-assessment of health and chronic illness both exerted an effect on general practitioner consultation that was independent of minor psychiatric morbidity in both sexes. The same applied to illness-related social impairment in men. For women, however, impairment and GHQ status exerted an interactive effect, i.e. the presence of self-rated social impairment increased the permeability of the first filter for GHQ negative women and not for GHQ positive women.

The above two investigations demonstrate, if anything, the complex structure of the first filter. The organisation of health care, people's attitudes and the character of morbidity (e.g. type or severity of psychological symptoms) interact in a way that is difficult to grasp and foresee by the primary-care provider. Comprehension of the nature of the first filter is a pre-condition for any attempt at increasing its permeability for defined high-risk groups in the population. At present, we are unfortunately a long way from being able to manipulate illness behavior!

Second Filter: GP Recognition of Cases.

The second filter has been investigated much more often than the first. It proved to be quite impermeable in most instances. Often not more than 50% of screened and probable cases are recognized by the general practitioner (Goldberg et al., 1987). To some extent this low rate of recognition may be more apparent than real, because follow-up of cases not detected by the GP at the time of their screening with the GHQ may still reveal psychological management immediately on encounter or during later visits (Jencks, 1985; Berwick et al., 1987; Shapiro et al., 1987). Failure of such cases to be detected could be an artifact of the research situation requiring an immediate diagnosis from the GP. In this respect, it might be better to

shift from a pre-occupation with the accuracy or inaccuracy of a clinician's diagnostic formulation alone to an additional concern for the processes whereby generalist physicians elicit, analyze, and synthesize or discard cues pertinent to mental illness (Schulberg et al., 1986).

This reorientation should include more emphasis on establishing the prevalence of co-morbidity of physical and emotional illness (Schulberg et al., 1987), obscuring the existence of one of the conditions. Blacker et al. (1987) mentioned that major depressives missed by their GP were more likely to be suffering from physical illnesses to which the depression seemed to be related.

Observations by Katon et al. (1986), regarding somatization, are along the same lines. They see the tendency for primary-care patients to somatize as resulting in an underestimate of psychiatric illness by epidemiologists and physicians who utilize screening questions that are primarily psychological in focus. Moreover, many primary-care patients have both medical and psychological illness, but often attribute psychological symptoms to their medical illness.

A much debated factor supposed to influence the permeability of the second filter is that of feeding the psychiatric screening results back to the GP (Hase et al., 1988; Rand et al., 1988; Kamerow, 1987; Campbell, 1987; Mari et al., 1987). The issue remains controversial, although for particular groups of patients, such as the elderly, blacks and men, there is ample evidence that feedback of screening results is effective (German et al., 1987; Shapiro et al., 1987). Using the SRQ and the CIS (Harding et al., 1980; Goldberg et al., 1970), Mari et al. (1987) calculated the benefit (the decrement in false negatives as compared with the GP's assessment only) to costs (the increment in false positives as compared with the GP's assessment only) ratio, which was optimal with the diagnostic strategy of using the SRQ score only and ignoring the GP's assessment.

Bellantuono et al. (1987) pointed out the influence of the presence alone of researchers in a practice on the diagnostic behaviour of the GP. The GP's case rate, sensitivity, bias and accuracy were higher when the research psychiatrist was present than after he had concluded his interviews, and his specificity and hidden morbidity were lower. In other words, the attitude of the GP is a crucial factor in opening up the second filter (Burns, 1985; Johnstone et al., 1976; Goldberg, 1985). This is revealed in his interest, knowledge and skills, and practice style, such as the length of visits and tendency to order diagnostic tests and to refer to specialists. The GP has to be prepared to make multiple diagnoses and to consider psychiatric illness not only in those patients for whom he has been unable to make a physical diagnosis. Of course, he has to be convinced that the effects of case detection and treatment are beneficial. In a controlled trial, Johnstone and Goldberg (1976) demonstrated that the duration of the episode was much shorter for patients whose disorder had been recognized by the general practitioner. For patients with more severe disorders, there were significant differences still demonstrable between the groups one year later.

Up to this point we have mainly reviewed variables related to the primary-care provider which appear important in determining the permeability of the second filter. Another question regards what characteristics of primary-care patients themselves can serve as cues to alert the GP that he might be dealing with a psychiatric case. Vaillant et al. (1988) stated that even psychiatric epidemiologists lack a "gold standard" to establish psychiatric morbidity, and that the greatest obstacle to obtaining validity is that most psychiatric disorders are dimensional and not categorical. They applied different models for assessing psychiatric impairment and found the same power of discrimination whether impairment was assessed from categorical criteria (research caseness and DSM-III diagnosis), by adult adjustment, by inferred intrapsychiatric adaptation (immaturity of defenses), or by a scaled estimate of psychosocial impairment. Overlap was enormous. If a person's level of functioning and work is strongly related to psychopathology, that kind of information might serve more easily than psychiatric symptoms as a key for the primary-care provider to psychiatric caseness (Wright et al., 1987). Unfortunately, the literature does not provide much data on such concomitants of psychiatric morbidity.

A primary-care attender's history and sociodemographic profile appears to provide some relevant information. Previous mental disorder, low education and income, and widowhood increased detection of psychiatric morbidity (Hoeper et al., 1984). Boardman (1987) found a higher identification index (number of

patients identified as ill by GP and GHQ/number of high scorers (GHQ) × sensitivity), for example, in widowed, separated, and elderly adult patients, as well as in some non-British ethnic groups. We could find no data on biographic information related to GP case detection. More detailed sociodemographic and biographic research into high risk groups might help us to identify facts which could increase permeability of the second filter by alerting the GP. Such studies should include not only previous but also subsequent illness behavior of primary-care attenders to discover more subtle indicators of psychiatric morbidity, such as disease conviction (Pilowsky, 1987).

In summary, it appears that permeability of the second filter can be influenced by increasing the GP's awareness of the nature and prevalence of mental health problems amongst his attenders, and of the existence of high risk groups.

Third Filter: The Decision to Refer

Permeability of the third filter should be adequate and not necessarily greater. We have already seen that approximately 10% of morbidity reaches the mental health sector. They should be the right type of cases and not necessarily more. Very few studies deal with this question, particularly with referral patterns of patients that were also involved in GP detection studies.

A multipractice study of depressive patients in the Netherlands (Sigling, 1984), involving 62 general practitioners, surveyed their reasons for referring patients. Feelings of incompetence, failure of the patient to respond to treatment and risk of suicide were cited most often. Rawnsley et al. (1962) found a wider range of factors: failure to respond to treatment, the need for inpatient care, type of illness, pressure from relatives, request by the patient to see a specialist, serious impairment of patient's working capacity, lack of emotional support for the patient from members of the family, and the opinion of the GP that his patient may find it more acceptable to be told that he has nervous trouble by a specialist, rather than by his own doctor. So far, these factors affecting permeability of the third filter, mainly concern competence of the GP. Their consideration could lead to attempts at increasing his competence, thereby decreasing permeability of the filter.

Another factor is the structure of the health care system and accessibility of the specialty sector, as we have mentioned in the discussion of the ECA study. Degrees of distress constitute a further factor in seeking mental health care. Berwick et al. (1987) found that especially persistent high scorers on the GHQ were more likely than low scorers to enter the system of care, not only for primary care but also for mental health care. Sashidharan et al. (1988) compared hospital-treated and general-population morbidity from affective disorder and provided useful indirect information on permeability of the third filter. Women who are single and over 55 years are more likely to arrive at the specialty sector, compared with other women with similar disorders. Ormel et al. (1990) found that recognition of a GHQ positive case increased the likelihood of referral (17%) compared with that of unrecognized GHQ positive cases (6%).

It appears to be the attitude of the GP, more in terms of insecurity, in combination with the nature of his cases which determine the permeability of the third filter. The ultimate test of the value of an increased permeability of this filter is an outcome study, with patients randomly assigned to treatment by

the GP or treatment by mental health professional. In the final part of the chapter we will return to factors affecting permeability of the second and third filter on the basis of a study conducted in Dutch general practice.

A Dutch Study of the Second and Third Filters

From the above review of the literature, no consistent profile regarding permeability of the second and third filters emerged. This is partly because the studies that were reviewed are not strictly comparable: for example, their health-care systems are quite different. More can be learned if the consecutive filters are examined in one and the same study. This was done in a panel study of primary care conducted from September 1985 to May 1987 in the province of Groningen, the Netherlands (see also Ormel et al., 1990; Wilmink, 1989).

Design

Table 3.1 describes the design of the study. In order to obtain a representative sample of GPs with regard to their basic attitude toward family medicine, a stratified sample of 25 GPs was selected from the total population of GPs practicing in the town of Groningen (population: 175,000), and in the surrounding villages. Each GP recruited all patients, aged 16 to 65 years, attending on any of 10

Table 3.1. Patient selection.

2237 patients from 25 GP's (25 series of approximately 90 consecutive GP attenders)
1994 returned GHQ (11% nonresponse)

	Presence of MHP in past 12 months according to GP				
	no		yes		
	1450 "new" patients		544 "old" patients		
GHQ/GP caseness:	GHQ-/GP-	GHQ-/GP+	GHQ+/GP-	GHQ+/GP+	
	847	46	397	160	n=1450
Sampling proportion:					
7%	100%		23%	100%	
62	46		91	160	n= 359
Nonresponse: (total 27%)					
15%	54%		12%	34%	
53	21		80	106	n= 260
Thus, 260 were assessed with the PSE/GSDS					

specified days. These were distributed in a systematic manner over four weeks in order to avoid bias. During this index consultation, the GP filled out a standard form about his patient, and handed out the GHQ to be completed at home and returned by mail to the Department of Social Psychiatry. The nonresponders did not differ from responders with respect to age and the presence of a mental health problem as assessed by the GP. However, males did more often fail to respond than did females (13% vs. 9%). We distinguished between "old" and "new" cases on the basis of a mental health problem having been diagnosed by the GP during the previous 12 months or not.

After the next sampling stage, those patients sampled were approached within 2 weeks of the index consultation for interviewing with the *Present State Examination* (PSE) and the *Groningen Social Disability Schedule* (GSDS). Following the index consultation the GPs kept a record on their management of cases.

Caseness and Other Measurements

Three definitions of caseness were used:

1) *GP cases.* On the basis of information collected during the index consultation, the GP assessed the presenting complaints as indicating (1) physical illness, (2) specific psychiatric disorder, (3) physical or psychological complaints from psychosocial problems or stress, or (4) a health visit. Categories (2) and (3) were considered GP-cases.

2) *GHQ-caseness.* This was determined with the GHQ-30 version at cutting points 4/5 and 8/9.

3) Finally, *psychiatric caseness* followed the *Present State Examination Index* of Definition of 5+.

Social disability was assessed with *Groningen Social Disability Schedule* (Wiersma, 1986). Some problems in at least two roles or major problems in at least one counted as disability. Other measurements included the attitude of the GP (Verhaak, 1986); the reason for encounter, as psychological or other; neuroticism and extraversion (Wilde, 1962), and total unpleasantness because of long-term difficulties. We also applied Brown and Harris' (1986) method of assessing *life events and long-term difficulties.*

Findings Regarding the Second Filter

Those giving a psychological reason for encounter to the GP were 150 times as likely to be detected as cases than those giving other reasons. This is measured as an *odds ratio* of 150.[1] This effect appeared so overwhelming that the next analysis of the second filter concerns only patients with other reasons for their visit.

Table 3.2 gives the odds ratios of the GP detecting a GHQ-case for variables that had a significant effect, for the 712 patients without a psychological reason for their encounter. (Age, sex, level of education and attitude of the GP had no significant effect and are therefore not included in the table.) It can be seen that if the case is "old," if the patient is married or widowed, and for each one-point increment in GHQ score, there is a positive effect on detection. In the second column results are recalculated correcting for the effect of "old" cases, while in the third column results are given correcting for the effect of

---

1   An odds ratio of a given event is the *ratio of the probability of its occurrence to the probability of its nonoccurrence.* An example may make this clearer: Let us suppose we were interested in the effect of neuroticism on referral. In the present study of the 33 individuals with high neuroticism, 7 were referred and 26 were not, so that for these patients the probability of referral was 7/33, or 1:4.7. However, of the 58 individuals with low neuroticism, 8 were referred and 50 were not, so that the probability of referral was 8/58, or 1:7.2. The ratio of these two probabilities is the odds ratio, 1.67 in this example. Thus, if you are neurotic, you have a 1.67 times greater chance of referral than if you are not.
    When interpreting odds ratios three things are important: (1) No effect gives an odds ratio of 1 (not zero: an odds ratio of zero would be a very strong negative effect!); (2) the odds ratio is not a symmetrical measure: its range is from zero to infinity; (3) the odds of referral is the reciprocal of the odds of nonreferral, and this facilitates interpretation of odds ratios of less than unity. Thus, an odds ratio of 0.10 for the relationship between education and referral means that those with high education have one-tenth the chance of referral than those with low education; or, those with low education are ten times as likely to be referred as those with high education.

Table 3.2. Odds ratios (OR) of GP recognizing cases with GHQ-5+ and reasons for encounter other than psychological (N=712).

Variable	OR	OR₁	OR₂
Old cases	5.44**	—	—
One point increment in GHQ			
total score	1.03**	1.00	—
Type of occupation: student	.60*	.82	1.21
On social assistance	.77	.66*	.66
Marital state			
— single	1.00	1.00	1.00
— married	1.51**	1.33**	1.33*
— divorced	.63	.46*	.46*
— widowed	4.25**	3.96**	3.96**

OR₁   effect of variable corrected for newness of case
OR₂   effect of variable corrected for newness of case and
      increment in GHQ total score
* $p<0.10$, ** $p<0.05$, *** $p<0.01$

GHQ score. (When we considered only GHQ-8+ cases, the effect of the GHQ total score disappeared, and age 45 years or more gained some effect: 1.85**, 1.58* and 1.58* respectively).

In Table 3.3, the analysis of the second filter is continued only for the 179 new patients—whatever their reason for encounter—who had an interview and, therefore could be assessed in more detail. GP attitude, neuroticism, extroversion, social support, life events and their total unpleasantness, long-term difficulties and their total unpleasantness, and age did not appear to have a significant effect on detection. Once more, psychological reasons for the encounter had a strong effect, as did PSE caseness, and to a lesser extent social disability.

Long-term difficulties resulting from an event seemed to have an effect only for cases with a score of 8+. It can be seen that youth has an effect after corrections have been made for reason for the encounter, caseness and social disability.

So far, with few exceptions, primarily psychiatric features of a case appear to affect permeability of the second filter, while sociographic and biographic characteristics seem to play a less important role.

Findings Regarding the Third Filter

Table 3.4 deals with the new cases—whatever their reason for encounter—who were detected by the GP and were interviewed.

Table 3.3. Odds ratios (ORs) of GP recognising new cases with GHQ-5+, and followed up for PSE and GSDS interview (N=179).

Variable	OR	OR₁	OR₂	OR₃
Age 45 yrs. or more				
vs. 16–30 yrs.	0.43	0.23**	0.25**	0.20**
Psychol. reason encounter	40.90***	—	—	—
PSE-5+ case	7.18***	3.48***	—	—
Social disability	3.15***	2.38**	1.88	—
Event related difficulty	3.31**	1.93	2.06	2.08

OR₁   effect of variable corrected for reason for encounter
OR₂   effect of variable corrected for reason and PSE-caseness
OR₃   effect of variable corrected for reason, PSE-caseness and social disability
** $p<0.05$, *** $p<0.01$

Table 3.4. Odds ratios of referral for mental health problem of new GHQ-5+ cases, who had been recognized by GP (N=100).

Variable	OR	OR₁	OR₂	OR₃
Psychological reason encounter	9.58***	—	—	—
PSE-caseness	3.48***	2.44	—	—
Social disability	2.00	1.70	1.33	—
Long-term difficulty	3.79**	3.84**	3.62**	3.60**
Event related difficulty	3.17**	2.40	1.94	1.88
Family orientation GP	4.19*	4.82*	4.81*	4.82*

OR₁   effect of variable adjusted for reason
OR₂   effect of variable adjusted for reason and PSE-caseness
OR₃   effect of variable adjusted for reason, PSE-caseness and social disability
* p<.1, ** p<.05, *** p<.01

Referral—and thus permeability of the third filter—was not only influenced by psychiatric features of the case but apparently also by his or her social problems as well as the "family orientation" of the GP. When allowance has been made for reason for the encounter, caseness and social disability, there are still effects from long-term difficulties and the family orientation of the GP. However, age, sex, social disability, neuroticism, extroversion, social support, life events and their total unpleasantness as well as the total unpleasantness of long-term difficulties did not exert a significant effect on referral for a mental health problem. It appears that GPs tend to refer patients with psychiatric symptoms, who also have life problems; and that the family orientation of the GP is also an important factor.

Conclusions

Today, the emphasis is on treating mental health problems as much as possible at the primary-care level. Most of our knowledge regarding mental disorder was gathered during clinical epidemiological studies first at the fifth and then gradually more and more at the fourth level of morbidity. Goldberg and Huxley's model of the pathway down to this level indicates that morbidity filtered through as far down as this constitutes only a fraction of morbidity in the community. This is important knowledge, as it provides insight into the GP's diagnostic behaviour and his or her management of cases. Crucial to this management are the illness behaviour of the patient, reflected in the decision to visit the GP and the reasons presented during this encounter; and the decisions of the GP, reflected in his recognition of a mental health problem and its eventual referral to the specialty sector. Such insight has already been incorporated into training programmes (Gask, 1989).

This review of the literature on the filters provided hardly any study observing and describing directly the decisions and resulting actions of the GP in individual cases, i.e. describing the process in longitudinal studies of groups of patients. Most studies try to elucidate the process by looking at indirect indicators of illness behaviour of the patient and of the decision behaviour of the GP. Findings suggest that psychiatric symptoms and complaining behaviour, and to some extent social disability, play a greater role than does the biographic and socio-graphic context of patients, as far as detection and referral are concerned. The impression is that the more disordered patients are recognized, and the more disordered and troubled are referred to the specialty sector. Whether this is desirable depends on the organisation of the general and mental health services. The impression from the Dutch study is that GPs do not respond to such cues as life events or social support—features of a case that appear important for treatment and could easily be incorporated in a management protocol.

References

Bellantuono, C., Fiorio, R., Zanotelli, R., & Tansella, M. (1987). Psychiatric screening in general practice in Italy. *Social Psychiatry, 22,* 113–117.

Berwick, D. M., Budman, S., Damico-White, J., Feldstein, M. & Klerman, G. L. (1987). Assessment of psychological morbidity in primary care: Explorations with the General Health Questionnaire. *J. Chron. Dis., 40,* 71S–79S.

Blacker, C.V.R., & Clare, W. (1987). Depressive disorder in primary care. *Brit. J. of Psychiatry, 150,* 737–751.

Boardman, A. P. (1987). The General Health Questionnaire and the detection of emotional disorder by general practitioners. *Brit. J. of Psychiatry, 151,* 373–381.

Brook, F.G., Giel, R., ten Horn, G.H.M.M., Ormel, J., & Wiersma, D. (1985). Epidemiologische beschouwingen over vraag en aanbod in de geestelijke gezondheidszorg. In J. W. B. M. van Berkestijn, R. Giel & R. A. van de Hoofdakker (Eds.), *Stukken van de Puzzel* (31–61). Groningen: v. Denderen.

Brown, G. W., & Harris, T. (1986). Establishing causal links: The Bedford studies of depression. In H. Katschnig (Ed.), *Life events and psychiatric disorders: Controversial issues.* London: Cambridge University Press.

Burns, B.J., & Burke, J. D. (1985). Improving mental health practices in primary care: findings from recent research. *Public Health Reports, 100*(3), 294–300.

Campbell, T. L. (1987). An opposing view. *The Journal of Family Practice, 25,* 184–187.

Gask, L. (1989). Bibliography of training courses for primary-care physicians. In N. Sartorius, D. P. Goldberg et al. (Eds.), *Psychological disorders in general medical settings (App. 1).* Toronto: Hogrefe & Huber.

German, P. S., Shapiro, S., Skinner, E. A., v. Korff, M., Klein, L. E., Turner, R. W., Teitelbaum, M. L., Burke, J., & Burns, B.J. (1987). Detection and management of mental health problems of older patients by primary care providers. *JAMA, 257,* 489–493.

Goldberg, D. (1985). The detection of psychiatric disorder in primary care settings. Implications for the taxonomy of neurosis. *Isr. J. Psychiatry Relat. Scie., 22,* 245–255.

Goldberg, D., & Blackwell, B. (1970). Psychiatric illness in general practice. A detailed study using a new method of case identification. *Br. Med. J.,* 439–443.

Goldberg, D., & Huxley, P. (1980). *Mental illness in the community, the pathway to psychiatric care.* London, New York: Tavistock.

Goldberg, D., & Bridges, K. (1987). Screening for psychiatric illness in general practice: The general practitioner versus the screening questionnaire. *J. of the Royal College of General Practitioners, 37,* 15–18.

Harding, T. W., Arango, M. V., Baltazar, J., Climent, C. E., Ibrahim, H. H. A., Ignacio, L. L., Murthy, R. S., & Wig, N. N. (1980). Mental disorders in primary health care: A study of their frequency and diagnosis in four developing countries. *Psychol. Med., 10,* 231–241.

Hase, H. D., & Luger, J. A. (1988). Screening for psychosocial problems in primary care. *The J. of Family Practice, 26*(3), 297–302.

Hodiamont, P., Peer, N., & Syben, N. (1986). Epidemiological aspects of psychiatric disorder in a Dutch health area. *Psychological Medicine, 17,* 495–505.

Hoeper, E. W., Nycz, G. R., Kessler, L. G., Burke, J. D. & Pierce, W. E. (1984). The usefulness of screening for mental illness. *The Lancet, I,* 33–35.

Jencks, S. F. (1985). Recognition of mental distress and diagnosis of mental disorder in primary care. *JAMA, 253*(13), 1903–1907.

Johnstone, A., & Goldberg, D. (1976). Psychiatric screening in general practice. *The Lancet, 20,* 605–609.

Kamerow, D. B. (1987). Is screening for mental health problems worthwhile in family practice? An affirmative view. *The J. of Family Practice, 25*(2), 181–183.

Katon, W., Vitaliano, P. P., Russo, J., Cormier, L., Anderson, K., & Jones, M. (1986). Panic disorder: Epidemiology in primary care. *The J. of Family practice, 23*(3), 233–239.

Mari, J. de J., Iacoponi, E., Williams, P., Simoes, O., Silva, J. B. T. (1987). Detection of psychiatric morbidity in the primary medical care setting in Brazil. *Rev. Saude public., 21*(6), 501–507.

Ormel, J., v.d. Brink, W., Koeter, M. W. J., Giel, R., van der Meer, K., van de Willige, G., Wilmink, F. W. (1990). *Recognition, management, and outcome of mental health problems. A naturalistic study in 25 Dutch general practices.* Submitted.

Pilowsky, I., Smith, Q. P., & Katsikitis, M. K (1987). Illness behaviour and general practice utilisation: A prospective study. *J. of Psychosomatic Research, 31,* 177–183.

Rand, E. H., Badger, L. W., & Coggings, D. R. (1988). Toward a resolution of contradictions—Utility of feedback from the GHQ. *Gen. Hosp. Psychiat. 10*(3), 189–196.

Rawnsley, K., & Loudon, J. B. (1962). Factors influencing the referral of patients to psychiatrists by general practitioners. *Brit. J. Prev. Soc. Med., 16,* 174–182.

Sashidharan, S. P., Surtees, P. G., Kreitman, N. B., Ingham, J. G., & Miller, P. Mc C. (1988). Hospital-treated and general-population morbidity from affective disorders. Comparison of prevalence and inception rates. *Brit. J. of Psychiatry, 152,* 499–505.

Schulberg, H. C., McClelland, M., Coulehan, J. L., Block, M., & Werner, G. (1986). Psychiatric deci-

Section II   Chapter 3

sion making in family practice. Future research directions. *Gen. Hosp. Psychiat. 8*, 1–6.

Schulberg. H. C., McClelland, M., & Burns, B. J. (1987). Depression and physical illness: The prevalence, causation, and diagnosis of comorbidity. *Clinical Psychology Review, 7*, 145–167.

Shapiro, S., Skinner, E. A., Kessler, L. G., von Korff, M., German, P. S., Tischler, G. L., Leaf, P. J., Benham, L., Cottler, L., Regier, D. A. (1984). Utilization of health and mental health services—Three epidemiologic catchment area sites. *Arch. Gen. Psychiatry, 41*, 971–977.

Shapiro, S., German, P. S., Skinner, E. A., von Korff, M., Turner, R. W., Klein, L. E., Teitelbaum, M. L., Kramer, M., Burke, J. D., & Burns, B. J. (1987). An experiment to change detection and management of mental morbidity in primary care. *Medical Care, 25*(4), 327–339.

Sigling, H. O. (1984). *Herkenning en benadering van patienten met een depressief syndroom*. Publikatie onderzoeksprojekt van het Huisartseninstituut van de V.U. i.s.m. het Peilstationsproject Nederland.

Vaillant, G. E., & Schnurr, P. (1988). What is a case? A 45-year study of psychiatric impairment within a college sample selected for mental health. *Arch. Gen. Psychiatry, 45*, 313–376.

Verhaak, P. F. M. (1986). *Interpretatie en behandeling van psychosociale klachten in de huisartsenpraktijk: een onderzoek naar verschillen tussen huisartsen*. Utrecht: Nivel.

Wiersma, D. (1986). *Groningen Social Disabilities Schedule: Manual for the use of the instrument*. Department of Social Psychiatry, University of Groningen.

Wilde, G. J. S. (1962). *Neurotische labiliteit gemeten volgens de vragenlijstmethode*. Amsterdam: v. Rossen.

Williams, P., Tarnopolsky, A., Hand, D., & Shepherd, M. (1986). *Minor psychiatric morbidity and general practice consultations: The West London Survey*. Supplement to *Psychological Medicine 9* (1–37). Cambridge: University Press.

Wilmink, F. W. (1989). *Patient, physician, psychiatrist. Assessment of mental health problems in primary care*. Thesis, Dept. of Social Psychiatry, State University Groningen, The Netherlands. UKKA Books.

Wright, A. F., & Perini, A. F. (1987). Hidden psychiatric illness: Use of the general health questionnaire in general practice. *J. of the Royal College of General Practitioners, 37*, 164–167.

Wijkel, D. (1986). *Samenwerken en verwijzen*. Utrecht: Nivel.

Chapter 4
Mental Health in Primary-Care Settings

J. L. Vázquez-Barquero

The way in which illness expresses itself is shaped, to a great extent, by socio-cultural and psychological factors. This point of view has been incorporated in the construct "illness behaviour" developed by Mechanic (1962). The act of consulting a doctor and being "labelled" and treated as mentally ill is part of this process of illness behaviour and is in itself also influenced not only by the presence of symptoms but also by a range of non-medical factors. Since the pioneering work of Shepherd et al. (1966), it has been accepted that the general practitioner plays a very relevant role in the process that starts with the patient's recognition of being ill and ends in the act of receiving psychiatric treatment. It is thus pertinent to discover whether primary care is used in an adequate manner and according to the needs of the consultees. In order to explore the way in which this is achieved in Spanish primary-care settings, we analyze some of our recent research findings. For this we follow the model put forward by Goldberg and Huxley (1980) to describe psychiatric disorders in the community and the pathway they follow in the pursuit of specialist care.

Psychiatric Morbidity in the Community

Using the *Clinical Interview Schedule* (CIS) (Goldberg et al., 1970), the *General Health Questionnaire* (GHQ) (Goldberg & Williams, 1988) and the *Present State Examination* (PSE) (Wing et al., 1974), we have, in the last few years, explored the extension and nature of mental illness in two different Spanish communities. We were able to show in the Community Survey of Cantabria (Table 4.1) that 14.7% of the total population (8.1% of men and 20.6% of women) had psychiatric disorders as measured by the PSE-ID-CATEGO system (Vázquez-Barquero et al., 1987). These morbidity figures are much lower than those detected by us with a similar two-stage design in a different community, the Baztan Valley (Vázquez-Barquero et al., 1981, 1982). Although there are clear sociological differences between the two communities, the variation in morbidity figures appears to be due to having applied different psychiatric interviews, i.e. the *Clinical Interview Schedule* (CIS) in the Baztan Valley and the *Present State Examination* (PSE) in the Cantabria Survey. We therefore feel that in order to obtain comparability between surveys, it is necessary to use not only similar methodological designs, but also comparable measures of morbidity—something that is often forgotten and should be taken into account in future comparisons of research findings.

We can also see in Table 4.1 that our morbidity figures in the Cantabria Survey are, for males, very similar to those detected with similar methodology in other communities (Bebbington et al., 1981; Henderson et al., 1981; Hodiamont et al., 1987). This is, however, not the case with females, among whom our prevalence rates are much higher. This higher female morbidity, which is due to a significant rise of phobic disorders, is associated with another relevant finding: the reversal in females of the predominance of depression upon anxiety described in the majority of the community surveys. This reversal, also detected by Brown and Harris (1978)

This investigation was supported by grants Exp. N 88/2147 and 89/0361 from the Spanish National Institute of Health, F.I.S.

Table 4.1. Description of the characteristics of some recent two-stage community surveys.

Author & area	First stage		Second stage		Weighted psychiatric prevalence %		
	N in sample	Instru.	N in sample	Instru.	Male	Female	Total
Vázquez-Barquero et al. (1981) Spain (rural)	1156	GHQ-60	415	CIS	19.1	28.3	23.8
Henderson et al. (1981) Australia (urban)	756	GHQ-30	157	PSE-140	7.1	11.1	9.0
Bebbington et al. (1981) England (urban)	800	PSE-40	310	PSE-140	6.1	14.9	10.9
Hodiamont et al. (1987) Holland (urban)	3232	GHQ-60	482	PSE-140	7.2	7.5	7.3
Vázquez-Barquero et al. (1987) Spain (rural)	1232	GHQ-60	425	PSE-140	8.1	20.6	14.7

in the New Hebrides and by Mavreas et al. (1986) in southern Europe, suggests the existence of cultural variations in the depressive/anxiety style of expressing psychological distress. This point of view has been confirmed by recent comparison of the symptoms profiles obtained in different European community surveys (Mavreas & Bebbington, 1988; Vázquez-Barquero et al., 1988).

As in other surveys we found that age maintained an interactive relationship with sex in relation to the presence of mental illness. In fact, while in males disorders were more common in those over the age of 35 in females the rise in prevalence occurred above

the age of 45. This trend, which is largely due to married women, is interpreted by Bebbington et al. (1981) as a consequence of children leaving home. The fact that we could not show a significant association with child care, unemployment or low social class for females contradicts the findings of other surveys conducted in urban areas of Northern Europe (Brown & Harris, 1978; Bebbington et al., 1981). It is conceivable that differences between the social structures of northern European and Mediterranean countries or between the urban and rural lifestyles account for these variations. We thus suggest that the way in which socio-demographic variables

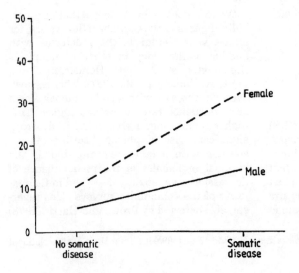

Figure 4.1. Weighted prevalence of psychiatric disorders (PSE-CATEGO-ID system) by sex and somatic disease.

condition the prevalence of mental disorders in each sex is cultural in nature and should be interpreted in the light of the idiosyncrasies of each community (Vázquez-Barquero et al., 1987; De Santiago et al., 1987).

Irrespective of differences in methods, most surveys demonstrate that in the community there is a clear interaction between physical and mental disorders. This has also been unequivocally confirmed by us both in the Baztan Valley and in the Cantabria surveys (Vázquez-Barquero et al., 1981, 1988). The data of the Community Survey of Cantabria shows in this respect that sex and physical illness exerted a significant influence on psychiatric morbidity (Figure 4.1). These variables, however, are by no means independent in their effects. The association of feminine status with somatic disease creates the condition of maximum risk of mental illness, while the absence of somatic disease tends to level out the sexual differences in psychiatric morbidity. We have also shown that this interaction between physical and psychiatric disorders is influenced by social factors in a "sex-specific" manner (Vázquez-Barquero et al., 1988). These findings are, therefore, in line with the theory put forward by Goldberg and Huxley (1980), who suggest that the predominance of mental disease in females is mainly the result of differences in the pattern of illness behaviour adopted by each sex. There is now good evidence to show that females are systematically more willing to acknowledge illness, to present physical and psychological complaints, and to establish contact with a medical agency.

What are the consequences of all these general findings?

- *First*, that, irrespective of the characteristics of the community, between 7% and 15% of the general population should formulate demands for mental health care, the extension of these demands being at least as twice as great in females than in males, and tending to increase with age.

- *Second*, that these demands will be in the majority of cases the expression of a combination of mental and physical needs, and therefore will tend to be formulated in a "bodily language."

- *Third*, that all these needs and demands

may be largely influenced by socio-cultural factors.

Considering that in most countries, and certainly in Spain, primary care is the first line of contact with the health system, it appears relevant to focus our attention on the analysis of the way in which these variables condition the process of establishing contact with primary-care services.

The Influence of Needs in Primary-Care Consultation

A conceptual model has been set out by Andersen in an attempt to integrate the many possible factors which influence the utilization of medical services in the community (Andersen & Newman, 1973; Andersen et al., 1975; Andersen & Laake, 1985). According to this model, physician utilization is determined by three sets of factors: "societal," "system" and "individual."

Societal factors include aspects such as attitudes and beliefs about illness. *System factors* are related to aspects like health service structure and organization. Both are postulated to influence *individual determinants*, which directly condition the utilization of resources. They also describe three subsets of variables related to individual determinants:

1) *illness variables*, which includes both physical and mental illness;

2) *predisposing variables*, which indicate how disposed a person is to establish medical contact;

3) *enabling variables*, which refer to conditions that facilitate or inhibit the use of services.

Despite the fact that the majority of surveys have shown that almost all the explained variance in consultation results from illness variables, it still appears useful to use this model as a framework for exploring the utilization of primary-care services.

Although physical illness is expected to be the best predictor of primary-care utilization, psychiatric disorders have also emerged as a powerful determinant of medical contact. Finlay-Jones and Burvill (1978), by comparing data from a community and a general practice survey, showed that while in respondents scoring 0–11 on the *General Health Questionnaire* ("noncases") the chances of consulting a general practitioner were 1 in 130, in those scoring 12+ ("cases") they were 1 in 60. These findings were confirmed by Burvill and Knuiman (1983) in a subsequent reanalysis of the same data using a logistic modelling technique. Studies like these present data at the aggregate level: it is community and general practice surveys, and not individuals, that are compared. Consequently, as Williams et al. (1986) emphasize, care must be exercised to avoid making inferences of individual levels on the basis of such comparisons.

Individual-level studies on the correlates of general practice consultation have been carried out in recent years in general practice settings, showing basically the same results as aggregate-level studies (Briscoe, 1987; Corney & Murray, 1988). Although these designs offer a clear view of the characteristics of persons who passed Filter 1 of the model proposed by Goldberg and Huxley (1980), they have the disadvantage of not allowing generalization of findings to the general population, and also of not permitting comparisons between persons who establish and those who do not establish medical contact. The only way to overcome these disadvantages is by conducting investigations in the community at an individual level. One such study is the secondary analysis carried out by Williams et al. (1986) on the data of the West London Survey (Tarnopolsky & Norton-Williams, 1980). They found that the presence of psychiatric morbidity, as measured by the GHQ-30, doubled the probability of consulting, and that about one-fifth of consultation could be attributed to it.

Similarly, in an analysis of a community sample using the 60-item *General Health Questionnaire* (Goldberg & Williams, 1988), we found that 25% of male and 34% of female probable cases had consulted a general practitioner in the 2 weeks prior to the survey (Table 4.2). This positive relationship between GHQ status and the likelihood of consulting a general practitioner is also demonstrated in our data by calculating "Levin's attributable risk" (Levin, 1953). We found that 15.5% of the consultation by the men and 20.3% of the consultation by the women could be attributed to psychiatric morbidity. These findings, which are remarkably similar to those obtained by Williams et al. (1986) in their secondary analysis of the West London Survey, could be used as an indicator of the effect of GHQ status on consultation. We have to point out, however, that in spite of the relevance of this effect, a high percentage (around 50%) of GHQ positive respondents have still not had recent contact with a medical agency. These results, which are again similar to those found by Williams et al. (1986) in a community with highly developed primary-care services, have important health implications and suggest that regardless of the level of complexity of the health service structure, a large proportion of probable psychiatric cases remain in the community without establishing medical contact.

Table 4.2. GHQ scores and general practice consultation in a community sample by sex.

GHQ SCORE	Male*			Female**		
	N in sample	G.P. consult.		N in sample	G.P. consult.	
		N	%		N	%
0–5	428	38	8.9	347	49	14.1
6–11	85	12	14.	136	32	23.5
12–19	45	7	15.6	91	29	31.9
20 +	23	10	43.5	68	25	36.8
TOTAL	581	67	11.5	642	135	21.0

* $\chi = 27.3$, df = 3, p<0.001
** $\chi = 27.1$, df = 3, p<0.001

Table 4.3. The statistically significant joint main effects on general practitioner consultation: linear-logistic model.

	Estimate	(S. E.)	Difference in deviance	d. f.,p
GM	−2.824	0.1861	—	
Sex2	0.5242	0.1625	11.42	1, <0.001
Age2	1.100	0.1782	42.19	1, <0.001
GHQ2	0.9607	0.1711	28.78	1, <0.001

Sex1, Age1, and GHQ1, were all constrained to be zero by the model.

The Influence of Predisposing and Enabling Factors in General Practice Consultation

There is widespread opinion that the decision to consult a general practitioner may be influenced not only by the presence of physical and psychological symptoms, but also by a range of socio-demographic factors. This point of view has been investigated in the Community Survey of Cantabria by analyzing the influence of six socio-demographic variables (sex, age, marital status, social class, educational level, urban/rural area of residence) in the interaction between psychiatric morbidity and general practice consultation. For this, first the association between GHQ status and consultation was independently assessed (Table 4.2), and secondly the joint effect of GHQ status and the six socio-demographic variables on consultation was evaluated through linear-logistic modelling (Table 4.3). Our findings confirmed that sexual differences do have a significant influence on the probability of consulting a general practitioner. In fact, women were more likely to consult irrespective of the presence or absence of psychiatric morbidity. At the same time, the effect of psychiatric morbidity, as measured by the GHQ, on the probability of consulting a general practitioner did not vary according to sex. Thus, in our survey sex and GHQ status exerted a main independent effect on consultation. These results are in accordance with the findings of other authors who suggest that women are more predisposed to consult especially with vague complains, for psychological symptoms or when looking for reassurance (Waldron, 1983; Briscoe, 1987).

Our data also indicated that age exerted a main effect on general practitioner consultation, an effect that was independent of psychiatric morbidity. The direction of the effect was toward an increase of consultation with increasing age. This association has been reported in numerous previous studies and appears to be largely accounted for by the increase of medical problems accompanying longevity (Barsky et al., 1986; Vázquez-Barquero et al., 1988).

Socio-cultural factors affect demand for medical care in a complex way, and contradictory results have been reported. While different authors have found a significant association between social class, educational level, employment status and the likelihood of consulting (Ingham & Miller, 1983), others have not found such an association (Wolinsky, 1978; Tanner et al., 1983; Andersen & Laake, 1987). We found that the effect of these predisposing variables in the logistic model analysis conducted with our data was not significant (Table 4.3). The analysis of the way in which urban/rural area of residence conditions the utilization of services deserves special consideration. The reason for this is that they represent one of the few "enabling" conditions that may facilitate or inhibit health service use. Our data indicate that the urban/rural area of residence did not exerted a significant effect on consultation, thus confirming that—as with the predisposing factors—the enabling variables are also irrelevant to health service use.

We conclude by saying that the most important finding to emerge from our data was the main independent effects of sex, age and psychiatric morbidity on general practice consultation. Furthermore, as in the secondary analysis conducted by Williams et al. (1986), we did not observe any significant interaction between psychiatric morbidity and the enabling or predisposing variables examined. Thus sexual differences and psychiatric morbidity appear to be the main determinants of the process of passing through the first filter of the model proposed by Goldberg and Huxley (1986). We have to point out, however, that there are potentially relevant variables that have gone unmeasured in our survey, such as attitudes, subjective evaluation of symptoms and appraisal of health system characteristics, and that may be very relevant in primary-care utilization (Tanner et al., 1983; Wolinsky, 1978).

The Detection and Treatment of Psychiatric Disorders by General Practitioners

The performance of the general practitioner in managing patients afflicted by psychiatric illness could be analysed from two independent but complementary perspectives: one centred around the study of their ability to identify psychiatric disorders and the second related to the analysis of their prescription habits for psychotropic drugs.

There have been a considerable number of surveys conducted in primary-care centres which have shown great variations in the rates of psychiatric disorders. In fact, the mean rates ranged from 9.0% to 39% (Goldberg & Huxley, 1986). These variations are not a reflection of real morbidity differences but rather the result of the various concepts of psychiatric illness and thresholds for case identification adopted by the general practitioner. Furthermore, as these surveys present information gathered in the context of a primary-care centre, their findings should not be unduly generalized to the general population. It is conceivable that data from primary-care studies may be influenced by an *assessment bias* derived from the general practitioner, who was aware that his clinical routine would be scrutinized in a research project. It is thus preferable to investigate the general practitioners' diagnostic habits from information obtained in community surveys. This we have done in Table 4.4, in which, on the basis of data from the Community Survey of Cantabria, we analyse the general practitioner's ability to detect the presence of psychological disorders in those patients who had established contact with their centre in the previous 2 weeks. The rate of conspicuous psychiatric morbidity presented in Table 4.4 is 9.9%, which is much lower than the one reported in the majority of the surveys conducted in general practice settings (Goldberg & Huxley, 1986) and also lower than the prevalence of psychiatric morbidity detected in the general population from which this data was extracted (Vázquez-Barquero et al., 1987). It should also be emphasized that a comparison between the rates of psychiatric morbidity detected by the general practitioner and those obtained in a community survey says nothing about the doctor's accuracy in assessing the patient's psychopathological status. Despite the fact that the doctor may detect a similar

Table 4.4. Evaluation of general practitioner's ability to identify psychiatric disorders.

GHQ STATUS	General practitioner's assessment	
	"No psych. case"	"Psych. case"
"Probable cases" (N= 71)	55	16
"Probable normals" (N= 131)	127	4

General Practitioner's Performance:	
"Accuracy"	= 70.8%
"Bias"	= 0.32
"Identification Index"	= 0.26
"Conspicuous Psychiatric Morbidity"	= 9.9%

Table 4.5. Rates of psychotropic drug prescribing in a community sample by GHQ-score.

| | | GHQ-60 Score | | | | |
		0–5	6–11	12–19	20+	K-S test
Male	Total N in sample	428	85	45	23	
						D= 0.51 P<0.01
	Consuming Psychotr.	6	2	2	5	
		1.4%	2.4%	4.4%	21.7%	
Female	Total N in sample	347	136	89	70	
						D= 0.33 P<0.01
	Consuming Psychotr.	13	11	16	29	
		3.7%	8.1%	17.9%	41.4%	

rate of psychopathology than is present in the "referring community," he could still be diagnosing the wrong sort of patients as psychiatrically ill. Thus, from the point of view of assessing a physician's performance as a case detector, the most adequate measure of all is the identification index, which is the ratio of "cases" correctly identified by the general practitioner to the expected "true positives." This index, however, is not in any sense independent of "accuracy" and "bias" of the general practitioner, and thus they both also have to be calculated. The identification index and the bias obtained from our data are lower than the ones reported in the surveys reviewed by Goldberg and Huxley (1986). This may be due to the fact that, at the time of assessing the patients' mental health status, the general practitioners were not aware that their diagnostic performance was going to be verified, and thus they may not have adopted a special focus on the psychopathological aspects of their patients. Similarly, our higher accuracy index could be interpreted as the consequence of the confluence of a low percentage of "probable cases" together with a doctor's low bias toward making psychiatric diagnosis. Our findings thus appear to indicate that not only a considerably low percentage of those "probable psychiatric cases" are correctly identified by the general practitioner, but that the figures in real life could be even lower than those studies conducted in general practice settings seem to suggest.

Table 4.6. Rates of psychotropic drug use in a rural area of Cantabria by the combined presence or absence of Psychiatric and Physical illness.

| Illness combination | N in the sample | Consuming psychotropic drugs | |
		N	%
Psychiatric and physical illness	89	32	35.9
Psychiatric without physical illness	33	6	18.2
Physical without psychiatric illness	135	23	17.0
Neither psychiatric nor physical illness	195	2	1.0

Indirect information about the general practitioner's diagnostic performance of mental disorders could be obtained by analyzing his psychotropic prescription habits. Most studies in this area have investigated the proportion of patients receiving psychotropic drugs in general practice settings. The prescription rates reported vary between 9.4% and 15.5% (Williams, 1979). Our survey in the general population of Cantabria reveals that 10.7% of the females and that 2.6% of the males were consuming psychotropic drugs (Vázquez-Barquero et al., 1989). This female predominance of consumption was significantly enhanced with increasing age, lower educational level, married marital status, absence of work, and housewife activity, while it disappeared with younger age, single marital status, and outside-the-house working activity. These findings lend support to social theories which suggest that women's greater tendency to receive psychotropic prescriptions may be associated with either the fact that they are more likely to be under the influence of social and family stressors or because they are more sensitive to stress (Cafferata et al., 1986; Cooperstock, 1978). The assumption that mental illness is the mediating mechanism between stress and psychotropic prescription might be postulated. Our data, however, did not confirm this entirely, since it showed that the female predominance in psychotropic prescription was higher in the group without mental illness. Our findings, therefore, support the opinion that sex differences in psychotropic drug use could not be accounted for solely by women being more mentally ill.

As expected, a number of studies have found a relationship between psychotropic prescription and emotional disorders (Gabe & Thorogood, 1986). This has been confirmed in our data, in which we found a tendency for psychotropic prescribing to increase throughout the scores in the GHQ-60 (Table 4.5; Vázquez-Barquero et al., 1989). This tendency, which is more marked above the cut-off point, suggests that "caseness" may not be the only relevant factor on prescription, and that we have also to take into account the severity of symptomatology. The table also shows that in this community only a small proportion of "probable cases" are receiving psychotropic

drugs. The general practitioner's low rate of psychotropic prescribing for the mentally ill, which is more marked in males than in females (male = 18.5%; female = 34.7%), has important public health implications, more so if we consider that our findings also demonstrate that depression is exclusively treated in these settings with anxiolytics (Vázquez-Barquero et al., 1989). Thus, our data confirmed the findings of other authors demonstrating that in the general population only a small proportion of those afflicted by psychiatric disorders receive psychotropic treatment, and also that anxiolytics are very often prescribed by the general practitioner as the treatment for depression (Mellinger et al., 1978; Gullick & King, 1979; Murray et al., 1981).

Although psychopathology should be the main reason for psychotropic consumption, in our survey these drugs are also widely prescribed for physical conditions. As shown in Table 4.6, the coexistence of physical and psychiatric disease accounted for substantially more psychotropic prescription than did psychiatric or physical illness individually. Furthermore, it was our observation that the presence of any of these diseases alone produce an almost equal rate of prescribing. Our data therefore support the finding of other authors demonstrating that physical illness is as relevant as psychiatric disease for determining the general practitioner's psychotropic prescription habits (Mellinger et al., 1978; Williams et al., 1978).

Conclusions

In summary, we have presented data illustrating that:

1) a great proportion of persons afflicted by psychiatric disorders remain in the community without establishing contact with a medical agency and without receiving adequate psychotropic treatment;

2) that the process that conditions the act of establishing medical contact, being correctly identified as "psychiatric case," and receiving psychotropic treatment, is related to a large extent to socio-demographic factors;

3) that physical and mental disease are seldom presented in an isolated form, and that they tend to interact in a complex way when conditioning the use of health resources.

These findings—which have important public health implications—demonstrate the need to develop "research-intervention" studies geared, in the first place, to identifying more precisely the factors that condition the inadequate use of health resources by the mentally ill, and secondly to develop health and educational strategies directed to improve, in the general practitioner and also in the general population, the process by which mental disorders become identified and treated.

References

Andersen, R., & Newman, J. (1973). Societal and individual determinants of medical care utilization in the United States. *Millbank Memorial Foundation Quarterly. 51*, 91–124.

Andersen, R., Kravits, J., & Anderson, O. (1975). *Equity in health services: Empirical analyses in social policy.* Cambridge, MA: Ballenger Publishing Company.

Andersen, A. S., & Laake, P. (1987). A model for physician utilization: Analysis of Norwegian data. *Medical Care, 25,* 300–310.

Barsky, A. J., Wyshak, G., & Klerman, G.L. (1986). Medical and psychiatric determinants of outpatient medical utilization. *Medical Care, 24,* 548–560.

Bebbington, P., Hurray, J., Tennant, C., Sturt, E., & Wing, J.K. (1981). Epidemiology of mental disorders in Camberwell. *Psychological Medicine, 11,* 561–579.

Briscoe, M. E. (1987). Why do people go to the doctor? Sex differences in the correlates of GP consultation. *Social Science and Medicine, 25,* 507–513.

Burvill, P. W., & Knuiman, M. W. (1983). Minor psychiatric morbidity and general practitioner consulting rates. *Psychological Medicine, 13,* 635–643.

Brown, G. W., & Harris, T. (1978). *Social origins of depression: A study of psychiatric disorder in women.* London: Tavistock.

Cafferata, G. L., Kasper, J., & Berstein, A. (1986). Family roles, structure and stressors in relation to sex differences in obtaining psychotropic drugs. In J. Gabe & P. Williams (Eds.), *Tranquilizers, social, psychological and clinical perspectives.* London, New York: Tavistock.

Cooperstock, R. (1978). Sex differences in psychotropic drug use. *Social Science and Medicine, 12,* 179–186.

Corney, R., & Murray, M. (1988). The characteristics of high and low attenders at two general practices. *Social Psychiatry and Psychiatric Epidemiology, 23,* 39–48.

De Santiago Diaz, A., Vázquez-Barquero, J. L., Diez Manrique, J. F. (1987). La enfermedad mental en la mujer. *Anales de Psiquiatria, 3,* 191–200.

Finlay-Jones, R., & Burvill, P. W. (1978). Contrasting demographic patterns of minor psychiatric morbidity in general practice and the community. *Psychological Medicine, 8,* 455–466.

Gabe, J., & Thorogood, N. (1986). Tranquilizers as a resource. In J. Gabe & P. Williams (Eds.), *Tranquilizers, social, psychological and clinical perspectives.* London, New York: Tavistock.

Goldberg, D., Cooper, B., Eastwood, M. R., Kedward, H. B., & Shepherd, M. (1970). A standardized psychiatric interview suitable for use in community surveys. *British Journal of Preventive and Social Medicine, 24,* 18–23.

Goldberg, D., & Huxley, P. (1980). *Mental illness in the community. The pathway to psychiatric care.* London, New York: Tavistock.

Goldberg, D., & Williams, P. (1988). *A user's guide to the General Health Questionnaire.* Windsor, Berkshire: NFER-NELSON.

Gullick, E. L., & King, L. J. (1979). Appropriateness of drugs prescribed by primary care physician for depressed outpatients. *Journal of Affective Disorders, 1,* 55–58.

Henderson, A. S., Duncan-Jones, P., Byrne, D. G., Scott, R., & Adcock, S. (1979). Psychiatric disorders in Canberra. A standardized study of prevalence. *Acta Psychiatrica Scandinavica, 60,* 355–374.

Henderson, A. S., Byrne, D. G., & Duncan-Jones, P. (1981). *Neurosis and the social environment.* London: Academic Press.

Hodiamont, P., Peer, N., & Sybe, N. (1987). Epidemiological aspects of psychiatric disorders in a Dutch health area. *Psychological Medicine, 17,* 495–506.

Ingham, J. G., & Miller, P. Mc C. (1983). Self-referral: Social and demographic determinants of consulting behaviour. *Journal of Psychosomatic Research, 27,* 233–239.

Levin, M. L. (1953). The occurrence of lung cancer in man. *Acta Unio Internationale Contra Cancrum, 19,* 531–541.

Mavreas, V. G., Beiss, A., Mouyias, A., Rigoni, F., & Lyketsos, G. (1986). Prevalence of psychiatric disorders in Athens: A community study. *Social Psychiatry, 21,* 172–181.

Mavreas, V. G., & Bebbington, P. E. (1988). Greeks, British Greek Cypriots and Londoners: A comparison of morbidity. *Psychological Medicine, 18,* 433–442.

Mechanic, D. (1962). The concept of illness behaviour. *Journal of Chronic Disease, 15,* 189–190.

Mellinger, G. D., Balter, M. B., Manheimer, D. I., Cisin, I. H., & Parry, H. J. (1978). Psychiatric distress, life crisis, and use of psychotherapeutic medications. *Archives of General Psychiatry, 35,* 1045–1052.

Murray, J., Dunn, G., Williams, P., & Tarnopolsky, A. (1981). Factors affecting the consumption of psychotropic drugs. *Psychological Medicine, 11,* 551–560.

Shepherd, M., Cooper, B., Brown, A. C., & Kalton, G. W. (1966). *Psychiatric illness in general practice.* London: Oxford University Press.

Surtees, P. G., Dean, C., Ingham, J. G., Kreitman, N. B., Miller, P. Mc C, & Sashidharan, S. P. (1983). Psychiatric disorder in women from an Edinburgh community: Association with demographic factors. *British Journal of Psychiatry, 142,* 238–246.

Tanner, J. L., Cockerham, W. C., & Spaeth, J. L. (1983). Predicting physician utilization. *Medical Care, 21,* 361–369.

Tarnopolsky, A., & Norton-Williams, J. (1980). *Aircraft noise and the prevalence of psychiatric disorders.* London: Social and Community Planning Research.

Vázquez-Barquero, J. L., Muñoz, P. E., & Madoz Jauregui, V. (1981). The interaction between physical illness and neurotic morbidity in the community. *British Journal of Psychiatry, 139,* 328–335.

Vázquez-Barquero, J. L., Muñoz, P. E., & Madoz Jauregui, V. (1982). The influence of the process of urbanization on the prevalence of neurosis. *Acta Psychiatric Scandinavica, 65,* 161–170.

Vázquez-Barquero, J. L., Diez Manrique, J. F., Peña, C., Aldama, J., Samaniego Rodriguez, C., Menendez Arango, J., & Mirapeix, C. (1987). A community mental health survey in Cantabria: A general description of morbidity. *Psychological Medicine, 17,* 227–241.

Vázquez-Barquero, J. L., Peña, C., Diez Manrique, J. F., Arenal, R., Quintanal, R. G., & Samaniego, C. (1988). The influence of sociocultural factors on the interaction between physical and mental disturbances in a rural community. *Social Psychiatry and Psychiatric Epidemiology, 23,* 195–201.

Vázquez-Barquero, J. L., Bebbington, P., Diez Manrique, J. F., Mavreas, V. G., Peña Martin, C., & Arenal, G. (1988). Estructura sindromica de la enfermedad mental en Londres y Cantabria. *Actas Luso Españolas de Neurologia y Psiquiatria, 16,* 347–355.

Vázquez-Barquero, J. L., Diez Manrique, J. F., Peña, C., Arenal Gonzalez, A., Cuesta, M. J., & Artal, J. A. (1989). Patterns of psychotropic drug use in a rural community. *British Journal of Psychiatry, 155,* 633–641.

Waldron, I. (1983). Sex differences in illness incidence, prognosis and mortality: Issues and evidence. *Social Science and Medicine, 17,* 1107–1123.

Williams, P. (1978). Physical ill-health and psychotropic drug prescription: A review. *Psychological Medicine, 8,* 683–693.

Williams, P. (1979). The extent of psychotropic drug prescription. In P. Williams & A. Clare (Eds.), *Psychosocial disorders in general practice.* London: Academic Press.

Williams, P., Tarnopolsky, A., Hand, D., & Shepherd, M. (1986). Minor psychiatric morbidity and general practice consultation: The West London survey. *Psychological Medicine* (Suppl. 9).

Wing, J. K., Cooper, J. E., & Sartorius, N. (1974). *Measurement and classification of psychiatric symptoms.* Cambridge: Cambridge University Press.

Wolinsky, F. D. (1978). Assessing the effect of predisposing, enabling, and illness-morbidity characteristics of health service utilization. *Journal of Health and Social Behaviour, 19,* 384–394

Chapter 5
Mental Health in General Medical Clinics

Antonio Lobo

He did more for me than was necessary in a physician:
he was worried about me, not the prestige of his art . . .
no task was burdensome for him,
no task was upsetting: my suffering moved him:
I was his first concern
among the multitude of patients that asked for his help:
he took care of others only when my health permitted it.
I am obliged to this one,
not so much because he is a physician
but because he is a friend.
Seneca, *De Beneficiis*

Seneca, the Spanish-Roman philosopher, refers to a humanistic approach in medicine that has a long tradition in Spain. It is the main spirit that pervades the influential "psychosomatic movement" in this country (Rof Carballo, 1954; Lain-Entralgo, 1955). We have also been influenced by "psychosomatic" views in our approach to mental health problems in general medical settings . Although these views have stirred considerable international interest (Temoshock, Fox & Dienstfrey, 1986), they have also led to much uncritical literature (Shepherd,1978) . We have previously argued in favour of a psychosomatic perspective that takes into consideration not only philosophical and medical humanism, but also empirical science (Lobo, 1986).

Epidemiological research has documented the relationship between psychological and somatic morbidity (Shepherd, Davies & Culpan, 1960; Eastwood & Trevelyan, 1972). These type of studies are fundamental to the study of psychological disorders as they occur in general medical settings (Shepherd, 1978). The documentation of prevalence rates for disorder has implications for services organization—including the so-called liaison services; and the search for associated elements might give clues about risk factors. Obviously,

this is of interest in public health and preventive medicine.

In fact, early reviews, in the 1960s, suggested psychological morbidity as an important health problem in medical patients (Lipowski, 1967). Oncological patients were but one example of persons with high rate of disturbance who initially attracted our interest. However, the discrepant rates reported suggested methodological flaws and differences in case definition and case identification which could invite epidemiological analysis (Lobo, Folstein & Abeloff, 1979). This led us to the use of standard methods of assessment in the patients admitted to an American cancer centre: a two-phase screening procedure was designed, with the *Present State Examination* being used in the second phase. Later on, similar designs in Spanish patients have permitted cross-cultural comparisons (Lobo & Gimeno-Aznar, 1981; Salvador, 1987).

Psychiatric Morbidity in Medical Populations

Recent reviews show that morbidity studies in the last decade have generally been more carefully executed than in the 1960s and early

The author would like to thank all the researchers in our group who made this work possible. This study was supported in part by a grant for Mental Health Research from the Diputacion General de Aragon.

1970s (Cavanaugh & Wettstein, 1984; Mayou & Hawton, 1986). Standardized methods and well-validated instruments tend to be the norm rather than the exception. Some studies were one-phase screening procedures (Worsley et al, 1977; Cavanaugh, 1983), while all European studies presented in Table 5.1 used two-phase designs. In hospital samples, the prevalence ranges from 23% in the well-known study of Maguire et al. (1974) or even less, to 61% in the study by Cavanaugh (1983). It tends to be lower in two-stages studies and outpatient clinics, but some of them report rates around 50% (Ballinger, 1977). More recent investigations in different countries have shown similar findings (Ormel et al., 1989; Likouras et al., 1989). Several studies conducted in Spain by our group (Perez-Echeverria, 1985; Salvador, 1987; Lobo et al., 1988b) and others (Vázquez-Barquero et al., 1985a) have shown particularly high prevalence of psychiatric disorders (see Table 5.1).

Affective disorders are most frequently found; they are often of mild intensity, especially among outpatients, where mixed anxiety and depression may be the most prominent psychopathology. Among inpatients, such affective disorders can be of severe intensity, and organic psychosyndromes are also observed. So far no investigators have attempted to account for the wide variation between the reported rates, yet as Holland points out in Chapter 2 of this volume, it is a public health task to test hypotheses that may account for such variations. Such findings also have implications for the organisation of "liaison services."

Implications

The high rates of disorder observed in different studies and different cultures and medical settings seem to confirm the association between somatic disease and psychological disturbances. This has obvious public health implications. Patients with delirium or cognitive impairments are of medical interest, since several authors (Rabins et al., 1983; Popkin, Mackenzie & Callies, 1984) and ourselves (Lobo et al., 1979, 1988a), have reported *high mortality rates* in these groups. Affective disorders are distressing and may complicate the course and management of physical illness. It remains uncertain what kind of disorders are likely to respond to treatment; it might well be, as Mayou and Hawton (1986) pointed out, that the majority of patients require only some kind of psychological support. There is some evidence, however, that the affective disturbances seen by nonpsychiatric physicians may respond to pharmacological (Ashcroft, 1986), formal psychological (Ryle, 1986) or social work interventions (Corney, 1984).

It has recently been shown—in several different countries—that psychological disorders frequently go *unrecognized by the medical staff* (Maguire et al., 1974; Knights & Folstein, 1977; Lobo et al., 1979). In our own study, 50% of medical outpatients with psychological disturbances had not been detected as such by the internist (Lobo et al., 1988b). It might be argued that the detection of disturbance in these patients requires extensive training. However, after ten supervised interviews with the internist, the rate of unrecog-

Table 5.1. Studies of psychiatric morbidity in medical patients.

Reference	Medical setting	Case identification		Prevalence
Inpatients:				
Maguire et al. (1974)	Medicine	GHQ-60,	CIS	23%
Bridges & Goldberg (1984)	Neurology	GHQ-28,	CIS	39%
Perez-Echeverria (1985)	Endocrine	GHQ-28,	CIS	91%
Salvador (1987)	Oncology	GHQ-28,	PSE	53%
Outpatients:				
Kirk & Saunders(1979)	Neurology	GHQ-60, Interview		27%
MacDonald & Bouchier(1980)	Gastroenterol. and Gen. Med.	GHQ-60,	CIS	26%
Byrne (1984)	Gynaecology	GHQ-60,	PSE	29%
Lobo et al. (1988)	Internal Med.	GHQ-28,	CIS	47%

nized disturbance was reduced to 19.1% (p<0.01). Since reported depression correlated quite well in this study with anxiety, and these were the most frequent psychological disturbances, we have suggested that a single question about the patient's mood would greatly improve detection rates by nonpsychiatrists (Lobo et al., 1988b).

Technical factors concerned with the doctor's interview techniques are involved in the recognition problem (Marks, Goldberg & Hillier, 1979; Wilmink et al., 1988). These authors and others (Diaz-Manrique et al., 1983; Sivakumar et al., 1986) have shown that the doctor's attitudes are also important. Some investigators have shown that improved detection improves the prognosis of the patients' disturbances (Johnstone & Goldberg, 1976; Ormel et al., 1989). Thus, attempts to improve the attitudes and interview techniques of general physicians are of more than academic interest. Consultation-liaison services have shown a potential to change the pattern of referrals (Brown & Cooper, 1987) and have a role in improving the physician's abilities and attitudes. However, evaluation of the efficacy of such services is mandatory (Sensky, 1986), and the advent of systematic modern interventions are promising in this respect (Huyse, 1989).

Factors Associated with Psychiatric Morbidity in Medical Settings

Some reviewers have suggested that little is known concerning associations between psychiatric disorders in these settings and other factors (Mayou & Hampton, 1986). We have already seen that there are wide variations between reported rates, and we shall now consider possible explanations for this. First of all, the investigators had different backgrounds, methodologies are not always comparable, and the samples studied came from different medical settings. The Spanish rates tend to be higher than in other European studies, and it is possible that different case finding procedures or thresholds were used.

However, the protocol in the medical outpatients' study, which may be taken as an example of our methods, was similar to that used elsewhere (Lobo et al., 1988b). The patients were examined independently, in different phases, by the internist, by auxiliary personnel or lay interviewers administering a battery of instruments such as the GHQ and social and personality schedules; and, finally, by standardized psychiatrists who administered the *Clinical Interview Schedule* (CIS) to the patients and diagnosed them according to predetermined operative criteria. The senior author had been personally standardized in the use of the CIS with the original authors. Our rating of a psychiatric "case" developed during the initial studies. A global or psychiatrist's severity rating derived from the CIS scoring method has been used: subjects with scores of 0 and 1 were considered to be "noncases;" "cases" received scores of 2, 3 or 4, according to their severity. Coefficients of interrater reliability calculated for the "case"/"noncase" distinction were as follows: Overall agreement, 92%; correlation (r), 0.95; Weighted kappa, 0.93. (Lobo et al., 1984).

Even if it is difficult to compare our studies with other countries, it may be worthwhile comparing results of studies inside our own group, since the protocols were always similar and the investigators had a common background. Taken together, the studies reviewed until now and other studies in our group (Artal, 1983; Muro, 1983; Pavon, 1985; Marco, 1989) suggest that different diseases or degrees of severity could account for different morbidity rates. Some other data support this interpretation.

Type of Illness

Figures 5.1 and 5.2 refer to CIS psychopathological profiles of endocrine patients and medical controls examined in one of our studies (Perez-Echeverria, 1985). The same psychiatrists, with exactly the same method, studied the following groups of patients: endocrine inpatients and outpatients, medical inpatients in the same ward and, finally, medical outpatients. It can be seen that the percentage of patients having CIS scores of greater than two both in the reported and observed abnormalities sections, or in the final global evaluation, were clearly higher in the endocrine inpatients as compared to en-

Figure 5.1. Psychopathological CIS profiles of endocrine patients and Medical controls: Reported symptoms section (SS: Somatic symptoms; F: Fatigue; IN: Insomnia; I: Irritability; C: Concentration; DR: Depression, reported; AR: Anxiety, reported; O: Obsessions; PH: Phobias).

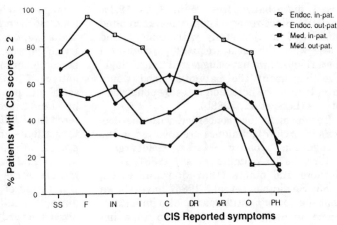

Figure 5.2. Psychopathological CIS profiles of endocrine patients and medical controls: observed abnormalities section (S: Slowness; SU: Suspiciousness; H: Histrionic; DO: Depression, observed; AO: Anxiety, observed; DE: Delusions; ID: Intellectual deterioration; DT: Depressive thoughts; HY: Hypochondriasis. GB: "Global" CIS rating).

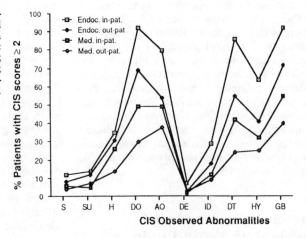

docrine outpatients and medical controls.

It might be argued with some justification that endocrine diseases are not a homogeneous group; however, the above findings suggest that such patients are at a higher risk of developing psychiatric disorders. Contrary to common expectations (Lloyd, 1980)—and, indeed, our own—cross-sectional studies in our group suggest that prevalence of disorder in oncological patients is not higher than in general medical samples (Lobo & Gimeno-Aznar, 1981; Salvador, 1987).

Other factors that might influence psychological morbidity rates are also related to the somatic illness, for example, type and localization of the somatic pathology. Muro (1983)

examined patients referred to endoscopic gastro-duodenal procedures because of gastric pains or discomfort. Documented duodenal ulcers, as expected, produced more morbidity in the acute stage than in the nonacute stage, 6 months to 1 year after the initial examination: 74% of "cases" compared with 56%. However, the morbidity rate was still significantly lower in this nonacute stage among the patients with ulcers located in the lesser curvature of the stomach (30%, p<0.01). Tennant, Goulston and Langeluddecke (1986) have also suggested that anxiety and depression in gastric and duodenal ulcer patients seemed to reflect severity or chronicity of G.I. symptoms or the impending endoscopy procedure.

Table 5.2. Relationship between severity of psychological disturbance (CIS "Global" scores) and mean values of hormonal levels for different endocrine diseases. (Mean hormonal values are higher [with the exception of cortisol and 17-OHCS in Addison's patients] in patients with higher CIS severity scores (Mann-Whitney test.)

Disease	Comparisons between CIS "global" scores	Hormone	Mean hormonal value in pts with higher CIS severity	Mean hormonal value in pts with lower CIS severity	p
Cushing	3 vs.2	ACTH	117.6 (6.1) pg./ml	27.3 (2.6) pg/ml	0.03
(N=14)	4 vs.3	ACTH	142.0 (7.7)	117.6 (4.6)	0.06
	4 vs.2	ACTH	142.0 (6.0)	27.3 (2.0)	0.01
Addison	3 vs.2	ACTH	521.3 (0.8) pg/ml	102.8 (2.0) pg/ml	0.04
(N=12)	3 vs.2	Cortisol	1.3 (4.0) µg/ml	2.45 (8.5) µg/ml	0.02
	3 vs.2	17-OHCS	2.3 (4.1) mg/24hr	6.10 (8.0) mg/24h	0.04
Hyperprolactinaemia					
(N=15)	2 vs.1	Prolactin	1135.6 (4.0) ng/ml	580.2 (1.0) ng/ml	0.06
	3 vs.1	Prolactin	1410.3 (5.0)	580.2 (1.0)	0.03
	3 vs.2	Prolactin	1410.3 (8.1)	1135.6 (4.2)	0.05

Group 1 = mild; 2 = moderate; 3 = severe severity of disorder

Severity of illness

Studies reviewed so far suggest that severity of illness is a possible risk factor for psychological morbidity, since inpatients tend to show higher morbidity rates, even when considering the same type of illness. Similarly, in the study of endocrine patients, correlations have been found between psychopathological levels and endocrine deviations (Perez-Echeverria, 1985; Lobo et al., 1988c). Table 5.2 shows some results of nonparametric statistical calculations: in Cushing's Disease or hyperprolactinemia, mean hormone values (and mean ranks), as hypothesized, are higher in patients with moderate or severe levels of psychopathology (CIS "global" scores 3 or 4, respectively) when compared to patients with mild or borderline psychopathology levels (CIS "global" scores 2 or 1, respectively). The opposite is true, as expected, for cortisol and 17-OHCS mean hormone values in Addison's disease. Although Abed et al. (1987) failed to find a relationship between growth hormone and psychological symptoms in acromegaly patients, Starkman and Schteingart (1981) are among the authors who have managed to do so.

Other authors have suggested an association between somatic disease severity and psychopathological symptoms in peptic ulcer patients (Tennant et al.,1986), in angina pa-tients (Tennant & Langeluddecke, 1985) and in medical inpatients (Moffic & Paykel, 1975). These findings cannot be generalised to primary care or outpatient settings, where some of our studies show that those *without* somatic disease may have high levels of psychological disturbance.

In the outpatients medical sample mentioned earlier (Lobo et al., 1988b), the internist initially examined the patients blind to the psychiatrists. On the basis of his clinical history and examination, in the first visit, he suspected 47.3% of the patients considered to be psychiatric "cases" to have no "organicity" to justify the presenting somatic symptoms, while the same was true in only 12.6% of "noncases" (p<0.001). Once the laboratory work-up was completed, he still felt 37% of the "cases" and 19.8% of the noncases" to have an absence of organicity (p<0.001). Muro (1983) and Pavon (1985) found similar results in their endoscopy clinic and rural general practice, respectively.

Vázquez-Barquero et al. (1985b) in Spain and several other authors in the international literature (Goldberg & Huxley, 1980; McDonald & Bouchier, 1980; Bass & Wade, 1984; Bridges & Goldberg, 1985) have reported results in the same direction. To complicate the issue, however, in several of the studies reviewed (Muro, 1983; Pavon, 1985; Vázquez-Barquero et al., 1985b) and similarly in other reports (Magni, 1984; Nielzen et al., 1986), both the presence of important somatic findings and the absence of "organicity" have been associated with psychiatric disturbances.

The Time of Examination

The time of the examination also seems to influence morbidity rates. In the endocrine sample referred to above, we studied the patients on two occasions: within the first 3 days after admission and at the time of discharge. Initially, the GHQ-28 showed that 88% had high scores, but this figure fell to 55% at the time of their discharge (p<0.001), although very few had any psychiatric treatment. The psychiatrists who administered the CIS interview classified 90% as "cases" initially, and 58% of them at discharge (p<0.001) (Perez-Echeverria, 1985; Lobo et al., 1988c).

Other authors have also shown psychological disturbances to improve without formal psychiatric treatment, so one wonders whether to consider such disorders as "illnesses" or merely as distress. Lloyd and Cawley (1983), for example, examined with the CIS interview 100 men who had recently suffered an acute myocardial infarction and diagnosed 35 of them as having psychiatric morbidity. This morbidity was judged to have been precipitated by the infarction in 19 patients. Since only 25% of these were still assigned a psychiatric diagnosis 12 months later, it was suggested they suffered transient syndromes that might better be regarded as normal distress. Hawton (1981), however, among other authors, has reported the maintenance of morbidity during long periods of time. One other study in our group has addressed the important issue of the course and natural history of the disturbances.

Bailon (1989) examined breast cancer patients 1 month after their mastectomy and followed them up during the 6 monthly chemotherapy cycles. Her results partially coincided with other European authors (Vauhkonen et al., 1985), who consider this postsurgery period a very stressful one: close to 80% of the patients were initially considered to be "cases" on the basis of the PSE and psychiatric history administration.

Most of these cases were depressive ill-nesses, but the rates decreased steadily during the follow-up period, to 12% during the last chemotherapy cycle. An ironic interpretation might suggest chemotherapy to be a wonderful antidepressant. However, she suspected that the continued supervision and care by the medical team during the patients' treatment to be psychologically helpful. In support of this, when the patients were examined a year later, after care by the medical team had lapsed, there were higher rates of disorder once more (Bailon, 1989). Mann (1984) also reported the beneficial effect of regular clinic attendance and a warm and supportive atmosphere in his hypertension patients.

Psychosocial Factors

So far we have reviewed data related to the somatic illness that might influence the psychological health of medical patients. We considered the hypothesis that personality and social problems should also be considered risk factors, and some data tend to support these conjectures. Abnormal personality traits, especially neuroticism measured with the Spanish version of Eysenck's personality questionnaire (Escolar, 1981), have been correlated with psychopathological scores in several of our studies (Escolar, 1981; Artal, 1983; Perez-Echeverria, 1985; Muro, 1983; Pavon, 1985; Lobo et al., 1988b). Other authors in Spain (Padierna-Acero et al., 1984) and in other countries (Tennant et al., 1986) have reported similar findings.

In view of the risk of contamination in instruments such as the EPQ, we clinically examined the premorbid personality of the medical outpatients referred to earlier with outside informants. Abnormal personality was operationally defined. Close to half of the patients considered to be "cases" according to CIS criteria had an abnormal premorbid personality, while the same happened only in 5% of the "noncases" (p<0.001). (Lobo et al., 1988b). Although the assessments of personality were carried out by the psychiatrists who had administered the CIS, this nevertheless tends to support our working hypothesis.

Similarly, in this same study, the social problems considered to be "intense" with operational criteria based on our original structured interview were significantly more frequent among the "psychiatric cases" compared to the "noncases" (25.5% to 8.2%; $p<0.05$). The social problems severity score, on the other hand, correlated with the CIS severity score ($r = 0.4$; $p<0.001$; Lobo et al., 1988b). Other authors have also reported associations between social factors and psychological disturbance (Logsdail et al., 1988), although previous reviewers have implied the association is not strong (Mayou & Hawton, 1986).

Conclusion

Although disorders found in medical practice are often minor, their prevalence is considerable. The patients appear despondent, preoccupied, anxious, dysphoric or clearly depressed. At times, they appear quite impaired cognitively. All this has implications for medical practice and for public health.

In terms of *secondary prevention*, an impor-
tant proportion of psychological disability remains undetected by medical staff. At the present time, however, it remains uncertain which disorders would benefit from formal treatment. Primary prevention is even more complicated, since the causes of these disorders are unclear. The problem is a multifacetted one and thus escapes an easy solution. Rates of disorder are higher in some physical diseases than in others, and generally tend to be higher with more severe physical diseases: although among outpatients this does not hold. Rates of disorder are higher at the beginning of a period of inpatient care, and tend to co-vary with social problems. Rates for abnormal personality are higher among those with psychological disorders.

These are the kinds of findings calling for multiaxial classificatory systems (Jenkins, Smeeton & Shepherd, 1988; Lobo, 1989). The identification of well-defined groups of disordered patients and the testing in them of specific hypothesis is advisable if aetiological knowledge is to advance, and prevention and treatment to be made possible.

References

Abed, R. T., Clark, J., Elbadawy, M. H. F., & Cliffe, M. J.(1987). Psychiatric morbidity in acromegaly. *Acta Psychiatrica Scandinavica, 75*, 635–639.

Artal, J. A. (1983). *Epidemiologia de trastornos psicologicos en jovenes soldados con patologia medicoquirurgica*. Doctoral thesis. Zaragoza: Universidad de Zaragoza.

Ashcroft, G. W. (1986). Treatment effectiveness. In M. Shepherd, G. Wilkinson & P. Williams (Eds.), *Mental illness in primary care settings* (pp. 115–122). London, New York: Tavistock.

Bailon, M. J. (1989). *Trastornos psiquicos y correlaciones en pacientes con cancer de mama*. Doctoral thesis . Zaragoza: Universidad de Zaragoza.

Ballinger, C. B. (1977). Psychiatric morbidity and the menopause: Survey of a gynaecological outpatient clinic. *British Journal of Psychiatry, 131*, 83–89.

Bass, C., & Wade, C. (1984). Chest pain with normal coronary arteries: A comparative study of psychiatric and social morbidity. *Psychological Medicine, 14*, 51–61.

Bridges, K. W., & Goldberg, D. P. (1984). Psychiatric illness in inpatients with neurological disorders: Patients' views on discussion of emotional problems with neurologists. *British Medical Journal, 289*, 656–658.

Bridges, K. W., & Goldberg, D. P. (1985). Somatic presentation of DSM-III psychiatric disorders in

primary care. *Journal of Psychosomatic Research, 29*, 563–569.

Brown, A., & Cooper, A. F. (1987). The impact of a liaison psychiatry service on patterns of referral in a general hospital. *British Journal of Psychiatry, 50*, 83–87.

Byrne, P. (1984). Psychiatric morbidity in a gynaecology clinic: An epidemiological survey. *British Journal of Psychiatry, 144*, 28–34.

Cavanaugh, S. A. (1983). The prevalence of emotional and cognitive dysfunction in a general medical population using the MMSE, GHQ and BDI. *General Hospital Psychiatry, 5*, 15–24.

Cavanaugh, S. A., & Wettstein, R. M. (1984). Prevalence of psychiatric morbidity in medical populations. In L. Grinspoon (Ed.), *Psychiatry update*. Washington DC: American Psychiatric Press.

Corney, R. H. (1984). The effectiveness of attached social workers in the management of depressed female patients in general practice. *Psychological Medicine* (Monograph Supplement 6).

Diez-Manrique, J. F., Menendez-Arango, J., Samaniego-Rodriguez, C., Vázquez-Barquero, J. L., Guillen-Acedo, J., Lequerica-Puente, J., Llano-Rincon, A., Garcia-Quintanal, R., & Pena-Martin, C. (1983). Actitudes hacia el enfermo psiquiatrico. *Actas Luso-Espanolas de Neurologia y Psiquiatria, 11*(4), 295–312.

Eastwood, M. R., & Trevelyan, M. H. (1972). Relationship between physical and psychiatric disorder. *Psychological Medicine, 2,* 363–372.

Escolar, V. (1981). *Aportaciones al uso del cuestionario de Eysenck (EPQ) para adultos en la poblacion espanola.* Doctoral thesis . Zaragoza: Universidad de Zaragoza.

Goldberg, D., & Huxley, P. (1980). *Mental illness in the community. The pathway to psychiatric care.* London, New York: Tavistock.

Hawton, K. (1981). The long-term outcome of psychiatric morbidity detected in general medical patients. *Journal of Psychosomatic Research, 25*(3), 237–243.

Huyse, F. J. (1989). *Systematic interventions in consultation/liaison psychiatry.* Amsterdam: Free University Press.

Jenkins, R., Smeeton, N., Marinker, M., & Shepherd M. (1985). A study of the classification of mental ill-health in general practice. *Psychological Medicine, 15,* 403–409.

Johnstone, A., & Goldberg, D. (1976). Psychiatric screening in general practice. *Lancet, 1,* 605–608.

Kirk, C. A., & Saunders, M. (1979). Psychiatric illness in a neurological outpatient department in North East England: Use of the General Health Questionnaire in the prospective study of neurological outpatients. *Acta Psychiatrica Scandinavica, 60,* 427–437.

Knights, E. B., & Folstein, M. F. (1977). Unsuspected emotional and cognitive disturbance in medical patients. *Annals of Internal Medicine, 87,* 723–724.

Lain-Entralgo, P. (1955). *Mind and body: Psychosomatic pathology.* (Espinosa A. M., trans.). London: Harrill.

Lipowski, Z. J. (1967). Review of consultation psychiatry and psychosomatic medicine. II. Clinical aspects. *Psychosomatic Medicine, 29,* 201–224.

Lloyd, G. G. (1980). Whence and whither "liaison" psychiatry?. *Psychological Medicine, 10,* 11–14.

LLoyd, G., & Cawley, R. H. (1983). Distress or illness? A study of psychological symptoms after myocardial infarction. *British Journal of Psychiatry, 142,* 120–125.

Lobo, A., Folstein, M. F., & Abeloff, M. D. (1979). Incidencia, prevalencia y deteccion de morbilidad psiquiatrica en un hospital oncologico. *Folia Neuropsiquiatrica, 14,* 1–4, 270–284.

Lobo, A., & Gimeno-Aznar, J. L. (1981) Estudio transcultural de los problemas psiquiatricos en pacientes oncologicos. *Oncologia 80, 136*(5), 24–30.

Lobo, A., Gomez-Burgada, F., Perez-Echeverria, M. J., Miranda, M., & Clare, A. (1984). Estudio de la entrevista psiquiatrica estructurada CIS en pacientes espanoles. *Comunicacion Psiquiatrica, 11,* 43–60.

Lobo, A. (1986). Philosophical humanism and empirical science: Spanish perspectives on psychosomatics. *Advances, Institute for the Advancement of Health, 3, 4,* 58–76.

Lobo, A., Folstein, M. F., Escolar, V., Morera, B.,

Fetting, J., & Bailon M. J. (1988a). Higher mortality and diagnostic validity of "delirium" syndromes in oncological patients. In A. Lobo & A. Tres (Eds.), *Psicosomatica y cancer* (pp. 89–103). Madrid: Ministerio de Sanidad y Consumo.

Lobo, A., Perez-Echeverria, M.-J., Artal, J., Rubio, L., Escolar, M.-V., Gonzalez-Torrecillas, J.-L., Morera, B., Dia, J.-L., & Miranda, M. (1988b). Psychiatric morbidity among medical outpatients in Spain: A case for new methods of classification. *Journal of Psychosomatic Research, 32,* 355–364.

Lobo, A., Perez-Echeverria, M.-J., Jimenez-Aznarez, A., & Sancho, M.A. (1988c). Emotional disturbances in endocrine patients: Validity of the scaled version of the General Health Questionnaire (GHQ-28). *British Journal of Psychiatry, 152,* 807–812.

Lobo, A. (1989). On multiaxial psychiatric diagnosis for general medical patients. *British Journal of Psychiatry, 155* (Suppl. 4), 38–41.

Logsdail, S. J., Callanan, M. M., & Ron, M. A. (1988). Psychiatric morbidity in patients with clinically isolated lesions of the type seen in multiple sclerosis: A clinical and MRI study. *Psychological Medicine, 18,* 355–364.

Lykouras, E., Ioannidis, C., Voulgari, A., Jemos, J., & Tzonou, A. (1989). Depression among general hospital patients in Greece. *Acta Psychiatrica Scandinavica, 79,* 148–152.

MacDonald, A. J., & Bouchier, I. A. D. (1980). Nonorganic gastrointestinal illness: A medical and psychiatric study. *British Journal of Psychiatry, 136,* 276–283.

Magni, G. (1984). Chronic low-back pain and depression: An epidemiological survey. *Acta Psychiatrica Scandinavica, 70,* 614–617.

Maguire, G. P., Julier, D. L., Hawton, K. E., & Bancroft, J. H. J. (1974). Psychiatric morbidity and referral on two general medical wards. *British Medical Journal, I,* 268–270.

Mann, A. (1984). Hypertension: Psychological aspects and diagnostic impact in a clinical trial. *Psychological Medicine* (Monograph Supplement 5).

Marco, C. (1989). *Morbilidad psiquiatrica y conducta de enfermedad enenfermos hipertensos.* Doctoral thesis . Zaragoza: Universidad de Zaragoza.

Marks, J. N., Goldberg, D. P., & Hillier, V. F. (1979). Determinants of the ability of general practitioners to detect psychiatric illness. *Psychological Medicine, 9,* 337–353.

Mayou, R., & Hawton, K. (1986). Psychiatric disorder in the general hospital. *British Journal of Psychiatry, 149,* 172–190.

Moffic, H. S., & Paykel, E. S. (1975). Depression in medical inpatients. *British Journal of Psychiatry, 126,* 346–353.

Muro, C. (1983). *Trastornos psicologicos en pacientes digestivos: Epidemiologia y correlaciones.* Doctoral thesis . Zaragoza: Universidad de Zaragoza.

Nielzen, S., Petteersson, K. I., Regnell, G., Svensson, R. (1986). The role of psychiatric factors in symptoms of hiatus hernia or gastric reflux. *Acta Psychiatrica Scandinavica, 73,* 214–220.

Ormel, J., van den Brink, W., Koeter, M. W. J., Giel, R., van der Meer, K., van de Willige, G., & Wilmink, F. W. (in press). Recognition, management and outcome of mental health problems. A naturalistic study in 25 Dutch general practices.

Padierna-Acero, J. A., Vázquez-Barquero, J. L., Pena, C., & Ochoteco, A. (1984). Neuroticismo y coronariopatia. *Actas Luso-Espanolas de Neurologia y Psiquiatria, 12,* 340–346.

Pavon, A. (1985). *Trastornos psiquiatricos entre los pacientes medicos de un medio rural aragones.* Doctoral thesis. Zaragoza: Universidad de Zaragoza.

Perez-Echeverria, M. J. (1985). *Correlaciones entre trastornos endocrinologicos, niveles hormonales en sangre, variables de personalidad y alteraciones psicopatologicas.* Doctoral thesis . Zaragoza: Universidad de Zaragoza.

Popkin, M. K., Mackenzie, T. B., & Callies, A. L. (1984). Psychiatric consultation to geriatric medically ill inpatients at a university hospital. *Archives of General Psychiatry, 41,* 703–707.

Rabins, P. V., & Folstein, M. (1982). Delirium and dementia: Diagnostic criteria and fatality rates. *British Journal of Psychiatry, 140,* 149–53

Rof-Carballo, J. (1954). *Patologia psicosomatica.* Madrid: Paz Montalvo.

Ryle, A. (1986). Efficacy of treatment of mental illness in primary care settings. In M. Shepherd, G. Wilkinson & P. Williams (Eds.), *Mental illness in primary care settings* (pp. 123–130). London, New York: Tavistock.

Salvador, L. (1987). *Morbilidad psiquica en pacientes oncologicos.* Doctoral thesis . Zaragoza: Universidad de Zaragoza.

Sensky, T. (1986). The general hospital psychiatrist: Too many tasks and too few roles?. *British Journal of Psychiatry, 148,* 151–158.

Shepherd, M., Davies, B., & Culpan, R. H. (1960). Psychiatric illness in the general hospital. *Acta Psychiatrica et Neurologica Scandinavica, 35,* 18–525.

Shepherd, M. (1978). Epidemiological perspective: Psychosomatic medicine. *International Journal of Epidemiology, 7*(3), 201–205.

Sivakumar, K., Wilkinson, G., Toone, B. K., & Greer, S. (1986). Attitudes to psychiatry in doctors at the end of their first post-graduate year: Two-year follow-up of a cohort of medical students. *Psychological Medicine, 16,* 457–460.

Starkman, M. N., & Schteingart, D. E. (1981). Neuropsychiatric manifestations of patients with Cushing's syndrome. *Archives of Internal Medicine, 141,* 215–219.

Temoshock, L., Fox, B. H., Dienstfrey, H. (1986). Reports and discussions about mind-body-health investigations. International Issues Advances. *Institute for the Advancement of Health, 3, 4.*

Tennant, C. C., & Langeluddecke, P. M. (1985). Psychological correlates of coronary heart disease. *Psychological Medicine, 15,* 581–588.

Tennant, C., Goulston, K., & Langeluddecke, P. (1986). Psychological correlates of gastric and duodenal ulcer disease. *Psychological Medicine, 16,* 365–371.

Vauhkonen, M. L., Achte, K., Salokari, M., Lindfors, O., & Lehvonen, R. (1985). The psychological impact of cancer on the patient's life during the first year after mastectomy. In O. Lindfors, R. Lehvonen., M.L. Vauhkonen & K. Acht (Eds.), *Psychosomatics of cancer* (pp. 51–60). Helsinki: Reports of Psychiatria Fennica, No. 65.

Vázquez-Barquero, J. L., Padierna-Acero, J. A., Ochoteco, A., & Diez-Manrique, F. (1985a). Mental illness and ischaemic heart disease: Analysis of psychiatric morbidity. *General Hospital Psychiatry, 7,* 15–20.

Vázquez-Barquero, J. L., Padierna Acero, J. A., Pena Martn, C., & Ochoteco, A. (1985b). The psychiatric correlates of coronary pathology: Validity of the GHQ-60 as a screening instrument. *Psychological Medicine, 15,* 589–596.

Wilmink, F. W., Ormel, J., Giel, R., Krol, B., Lindeboom, E. G., van der Meer, K., & Soeteman, J. H. (1988). General practitioners' characteristics and the assessment of psychiatric illness. *Journal of Psychiatric Research* (in press).

Worsley, A., Walters, W. A. W., & Wood, E. C. (1977). Screening for psychological disturbance amongst gynaecology patients. *Australian and New Zealand Journal of Obstetrics and Gynaecology, 17,* 214–219.

Section III
Public Health Aspects of Specific Conditions

Schizophrenia and Allied Disorders

A recent World Health Organization study demonstrated that, although the annual inception rate of the core syndrome of schizophrenia was distributed around a mean of 1 per 10,000 in eight centres on three continents, there were much wider variations in the inception rates when a "broad" definition of the disorder was used (Sartorius, Jablensky, Korten et al. 1986). There are also up to 10-fold variations in prevalence between countries (Torrey, 1989). One likely explanation is that schizophrenia has a better prognosis in developing countries.

When data are analysed within countries, a similar picture emerges. Yrjö Alanen shows in Chapter 17 that while the inception rate for schizophrenia was fairly constant across Finland at 16–19/100,000 at risk, prevalence was proportional to the number of long-stay beds made available in various parts of the country, and was higher in areas of low socioeconomic status. Many studies report positive associations with lower social class, emigration, unemployment, residence in areas with high transient population and residence in isolated areas. The evidence tends not to support a causal association for these factors, but is in favour of a drift into more marginal life situations by individuals either in the prodrome or the residual phase of the illness.

Schizophrenia is particularly disabling since it gives rise to defect symptoms; these may result in poor nutrition and self-neglect, with a consequent increase in infections such as tuberculosis. Although this is not a significant cause of increased morbidity in places with well-developed health services, it may become so with the closure of psychiatric hospitals and other well-supervised residential institutions. Schizophrenia has an increased mortality with a standardised mortality ratio of 2.53 (Black, 1988), with many of the additional deaths occurring in the period immediately after hospital discharge.

Most of the adverse consequences of schizophrenia are social rather than medical. They particularly accrue to the quarter of all persons with schizophrenia who have persistent and severe illnesses. They include poverty, substandard housing or actual homelessness, and an increased risk of imprisonment. Schizophrenia is also a potent cause of anxiety and depression in the close relatives of an affected person.

Schizophrenia imposes a severe economic burden on a country with high employment and well-developed health services. Gunderson and Mosher (1975) estimated that the annual cost of schizophrenia to the U.S. economy (at 1975 prices) to be $ 19.5 billion— approximately equivalent to the industrial output of the city of Chicago. Direct health costs accounted for only 20% of this figure. In countries with more agrarian economies and with high unemployment, the costs are of course likely to be substantially lower. Community care is not much, if at all, cheaper for an equivalent quality of care. As more patients are discharged from hospital, the more disabled are those that remain, so that the marginal cost of community care increases as the hospitals are run down in size.

There is clearly a public health task in attempting to account for the wide range in inception rates for "broad" schizophrenia, and in endeavouring to reduce the mean duration of episode for schizophrenic illnesses, and thus reduce the high prevalence rates still encountered in some developed countries. Much work remains to be done in understanding the factors responsible for the variation in inception rates, although Sartorius and his colleagues (1986) have shown that some unusual biological or psychological stress commonly precedes transient episodes of schizophrenia-like illnesses in the developing world.

The task of reducing prevalence rates in developed countries should be thought of as tertiary prevention, and is covered by Alanen and his colleagues in Chapter 17: we return to this theme in our introduction to the next section. In developed countries, it has been shown that family atmosphere affects the risk of relapse in those patients who have high contact with their families; but there are differences between cultures over which characteristics of the relationship are associated with greater risk, and how much risk can be attributed to this factor. The generally better prognosis of schizophrenia in developing countries may be partly due to greater acceptance of deviance within families in some cultures. Other possible explanations are that

- better-prognosis, symptomatic schizophrenia is more common in the developing world;

- those destined to develop poor prognosis schizophrenia are less likely to survive infancy in the developing world; or

- developing economies are more likely to offer opportunities for social reintegration.

Most authorities accept that it is social deterioration that is the most significant determinant of outcome, and that psychosocial treatments are the most appropriate for preventing this. In one study, social and occupational functioning at outset, combined with the extent of defect symptoms and the quality of housing, accounted for 47% of the variance of social outcome and made a substantial contribution to symptomatic outcome 5 years after the initial episode (Prudo & Blum, 1987). However, psychosocial treatments have been less thoroughly evaluated than drug treatments, so that this is also an important public health task where future research is needed.

Depression

Depression ranges from relatively rare severe forms of illness like bipolar illness (or manic-depressive psychosis) which have been well researched, to much more common forms of depressive illness, which are of correspondingly greater public health importance. A study organised by WHO showed that all countries studied have both forms of the illness, with the less severe form invariably being associated with somatic symptoms (Sartorius, Jablensky, Gulbinat & Ernberg, 1980). Regier, Boyd, Burke, Rae and others (1989) have compared results of the Epidemiologic Catchment Area (ECA) study with results from other countries, and report 1-month period prevalence rates for depression of between 4.8 and 7.4% in most centres. Brown, in this volume, reports much higher annual figures for urban women.

These high prevalence figures, combined with the fact that there are much higher rates for depressive illness among the physically ill (see Antonio Lobo's chapter in this volume), and that even when they are not physically ill depressed patients often present to doctors with somatic symptoms, make depression an illness with very great public health importance. Murphy, Monson, Olivier and others (1987) have shown that depressed patients seen on a community survey will have a 50% increased mortality over the next 16 years, and have an 82% chance of a poor outcome, the latter being defined as continuing evidence of affective symptoms over the follow-up period or death. It is evident that even the "minor" forms of depressive illness have serious consequences.

Genetic factors are undoubtedly important in determining the vulnerability to the severe forms of depressive illness, but twin studies indicate that they are of much less importance in determining the common forms of the disorder. Kendler and his colleagues (1987) have argued that genes act in a largely nonspecific way to influence the general level of an individual's symptoms—be they depressive or anxious symptoms—and that the role of genes is to make one sensitive to environmental stress: the form of symptoms then depending upon the environment.

It is clear that social factors are of great importance in the aetiology of the common form of depression. In Chapter 6, George Brown argues that for most populations studied there have been differences in terms of either social class or integration into the traditional way of life, with greater rates being found in the lower social classes and in the less well-integrated. About half of the depression cases will be chronic in the sense of having lasted at least 1 year. Having put forward a complex psychosocial model for the aetiology of depressive illness, he concludes that it may be impossible, despite the knowledge we have gained, to do much about the depressogenic currents in urban, inner-city settings without major structural changes.

He reaches three major conclusions:

- Psychiatrists are advised to think more in terms of delegation, education and example, since they are too few in number to restrict their activity just to the individual and his or her family. It is essential that, as part of their job, they help to motivate and to guide others outside the immediate psychiatric milieu. They are advised to alert others to the problems posed by chronic depressive illness.

- Secondary *prevention* should be aimed at high-risk groups, and it is a straightforward matter to describe the factors that contribute to increased risk from the model proposed.

- Finally, he argues that there is a *central role for women themselves* through voluntary activity exemplified by befriending schemes, albeit with these needing to be set up and run by a small core of trained personnel.

Suicide and Attempted Suicide ("Parasuicide")

In Chapter 7, Norman Kreitman considers public health aspects of parasuicide and suicide. There was an increase of both parasuicide and unemployment in the United Kingdom during the 1970s, and the relative risk of parasuicide increased with duration of unemployment. If the economy is thriving, there is a high rate of parasuicide among the unemployed, but as unemployment rises parasui-cide depends much less on personal characteristics. Although there are more repeaters than first attempters in middle age, first attempters over age 65 predominate once more.

Kreitman shows that in recent years suicide has halved in the elderly but increased in the younger age groups, and that social class and age are equally important as putative explanatory variables. These findings are used as a basis for putting forward a programme of future research which needs to be done in this area.

AIDS and Drug Abuse

In Chapter 8, Peter Jepsen and Anne Hjorther consider the epidemiology of AIDS and present evidence for the growing public health problem presented by the spread of the virus. Three different world patterns are discerned, and in Northern Europe and the United States intravenous drug abusers are seen as an important bridge in the spread of the virus. To prevent AIDS, it is necessary for people to change their lifestyle. In the Third World, people should limit their degree of sexual activity with multiple partners, which will also become important elsewhere.

Intravenous drug abusers are especially important in the spread of AIDS among heterosexuals in Europe and the USA. If AIDS is to be reduced among drug abusers, they will need not merely clean needles and syringes, but must be offered treatment for their addiction. Thus, a greatly increased treatment programme for drug abusers is seen to be a major public health task in the control of AIDS in Europe and the USA.

In his chapter on psychological and social aspects of AIDS, Michael King argues against mandatory HIV testing for immigrants or for those about to be married. He reports a rate of minor psychiatric morbidity of only 31% in AIDS patients surveyed in an STD clinic and argues that this rate—no higher than that expected in other outpatients clinics—probably owes much to the enlightened public health measures already taken in the clinic. The only factors that predicted psychological disorder were previous history of such disorders or excessive concern about health. He reviews evidence that suggests that psychological stress lowers immunity and hastens progress of the disease. Further research is needed about the effects of attempts to provide health education concerning AIDS, and the effectiveness of counselling.

Alcohol-Related Problems

In Chapter 10, Rachel Jenkins and Sharon Harvey consider public health aspects of alcohol consumption, and identify early intervention as the major public health task in the area. Alcohol consumption is increasing in the United Kingdom at a time when tobacco consumption is declining; and average per capita alcohol consumption correlates both with the proportion of heavy drinkers and mortality from alcohol-related diseases. The cost of alcohol is falling relative to disposable income, and "problem drinkers" have three times as many accidents, and five times as much sickness absence, as others.

The authors conducted a longitudinal survey among civil servants and found that even moderate alcohol consumption has measurable public health consequences. Among men, those who had been psychiatric "cases" at the time of the first survey increased their alcohol consumption by the time of the second survey, though this effect did not occur among the women. The authors confirm that the relative risk of sickness absence is greater among men who take more than 30 units per week, and women who take more than 10 units per week—and they observe that none of the sickness certificates mentioned alcohol! They conclude by arguing for early intervention at an individual level and briefly discuss the need to control alcohol consumption nationally by means of price rises and the limitation of advertising.

Dementia

Regier et al. (1988) have used ECA data to estimate that severe cognitive impairment occurs in about 1.3% of the adult US population, with the 1-month prevalence being equal to the "life-time prevalence." The prevalence of dementia rises sharply with age, from about 2% in persons in the age-group 65–70 to about 20% in those over 80, and to 50% for those over 90. As the human lifespan increases, the age structure of the population changes with

a greater proportion of the population surviving beyond the age of 75 and thus entering the years of maximum risk. The forthcoming epidemic of AIDS will also be adding cases of dementia in younger age groups.

From the public health standpoint, multiinfarct dementia might be prevented with better and earlier intervention for hypertension, and AIDS dementias might be prevented in ways discussed in Chapters 8 and 9. The advent of gene probes for Huntington's chorea may lead to some reduction in inceptions over the long term, although early experiences have not been encouraging. We discuss the chapters in this volume on early detection by Brian Cooper, and on the use of services by the elderly in the community by Anthony Mann, in our introduction to Section V.

References

Black, D. W. (1988). Mortality in schizophrenia. The Iowa record linkage study. *Psychosomatics, 29,* 55–60.

Gunderson, J. G., & Mosher, L. (1975). The cost of schizophrenia. *American Journal of Psychiatry, 132,* 901–906.

Hafner, H. (1989). Epidemiology of schizophrenia. In H. Hafner, W. F. Gattaz, & W. Janzarik (Eds.), *Search for the causes of schizophrenia.* Heidelberg: Springer-Verlag.

Kendler, K. S., Heath, A. C., Martin, N. G., & Eaves, L. J. (1987). Symptoms of anxiety and symptoms of depression. *Archives of General Psychiatry, 122,* 451–457.

Murphy, J., Monson, R., Olivier, D., Sobol, A., & Leighton, A. (1987). Affective disorders and mortality. *Archives of General Psychiatry, 44,* 473–479.

Prudo, R., & Blum, H. M. (1987). Five year outcome and prognosis in schizophrenia. *British Journal of Psychiatry, 150,* 345–354.

Regier, D., Boyd, J., Burke, J., Rae, D., Myers, J., Kramer, M., Robins, L., George, L., Karno, M., & Locke, B (1988). One month prevalence of mental disorders in the US: Based on five ECA sites. *Archives of General Psychiatry* (in press).

Sartorius, N., Jablensky, A., Gulbinat, W., & Ernberg, G. (1980). WHO collaborative study: Assessment of affective disorders. *Psychological Medicine, 16;* 909–928.

Sartorius, N., Jablensky, A., Korten, A. et al. (1986). Early manifestations and first contact incidence of schizophrenia in different cultures. *Psychological Medicine, 16,* 909–928.

Torrey, E. F. (1989). Schizophrenia: Fixed incidence or fixed thinking? *Psychological Medicine, 19,* 285–289.

Chapter 6
Some Public Health Aspects of Depression

George Brown

Public health planning ideally requires knowledge about distribution, aetiology and course of specific disorders. For those disorders of concern to psychiatry, this usually requires the study of total populations, as the majority of clinically relevant conditions are not seen by specialists. Fortunately, knowledge about depression, particularly concerning women, is now probably sufficient to begin consideration of its lineaments in public health terms. Indeed, given present knowledge, it would be unethical not to pursue the possibility of preventive intervention with vigour. The whole point of the following presentation of material about what is known of clinical depression in psychosocial terms is to deal with its implication in public health terms. Only depression is discussed. Given this concentration and the ensuing development of a complex model dealing with depression, the presentation is bound to appear to conflict with an alternative, general, radical, approach to public health, which has a good deal to commend it (e.g. MacIntyre, 1988):

- First, this alternative emphasises the *non-specific aspects of disease*—that certain general social factors relate to an overall high rate of disorder. By contrast, the more specific approach to be outlined emphasises the fact that psychosocial factors involved in the development of specific disorders (such as depression, anxiety and schizophrenia) can be very different.

- Second, this alternative emphasises the *wider social structure* rather than the circumstances of individuals. For example: "The decisions made by industrial companies also affect the lives of thousands of people. The economic consequences of a factory closure, the use of poor quality building materials, the disregard of the already lax regulations governing the dis-

charge of chemicals into the water and air, the strain associated with low wages of pay and an uncertain future, may all have significant repercussions on public health" (Research Unit in Health and Behavioural Change, 1989, pp. 154).

However, while such a perspective makes a good deal of sense, it is equally clear that much of our recent advance in understanding in social psychiatry would have been impossible without an emphasis on both the individual (and his or her immediate milieu) and on specific disorders.

In fact in research terms there is probably no conflict between a general and specific perspective: it is, for example, not difficult to conceive how a general improvement in certain social conditions might well lower the risk of say, both depressive and anxiety disorders (and perhaps even schizophrenia) via its ability to effect a *range* of quite different changes in the settings of individual men and women. There is nothing inherently wrong in such a more general blunderbuss approach if it obtains results. In any case, research of the kind outlined is also uncovering general, non-specific, effects. The events involved in onset of depression for example, appear to be also important in the onset of "functional" gastro-intestinal disorders (Craig, 1989; Creed, 1989), in certain menstrual disorders (Harris, 1989), in multiple sclerosis (Grant et al., 1989), and the course of breast cancer (Ramirez & Craig, 1989).

The danger, of course, is that the very success of a research approach concentrating on the individual and his or her milieu (past and present) will lead to the neglect of critical structural influences. The case made by the feminist movement about the general status of women would appear to be generally correct: as a society in the UK we are shamefully negligent in day-to-day matters, and at a policy level of the needs of mother and child. Many issues join at this point, including the "feminisation of poverty." At heart in the light of the material presented it is necessary to increase the control women have and feel they have over their lives as well as to improve the quality of the male-female relationship—a tall order! In more analytical terms, there is a need to increase the range of strategies that they can employ to receive and give comfort, and support and gain some sense of their own value.

Unfortunately, relevant knowledge, whether couched in specific or general terms, will not be enough. Such knowledge, and even that of how pathological processes may be reversed, is a good deal short of showing how to arrange matters so that suffering can be reduced in population terms. The problem of the organisation of effective services is, of course, one faced by medicine as a whole. But it is particularly so for psychiatry given the large numbers involved, when contrasted with the size of the profession, and the ambiguous views held by both medical and lay persons about the nature of the conditions encompassed. And here it is not only a matter of organising services and acquiring the resources to do so. It is also a matter of creating social structures capable of pursuing such activity effectively over the long haul. Alexander Leighton's (1982) fascinating account of the fate of one community mental health centre in Canada, where after a decade physicians were no longer even keeping proper medical records, is perhaps a not too extreme example of the kind of decay in reform and enthusiasm that is possible. But with depression we are only at the beginning of a spurt of new knowledge and innovation, and it is with the nature of *possible* interventions rather than their organisation and delivery that we will be primarily concerned.

Depression and Its Distribution

First, by way of background, the measurement of depression employed in the studies reviewed is described briefly and then the distribution of depression in these terms. The review deals largely with studies employing the Bedford College criteria of caseness; this is fairly comparable to, though somewhat more conservative than, the category of major depression defined by DSM-III or that provided by the ID system of the *Present State Examination*. It deals only with measurement of recent disorder and avoids the fashionable but suspect notion of lifetime disorder now commonly used in populations studies, especially in the United States.

The Bedford College scheme uses the 40-item shortened version of the *Present State Examination* (PSE) to collect material about basic symptomatology. The PSE was originally developed on hospital inpatients, and therefore tends, if anything, to have high thresholds for inclusion of particular symptoms. Although not originally designed for population surveys it is probably useful that any bias would tend to act against the inclusion of "normal" reactions to stressful circumstances. In the surveys reviewed, the PSE was extended from the consideration of a 1-month period to cover the 12 months before interview, the interviewer dating the onset as accurately as possible within the year (Brown & Harris, 1978; Brown, Craig & Harris, 1985).

Interviewers were trained in the use of the shortened version of the 9th edition of the PSE (Wing et al., 1974). Although initially designed to be administered by clinicians, there is now extensive evidence to support its use in surveys by trained lay interviewers (e.g. Cooper et al., 1977; Wing et al., 1977). The threshold for caseness used in the surveys was designed to contrast "cases," who would have syndromes comparable to those of women seen in outpatient clinics, with "borderline cases." The latter have had symptoms that are not sufficiently typical, frequent or intense to be rated as cases, but still are more than isolated symptoms. There are also women with odd psychiatric symptoms such as fatigue, sleep disorder and nervous tension which are not sufficient to warrant even a borderline case rating. Essential to the whole procedure has been the development of reference examples of cases and borderline cases for different diagnostic groups. In the general population, those of depression and anxiety or phobic states are much the most important, although we also record obsessional, tension, alcoholic and drug dependent categories. This diagnostic system has been shown to have good inter-rater reliability; there is also evidence for its construct validity in the context of aetiological research (Brown & Harris, 1978; Finlay-Jones et al., 1980; Finlay-Jones & Brown, 1981; Brown & Prudo, 1981; Prudo et al., 1981).

Major syndromes are treated nonhierarchically. This permits an anxiety state to be rated separately from a depressive disorder and allows a subject to be characterised by separate diagnoses at different levels of severity, for example, case depression: borderline case anxiety (see Brown, Craig & Harris, 1985, for further details).

Using this scheme the overall rate of caseness (primarily of depression) in women between 18 and 65 has, in a number of surveys, proved to be similar in overall terms. The rate of caseness in the course of one year was 17% in a survey of 458 in Camberwell in the early 1970s and 14% in a study of a rural population in the Outer Hebrides 5 years later (Brown & Harris, 1978; Brown & Prudo, 1981). Studies by other workers in London and Edinburgh using the PSE and somewhat similar diagnostic schemes have essentially confirmed a yearly rate of around 15% for women (Bebbington et al., 1981, 1984; Dean et al., 1983; Surtees et al., 1983). There is also general agreement that the great majority of cases involve a diagnosis of depression, although this not infrequently goes with another condition.

There is general agreement that in urban settings at least, the experience of depression among men is a good deal less (e.g. Bebbington et al., 1981; Weissman & Myers, 1978). However, the matter is not beyond dispute, as men are typically more difficult to contact and interview than women. Researches with women are reviewed for whom findings are far more plentiful; however, there is good evidence that the model of depression to be outlined is in broad terms equally applicable to men (e.g. Bebbington et al., 1981; Bolton & Oatley, 1987; Eales, 1988).

Despite this broad comparability, there are typically large differences *within* populations in recent estimates of prevalence of depression among women. For most of the populations studied there have been *differences in terms of either social class* (e.g. Camberwell) or *integration into the traditional way of life* (e.g. Outer Hebrides). The differences in rates are of the order of two or three in favour of the middle classes or the socially integrated. The only exception appears to be Bilbao, an industrial city in the Basque country in Spain, where social class differences are modest (Gaminde & Uria, 1988). Occasionally, the rate in a population as a whole has differed markedly from the round figure of 15%. A low rate, for example, has been reported in Nijmegen in Holland (Hodiamont, 1986). In a recent study of a Basque-speaking rural population of women living in fairly large family households, there was only a 2% rate of caseness of depression (4/167) in 1 year, a six-fold difference compared with Camberwell (Gaminde & Uria, 1988). There were no obvious differences among households in the degree of social integration. In the rural Outer Hebrides, by contrast, it was among those in council housing and small farms that were no longer farmed (i.e., the less integrated) that particularly high rates of depression were found (Prudo et al., 1981.)

Other demographic-type correlates have been found. In the UK it is women with children living at home who are at greatest risk of developing a depressive disorder, but in Bilbao, in Spain, and in Milan, in Italy (Lora, 1989), women with children did not appear to be at greater risk. These are, of course, results that might well reflect the effect of cultural differences surrounding the care of young children and the value placed on the role of mother.

In this introduction it is important to emphasise issues surrounding course as well as aetiology. Perhaps the most melancholy statistic about depression is the finding in most population studies that at any one time *about half the cases of depression will be chronic* in the sense of having lasted at least 1 year. (A survey in a prosperous Canadian population reports a much lower rate [Costello, 1982].) When viewing depression in public health terms, the frequency of chronic disorders is perhaps the most challenging distributional statistic.

A Psychosocial Model of Depression

Knowledge about aetiology and course of depression are discussed in terms of possible preventive strategies with the help of the schematic causal diagram shown in Figure 6.1. The commentary adds a little more detail to the critical junctures outlined in the diagram; but the model as it stands summarises reasonably well current knowledge about psychosocial factors. It includes the insights gained in a recent longitudinal study of a relatively high-risk group of women living in Islington, an inner-city district of London, and the review, in fact, relies a good deal on results of this enquiry.

Working-class women with a child living at home and single mothers irrespective of social class were selected for the Islington study because they were expected to be particularly at risk. This is reflected in a rate of onset of new cases of depression in the follow-up year of 10.6% (32/303) once those with depression at a caseness level at time of first contact were excluded. A quarter of these onset conditions went on to become chronic in the sense they lasted 12 months or more. As anticipated in the earlier review, just short of half the cases present at the point of first interview were chronic (Brown, Craig & Harris, 1985). The situation among the Islington women was therefore one of a high rate of onset of depressive disorders, but with the majority of the new onsets clearing up within a year, leaving a core of chronic conditions. (Subclinical depressive and anxiety conditions, however, quite often persisted after a caseness depressive condition had subsided.)

The model as far as aetiological processes are concerned is essentially based on negative influences, in the sense that almost all the factors of importance concern some aspect of deprivation. However, when the issues of course and recovery are considered, there are a number of clear positive effects. All such effects are displayed in the bottom half of the diagram. The model consists of four sets of causal linkages ("past," "background," "crisis" and "post onset") involved in either the development, course and recovery from depression; these are briefly outlined and each discussed

in terms of possible intervention.

There are 11 links in the model as a whole. The effect of each has been calculated in terms of path analyses showing direct and indirect effects. However, detailed numerical results are not presented as an approximate estimate of the effect of each set of linkages is all that is necessary in a general overview.

The Crisis Situation

The situation immediately before onset is intimately involved in almost all of the depressive onsets. Of critical importance in this crisis situation are provoking life events, shown as link 1 in Figure 6.1. A number of studies have now confirmed the importance of "severely threatening events" for the genesis of depression (Brown & Harris, 1986a). Such events are defined by means of the *Life Event and Difficulty Schedule* (LEDS), which attempts both to establish the presence of life events in general and to assess their likely meaning. In the Islington survey, 130 of the 303 women without depression at a caseness level at the time of first interview experienced a severe event in the follow-up year, and for 29 of the women depression at a caseness level followed at some point after a severe event. Therefore, almost all the 32 onsets were preceded by such an event.

There is now, in fact, a general agreement about the critical importance for depression of the experience of loss (e.g. Bibring, 1953; Beck, 1967; Paykel, 1974; Finlay-Jones & Brown, 1981; Miller & Ingham, 1983; Dohrenwend et al., 1986), and among the Islington women the majority of severe events occurring in the 6 months before a depressive onset did involve a loss, disappointment or failure (see Brown et al., 1987; Brown, 1989). For just over one-third of the 29 women with both a severe event and onset, the crisis presented a *threat to their identity as a wife or mother* about which very little could be done—at least in the immediate future—and for most it was part of a long history of failure and disappointment in one or both of these roles. A second set of women, just under the size of the first, had a more diverse set of experiences. But common to all appeared to be a sense of *imprisonment in a nonrewarding and deprived setting*, with the event itself underlin-

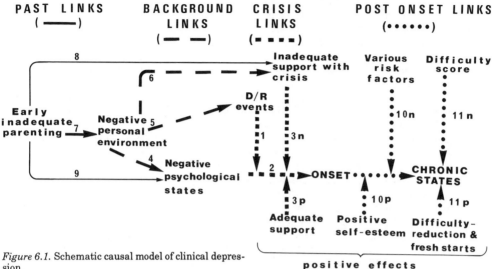

Figure 6.1. Schematic causal model of clinical depression.

ing how little they could do about extracting themselves. Any way forward appeared to be blocked. Events concerning poor housing, or debt or both were common, although there were usually wider ramifications—for example, one was a single mother pregnant by a man who had let her down when her flat had been set on fire (the severe event), so that she had been left homeless. The distinction between the first two groups is one of degree: the *dominant theme* for both was one of *loss, failure and disappointment*. A final set of women, of much the same size as the second, *lost a core person* they had known for some time; for some it appeared to be no more than a break in the contact, but they had good grounds to feel rejected. Most of the crises, in fact, continue the same theme of failure and disappointment, for example, learning of the infidelity of a lover, although a few of the women experienced a death of a core tie for which there was no obvious reason for them to feel in any way responsible, or for that matter rejected. But overall, there was not much doubt about the conclusion to be drawn: the events presented for the most part an integral threat to core aspects of the sense of identity and self-worth of the women.

The strength of this link between onset and severe event was increased when their classification was further refined. In the context of

prevention one set of results is of particular interest since it relates to circumstances that had usually existed for some time. A severe event matching an ongoing marked difficulty present at the time of the first interview was particularly likely to lead to depression. For example, the threat of eviction because of rent arrears, experienced by one woman, matched the ongoing difficulty she had concerning such payments. The majority of difficulties involved in such matching *D-events* (D standing for difficulty) had been going on for well over a year (Brown et al., 1987).

There was a similar effect for severe events matching a prior role conflict (called *R-events*). Conflicting demands of work and domestic responsibilities were usually involved; for example, a child found to be stealing would match a woman's earlier worry at the time of first interview about work demands and care of her child. When the two types of event are combined, risk of depression is increased threefold for those with a *D/R-event* compared with those with an ordinary severe event, and just over half of all the 32 women developing depression had such an event not long before onset.

Other factors of importance in the crisis situation immediately before onset can be divided into two factors relating to self (link 2) and one relating to support with the event itself (link 3). (All references to links relate to Figure 6.1.) In terms of link 2, the presence of negative psychological states (either low self-esteem or a chronic subclinical condition, usually of depression or anxiety) at the time of first interview was highly related to subsequent development of a depressive caseness condition, but only among those with a severe event. The relationship of the two negative psychological states to depression was roughly equal, with an onset rate in the presence of a severe event of approximately one-third given one or the other (25/65) and only 6% (4/65) for those with just a severe event. But, perhaps surprisingly, these psychological states were not usually enough to produce depression. In almost every instance of onset, their presence went along with either inadequate support with the severe event (link 3) or the presence of a D/R-event (link 1). A D/R-event has already been defined. Adequacy of support, otherwise called *crisis support,* was defined as confiding about the severe event, receiving at least "moderate" active emotional support from the same person, and with no negative reaction concerning the woman's help seeking on the other person's part at some point in the crisis (Brown et al., 1986b).

Table 6.1 deals with married women who had experienced a severe event and illustrates the basic findings concerning crisis support. Cell "d" shows those who received no support from their husband on either occasion, and, as expected, they have a high rate of depression. Cell "b" shows women who did confide in their husband at the earlier point, but who failed to obtain support from him. They were, in other words "let down," and they had a particularly high rate of depression. Both forms of inadequate support are represented by the negative link 3n in Figure 6.1.

Only those in cell "a," receiving adequate support on both occasions, were at low risk. This effect is represented by a separate positive link 3p in the bottom half of the figure. A further point is not shown about cell "d": among women receiving no support on either occasion from

their husband, there was a complete absence of depression for 18 who received adequate support in the crisis from someone named earlier as very close—usually a woman. But this only occurred as long as a woman had not been let down by her husband—that is, the effect was restricted to cell "d." This second "positive" effect is also represented by the positive link 3p in the bottom half of the figure.

The full material shows that married women were particularly prone to be "let down"—either by a husband or someone whom they had named as "very close." By contrast, single mothers who were confiding in someone named as "very close" at the time of first interview and seen fairly regularly, practically always received support in the crisis from at least one such person. Their high risk of depression was related less to being let down than to lacking support in the first place (Brown et al., 1986b).

In the crisis situation, therefore, negative psychological states present at the time of first interview are carried forward into the crisis situation involving a severe event. But high risk itself is associated with the further presence of an *aetiological complex* of at least two of three risk factors: an internal one of low self-esteem *or* chronic subclinical symptoms, and two external ones of D/R-event and inadequate support (links 1, 2 or 3). As many as 24 of the 29 onsets following a severe event experienced two of the three, and 57% (24/47) of those positive on the complex, developed depression.

To sum up:

Some women were at very high risk. Given the presence of a severe event, at least one of

Table 6.1. Confiding in husband at first interview, Crisis support during the follow-up year, and onset of depression among those with a provoking agent (of married women).

Confiding in husband at 1st interview	Crisis support from husband during follow-up		
	YES % onset	NO % onset	TOTAL % onset
YES	a 4 (1/23)	b 40 (6/15)	15 (7/38)
NO	c 20 (2/7)	d 26 (10/38)	27 (12/45)

Crisis support not known for 3

the two internal and one of the two external factors had to be present for there to be this risk. It is important to note that it was rare for either the internal factors alone or the external alone, to be followed by a depressive onset.

The employment experiences of the women at the time of the severe event can almost certainly be fitted into this scheme. There was a high risk of depression among those working full-time, and single mothers were more likely to work full-time than married women. The key element appears to have been the way full-time employment served to underline the depressogenic implications of certain severe events involving the "deviancy" of children or husband (and sometimes lover) (Brown & Bifulco, 1989). For example, even among the mothers who enjoyed working full-time, there were frequent feelings of strain and conflict over the care of their children, and "delinquency" events in the children were associated with a particularly high risk among such women—but not among those working part-time or not working.

Married women working part-time were at low risk compared with married women who did not work, and this appears to have been related in some way to the quality of their marriages. Those working were less likely to feel insecure about their marriage than those not working even when "objective" sources of insecurity in their marriage were taken into account (Brown & Bifulco, 1989). There is therefore a possibility that part-time work served to improve the marital relationship or at least protect the woman somewhat from any negative effects. However, what exactly is going on is unclear; the important point for the present is that there is no reason to think that such effects cannot be accommodated in the model so far outlined that has emphasised the key importance of core ties. Unfortunately, given these apparently powerful effects, the crisis situation itself would not appear to be an effective entry point for prevention. Onset typically occurred within a matter of weeks of a severe event of any type. Moreover, it is possible that by the time this point is reached, some kind of depressive response may be in some way functional. But this possibility need not concern us, as the chances of successful intervention on a large

scale at this point would appear to be almost nil. However, the results do have implications for intervention if a somewhat different time perspective is taken. The same aetiological complex can be seen from the vantage point of the first interview (and often much earlier) that has more interesting implications.

Intervention in Terms of Background Factors

An index of "negative elements of core relationships" at the time of first interview predicts well both immediate risk factors just discussed, i.e. the quality of support in a crisis (link 3a), and the occurrence or nonoccurrence of a D/R-event (link 1). It is also highly related to negative psychological states (low self-esteem and chronic subclinical conditions—link 2 (Brown, 1989). For married women, the index is largely made up of items relating to the quality of their marriage. For single mothers, quality of tie with children at home as well as those with anyone named as "very close" outside the home is predictive. The upshot is that if the quality of core ties is taken into account, it is possible to predict depression just as well from the vantage point of measures made at the point of first interview as from the aetiological complex of the follow-up period itself. The importance for prevention is that the background factors have typically persisted for some time.

The predictive power of the index is remarkable. Eighty women had both "negative elements in core relationships" *and* either low self-esteem or chronic subclinical symptoms, and 31% (25/80) subsequently developed depression. Put another way, 78% of onsets occurred among a quarter (80/303) of the women at risk. The index has been called *conjoint* to emphasise the importance of both internal and external components.

To sum up:

Depression is intimately related to the "negative quality of core relationships," both in terms of the severely threatening events they tend to throw up and the feelings of low self-esteem and chronic subclinical conditions they can generate. There is obvious potential here for intervention, bearing in mind the background factors have typically persisted for several years at least. The finding that both an internal and an external negative factor (i.e. the Conjoint Index) must be present is intriguing. A suitably cautious interpretation would appear to be twofold. Where the interpersonal environment is clearly poor, the internal state of a woman will usually also be affected (in terms of low self-esteem or low-grade symptoms). To talk about the one is therefore to talk about the other. Where the environment is more marginal in terms of its implications, the presence of "negative psychological factors" helps the investigator to pick out the potentially more depressogenic environments. However, it should be noted that neither interpretation rules out that low self-esteem and subclinical symptoms play a direct causal role in any subsequent depression (Brown, Bifulco & Andrews, 1989).

However, in terms of prevention, it should be borne in mind that in about one-third of the high-risk married women, the "negative elements in core relationships index" probably represented—in the light of the follow-up material—somewhat minor blips in an otherwise successful relationship. It just so happened that on occasions among a group of such somewhat marginal relationships one of the component ratings of the index (e.g. a "moderate" rating on "negative interaction with husband") predicted either a crisis in the follow-up year or being "let down" in terms of one or both of these. One husband, for example, in such an apparently somewhat marginal relationship turned out at follow-up to have been having an affair at the time of first interview, and in another the woman had hidden from us the full extent of her husband's past irresponsible behaviour; in the following year he developed a severe paranoid disorder that created serious problems for her. However, in most instances such somewhat marginal marriages continued to be unexceptional.

Almost all the single mothers at high risk in terms of the Conjoint Index were without someone named as very close, whom they saw quite often and in whom they could confide. And depression among such women was almost entirely restricted to those without such a "true" very close tie (Brown et al., 1986b; O'Connor & Brown, 1982; Brown & Andrews, 1986).

Past Intervention in Terms of Past Factors

There has a been a good deal of research on the impact of experiences in childhood, adolescence and early adulthood on chances of depression in adulthood and a reasonably clear picture of the importance of long-term effects begins to emerge.

The original version of the model shown in Figure 6.1 included loss of mother before 11 (Brown, Harris & Copeland, 1977). While there has been controversy about its aetiological role (Brown & Harris, 1986a; Harris & Brown, 1985; Crook & Eliot, 1980; Tennant, Bebbington & Hurry, 1980; Harris, Brown & Bifulco, 1986), the basic effect has now been replicated in two further studies (Brown, Harris & Bifulco, 1986; Harris, Brown & Bifulco, 1986, 1987; Bifulco, Brown & Harris, 1987). Recent research suggests, however, that more fundamental than the early loss is the quality of replacement parental care. If this is inadequate (in terms of an index of parental indifference and lax control, termed *lack of care*), risk of current depression is doubled irrespective of loss of a mother.

A measure of antipathy of mother in childhood has also been included to form an index of *early inadequate parenting*. This index, like lack of care alone, shows important links with subsequent factors—for example, women positive on it have double the rate of low self-esteem. In terms of a path analysis, the most important link is with negative personal environment represented by the "negative elements in core relationship index" (link 7 in Figure 6.1). Via this link early inadequate parenting has its main link with the negative psychological states of low self-esteem and chronic subclinical conditions (link 4 in Figure 6.1) and the external factors in the crisis situation. Its direct links with subsequent factors in the model are less substantial (links 8 and 9).

To sum up:

Early inadequate parenting is linked to risk of depression in adulthood, but largely via an adverse current environment represented by the background risk factors. As an approximate estimate, the past accounts for a third of current depression—that is, only 2 rather than 3 women in Islington would have depression in the follow-up year were it not for the much earlier inadequate parenting. Given problems of measurement this figure may even turn out to be somewhat conservative.

Again the potential here for *prevention* is obvious. This might be through some influence on the quality of parental care itself or substitute parental care. Some existing services, such as the Newpin befriending scheme in Southwark, were set up with just the apparent link of depression in mothers with child abuse and neglect in mind. However, it may also prove effective to intervene at some point in the subsequent conveyor belt of adverse experiences that typically follows such poor parenting if it is to lead to depression—experiences often bound up with choice of men, premarital pregnancy, and problems of housing and employment. The evidence for the importance of this strand is now fairly well established. There is also some evidence for a parallel internal strand concerning cognitive and emotional development, including not only cognitive sets such as self-esteem and helplessness, but also styles of attachment along the lines outlined by Bowlby (Harris et al., 1989).

Post-Onset Intervention

The Transition to Chronicity

As already noted, some quarter of the depression developing in the follow-up year in Islington lasted for at least 1 year, and this appears to be much the kind of proportion to be expected—at least in urban settings. We know surprisingly little about the determinants of this transition (link 10). In the Islington survey, the numbers involved were small, and this may explain why poor parenting turned out to be unrelated to the transition to chronicity. (Such a link would have been expected if only because such a background of early inadequate parenting was high among the larger sized group of women who were chronically depressed at the time of our first contact with them.)

Current psychosocial factors do appear to be of some relevance for determining chronicity. A measure of self-esteem based on positive comments predicted length of episode among the 32 onset cases in Islington (Brown, Andrews & Bifulco, 1989). In addition, an onset provoked by a D/R-event more often became chronic.

Chronic States

Finally, there is the chronic population itself. Of the women in the Islington sample, 8% suffered from a chronic state at the time we first saw them (Brown, Craig & Harris, 1985). A follow-up of a small subsample 8 years later suggests that as many as 18% had suffered from a chronic state in the 9-year period (Andrews, 1989). In other words, the problem is probably a considerable one.

Material collected over a 3-year period in Islington has confirmed findings of earlier research in Camberwell that ongoing difficulties do play a role in perpetuating depression at a caseness level (link 11n in Figure 6.1). However, equally important is a finding that recovery from chronic depression (including any major improvement) is related either to a reduction in ongoing difficulties or to the occurrence of a *fresh start event,* involving the idea of starting again—link 11p in Figure 6.1 (see also Table 6.2). While a fresh start often goes with a reduction in difficulties, the two by no means always go together. Perhaps surprisingly, fresh start events often involve a significant degree of threat (a quarter were rated severe). The important thing appears to be that they convey some

Table 6.2. Recovery or improvement among 48 Islington women with chronic depression in terms of a fresh start event or difficulty-reduction.

Initial difficulty score	Fresh-start event or difficulty reduction	
	YES	NO
	(% recovered or improved)	
0–2 (low)	100 (6/6)	63 (5/8)
3–6	71 (5/7)	50 (2/4)
	60	21
7 (high)	54 (7/13)	10 (1/10)

hope that things could be better, such as reconciliation with an estranged son and daughter-in-law after the birth of a second grandchild, starting divorce proceedings by taking out an injunction against a violent husband, husband getting a job that relieves considerable financial difficulties and tension at home, or an extremely violent husband being sent to prison for several years because of his attack on the woman and her mother (Brown et al., 1988).

The majority of women in Islington recovering from chronic depression had either experienced difficulty reduction or a fresh-start event, and in this sense, the general importance of a cognitive-affective approach to depression is confirmed: the changes either involved relief from ongoing adversity or state of deprivation, or the hope of this. Among women who recovered without either experience were a number whose depression had been brought about by a death (of a husband or child), and there may well be a small group of chronic depressions following a bereavement that dissipate with time alone.

There was also a hint that under certain circumstances, the level of social support played a role (link 11p). There have been other suggestive studies (Surtees & Ingham, 1980; Tennant et al., 1981a, 1981b; Parker et al., 1985; Miller et al., 1987), and it is possible to make a provisional case that the process of recovery is often the mirror-image of the psychosocial processes leading to onset.

The challenge of the high rates of chronicity makes this perhaps the most obvious point in the model to start any intervention in the population at large. There can be no doubt about the suffering involved, nor, for that matter, the consequences for others—either from the depression itself or the circumstances that gave rise to it. To take just one example: Islington women have now been followed up 8 years after they were first seen, together with any daughters in their late teens and early 20s. Current psychiatric disorder including depression, anxiety and eating disorders in the daughters at a case level is already far from negligible and is highly related to a history of either chronic or episodic depressive disorders in the mother during the daughter's life time (Andrews, Brown & Creasey, 1989). Such conditions are even

more highly related to the experience of early inadequate parenting by the daughter. Such results (and others could be cited) underline the potential gain from any programme of intervention capable of heading off such generational effects.

Some Final Comments

Any discussion of issues of methodology and validity has been deliberately omitted in presenting these results. A good deal has now been replicated, but other parts urgently need further study—for example, the predictive role of the Conjoint Index in onset, the predictive role of positive self-esteem in length of episode and the role of fresh-start events in recovery from chronic states. But even if replicated, there are bound to be cultural differences. However, there has already been sufficient replication of certain core findings across populations, and the theoretical perspective is sufficiently general for a case to be made for beginning to think in preventive terms and for the planning of limited kinds of preventive research.

Specific and more general approaches to public health issues were earlier contrasted. In terms of the more general, structural, approach there can be no argument that *there is a role for psychiatric opinion and knowledge to inform political decisions relevant to health*—and many do have such implications. There is also a general need for *psychiatrists to think more in terms of delegation, education and example*—and there are already stimulating examples in this volume. Psychiatrists are too few in number to restrict their activity just to the individual and his or her family. It is essential that, as part of their job, they help to motivate and to guide others outside the immediate psychiatric milieu. Here it would be equally fool-hardy to neglect the more individual perspective. There are times when it is critical to know that, say, the intervention required in terms of immediate the environment by someone with schizophrenia is likely to be different from someone suffering from depression. Moreover, although the issue of deprivation is obviously critical, it would be misguided to reduce the psychosocial factors of relevance to psychiatric disorder to this—at least as this is usually understood in a political context. Many in the middle classes also develop affective disorders; and, continuing in stereotypical terms, many working-class women have middle-class problems in their marriages. We need to face the fact that our general way of life and cultural practices as a whole need to come under scrutiny—not necessarily to change them in any straightforward sense, but perhaps to offer some comment on the possibility of amelioration and support.

It may prove impossible, despite the knowledge we have gained, to do much about the depressogenic currents in urban, inner-city settings without major structural changes. But it is too soon to conclude that nothing can be done at an individual level if these do not occur, or occur very slowly. Present knowledge in any case has reached a point where there is a moral necessity to explore the various possibilities for intervention at every level. It is also possible that even modest demonstrations of effectiveness at an individual level may favourably influence political initiatives.

What, therefore, might be accomplished in the short term and on a more individual level? There is, for a start, an obvious need to improve the efficacy and coverage of existing services, using this term in the broadest sense. Those linked to general practice, education and employment come readily to mind. An interesting current example of an apparently effective intervention carried out on a large scale and with surprisingly little cost has been the reduction in bullying in Norwegian schools. The intervention followed widespread concern following two cases of suicide and was made largely via the teachers. It may well, within the space of 2 years, have cut the incidence of bullying by a half (Olweus, 1989). Of course, in terms of preparation for life outside school a great deal more might be done.

However, Newton's (1988) recent emphasis on the conventional public health argument is persuasive: that is, that, by and large, interventions are likely to prove more effective if *effort is concentrated on high-risk groups* rather than to try to change the quality of life for the population as a whole. In these terms, another obvious example is the critical area of contraception and abortion; and here there may have already been important advances over the last 20 years. The only vulnerability factor established in earlier research in Camberwell that gained no support from the Islington survey was the presence of 3 children aged less than 14 at home. Indeed, in Islington such women were, if anything, *protected* from depression. We have argued that this may well be the direct result of the greater control of women over contraception, and that today more women have the number of children they ideally require than in Camberwell in the 1960s (Harris et al., 1989).

There also needs to be greater awareness of the possible *depressogenic implications* of "events" and ongoing "difficulties" occurring to the individual woman: what do they reflect about long-term environments? Here, it should be recalled the apparent remarkable degree of prediction of depression possible in the short term at least. Here, general practice, health visitors and the police may prove vital in their potential for carrying out initial appraisals. Of course, it will still be necessary to do something once a depressogenic situation has been assessed. And it may be asked whether there is here a case to be made for new services. And, if so, what would be the role of psychiatry? It will perhaps prove easiest in the first place to make a case in terms of the problem presented by chronic depressive conditions. Everyone is likely to have his or her own favourites. However, it is doubtful whether psychiatrists should (or could) play more than a facilitating and guiding role. There is by contrast likely to be a central role for women themselves through voluntary activity exemplified by befriending schemes, albeit with these needing to be set up and run by a small core of trained personnel (e.g. Pound & Mills, 1985).

Inevitably, at this point, with current resources so thin, such suggestions must take on a somewhat vacuous air. But I am not arguing for immediate *general* implementation. Much still needs to be established—not the least about the effectiveness of specific interventions. We are at best at the beginning of a wave of effort (and , it is hoped, enthusiasm), together perhaps with the release of resources and opportunities the increasing closure of large mental hospitals. If we do our job well over the next decade it is possible that "services" that do emerge will not suffer the fate of Leighton's mental health centre. But how this might be prevented is an issue equally as complex as the one just explored. My own choice would be to move somewhat away from reliance on professional or quasi-professional help to one of facilitating ordinary women (or men for that matter) to help each other. Insofar as a good deal of the depression seen in medical (not simply psychiatric) practice is the direct result of problems of living, the problem needs to be also tackled from a nonmedical perspective.

Although the biological outcroppings of depression present an obviously important focus for intervention, if the aetiological model arising from current research proves even halfway correct, this will not be enough. One al-

ternative (and, of course, there are others) is to encourage the development of "services" based on the *provision of social support,* something women can give to each other and something that is understood and appreciated and, by and large, wanted—often desperately. It is a commodity that can in time release energies in both those that give and those who receive it. Given suitable professional guidance, such services may well prove to provide an inexhaustible supply of necessary support and one, since it is one to one and voluntary, that need not have the built-in decay in effectiveness that is the history of so much in the public sector. On the assumption that such schemes are in place and are effective, it will be easier to assess the need for specialist services based on more traditional therapeutic lines.

References

Andrews, B. (1989). Personal communication.

Andrews, B., Brown, G. W., & Creasey, L. (1989). *Intergenerational links between psychiatric disorder in mothers and daughters: The role of social factors.* Unpublished manuscript.

Bebbington, P. W., Tennant, C., & Hurry, J. (1981). Adversity and the nature of psychiatric disorder in the community. *Journal of Affective Disorders, 3,* 345–366.

Bebbington, P. W., Hurry, J., Tennant, C. & Sturt, E. (1984). Misfortune and resilience: A community study of women. *Psychological Medicine, 14,* 347–363.

Beck, A. T. (1967). *Depression: Clinical, experimental and theoretical aspects.* London: Staples Press.

Bifulco, A., Brown, G. W., & Harris, T. (1987). Childhood loss of parent and adult psychiatric disorder: The Islington study. *Journal of Affective Disorders, 12,* 115–128.

Bibring, E. (1953). Mechanisms of depression. In P. Greenacre (Ed.), *Affective disorders: Psychoanalytic contributions to their study.* New York: International Universities Press.

Bolton, W., & Oatley, K. (1987). A longitudinal study of social support and depression in unemployed men. *Psychological Medicine, 17,* 453–460.

Brown, G. W. (in press). Etiology of depressive disorder. In D. Bennett & H. Freeman (Eds.), *The practice of social psychiatry.* London: Churchill Livingstone.

Brown, G. W., Adler, Z., & Bifulco, A. (1988). Life events, difficulties and recovery from chronic depression. *British Journal of Psychiatry, 152,* 487–498.

Brown, G. W., & Andrews, B. (1986). Social support

and depression. In M. H. Appleby & R. Trumbull (Eds.), *Dynamics of stress* (pp. 257–282). New York; Plenum.

Brown, G. W., Andrews, B., Bifulco, A., & Veiel, H. (1989). Self-esteem and depression: *1. Measurement issues and prediction of onset.* Unpublished manuscript.

Brown, G. W., Andrews, B., Harris, T., Adler, Z., & Bridge, L. (1986). Social support, self-esteem and depression. *Psychological Medicine, 16,* 813–831.

Brown, G. W., & Bifulco, A. (1990). Women, employment and the development of depression: A replication of a finding? *British Journal of Psychiatry, 154,* in press.

Brown, G. W., Bifulco, A., & Andrews, B. (1989). *Self-esteem and depression: 4. Effect on course and recovery.* Unpublished manuscript.

Brown, G. W. , Bifulco, A., & Harris, T.O. (1987). Life events, vulnerability and onset of depression: Some refinements. *British Journal of Psychiatry, 150,* 30–42.

Brown, G. W., Craig, T. K. J., & Harris, T. O. (1985). Depression: disease or distress? Some epidemiological considerations. *British Journal of Psychiatry, 147,* 612–62.

Brown, G. W., Harris, T.O., & Copeland, J. R. (1977). Depression and Loss. *British Journal of Psychiatry, 130,* 1–18.

Brown, G. W., & Harris, T.O. (1978). *Social origins of depression.* London: Tavistock.

Brown, G. W., & Harris, T. O. (1986a). Establishing causal links: The Bedford College studies of depression. In H. Katschnig (Ed.), *Life events and psychiatric disorders: Controversial issues* (pp. 107–187). Cambridge, England: Cambridge University Press.

Brown, G. W., Harris, T. O., & Bifulco, A. (1986). Long-term effect of early loss of parent. In M. Rutter, C. Izard & P. Read (Eds.), *Depression in childhood: Developmental perspectives*. New York: Guilford Press.

Brown, G. W., & Prudo, R. (1981). Psychiatric disorder in a rural and an urban population: 1. Aetiology of depression. *Psychological Medicine, 11,* 581–599.

Cooper, J. E., Copeland, J. R. M., Brown, G. W., Harris, T. & Gourley, A. J. (1977). Further studies on interviewer training and inter-rater reliability of the present state examination (P.S.E.). *Psychological Medicine, 7,* 517–523.

Costello, C. G. (1982). Social factors associated with depression: A retrospective community study. *Psychological Medicine, 12,* 329–339.

Craig, T. K. J. (1989). Abdominal pain. In G. W. Brown & T. O. Harris (Eds.), *Life events and illness*. London: Unwin Hyman/New York: Guilford Press.

Creed, F. (1989). Appendectomy. In G. W. Brown & T. O. Harris (Eds.), *Life events and illness*. London: Unwin Hyman/New York: Guilford Press.

Crook, & Eliot (1980). Parental death during childhood and adult depression: A critical review of the literature. *Psychological Bulletin, 87,* 252–259.

Dean, C., Surtees, P. G., & Sashidharan, S. D. (1983). Comparison of research diagnostic systems in an Edinburgh community sample. *British Journal of Psychiatry, 142,* 247–256.

Dohrenwend, B. P., Shrout, P. E., Link, B. G., Martin, J. L., & Skodol, A. E. (1986). Overview and initial results from a risk-factor study of depression and schizophrenia. In J. E. Barrett & R. M. Rose (Eds.), *Mental disorders in the community* (pp. 184–215). New York: Guilford Press.

Eales, M. J. (1988). Depression and anxiety in unemployed men. *Psychological Medicine, 18,* 935–946.

Finlay-Jones, R., & Brown, G. W. (1981). Types of stressful life event and the onset of anxiety and depressive disorders. *Psychological Medicine, 11,* 803–815.

Finlay-Jones, R., Brown, G. W., Duncan-Jones, P., Harris, T., Murphy, E., & Prudo, R. (1980). Depression and anxiety in the community. *Psychological Medicine, 10,* 445–454.

Gaminde, I., & Uria, M. (1988). *Desordenes afectivos y factores sociales en la comunidad automona vasca—3.*

Grant, I. W., McDonald, I., Patterson, T., & Trimble, M. R. (1989). Multiple Sclerosis. In G. W. Brown & T. Harris (Eds.), *Life events and illness*. London: Unwin Hyman/New York: Guilford Press.

Harris, T. (1989). Disorders of menstruation. In G. W. Brown & T. Harris (Eds.), *Life events and illness*. London: Unwin Hyman/New York: Guilford Press.

Harris, T., Adler, Z., Bridge, L., & Brown, G. W. (1989). *Instability of indicator variables and replication studies: Depression in women and number*

of children at home. Unpublished manuscript.

Harris, T., & Brown, G. W. (1985). Interpreting data in aetiological studies: Pitfalls and ambiguities. *British Journal of Psychiatry, 147,* 5–15.

Harris, T., Brown, G. W., & Bifulco, A. (1986). Loss of parent in childhood and adult psychiatric disorder: The role of parental care. *Psychological Medicine, 16,* 641–659.

Harris, T., Brown, G. W., & Bifulco, A. (1987). Loss of parent in childhood and adult psychiatric disorder: The role of social class position and premarital pregnancy. *Psychological Medicine, 17,* 163–183.

Harris, T., Brown, G. W., & Bifulco, A. (1989a). Loss of parent in childhood and adult psychiatric disorder: The role of social class position and premarital pregnancy. *Psychological Medicine, 17,* 163–183.

Harris, T., Brown, G. W., & Bifulco, A. (1989b). *Loss of parent in childhood and adult psychiatric disorder: The role of situational helplessness.* (in press).

Leighton, A. (1982). *Caring for mentally ill people*. Cambridge: Cambridge University Press.

Lora, A. (1989). Personal communication.

MacIntyre, S. (1986). The patterning of health by social position in contemporary Britain: Directions for sociological research. *Social Science & Medicine, 23,* 393–415.

Miller, P. M., & Ingham, J. G. (1983). Dimensions of experience. *Psychological Medicine, 13,* 417–429.

Miller, P. M., Ingham, J. G., Kreitman, N. B., Surtees, P. G., & Sashidharan, S. P. (1987). Life events and other factors implicated in onset and in remission of psychiatric illness in women. *Journal of Affective Disorders, 12,* 73–88.

Newton, J. (1988) *Preventing mental illness*. London, New York: Routledge & Kegan Paul.

O'Connor, P., & Brown, G. W. (1984). Supportive relationships: Fact or fancy? *Journal of Social and Personal Relationships, 1,* 159–175.

Olweus, D. (in press). Bully/victim problems among school children: Basic facts and effects of a school based intervention program. In K. Rubin & D. Pepler (Eds.), *The development and treatment of childhood aggression*. Hillsdale, NJ: Erlbaum.

Parker, G., Tennant, C., & Blignault, I. (1985). Predicting improvement in patients with non-endogenous depression. *British Journal of Psychiatry, 146,* 132–139.

Paykel, E. S. (1974) Recent life events and clinical depression. In I. K. E. Gunderson & R. D. Rahe (Eds.), *Life stress and illness*. Springfield, IL: C.C. Thomas.

Pound, A., & Mills, M. (1988). A pilot evaluation of Newpin—a home visiting and befriending scheme in South London. *A.C.C.P. Newsletter* 7(4).

Prudo, R., Brown, G. W., Harris, T., & Dowland, J. (1981). Psychiatric disorder in a rural and an urban population: 2. Sensitivity to loss. *Psychological Medicine, 14,* 327–343.

Ramirez, A., Craig, T., Watson, J., Fentiman, I., North, W., & Reubens R. (1989). Stress and re-

lapse of breast cancer. *British Medical Journal,*
298, 291–293.

Research Unit in Health & Behavioural Change
(1989). *Changing the public health.* Chichester:
Wiley.

Surtees, P. G., & Ingham, J. G. (1980). Life stress
and depressive outcome: Application of a dissipa-
tion model to life events. *Social Psychiatry, 15,*
21–31.

Surtees, P. G., Dean, C., Ingham, J. G., Kreitman, N.
B., Miller, P. M., & Sashidharan, S. P. (1983).
Psychiatric disorder in women in an Edinburgh
community: Associations with demographic factors. *British Journal of Psychiatry, 142,* 238–246.

Tennant, C., Bebbington, P., & Hurry, J. (1980).
Parental death in childhood and risk of adult depressive disorder: A review. *Psychological Medi-*
cine, 19, 189–299.

Tennant, C., Bebbington, P., & Hurry, J. (1981a).
The natural history of neurotic illness in the community: Demographic and clinical predictors of remission. *Australian and New Zealand Journal of*
Psychiatry, 15, 111–116.

Tennant, C., Bebbington, P., & Hurry, J. (1981b).
The short-term outcome of neurotic disorders in
the community: The relation of remission to clinical factors and to "neutralising" events. *British*
Journal of Psychiatry, 139, 213–220.

Weissman, M. M., & Klerman, G. L. (1977). Sex
differences and the epidemiology of depression.
Archives of General Psychiatry, 34, 98–111.

Wing, J. K., Nixon, J. M., Mann, S. A., & Leff, J. P.
(1977). Reliability of the PSE (9th ed.) used in a
population study (1977). *Psychological Medicine,*
7, 505–516.

Chapter 7

Research Issues in the Epidemiological and Public Health Aspects of Parasuicide and Suicide

Norman Kreitman

The purpose of this contribution is to sketch some of the gaps in knowledge that currently confront those concerned with the public health aspects of self-damaging behaviour. Action may, of course, precede full understanding, but it is more likely to succeed when it is informed by knowledge of causal factors. Accordingly, the emphasis here will be on those epidemiological issues concerned with aetiology, broadly defined. The British research tradition since the time of Stengel has been to treat nonfatal self-harm, or parasuicide, separately from suicide per se. That important distinction is followed here.

Parasuicide

A striking feature of parasuicide is how very common it is. In some years, according to Edinburgh data, one girl in 100 between the ages of 15 and 19 is admitted to hospital with self-poisoning or self-injury, and the true rate of morbidity in the population must, of course, be higher. The central puzzle about parasuicide, however, is the substantial degree of fluctuation over time in the treated morbidity rates. Figures 7.1 and 7.2 from Mannheim, West Germany, and from Edinburgh, respectively, illustrate recent trends that are similar to those noted in other centres too.

Why have these changes occurred? Two hypotheses have been tested in our own group. The first concerns the role of unemployment in men, which has been closely investigated by my colleague Stephen Platt (Platt & Kreitman, 1985; Platt, 1986). To describe the development of the research, it is convenient to divide the study period into two phases, the first being in the 1970s when we first became

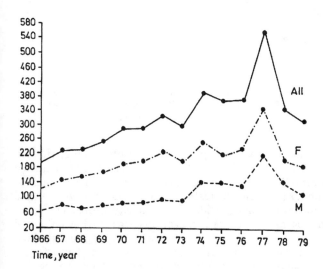

Figure 7.1. Attempted suicides in Mannheim 1966–1979 (Hafner, 1985).

Figure 7.2. Parasuicide rates (aged 15+) per 100,000 in Edinburgh.

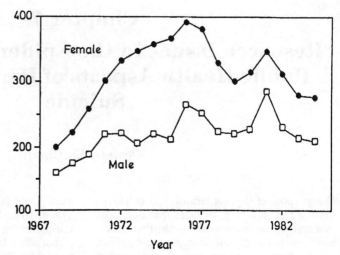

Figure 7.3. Edinburgh 1968–1984: Parasuicide and unemployment rates, males.

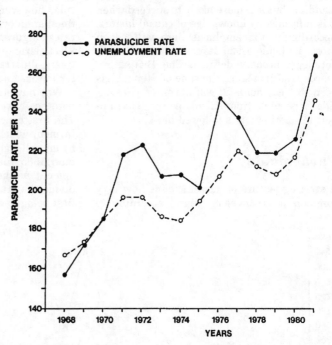

interested in the issue, and the second spanning the present decade. During the 1970s, up to and including 1981, there was a dramatic increase in the number of men in Edinburgh who were out of work, and coincident with that increase a rise in the rate of male parasuicides (see Figure 7.3).

It had long been known that the unemployed were overrepresented among male parasuicide patients (e.g. Kessel, 1965; Hawton & Rose, 1986). It was also well established that strong ecological correlations could be demonstrated between unemployment and parasuicide across the city wards. The possibility of a causal link was further enhanced when we demonstrated a conspicuously high parasuicide rate for the unemployed in the general population, and by the discovery that

Table 7.1. Parasuicide rates by duration of unemployment: Edinburgh City males, 1982.

Duration of unemployment	Parasuicide rate (per 100,000)	Relative risk
Less than 4 weeks	1012	8.8
5–26 weeks	615	5.4
27–52 weeks	1193	10.4
Over 52 weeks	2164	18.9
All unemployed	1345	11.8
All employed	114	

the relative risk of parasuicide increased dramatically with increasing duration of unemployment (Table 7.1), even after controlling for a number of possible confounding variables such as age, social class and residential area.

We went on to examine how the relation of parasuicide and unemployment changes over time. *When the economy is thriving the unemployed are a marginal group characterised by multiple handicaps and likely to demonstrate a high rate of parasuicide; with the advent of mass unemployment due to broad economic trends, membership of the unemployed category depends much less upon personal characteristics.* The rate of parasuicide among them might, therefore, be expected to fall as unem-

ployment becomes more widespread. That is precisely what happens (Figure 7.4).

Despite this fall in rate, the increase in the total numbers of unemployed has been such as to generate increasing numbers of unemployed parasuicides, and the population-attributable risk from unemployment has steadily increased (see Table 7.2).

We also considered the meaning of high unemployment for particular communities. It seemed plausible that in societies where high unemployment was endemic, and hence denoted less deviance, expectations and lifestyle would be moderated in such a way as to adapt as far as possible to unemployment-related stress. Conversely, a sudden increase in unemployment rates might be especially traumatic. In consequence, it would be predicted that for a given level of unemployment comparatively lower rates of parasuicide would occur where this was a long-standing state of affairs than when it was recent. Work from a number of centres (e.g. Furness et al., 1985) and from our own city gave general support to the hypothesis.

A credible causal model was thus beginning to emerge, but it needed to be supplemented by demonstrating a plausible mechanism.

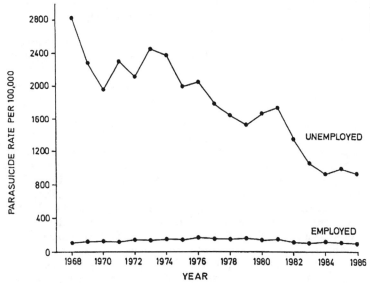

Figure 7.4. Parasuicide rates among employed and unemployed males.

Table 7.2. Population attributable risk of parasuicide arising from unemployment.

Year	Parasuicide rate/100,000		Population attributable risk (A-B)	Maximum % of overall rate attributable to unemployment ((A-B)/A) × 100
	Among all economically active (A)	Among employed (B)		
1969	188	117	71	38.1
1970	204	122	82	40.4
1971	238	115	123	51.5
1972	252	141	111	44.0
1973	240	134	106	44.2
1974	247	149	98	39.6
1975	239	139	100	42.1
1976	299	173	126	42.0
1977	284	153	131	45.9
1978	257	150	107	41.8
1979	253	160	93	36.6
1980	260	143	117	45.0
1981	322	154	168	52.3

Clinical experience furnished many possible psychosocial explanations for a link between unemployment and parasuicide. Though unemployed patients rarely cited unemployment per se as a precipitating cause for the act, it was evident that among this group loss of work had often led to increasing demoralisation, depression, violence, debts (affecting the wives as much or more than their unemployed husbands), increasing family friction and increasing alcohol consumption. However, more formal testing was required if clinical observations were to be confirmed.

The argument concerning the effect of mass economic causes, rather than individual psychopathology as the reason *why* an individual is unemployed, has already been mentioned, and the "dilution" effect illustrated in Figure 7.4 above. An attempt was made to test such changes directly, by comparing unemployed parasuicides in years when the population unemployment rates differed markedly. *Contra hypothesi* evidence of personal handicap and psychopathy was about the same (Platt & Duffy, 1986). But another study yielded positive evidence. Beck et al. (1975) had pointed to hopelessness rather than depressed mood as the primary correlate of self-damaging behaviour and of its degree of lethality, a finding that has been replicated by several workers. Platt and Dyer (1987) showed that

unemployed parasuicides were more hopeless in Beck's terms than were parasuicides in work, and the difference persisted when depression per se was partialled out. These findings were entirely in accord with the widespread documentation of negative evaluations of the future, with or without depressive symptoms, as a salient feature of the unemployed, especially if it is long-term (reviewed by Warr, 1984).

Overall, a causal role for unemployment in relation to parasuicide seemed to be if not established—it would be difficult to specify just what would constitute conclusive proof—at least highly plausible. The real difficulty arises when we move on from the 1970s to the 1980s. The data became complex (and are not presented here), but in essence the male parasuicide rate has remained static or, more recently, even begun to decrease. Conversely, the unemployment rates have fluctuated from their all-time high in the early part of the decade to steadily falling levels more recently, although it is uncertain how far this effects the short-term as against the long-term unemployed. At the aggregate levels, the two variables have ceased to be related.

It might be possible to accommodate these apparently anomalous facts within the main hypothesis, drawing on work such as that of Jackson and Warr (1987) showing that com-

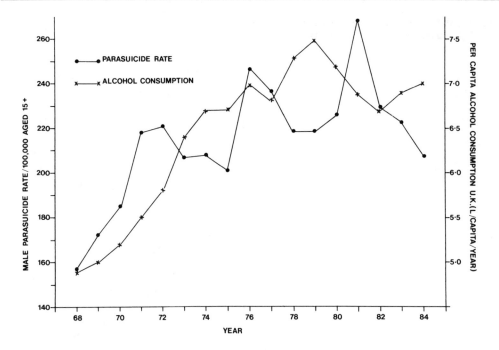

Figure 7.5. Edinburgh male parasuicide rate and U.K. alcohol consumption.

munities eventually adapt to the effects of unemployment. It is also possible that although the same causal relationship pertained in both decades the effect is more readily demonstrated in the 1970s when large shifts occurred in the unemployment rate than in the 1980s where less dramatic changes were evident. But such progressive refinements of the thesis would quite properly generate increasing scepticism. At present we would claim no more than that unemployment is or was a plausible reason for the changes within the earlier period, but that subsequently it has either ceased to operate in this way, or that its effect has been overlaid by other and quite different processes.

Much the same might be said for the *second hypotheses* we have considered, namely, that the *rising parasuicide rates, particularly for men, might be associated with rising levels of alcohol consumption.* The evidence both for and against this view cannot be rehearsed in detail; in summary, there was rather less direct evidence for a linkage than was found for unemployment, but nevertheless there did indeed appear to be a possible line of explana-

tion here. Once again, however, the hypothesis failed to hold up for the later years of the study period under discussion (see Figure 7.5).

Thus, the first problem to which I wish to draw attention is how to explain why the changes in the parasuicide rate over the past decade or so have followed their particular course. Efforts to test causal theories concerning temporal trends for any behaviour that is undoubtedly multifactorial in origin are bound to encounter such difficulties, and there are general issues here concerning longitudinal analysis which are taken up later. However, to recognise a difficulty is not to solve it.

A quite different set of questions arise when we move to consider the patterns of morbidity shown by parasuicides with respect to repetition. Parasuicide is rather unusual in being a more or less instantaneous event that, although it may signal an underlying state of abnormality (in some sense), is not in itself attended by any obvious sequelae, unlike, say, a cerebral vascular accident. This is not to deny that important psychological and social

Figure 7.6. Males, rates (person) per 100,000 (aged 15+) by category (average of 3 cohorts).

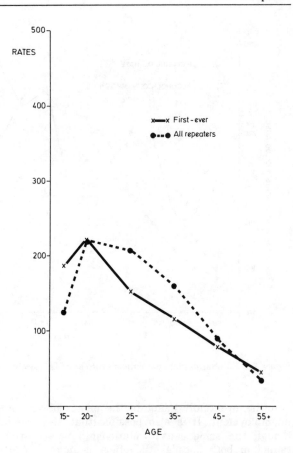

changes may follow the episode of self-harm, but most parasuicides do not receive, and arguably do not require, further hospital-based care. On the other hand, approximately 20% of cases will be re-admitted with a further episode within 12 months of their key admission; conversely, about half of all admissions have been preceded by an earlier hospital-treated episode. Repetition is thus a major issue. The aspect of repetition that has received most attention is, of course, the clinical problem of how to identify future repeaters. Other workers have used data on repetition within large data sets as a step toward deriving a polythetic taxonomy (Fahy et al., 1970; Bancroft & Marsack, 1977; Katschnig & Sint, 1973), but few appear to have considered the basic epidemiology of the repetitive parasuicidal individual.

When this is done, some rather surprising results and some unanswered problems

emerge. The strategy of an investigation of this kind poses some difficulties in that the defining characteristics of the individuals to be entered into the numerators of the rates (for first-ever or for repetitive parasuicide) are unstable, and in the course of a study period a patient may transfer from the former to the latter. Similarly, other characteristics such as his or her social context or marital status may be liable to abrupt fluctuation. Nevertheless, much can be learned even by a cross-sectional or snapshot approach. Some recent findings for men—those for women are similar—are illustrated in Figure 7.6. This shows two features of particular interest. The first is that *the individual characterised by multiple episodes occurs more frequently per unit of population in the middle-age band than in the younger group.* This could be viewed simply as a function of time, in that such a person would have been at risk for more years than will younger subjects. All the same, given that the age frequency distribution of parasuicide is so markedly skewed toward the younger age groups, the result is not one that could have been predicted with confidence. What is certainly surprising is that the rates for the repeaters are actually *higher* than for the first-ever individuals in the middle of the age range, emphasising the importance of repetition as a characteristic of patients at that time of life.

The second notable feature of the graph is that *among those aged 55 and older the pattern for the middle age group is reversed.* More parasuicides at this age are first-ever cases than repeaters. Their period at risk is greater than for the middle-aged, yet repetitive behaviour is less salient. A possibility to be considered here is that of a period of birth cohort effect, but separate analyses have failed to produce persuasive evidence that such effects do in fact occur. It seems much more likely the data reflect a different group of first-ever parasuicides who come to attention in later life. Clinical studies support this view; in terms of their formal psychiatric diagnosis and of their prognosis for completed suicide within the comparatively near future (Kreitman 1976), this group does indeed appear to be different in important respects from younger subjects and is in need of further study.

If the distinctions just noted are confirmed, then it is possible to put forward a series of questions concerning the epidemiological correlates of *inception* into a "career" of parasuicide as contrasted with the factors associated with the perseveration in this behaviour, along the lines now being formulated with regard to risk factors in affective disorders and schizophrenia for inception and chronicity. A comprehensive list of the two groups of risk factors is not yet available. Preliminary findings suggest that being young and being female are risk factors for first episodes, while being male and aged 35–54 are associated with multiepisode status. Conversely, membership of Social Class V is a potent risk factor for both inception and for repetition. How far further characteristics such as high alcohol consumption, so frequently reported by certain categories of repeaters, can be viewed epidemiologically is

going to depend on the adequacy of comparable data in the general population. It is evident that much work still requires to be done. This constitutes the second topic on my list of the issues needing attention.

Suicide

Given the horrified fascination suicide universally excites, it is not surprising that speculation on its causes date back to antiquity, nor that it was one of the first topics to be studied scientifically in the present area. Yet despite research since the early decades of the last century many outstanding problems await solution. There are indeed voices to be heard grumbling about the current lack of progress, suggesting that contemporary research is becoming repetitive and uninspired.

One reason, it seems to me, for the comparatively slow pace of present progress is the lack of a fresh theoretical approach to suicide. Notwithstanding the brief challenge offered by certain critics in the 1950s and 1960s, the field is still dominated by the Durkheimian approach, which, for all its merits, leads to difficulties in integrating the psychiatric with the sociological perspective. What is now required appears to be a step forward in which we attempt to combine the findings concerning the role of social factors with more recent studies by psychiatrists on the significant part played by psychiatric illness. The fusion of the two perspectives might be approached in two steps:

- First, we require descriptive work to improve the sophistication of existing data, specifically by the better use of operational criteria for both psychiatric and sociological variables.

- Second, an attempt should then be made at what may be called two-factor or multifactor epidemiology, leading to the construction of population models. This would imply dividing the general population by both psychiatric and social parameters simultaneously, and then determining the suicide rates within each segment of the community so defined.

Thus, we require to ascertain the suicide rates of the mentally ill and the mentally

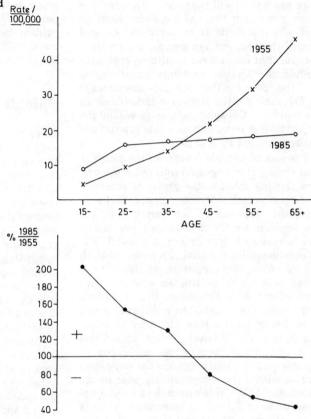

Figure 7.7. Suicide in males, England and Wales 1955 and 1985.

well, each subdivided by, say, level of social integration. It does not matter that in the first instance these variables are themselves probably correlated. What is needed is knowledge of the relative risks associated with each primary variable when the other is controlled and when they are jointly operative. Modern statistical methods offer techniques for dissecting out just such information. To speculate somewhat, it seems very likely that the pattern of suicide rates produced by population divided along the lines suggested would, as a preliminary, confirm the major role of mental illness. But since events such as wars or periods of high unemployment have profound effects on national suicide rates, we must then hypothesise that fluctuations because of wars, etc. (or in some convenient proxy measure) will only relevant among

those who are already mentally ill. Without an overview of the kind I have outlined, neither these not a host of similar theoretical issues can properly be addressed. Here, then, is a third programme for future work. (Of course, there are considerable technical problems to be faced in such work; but, then, epidemiology never was a discipline for the faint-hearted.)

There are other, more circumscribed questions urgently requiring attention either for theoretical reasons or because action is required. These two considerations do not always point in the same direction. Suicide among the elderly provides a case in point. In England and Wales, the suicide rates among both men and women aged 65 and over have halved over the past 30 years (see Figure 7.7), and there have been similar declines in the

United States (though, interestingly, not in Scotland). It would be of the greatest scientific value to know why this decline has occurred, yet perhaps because the problem appears to be going away, no one appears to be investigating the matter.

The converse is true of the increasing rates among the young and the middle-aged, so widespread a feature of Western societies over the past decade or so. Great attention is being devoted to this issue, though it is a little disappointing that much of it is still using aggregate data and ecological techniques. Other work demonstrates high suicide rates among newly emerging risk groups such as drug addicts or AIDS victims, but without going on to clinch the argument by showing that these additional cases explain the changes in the national trends.

Again, a two-phased approach appears to be necessary in the pursuit of causal explanations. The first would be to obtain what lawyers would term "further and better particulars" of the suicides occurring at different points in time. Currently description appears to be stuck with the ubiquitous and profoundly uninformative age-sex specification alone. Much more is needed. For example, a curiously neglected variable is that of social class. In a recent study on current data my colleagues and I have been surprised to find that among men of working age, age-standardised social class rates and social-class-standardised age rates, show about the same variance, that is to say, they are about equally important in "explaining" variations in suicide. Our next descriptive problem will be to determine how the "changes" now occurring can be characterised as age-specific or class-specific shifts, or both.

The further and more fundamental phase of research would be to propose and test putative causal mechanisms. Analytic studies, as distinct from simple monitoring—useful as that may be for other purposes—must be guided by specific hypotheses, and there are a number of possibilities that seem worth the considerable labour involved in their investigation. Both have already been touched on in the context of parasuicide. One is the role of rising alcohol consumption. It has been repeatedly shown that *per capita alcohol consumption in a community correlates closely with rates of alcohol-related harm* (Royal College of Psychiatrists, 1986), *of which suicide is an important example.* What would now be required, therefore, is to test whether heavy drinkers currently represent a higher proportion of contemporary suicides than was formerly the case, and to estimate of how far any such increase does in fact explain the difference of the total rates. (Ideally, the work should be extended to ascertain whether the suicide rate among heavy drinkers and alcoholics has itself increased or fallen.) Much the same strategy could be applied to another putative factor already discussed, namely, unemployment—one of the classical correlates of suicide. The work histories of suicide victims are difficult to study, although useful investigations have already been carried out (Shepherd & Barraclough, 1980). But studies of this kind on the role of alcohol, or unemployment, and perhaps of other variables similar in that they effect large segments of the population, pose two special problems that will briefly be mentioned.

The first concerns all work devoted to understanding longitudinal trends, namely, that of obtaining the relevant data from earlier periods. Various strategies may be adopted to get round this problem, such as drawing informal conclusions on whatever data are available, forming a hypothesis concerning the underlying mechanism, and then conducting prospective investigations on the effects of that variable in a new setting. This approach can be fruitful, but cannot, of course, yield a clear answer to the historical question: sociology and history are different, albeit complementary disciplines. An alternative solution would be to establish one or more national centres to collect continuous or periodic data on suicides as they occur in the general population, using the investigative methods now well established by pioneers in the field. Despite the shifts in researchers' interests that are bound to occur during the course of such long-term projects, such a system would, I suggest, be very rewarding. The only problem is that of political-administrative will.

Yet another point concerns the inadequacy of easily available general population data that are directly relevant to the public health. Of course, this problem is not unique to suicide studies. The present situation regarding such information is really most unsatisfactory, to put it mildly. Data on unemployment have been exiguous in the extreme until the last few years; the UK has no systematic system for repeated surveys of alcohol consumption—which some Scandinavian countries manage to achieve annually—and even the mid-decennial Census for 1986 was cancelled. On behalf of the public health we have a right to demand more interest by government in the attempt to advance knowledge.

This review has concentrated on scientific issues, but the importance of suicidal behaviour from the public health standpoint should not be underestimated. Among women, parasuicide is the commonest single cause among acute medical admissions to hospital, and among men it ranks second. In Britain, completed suicide is the second commonest cause of death among young men, exceeded only by accidents. In most Western countries, suicide is one of the top ten causes of mortality in the general population, and is likely to become increasingly important as the suicide rate rises. The urgency of these problems is scarcely in doubt; the challenge is to identify tractable issues and to develop appropriate research strategies. This chapter is intended as a contribution to just that end.

References

Bancroft, J., & Marsack, P. (1977). The repetitiveness of self-poisoning and self-injury. *British Journal of Psychiatry, 131,* 394–399.

Fahy, T., Brockleburk, J., & Ashby (1970). Syndromes of self-poisoning. *Irish Journal of Medical Science, 3,* 497–503.

Furness, J., Khan M., & Bickers, P. (1985). Unemployment and parasuicide in Hartlepool 1974–1983. *Health Trends, 17,* 21–24.

Häfner, H. (1985). Are mental disorders increasing over time? *Psychopathology, 18,* 66–81.

Hawton, K., & Rose, N. (1986). Unemployment and attempted suicide among men in Oxford. *Health Trends, 18,* 29–32.

Jackson, P., & Warr, P. (1987). Mental health of unemployed men in different parts of England and Wales. *British Medical Journal, 295,* 525.

Katschnig, H., & Sint, P. (1973). Are there different types of attempted suicide? A cluster analysis approach. *Proceedings of VII International Congress on Suicide Prevention, Amsterdam.*

Kessel, W. (1965). Self-poisoning. *British Medical Journal, 2,* 1265–70; 1336–1340.

Kreitman, N. (1976). Age and parasuicide. *Psychological Medicine, 6,* 113–121.

Platt S., & Kreitman, N. (1985). Parasuicide and unemployment among men in Edinburgh 1968–1982. *Psychological Medicine, 15,* 113–123.

Platt S. (1986). Parasuicide and unemployment. *British Journal of Psychiatry, 149,* 401–405.

Platt, S., & Duffy, J. (1986). Social and clinical correlates of unemployment in two cohorts of male parasuicide. *Social Psychiatry, 21,* 71–74.

Platt, S., & Dyer, J. (1987). Psychological correlates of unemployment among male parasuicides in Edinburgh. *British Journal of Psychiatry, 151,* 27–32.

Royal College of Psychiatrists (1986). *Alcohol—our favourite drug.* London: Gaskell.

Shepherd, D., & Barraclough, B. (1980). Work and suicide—an empirical investigation. *British Journal of Psychiatry, 136,* 469–78.

Warr, P. (1984). Economic recession and mental health: A review of research. *Tijdschrift voor Sociale Gezondheidszorg, 62,* 298–308.

Chapter 8
Public Health Aspects of AIDS—1

Peter W. Jepsen & Anne Hjorther

The Acquired Immunodeficiency Syndrome (AIDS) was described for the first time in medical literature in June, 1981. It is characterized by opportunistic infections and/or certain malignancies due to an, at that time unexplained, underlying cellular immunodeficiency (Melbye, 1988). This underlying cellular immunodeficiency has later been found to be caused by infection with the human immunodeficiency virus (HIV). Hitherto, illnesses resulting from immunodeficiency had been encountered in patients receiving immuno-suppressant drugs for transplants and malignancies and in infants suffering from congenital immuno-deficiency (Fenton, 1987). The HIV is a retrovirus belonging to the family of lentiviruses, which means that the virus has ribonucleic acid, RNA, for its genetic information. The HIV has a unique enzyme called reverse transcriptase that enables it to make a DNA copy of itself.

Retroviruses are the only known organisms in which a DNA copy is made of an RNA template; and because they can develop a DNA copy of themselves, this can integrate into our own genetic material. Free viral particles have to enter a susceptible cell, and by so doing must bind to a specific receptor on the cell surface. This receptor is a particular molecule called CD4 (T4). Because we know the distribution of the receptor (CD4 molecule) we also know which cells can be infected in vivo (Weber, 1987). About 60% of the lymphocytes in the body, particularly a subset of T-lymphocytes called the helper subset, are CD4+, which means that they have the specific HIV-receptor. The helper lymphocytes are responsible for the first recognition of foreign antigens and T-helper cell destruction, which may be the result of infection with HIV, paralysis the cellular immune system. This stage of the disease is recognized by the development of signs and symptoms of immune-deficiency disease. Possibly also some B-lymphocytes, i.e. antibody producing lymphocytes carry the receptor but certainly the group of monocytes or macrophages may carry the CD4 molecule on their surface (Weber, 1987).

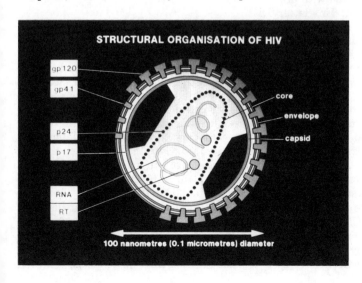

Figure 8.1. The structural organization of HIV.

Infected monocytes or macrophages may transfer HIV from the periphery to the central nervous system (CNS). The result may be development of CNS HIV disease including cognitive, motor and psychiatric symptoms, and in the later course of the illness frank dementia.

HIV causes a predictable, progressive derangement of immune function. Clinical AIDS appears to be just one, late manifestation of that process. The original case definition for AIDS only included clinical manifestations of the disease, i.e. certain opportunistic infections, e.g. pneumocystis carinii pneumonia, and certain neoplasms, e.g. Kaposi sarcoma, which—alone or in combination—accounted for 83% of the cases (Gerstoft, 1987). Earlier clinical manifestations of infection with HIV include chronic lymphadenopathy, severe lethargy and fatigue, significant weight loss, fever and/or night-sweats. Among the opportunistic infections are infection with toxoplasmosis, which often infects the brain causing CNS symptoms. The case definition has later been changed to include HIV seropositivity and HIV CNS disease in the definition (see below).

HIV CNS disease

Although dementia may result from cerebral opportunistic infections, it now seems certain that it is most commonly associated with primary HIV infection of the brain. This latter condition has been labelled the *AIDS dementia complex* (Fenton, 1987). It is known that the neurons are not infected in vivo. It is, however, also known that these changes can occur in the absence of other opportunistic CNS infections or neoplasms, or other signs of immuno-suppression in the body. These and other observations have led to the conclusion that AIDS is not only a viral immune disorder, but also a neuropsychiatric disorder. It has, moreover, been suggested that the virus can be transferred not only from the periphery to the CNS, it can also be transferred from the brain to other cells outside the CNS susceptible to HIV infection. The CNS then functions as a reservoir for HIV infection. The clinical consequence is that any treatment or prevention for HIV infection not effective in

the brain prove to be of only limited value to the AIDS patient (Bridge, 1988).

Bridge has also pointed out that there are similarities between the clinical profiles of the AIDS dementia complex and other subcortical dementias. The term subcortical dementia describes the intellectual deterioration secondary to diseases that are primarily distinguished by pathologic alterations in subcortical (i.e. striatum, thalamus and brainstem) rather than cortical structures. The classical cortical dementia is Alzheimer's disease. The subcortical dementias include progressive supranuclear palsy, Huntington's disease, Parkinson's disease and other extrapyramidal disorders. The prominent characteristics of cortical dementias usually involve progressive deterioration of memory (i.e. difficulty in learning new material) and high-order associative functions. The cardinal features of subcortical dementias include slowing of mental processes, progressive impairment of memory (i.e. difficulty in retrieving already stored material) and deficits in manipulating or using spontaneously acquired information (i.e. poor problem solving). Other clinical signs are personality and affective changes as well as dysfunction of the motor system, including speech, posture, gait, motor speed and movement disorder. However, unlike the cortical dementias, higher-order associative function is preserved, and intellectual impairment is milder in the subcortical dementias.

Epidemiology

The initial reports of AIDS described the key findings of the full-blown clinical syndrome and only minor additions have since been made. Included in the first reports was the suggestion that the clinical manifestations were secondary to a defect in cell-mediated immunity along with the observation that the patients belonged to specific groups, i.e. homosexual men, intravenous drug abusers or haemophiliacs (Gerstoft, 1987).

It has often been suggested that the original reservoir of AIDS might be found in Africa, where the disease might have existed long before the present epidemic (Melbye et al., 1984). The AIDS epidemic is, however, regarded as being of rather recent date—not only in Europe and the United States, but also in Africa (Melbye, 1988). In the Western part of the world, the United States seem to have been the absolute epicentre, from where HIV was spread to the corresponding European risk groups. Melbye has shown that HIV was introduced into the Danish homosexual milieu via sexual intercourse with American men, probably during the period 1978–1980, and that the haemophiliacs' sero-prevalence rates, which were very high and independent of national borders early in the epidemic, can be traced back to use of non-heat-treated, commercially produced factor VIII products made mainly from American donor blood (Melbye, 1988).

By the end of October 1988, a cumulative total of nearly 120,000 people had been officially reported as having AIDS in more than 140 countries. However, this number represents only a portion of the total cases of AIDS to date, which are estimated to be over 150,000 (Table 8.1). The WHO estimates that between 5 and 10 million persons may be currently infected with HIV.

Table 8.1. The global AIDS situation cumulative AIDS cases reported to the WHO by 30 October 1988.

Europe	14623
United States	84693
Africa	19141
Asia (May 1988)	241
Oceania (May 1988)	889
Total	120000

On the global level, three distinct epidemiologic patterns of infection and disease can be distinguished today. The relative frequencies and social features of the three types of transmission (sexual, parenteral and perinatal) and the possible date of HIV introduction of extensive spread account for these three patterns (Piot et al., 1988):

- *Pattern 1* is seen in Western Europe, North America, some areas in South America, Australia and New Zealand. The major affected groups are homo-/bisexual men and intravenous drug abusers. Sexual transmission is predominantly homosexual. In-

travenous drug abuse accounts for the next largest proportion of HIV infections, and even the majority of HIV infections in Southern Europe. Transmission in these groups is parenteral. A cohort of tens of thousands of persons has been infected from contaminated blood or blood products before 1985. Perinatal transmission is documented primarily among female intravenous drug abusers and the sexual partners of intravenous drug abusers.

- *Pattern 2* is seen in Africa, the Caribbean and some areas in South America, where heterosexuals are the main population group affected. Sexual transmission is predominantly heterosexual. As for parenteral transmission, transfusion of HIV-infected blood is a major public health problem. Nonsterile needles and syringes account for an undetermined proportion of HIV infections. Perinatal transmission is a significant problem in those areas where 5% to 15% of women are HIV-antibody-positive.

- *Pattern 3* is seen in Asia, the Pacific Region (except for Australia and New Zealand), the Middle East, Eastern Europe and some rural areas of South America. These areas are characterized by a very low prevalence of HIV infection even in persons with multiple sex partners. Transmission is both homosexual and heterosexual. Parenteral and perinatal transmission is currently not a problem.

HIV-2

In 1985, another human retrovirus, HIV-2, was identified. Antigenically and genetically, HIV-2 is more closely related to the so-called simian immunodeficiency virus (SIV) than to the original HIV, hereafter named HIV-1 (Piot et al., 1988). HIV-2 can cause an AIDS-like disease in humans. HIV-2 transmission appears to be occurring principally in West Africa. Data suggest that HIV-2 infects populations similar to those infected by HIV-1, with heterosexual activity being the dominant mode of spread (Piot et al., 1988). Like HIV-1, HIV-2 seems to spread rapidly and has been identified in Central Africa and in European patients in Europe (Piot et al., 1988). The simultaneous occurrence of HIV-1 and HIV-2 will have implications for diagnostic services, blood-donor screening programs and vaccine development (Piot et al., 1988).

HIV Antibodies

In connection with primary HIV infection, different clinical manifestations appear of which one of the ten most common appear to be an acute mononucleosis-like condition (Melbye, 1988). In the acute stage, high HIV-antigen titres may be found in the blood, reflecting the acute viremia. After the stage of primary infection follows in most cases a long incubation period during which the individual patient stays clinically healthy despite measurable changes in the immune parameters (Melbye, 1988). The incubation period from time of HIV infection to possible AIDS development is long, but because the epidemic is comparatively new, it is not yet fully clarified. For at least some time to come, longer observation periods will only lead to an extension of the mean incubation time already estimated. In some cases it may be as long as 10–15 years (Melbye, 1988). Early studies of disease progression suggested that only about 30–40% of patients infected with HIV progressed to AIDS. Subsequent studies have revealed less optimistic figures suggesting that in the absence of a scientific solution to HIV, most (and perhaps all) people who are infected with HIV will eventually develop end-stage disease and die prematurely (Redfield & Burke, 1988).

HIV antibodies against certain nuclear proteins are constantly present in the incubation period except in connection with the development of AIDS, where the antibody levels sometimes decline and sometimes even become unmeasurable (Melbye, 1988). In connection with the development of AIDS, the HIV-antigen titre may rise again. The role of possible modifying co-factors with respect to development of AIDS in sero-positive individuals is under discussion.

The Impact on Health and Society

The impact of HIV infection on health and society in the Third World will become seri-

ous. Since AIDS mainly affects people in their most productive years, effects of this disease on society may be as pernicious as its effect on individuals. The most visible impact of AIDS on the health system involves the direct cost of medical care for a disease that requires repeated hospitalization. But in addition, infection with HIV may have negative impact on ongoing health programmes and profound socio-economic and political consequences.

The most important lesson learned from the Third World may be the demonstration that HIV is primarily a sexually transmitted disease and that *the main risk factor for acquisition is the degree of sexual activity with multiple partners*—not sexual orientation. This is important to remember in the Western World where it is not unusual to look upon AIDS as a disease among homosexual men and intravenous drug abusers. It should also be remembered that although the prevention and control of AIDS are ultimately dependent on the decisions of individuals, these decisions are influenced by local, national and even international customs (Piot et al., 1988). It should be pointed out that not only have we learned how HIV is transmitted—through sexual contact, transfusion of contaminated blood or blood products, sharing HIV-contaminated needles or syringes, or transmission from infected mothers to newborns—more important is perhaps that it has been established how HIV is *not* transmitted, i.e. by casual contact; nor is there any evidence that it is transmitted by insects. This evidence is the basis for all the preventive measures that have been taken world-wide.

The AIDS epidemic in the Western European countries seems to have appeared about 2 years later than in the United States. Contrary to the American situation, a remarkably high percentage of the European AIDS cases in the early phase of the epidemic turned out to be Africans diagnosed in Europe. In addition, only a small number of the European AIDS cases at that time were parenteral drug users (Melbye, 1988). This is still true for the Northern European countries, although for the Southern European countries the proportion of intravenous drug abusers among the total AIDS cases is, for some reason, significantly higher. This fact cannot be explained by different access to clean needles or syringes or to methadone treatment programs.

In Denmark, HIV was probably introduced into intravenous drug abusers some 5 to 7 years later than into homosexual men. Most of the known drug abusers infected with HIV were probably infected during a relatively short period around 1985–1986. This explains why until now only a small proportion of the AIDS cases in Denmark has been intravenous drug abusers. The number of AIDS cases among intravenous drug abusers is therefore expected to increase in the years to come.

While observations seem to indicate that the incidence of sero-conversion among homosexual men in the Western world at present is much lower than in the beginning of the epidemic, it is still increasing among the intravenous drug abusers. Moreover, *as the control of the HIV epidemic among the intravenous drug abusers is considered the key to a general heterosexual epidemic,* there is increased interest in intravenous drug abusers.

In the United States, nation-wide 25% of the AIDS cases result from intravenous drug abuse. In 17% of these cases, intravenous drug abuse was the sole risk factor, the remaining 8% being homo- or bisexual men who are also intravenous drug users. There are an estimated 200,000 intravenous drug users in New York City, about 75,000 of them current users and approximately 125,000 with a history of intravenous drug abuse who are likely to resume using. Some 50–60% of the current intravenous drug abusers are already infected and test positive for antibodies to HIV (Citizens Commission on AIDS, 1988). At one time or another almost all intravenous drug abusers have sexual partners who are not themselves intravenous drug abusers. Of the documented cases of women who were infected by heterosexual transmission in New York City, 87% were infected by intravenous drug abusers. Of the paediatric AIDS cases in New York 80% are born to mothers who are either drug users themselves or sexual partners of drug users (Citizens Commission on AIDS, 1988). In New York City, there are an estimated 20,000 so-called "street kids"—youngsters below 21 of age whose use of crack is very prevalent, the use being financed by selling "sex for crack." Because of the level of

sexual activity that is needed to finance the drug abuse, this group is highly at risk of infection with HIV. It should be noted that crack is smoked, not injected. Transmission of HIV in this group is therefore solely sexual. The ratio of infected males to females is 1 to 1.

With only 4% of the total population in the United States, New York City has about half of the estimated 500,000 intravenous drug abusers in the country, and the number of AIDS cases among intravenous drug abusers is increasing. In the first 3 months of 1988, the number of newly reported AIDS cases among intravenous drug abusers for the first time exceeded the number of cases reported among homo- and bisexual men (Citizens Commission on AIDS, 1988).

Intravenous drug abusers in Europe have had proportionally fewer cases of AIDS than their American counterparts. These differences may be the result of less interaction between homosexuals and intravenous drug abusers in Europe than in certain areas of the United States (Melbye, 1988).

By 30 September 1988, 16,647 European AIDS cases had been reported. This represented an increase of 96% (8,139 new cases) since September 1987 and 16% (2,348 new cases)

Table 8.2. Cumulative AIDS cases by country reported to the WHO (23 January 1989).

Country	Total
Austria	236
Belgium	408
Denmark	358
Finland	37
France	5655
Germany (Federal Republic)	2779
Greece	151
Ireland	64
Israel	76
Italy	3008
Netherlands	694
Norway	100
Portugal	199
Spain	1850
Sweden	223
Switzerland	702
United Kingdom	1982
Yugoslavia	65
Other countries	50
Total	18637

since June 1988. The distribution of adult cases by transmission group showed an increase of 74% (3,709 newly reported cases) in a single year among homosexuals and bisexuals, and of 169% (2,529 newly reported cases) among intravenous drug abusers. 54.1% (1,009 of 1,864) of the female adult cases were intravenous drug abusers, and of the 400 paediatric cases, 165 (41.3%) had an intravenous-drug-using mother. The cases among intravenous drug abusers are reported mainly in Southern Europe. France, Italy and Spain reported 84.6% of the cases reported in this transmission group (WHO, 1988). Table 8.2 shows the cumulative number of AIDS cases in adults by transmission group and sex for 31 European countries as of 30 September 1988. Table 8.2 shows the cumulative AIDS cases reported by European countries to the WHO Collaborative Centre on AIDS as of 23 January 1989 (WHO, 1988).

Based on available evidence, the HIV situation among intravenous drug abusers in the Northern part of Western Europe seems less alarming, with an estimated 10–25% of the drug abusers being sero-positive. The estimate is, however, very insecure, because it is based on test samples from small materials, and because the total number of persons belonging to the risk group usually is not known. In South Europe, the situation seems more serious. It should, however, be pointed out that the distribution of known AIDS cases world-wide and within each country as well is very unequal, with the majority of cases having occurred in the big cities. Anyway, it can be concluded that at this stage of the AIDS epidemic in the Western World, the spread of HIV infection is linked to intravenous drug abuse. The problems of controlling the spread of HIV infection among intravenous drug abusers are discussed below in some detail.

HIV Testing

The role of HIV testing in the surveillance of the AIDS epidemic and in the prevention of AIDS is an issue of current discussion. While it is true that our epidemiologic knowledge of the spread of the HIV infection is very insufficient it is, however, *not necessarily true that the answer to the problem is mass screening of risk groups or the total population*—be it voluntary or involuntary. There are two main reasons for this:

- First, because of the latency time for sero-conversion, we could never be certain that a sero-negative tested person would not convert shortly after the testing, with the consequence that all test-negative persons should be retested, say, every 6 months.

- Second, how would we use such information when we lack of an effective treatment for HIV infection or the AIDS disease?

In some situations HIV testing may even have adverse consequences as some test-negative individuals with high-risk behaviour may falsely regard themselves as immune to the infection. At least in most parts of the Western world early questions about legal protection against the spread of the HIV infection are now balanced by questions about the rights of those infected and about confidentiality and nondiscrimination regarding access to health care, employment, housing, education, insurance and related interests (Dickens, 1988). The rights include the access to voluntary testing and confidentiality about the test result.

Treatment or Prevention

With our present knowledge, it is not very likely that within a few years we will have an effective treatment for AIDS or an effective vaccine for prevention of HIV infection. It should, however, be pointed out, first, that we do have treatments for many of the complications of HIV infection (for example, pneumonia); and second, that even if we had an effective vaccine today it is not very likely that we would be able to eradicate AIDS. We have effective treatments for diseases such as syphilis and gonorrhea and an effective vaccine for measles, and yet none of these diseases have been eradicated. An even better example is hepatitis B. An effective vaccine has been available for 5–6 years; since 1982 1.5 million people in the United States at risk for contracting the disease have been immunised—yet there has been a slight *increase* in the incidence of hepatitis B in the United States since 1978 (Nielsen, 1988). It seems likely that the same would happen if we had a vaccine for AIDS.

Where AIDS is concerned, *prevention means a change in lifestyle*. The means for accomplishing this change is information and counselling. With intravenous drug users, *prevention also means access to clean needles and syringes and treatment for their drug dependence*. Just informing the drug abuser about the adverse consequences of continued drug abuse may not be sufficient if not combined with an offer for treatment that implies an acceptable alternative to active drug abuse.

Drug Abuse Treatment as Prevention in the Spread of HIV

Drug-abuse treatment may reduce the spread of HIV infection directly, through the elimination or reduction of needle-sharing, or, indirectly, through control of sexual behaviour. The causal links between AIDS and drug use are clear and well understood (Citizens Commission on AIDS, 1988).

The *primary risk factors* include

- the number of drug injections,

- the number of needle-sharing partners,

- the sharing of needles and syringes,

- not being in treatment for drug abuse.

Additional risk factors are

- having an intravenous drug user as a sexual partner,

- prostitution,

- not using barrier protection (condom) in sex,

- geographic location (reservoir of HIV),

- (in the USA) being a member of a Black or minority group (e.g. Hispanic).

Some risk factors on this list (minority status and geographic location) are obviously not amenable to change, but others can be altered. Drug users in treatment, even if they relapse or are not totally free of drug use, are much more likely to inject drugs less frequently, to reduce the number of days of needle-sharing as well as the number of partners, and to use shared "cookers" less often (Citizens Commission on AIDS, 1988). Drug-abuse treatment that has an AIDS education

component can effect some of the other risk factors: increase the use of barrier precautions in sex (Hjorther et al., submitted for publication) and reduce prostitution, particularly among those who resort to prostitution for drugs or money to buy drugs (Citizens Commission on AIDS, 1988).

In reviewing data from a one-year follow-up study of clients from three different treatment modalities—outpatient methadone treatment programmes, residential programmes and outpatient drug-free (OPDF) programmes—Hubbard et al. (1988), in a paper prepared for the Committee on a National Strategy for AIDS, National Academy of Sciences, concluded:

> Drug-abuse treatment may have important direct and indirect effects on restricting the spread of infection with HIV by decreasing the prevalence of intravenous drug use and by decreasing regular drug use that impairs the immune system. Drug-abuse treatment results in substantial declines in the use of heroin, cocaine, prescription psychotherapeutic drugs, and other drugs in the year after treatment. Declines are closely related to length of time spent in treatment; treatment duration of >6 months has a significant impact on drug use after treatment. . . . Judging by the prevalence of regular use before and after treatment, methadone treatment appears to be the most effective modality for treatment of heroin use. Residential treatment is next most effective. Even after stays of 3 months in these modalities, there were large reductions in heroin rates. OPDF treatment appears to have little effect on heroin use (Hubbard et al., 1988).

As drug users have a varying characteristics and treatment needs, expansion of all types of drug treatment—drug detoxification, methadone maintenance, residential drug-free treatment and outpatient drug-free treatment—is needed (Citizens Commission on AIDS, 1988). Overall, the emphasis should be on developing specific treatment programmes that are appropriate for the particular needs of individual drug users, rather than on more global attempts to find a single treatment that works for all (Citizens Commission on AIDS, 1988). The goal must be to retain drug users in treatment for longer periods, since all evidence indicates that length of treatment influences social and personal stability. The longer drug users have been in treatment, the more likely they are to remain HIV-negative (Citizens Commission on AIDS, 1988).

Conclusions

AIDS and infection with HIV constitute *a world-wide public health problem*. In Western Europe and North America, transmission has occurred mostly among homosexual men and intravenous drug abusers, whereas in Africa HIV infection seems to be mainly heterosexually acquired. But heterosexual transmission appears to be increasing in some parts of the World, possibly also in United States and Western Europe. Perinatal transmission may be expected to increase equally.

The role of the *intravenous drug abusers* as a bridge in the heterosexual transmission is indisputable. That is one of the main reasons for the increasing interest in this group. AIDS has uncovered a number of problems regarding prevention and treatment of drug abuse that have existed for many years. It could be said that AIDS has done something good, in that it has brought the medical profession back into the treatment of drug abuse.

The *world-wide economic impact of AIDS* is very serious. It has been suggested that the lifetime cost of medical care per patient with AIDS in the USA will not exceed $ 80.000 (Bloom & Carliner, 1988). To that figure should be added the indirect cost of AIDS,

representing the discounted value of foregone earnings due to disability and premature death caused by AIDS. Estimates of foregone earnings are about six to eight times as large as the $ 80.000 in medical costs (Bloom & Carliner,1988).

The amount of human suffering caused by AIDS is immeasurable, and the costs of the disease are so high that every effort should be made to *prevent the spread of HIV*. Here, the salient fact is that the main risk factor for acquisition is the degree of sexual activity with multiple partners—not sexual orientation. For intravenous drug abusers, prevention of AIDS means treatment with the goal of retaining them in treatment for longer periods, and reducing the adverse medical and social consequences of continued drug abuse. Other measures include access to clean needles and syringes. However, merely informing the drug abusers about the adverse consequences of continued drug abuse is unlikely to be sufficient. It is necessary to combine counselling about risks with an offer for treatment, and if prevention is to be effective, it is important that the treatment offered is acceptable to as many of the drug abusers as possible. This is one of the reasons why treatment should always be voluntary.

References

Bloom, D. E., & Carliner, G. (1988). The economic impact of AIDS in United States. *Science, 239,* 604–610.

Bridge, T. P. (1988). AIDS and HIV CNS disease: A neuropsychiatric disorder. In T. P. Bridge, A. F. Mirsky & F. K. Goodwin (Eds.), *Psychological, neuropsychiatric, and substance abuse aspects of AIDS* (pp. 1–13). New York: Raven Press.

Citizens Commission on AIDS for New York City and Northern New Jersey. (1988). *AIDS and drug use. Breaking the link* (pp. 1–45). New York: Citizens Commission on AIDS (Stencil).

Dickens, B. M. (1988). Legal rights and duties in the AIDS epidemic. *Science, 239,* 580–586.

Fenton, T. W. (1987). AIDS-related psychiatric disorder. *British Journal of Psychiatry, 151,* 579–588.

Gerstoft, J. (1987). *AIDS in Denmark 1980–1984. Immunological, epidemiological and clinical studies among patients and high risk groups* (pp. 1–25). Copenhagen: Lægeforeningens forlag. (Thesis).

Hubbard, R. L., Marsden, M. E., Cavanaugh, E., Rachal, J. V., & Ginzburg, H. M. (1988). Role of drug-abuse treatment in limiting the spread of

AIDS. *Reviews of Infections Diseases, 10,* 377–384.

Melbye, M. (1988). *The natural history of human immunodeficiency virus infection (HIV). The cause of AIDS* (pp. 4–124). Thesis,. Århus.

Melbye, M., Biggard, R. J., & Ebbesen, P. (1984). AIDS epidemiology: Europe and Africa. In P. Ebbesen., R. J. Biggar & M. Melbye (Eds), *AIDS. A basic guide for clinicians* (pp. 29–41). Copenhagen/ Philadelphia/London: Munksgaard/ Saunders.

Nielsen, J. O. (1988). Behandling af AIDS. (Treatment of AIDS). *Ugeskrift for Læger, 150,* 3001–3002 (in Danish).

Piot, P., Plummer, F. A., Mhalu, F. S. Lamboray, J. L., Chin, J., & Mann, J. M. (1988). AIDS: An international perspective. *Science, 239,* 573–579.

Redfield, R. R., & Burke, D. S. (1988). HIV infection: The clinical picture. *Scientific Amer., 259,* 70–78.

Weber, J. (1988). The biology of HIV. In L. Paine (Ed.), *AIDS: Psychiatric and psychosocial perspectives* (pp. 1–11.) London Croom Helm.

WHO Collaborating Center on AIDS. (1988). *AIDS surveillance in Europe* (Quarterly report No. 19, pp. 1–25.) Paris: WHO.

Chapter 9

Public Health Aspects of AIDS—2 Psychological, Social and Ethical Factors

Michael B. King

AIDS has become the principal focus of international public health efforts in the 1980s. First reports of the disease emerged in 1981, and the agent responsible—the human immune deficiency virus (HIV)—was isolated in 1983. Developments have moved rapidly since with an elucidation of its structure and natural history. Drugs such as Zidovudine (AZT), which are active against retroviruses, have been widely used both in AIDS patients and those with asymptomatic viral infection, and recent attempts at vaccine development have been reported (Bolognesi, 1989). However, perhaps of greatest impact have been the voluntary and public efforts to prevent spread of the infection.

Prejudice and Discrimination

Earliest concern centred on those regarded as most at risk for infection, namely, homosexual men and intravenous drug users (IVDUs). Already largely unaccepted in Western society (Thompson et al., 1985; Richards, 1988), these people became the target of increasing discrimination (Deuchar, 1984; Ostrow, 1989). Only later, with the growing realisation of the extent of the heterosexual epidemic in North America, Africa and other developing countries was the conceptual shift made from at-risk group to at-risk behaviour. Nevertheless, discrimination has continued against people with AIDS and has greatly added to the medical and social burden of this disease (Summerfield, 1989). Homosexual men (Krajeski, 1984) and IVDUs (Glanz, 1987) have seldom been welcomed by the medical profession, but with the advent of AIDS it is imperative that doctors become more knowledgeable and skilled in their approach to these groups (Leach & Whitehead,

1985). Discrimination or prejudice in any form opposes public health efforts by forcing people with HIV underground, thereby rendering spread of the disease that much easier.

Prevention efforts in Africa are hampered by poor communications systems, lack of media coverage, reluctance to discuss sexual issues, and the unacceptability and unavailability of condoms. Little work has been done to assess the impact of the disease on families and communities, but anecdotal reports indicate that economic hardship, discrimination, rejection and resultant psychological disorder are common (Summerfield, 1989; Ngugi, 1989).

Intervention to Change Risk Behaviours

Behaviour changes are possible in people who are at risk. Although there has been public and governmental resistance, needle exchange schemes for IVDUs have been shown to reduce sharing without encouraging more widespread use of drugs (Coutinho, 1989). Furthermore, there are optimistic signs of other behavioural changes related to sharing of needles and syringes by drug addicts (Strang et al., 1987), as well as considerable evidence that education by the gay community of its own members has had a major impact in changing risk behaviours, thus limiting the spread of the virus in homosexual men (Bradbeer, 1987; Kelley et al., 1989).

Legal Sanctions

Despite its popularity with the general public, there is little public health sense in the mandatory HIV testing of immigrants (Edwards & Whitaker, 1989). Legislation in the United States currently bans HIV-positive people from entering that country, and many other nations have adopted similar regulations. The introduction of such measures has drawn an official response from The World Health Organisation, which has officially opposed governmental legislation on travel restrictions (WHO, 1988). Mandatory testing in other situations has also proved counter-productive. A recent report from the state of Illinois (Kelly & Turnock, 1989) has shown that mandatory premarital HIV testing simply does not work. In 1988, the state legislative passed a law requiring all marriage licence applicants to prove they had been tested for HIV antibodies within the past 30 days. Of 155,458 licence applicants over a 12-month period, 15 men and 11 women were found to be HIV antibody positive, of whom 62% reported some high-risk behaviour. Over the same time marriage applications declined by 22%, as couples crossed state borders to marry elsewhere. The annual cost of this mandatory testing programme was US $ 5.4 million, or US $ 217,641 per sero-positive individual identified, and can be contrasted with the US $ 770 per sero-positive individual identified through the state's counselling and testing programme. Needless to say, the legislation is in progress of repeal. Not only is mandatory public health intervention in HIV inefficient, it further compromises patient-doctor trust.

Psychological Health of People With HIV Infection

Early reports of high levels of psychiatric problems (Dilley et al., 1985) together with the recognition of an AIDS-associated dementia (Navia, 1986a, 1986b) led many to fear that the psychological services would be overwhelmed (Fenton, 1987). However, as in other "new" fields, earliest reports were often case series already referred for psychological help. When unselected populations of patients are assessed, lower levels of psychological distress are found.

Patients with HIV infection attending surveillance HIV clinics at two London teaching hospitals took part in a study to assess the prevalence of psychiatric disorder and the nature of associated risk factors (King, 1989a). They were also asked about their relationship with their family doctor regarding IVDU, homosexuality and HIV infection (King, 1988). Subjects were unselected and thus were representative of the clinic populations. Of the 192 patients (189 males, 3 females) who took part, 95 percent were bisexual or homosexual men. Each was interviewed with the *Clinical Interview Schedule* (Goldberg et al., 1970), a structured interview widely used to assess psychiatric disorder in nonpsychiatric patients in the community, as well as a further semistructured interview exploring their experiences regarding HIV and their relationship with their family doctor. Finally, all subjects completed two self-report scales exploring their psychological and physical health status.

Some 31% were psychiatric cases on the *Clinical Interview Schedule*, usually of depression and prolonged adjustment reactions. No patient had a psychotic illness. Twenty five percent of the patients reported verbal or physical rejection by at least one person in their social network because of their HIV infection. Only half of those registered with a family doctor had told him or her of their diagnosis, but almost all who had done so had received, at worst, neutral reactions while many doctors had been helpful. Rejection by GPs was extremely unusual. Patients who had not disclosed this information unnecessarily feared rejection by the GP, or perhaps more realistically feared the lack of confidentiality that might ensue.

Risk Factors For Psychiatric Disorder

Important risk factors for psychological disorder amongst these patients included past psychiatric disorder, excessive ruminations about physical health regardless of actual health status, inability to work or socialise as usual and knowing of the HIV diagnosis for less than 12 months, though only the first two reached statistical significance. Perhaps surprisingly, neither the stage of the HIV disease nor previous stigmatisation regarding either HIV or homosexuality was correlated with the presence of psychiatric disorder. However, some individuals had experienced feelings of guilt or self-blame regarding past sexual or drug activity, renewed ambivalence about their homosexual orientation, shame they perceived they had brought to others (particularly family) and a belief that they may have unwittingly infected others. Much of their concern was associated with the negative status of homosexuality in society. Nevertheless, the vast majority had adapted well to their diagnosis and were determined to learn more about their infection.

Neuropsychiatric Disorder

Of this population of patients with HIV disease, 12% showed some objective difficulty on brief tests of cognitive function (digit span, serial sevens, sentence recall), the majority of whom had AIDS. Although the study was limited by the brief nature of the neuropsychological tests employed, it confirmed recent findings that cognitive problems are usually only encountered when immunosuppression results in physical symptoms. Although occasional reports (Grant et al., 1987) had suggested that cognitive decline was common in asymptomatic HIV positive individuals, this work has not been confirmed subsequently (Selnes et al., 1989). Profound dementia is almost always a terminal event.

Significance of Psychiatric Problems

There seems little doubt that the level of psychiatric disorder present here, which is no different from other patient groups in hospital or primary medical care, owes much to early public health measures in clinics for sexually transmitted diseases (STDs), where effective education and counselling was instituted early in the history of HIV disease. However, the patients in this study were a reasonably highly educated, financially se-

cure population and may not reflect patient populations with the disease in coming years. There is considerable evidence that the epidemic is levelling off among homosexual men, almost certainly because of public health efforts of gay organisations and, more recently, government bodies. This is not the case, however, among poor, ethnic minorities and drug users in many Western inner city areas (Ostrow, 1989), who may be less economically and psychologically shielded from the impact of the infection—or in Africa, where the heterosexual epidemic continues unabated (Piot, 1989).

Importance of Other Sexually Transmitted Diseases

AIDS is increasingly becoming the scourge of disadvantaged groups in Western society (Harris, 1988; Summerfield, 1988), and prevention efforts need to be redoubled. Prevention and education is particularly important in STD clinics, where many patients who attend are at risk. There are strong associations between HIV infection and other STDs both in Africa and the West, and it is essential that we do not lose this opportunity for public health. It has been shown that psychological disorder among medical patients in hospitals or those attending their GP affects outcome of the physical disorder and compliance with treatment (Feldman et al., 1987). Furthermore, recognition of psychological distress by physicians can positively affect outcome (Johnstone & Goldberg, 1976; Sireling et al., 1985). It is crucial that the ability of venereologists to recognise psychological disorder is assessed—this core group of patients attending STD clinics may be most at risk for HIV infection and thus promote further spread of the epidemic. Appropriate intervention could have important public health consequences. Work to attempt to delineate this area is already underway (King et al., 1990).

Stress and Immunity

There is growing evidence that psychological or social stress may accelerate progression of symptomatic disease in people carrying the virus (Kessler et al., 1989; Coates et al., 1989). Although it is unclear whether immune mechanisms are directly involved, there is considerable evidence to link psychological and immune function (Temoshok, 1988). A woman with AIDS was awarded damages in a Canadian court when it was ruled that the stress of being sacked by her employer may have brought forward her symptomatic state (*La Presse*, Montreal, 9 June 1989, p. A3). It is important in prevention efforts that health workers be sensitive to possible psychological reactions and intervene. As noted earlier, past psychological health is a crucial risk indicator, as is excessive concern about possible physical symptoms. It has been shown that a limited social network, loneliness, absence of a primary partner and the deaths from AIDS of friends and acquaintances are all possible risk factors for the development of psychological distress (Coates et al., 1989) and are amenable to secondary prevention. Moreover, the drug and alcohol abuse that often accompany psychological distress may result in further immuno-suppression in persons with HIV disease (Donahoe & Falek, 1988; Jerrells et al., 1988).

Prevention of substance abuse is also important in increasing compliance with treatment and preventing careless behaviours that may result in further spread of the virus.

Confidentiality

With the advent of HIV disease, questions of confidentiality, particularly in the area of public health, have come under considerable scrutiny (AMA, 1988). The importance of confidentiality after death has resulted in a debate on the lack of privacy inherent to the methods of death certification in Britain (King, 1989b). Writers in medical journals have agonised over the need for informed consent for HIV antibody testing and the difficulties for doctors when recalcitrant patients place their sexual partners at risk by refusing either to divulge their HIV status or take precautions to protect them. Consensus around the world (Brennan, 1989) would seem to be in line with current ethical opinion in the UK (Sherrard & Gatt, 1987; GMC,

1988; Black, 1989), that although informed consent before an HIV test is essential, in the case of third parties doctors have a responsibility to break confidentiality as a last resort and warn "innocent" partners. Surprisingly, the average British doctor does not seem to agree. When 270 London doctors were interviewed in depth about their work with HIV patients, the vast majority claimed they would not break confidentiality with their patient by informing a partner at risk (King, 1989c). Perhaps they see the sense of ultimate confidentiality. If patients know that their doctor might at some point pass on information given as part of the medical contract, they will simply cease to inform him or her of sensitive facts. This evidence is backed up by other data recently reported from North America suggesting that doctors place a higher value on their patients welfare and keeping patients' confidences than truth-telling for its own sake (Novack et al., 1989), even when this involves deception.

Conclusions

There are many opportunities for public health efforts to solve the psychological, social and ethical problems in AIDS. However, they will only succeed if individuals are legally protected from stigma and irrational prejudice (Cole, 1989). Further research is needed to evaluate the effectiveness of education on changes in relevant behaviour (Darrow, 1987) as well as the role of counselling and support of patients (Bor et al., 1989). Many patients have successfully helped themselves through their own social networks and voluntary bodies in the community, and these efforts need to be reinforced. Family doctors, at least in Britain, have an important role in education and prevention and seem prepared to take it up (King, 1989c, 1989d). However, there is considerable evidence that the nature of the epidemic in Western countries is evolving with the likelihood of greater numbers of heterosexuals, particularly from among poorer ethnic minorities, being affected in the future. Public health efforts in the psychological and social domains must be bolstered to deal with people who possibly may be less help seeking than populations earlier in the epidemic.

References

American Medical Association (1988). Council report: Ethical issues involved in the growing AIDS crisis. *Journal of the American Medical Association, 259*, 1360–1361.

Black, D. (1989). Ethics of HIV testing. A personal view. *Journal of the Royal College of Physicians of London, 23*, 19–21.

Bolognesi, D. P. (1989). *Prospects and pitfalls of vaccination against HIV.* Paper presented to the Fifth International Conference on AIDS, Montreal, Canada, June 4–9, 1989.

Bor, R., Perry, L., Miller, R., Jackson, J. (1989). Strategies for counselling the "worried well" in relation to AIDS: Discussion paper. *Journal of the Royal Society of Medicine, 82*, 218–220.

Bradbeer, C. (1987). HIV and sexual lifestyle. *British Medical Journal, 294*, 5–6.

Brennan, T. A. (1989) AIDS and the limits of confidentiality. *Journal of General Internal Medicine, 4*, 242–246.

Coates, T. J., Stall, R. D., Ekstrand, M., & Solomon, G. F. (1989). *Psychosocial predictors as co-factors for disease progression in men infected with HIV: The San Francisco men's health study.* Paper presented to the Fifth International Conference on AIDS, Montreal, Canada, June 4–9, 1989.

Coutinho, R. A. (1989). *Epidemiology and control of AIDS among drug users.* Paper presented to the Fifth International Conference on AIDS, Montreal, Canada, June 4–9, 1989.

Darrow, W. W. (1987). A framework for preventing AIDS. *American Journal of Public Health, 77*, 778–779.

Deuchar, N. (1984). AIDS in New York city with particular reference to the psycho-social aspects. *British Journal of Psychiatry, 145*, 612–619.

Dilley, J. W., Ochitill, H. N., Perl, M., & Volberding, P. A. (1985). Findings in psychiatric consultations with patients with acquired immune deficiency syndrome. *American Journal of Psychiatry, 142*, 82–86.

Donahoe, R. M., Falek, A. (1988). Neuroimmunomodulation by opiates and other drugs of abuse: Relationship to HIV infection and AIDS. In T. P. Bridge, A. F. Mirsky, & F. K. Goodwin (Eds), *Psychological, neuropsychiatric and substance abuse aspects of AIDS* (pp. 145–158). New York: Raven Press.

Edwards, R. K., Whitaker, R. E. D. (1989). *AIDS and restriction on immigration and travel: US policy and its ramifications.* Paper presented to the Fifth International Conference on AIDS, Montreal, Canada, June 4–9, 1989.

Feldman, E., Mayou, R., Hawton, K., Ardern, M., & Smith, E. (1987). Psychiatric disorder in medical inpatients. *Quarterly Journal of Medicine, 241*, 405–412.

Fenton, T. W. (1987). Practical problems in the management of AIDS-related psychiatric disorder. *Journal of The Royal Society of Medicine, 80*, 271–274.

General Medical Council (1988). *HIV infection and AIDS: The ethical considerations.* London: GMC.

Goldberg, D. P., Cooper, B., Eastwood, M. R., Kedward, H. B., & Shepherd, M. (1970). A standardised psychiatric interview for use in community surveys. *British Journal of Preventive and Social Medicine, 24*, 18–23.

Gostin, L. O. (1989). Public health strategies for confronting AIDS. Legislative and regulatory policy in the United States. *Journal of the American Medical Society, 261*, 1621–1630.

Grant, I., Hampton Atkinson, J., Hesselink, J. R., Kennedy, C. R., Richman, D. D., Spector, S. A., & McCutchan, J. A. (1987). Evidence for early central nervous system involvement in the acquired immunodeficiency syndrome (AIDS) and other human immunodeficiency virus (HIV) infections. *Annals of Internal Medicine, 107*, 828–836.

Harris, M. (1988). "You have the virus." *The Spectator, August,* 9–11.

Jerrells, T. R., Marietta, C. A., Bone, G., Weight, F. F., & Eckardt, M. J. (1988). Ethanol-associated immunosuppression. In T. P. Bridge, A. F. Mirsky & F. K. Goodwin (Eds), *Psychological, neuropsychiatric and substance abuse aspects of AIDS* (pp. 173–185). New York: Raven Press.

Johnstone, A., & Goldberg, D. (1976). Psychiatric screening in general practice. A controlled trial. *Lancet, i,* 605–608.

Kelly, C., & Turnock, B. (1989). *Mandatory premarital HIV antibody testing: A twelve month experience.* Paper presented to the Fifth International Conference on AIDS, Montreal, Canada, June 4–9, 1989.

Kelly, J. A., St. Lawrence, J. S., Hood, H. V., & Brasfield, T. L. (1989). Behavioural intervention to reduce AIDS risk activities. *Journal of Consulting and Clinical Psychology, 57*, 60–67.

Kessler, R., Joseph, J., Ostrow, D., Phair, J., Chmiel, J., & Rusk, C. (1989). *Psychosocial co-factors in illness onset among HIV positive men.* Paper presented to the Fifth International Conference on AIDS, Montreal, Canada, June 4–9, 1989.

King, M. B. (1988). AIDS and the general practitioner: Views of patients with HIV infection and AIDS. *British Medical Journal, 297*, 182–184.

King, M. B. (1989a). Psychosocial status of 192 outpatients with HIV infection and AIDS. *British Journal of Psychiatry, 154*, 237–242.

King, M. B. (1989b). AIDS on the death certificate: The final stigma. *British Medical Journal, 298*, 734–736.

King, M. B. (1989c). Psychological and social problems in HIV infection: Interviews with general practitioners in London. *British Medical Journal, 299*, 713–717.

King, M. B. (1989d). London general practitioners'

involvement with human immunodeficiency virus infection. *Journal of the Royal College of General Practitioners, 39,* 280–283.

King, M. B., Mann, A., & Goldmeier, D. (1990). *Recognition of psychiatric disorder by physicians in a clinic for sexually transmitted diseases and its effect on outcome.* (Work in progress, St Marys Hospital, The Royal Free Hospital and the Institute of Psychiatry, London).

Krajeski, J. P. (1984). Acquired immune deficiency syndrome: The challenge to psychiatry. In S. E. Nichols & D. G. Ostrow (Eds), *Psychiatric implications of acquired immune deficiency syndrome* (pp. 131–137). Washington, DC: American Psychiatric Press.

Leach, G., Whitehead, A. (1985). AIDS and the gay community: The doctor's role in counselling. *British Medical Journal, 290,* 583.

Navia, B. A., Jordan, B. D., & Price, R. W. (1986a). The AIDS dementia complex: I. Clinical features. *Annals of Neurology, 19,* 517–524.

Navia, B. A., Cho, E. S., Petito, C. K., & Price, R. W. (1986b). The AIDS dementia complex: II. Neuropathology. *Annals of Neurology, 19,* 525–535.

Ngugi, E. N. (1989). *Social economic impact of AIDS in a home.* Paper presented to the Fifth International Conference on AIDS, Montreal, Canada, June 4–9, 1989.

Novack, D. H., Detering, B. J., Arnold, R., Forrow, L., Ladinsky, M., & Pezzullo, J. C. (1989). Physicians' attitudes toward using deception to resolve difficult ethical problems. *Journal of the American Medical Association, 261,* 2980–2985.

Ostrow, D. G. (1989). Psychiatry and AIDS: An American view. *Journal of the Royal Society of Medicine, 82,* 192–197.

Richards, T. (1988). Drug addicts and the GP. *British Medical Journal, 296,* 1082.

Selnes, O. A., McArthur, J. C., Miller, E. N., Sheridan, K., Becker, J. T., & Gordon, B. et al. (1989). *Further evidence of lack of HIV-1 related cognitive impairment during asymptomatic stages: the multicentre AIDS cohort study.* Paper presented to the Fifth International Conference on AIDS, Montreal, Canada, June 4–9, 1989.

Sherrard, M., Gatt, I. (1987). Human immunodeficiency virus (HIV) antibody testing. *British Medical Journal, 295,* 911–912.

Sireling, L. I., Paykel, E. S., Freeling, P., Rao, B. M., & Patel, S. P. (1985). Depression in general practice: Case thresholds and diagnosis. *British Journal of Psychiatry, 17,* 61–65.

Strang, J., Heathcote, S., & Watson, P. (1987). Habit moderation in injecting drug addicts. *Health Trends, 19,* 16–18.

Summerfield, D. (1989). HIV infection—discrimination and criminalisation. *Lancet, i,* 956–957.

Temoshok, L. (1988). Psychoimmunology and AIDS. In T. P. Bridge, A. F. Mirsky & F. K. Goodwin (Eds), *Psychological, neuropsychiatric and substance abuse aspects of AIDS* (pp. 187–198). New York: Raven Press.

Thompson, N. L., West, D. J., & Woodhouse, T. (1985). Social and legal problems of homosexuals in Britain. In D J. West (Ed), *Sexual victimisation* (pp. 93–159). Aldershot: Gower.

World Health Organisation Global Programme on AIDS (1988). *Avoidance of discrimination in relation to HIV-infected people and people with AIDS.* Resolution WHA41.24, Geneva, May, 1988.

Chapter 10
Public Health Implications of Mild to Moderate Alcohol Consumption

Rachel Jenkins & Sharon Harvey

This chapter briefly reviews some of the international public health literature on alcohol consumption, the social costs of alcohol consumption and the concept of safe limits of drinking. A longitudinal study of young mild-moderate drinkers in the Civil Service is described, their patterns of drinking over a period of 7 years and the consequences of their alcohol consumption in terms of psychological morbidity, sickness absence and labour turnover. The chapter concludes with a discussion of the implications of the study for the concept of safe limits, for possible early preventive strategies.

Mounting medical and political concern has been aroused concerning the steady rise of alcohol consumption in Britain and other Western countries. Alcohol intake per capita has almost doubled in Europe in the last 25 years (Office of Health Economics, 1988), with one-eighth of the world's population consuming one-half of the world's recorded alcohol consumption (WHO, 1986). In the UK, Godfrey et al. (1986) have demonstrated that real expenditure on alcohol rose from £ 5686 million in 1965 to £ 9905 million in 1984, an increase of 74% in two decades. (By contrast, expenditure on tobacco fell by 23% in the same time period.)

As Godfrey and her colleagues point out, these changes have to be assessed in the light of changes in expenditure on other items. The proportion of total expenditure spent on alcohol rose from 5.7% to 7.4%, whereas for tobacco it fell from 6.7% to 3.4%. It seems that tobacco is being viewed increasingly as a noxious, harmful substance by the general public in a way that alcohol is not.

The mean per capita consumption of alcohol in a country has been regarded as of overwhelming importance to public health for some decades because it has been suggested that *the proportion of heavy consumers in a society is directly proportional to the average consumption in that society* (e.g. Bruun et al., 1975). Popham et al. (1978) reviewed data from a number of European countries, the United States, Canada and Australia and showed the high correlation coefficients between per capita consumption of alcohol and mortality from alcohol-related disease. In a similar vein a decade later, Skog (1988) also reviewed the international literature from developed countries and demonstrated the strong association in different countries between per capita consumption and liver cirrhosis mortality, which was first hypothesised by Lederman 30 years earlier in 1956 (Lederman, 1956).

Liver cirrhosis is a leading cause of death in males aged 25 to 65. Furthermore, surveys from several European countries (WHO, 1986) have indicated that at least 20% of all males aged between 25 and 65 who are admitted to general hospitals are suffering from ailments related to their alcohol consumption, and that nearly 30% of all first admissions to psychiatric hospitals are alcohol related.

The reasons for increased alcohol consumption in Europe may not only relate to the greater availability of alcohol and to alcohol becoming relatively cheaper, but also to individuals developing drinking patterns that are new to their culture and that are added to existing drinking patterns. Two major examples of the latter phenomenon are the increase in wine drinking seen in Northern European countries as a result of exposure to Southern European countries and the increased recruitment of individuals who used to be abstainers or light drinkers, particularly women (Hore, 1988).

In the UK, relative to personal disposable income, the cost per litre of alcohol has fallen by 33% between 1960 and 1983 (Godfrey et al., 1986). Another way of looking at this phenomenon is to examine the number of hours of work needed to earn the price of, for example, a bottle of whisky. The average female nonmanual worker could purchase a bottle of whisky with 2.2 hours work in 1984, compared with over three times as much work (7.2 hours) 24 years earlier in 1960. The corresponding figures for the average male nonmanual worker are 1.4 hours in 1984 compared with 3.8 hours in 1960.

General evidence of a disproportionate increase in alcohol consumption in women has been described for the UK (Shaw, 1980; OPCS, 1988) and the United States (Leland, 1982), and is particularly prominent in employed women (Johnson et al., 1977; Parker et al., 1980). Women are responsible for a sizeable proportion of the recent expansion of the alcohol market, with the media portraying consumption of alcohol as a glamorous activity (Litman, 1986). As women may be more prone than men to alcoholic liver disease and alcohol-related brain damage, this trend is worrying (Dunne, 1988; Beary, 1986).

Such an increase in women's consumption has been attributed to the removals of constraints upon women's drinking, including greater freedom of access to alcohol, higher discretionary spending power and less social stigma than has hitherto pertained to women who drink regularly. The increase has also been attributed to the conflicts women particularly may experience between their domestic, family and occupational roles.

As is now widely accepted, alcohol causes not only physical illness, but also has considerable psychological and social effects. Alcohol-related traffic accidents account for up to 50% of road fatalities. Between one-third and one-half of all reported crimes are alcohol related. Heavy alcohol consumption can cause brain damage, psychosis and neurotic symptoms such as irritability, fatigue, poor concentration, anxiety, depression and impaired sleep.

It has long been recognised that many "problem" drinkers are at work (DHSS, 1980), and it has been estimated that their sickness absence is five times that of the average, and

that they are three times more liable to have accidents at work (Teher, 1986). However, as medical, political and industrial attention has focussed on these relatively visible severe problem drinkers, the majority of so-called "moderate" drinkers have been allowed to ignore the potential effects of alcohol on the occupational and social environment, despite the increasing evidence that even "moderate" levels of drinking are associated with accidents and absenteeism, which add to the cost of alcohol consumption misuse in the community (Grant, 1982).

The wider social costs of alcohol misuse in the UK have been estimated at 1.6 billion in 1985 and 2 billion in 1987 (McDonnell & Maynard, 1985; Maynard, 1987). A similar documentation of the costs of alcohol misuse in Minnesota (Parker et al., 1983) estimated the cost of alcohol misuse somewhere between 1.4 and 2.1 billion dollars, representing between 2.8% and 4.3% of all personal income of Minnesotans, and from 26 to 39 times the alcohol excise tax revenues generated in 1983. The documentation of the costs of alcohol abuse is an important initial step in the campaign to reduce alcohol-related deaths, morbidity and health-care costs.

Crofton (1987) has reviewed some of the British data documenting the extent and costs of alcohol problems in employment, and Kreitman (1986) pointed out the large contribution of light and moderate drinkers to work problems. A recent community survey in the United States has indicated that there are substantial proportions of employed men and women with alcohol problems even amongst occupational groups not hitherto considered to be at high risk for problem drinking (Parker et al., 1983).

The increase in per capita alcohol consumption, the increased recruitment of women to drinking, the documentation of the social hazards and costs of alcohol consumption all support the pressing need for an urgent reassessment of what might be a "safe" quantity of alcohol to consume for either sex, not only in terms of associated physical and psychological morbidity, but also in terms of occupational problems such as sickness absence, labour turn-over, impaired performance at work, impaired attitudes to work as well as in terms of other social problems for the individual and the family. This need can best be met by longitudinal epidemiological studies of male and female "moderate" and "light" drinkers to examine the natural history of different patterns of drinking, as well as to evaluate the social, psychological, physical and economic costs of relatively light and moderate alcohol consumption, particularly amongst employed men and women. Such studies should help to clarify the points at which preventive public health strategies might be most effective.

This chapter now describes one such study, a 7-year prospective study of a cohort of young male and female executive officers employed in the Home Office in the UK who were surveyed in 1980, 1981 and 1986. This longitudinal epidemiological study provided the opportunity to examine the stability of patterns of alcohol consumption, and the relationship between long-standing "moderate" alcohol consumption and the persistence of psychological symptomatology. It also allowed an evaluation of one of the economic costs of relatively moderate alcohol intake in terms of certified and uncertified sickness absence.

The project took advantage of research links developed with the Civil Service Medical Advisory Service and with the Home Office Establishment. The Home Office keeps strictly accurate and up-to-date records of the sickness absence of each of its employees whether medically certified or self-certified, and the previous surveys of the cohort demonstrated the feasibility and performance of epidemiological assessment techniques for minor psychiatric morbidity in this occupational setting (Jenkins, 1983, 1985a, 1985b, 1985c, 1986).

Study Population

A cohort of direct-entrant Executive Officers in the Home Office who had previously been assessed by one of the authors (RJ) in 1980 and 1981 were the subjects of the present follow-up study carried out in 1986/1987. The Home Office is a traditional hierarchical bureaucracy in which executive officers come from the core of the administration group of the Home Civil Service and carry out regular work in government departments according to laid down policy.

Direct-entrant executive officers all have either "A" levels or university degrees. They are selected according to the results of a civil service examination, and there is no selection or job allocation on the basis of sex. At the time of the initial survey of the cohort in 1980, the age group 20—35 was studied, and only those individuals who had been executive officers for less than 10 years were included. A letter was sent from the Establishment Office to each eligible executive officer, outlining the purpose of the survey and enclosing a consent form. The names of all respondents were then given to the authors. All respondents were interviewed in privacy in the relevant building of the Home Office using a structured standardised interview similar to that of the original study. Thus measures of psychiatric morbidity, alcohol consumption, social stress and supports, GP consultations and attitudes toward work were available on the cohort for the years 1980 and 1986. Sickness absence records were available for the whole 7 years under study. Blood investigations were only available for 1986.

Of the 184 executive officers in the Home Office who were interviewed in the original 1980 study and who formed the cohort for this follow up study 7 years later, only 75 were identified by the Establishment Division as still employed by the Home Office and available to be interviewed. This represents 41% of the original cohort.

Measures

All respondents were interviewed using the *Clinical Interview Schedule* (Goldberg et al., 1970), a standardised, semistructured interview that explores psychological symptoms in terms of their onset, duration and severity. Patients were divided into "cases" and "noncases" on the basis of their scores on the *Clinical Interview Schedule*. A score of 13 or below was designated a "noncase" and 14 or above a "case." In addition, all respondents completed the 30-item *General Health Questionnaire* (Goldberg, 1972, 1978), immediately following the clinical interview. This is self-administered and quickly completed. *Social stress and supports* were recorded by a brief screening interview following the *Clinical Interview* and examined the domains of occupation, finance, housing, social life, marriage and family (Jenkins et al., 1981).

Respondents were asked to quantify their alcohol consumption during the 7 days prior to the interview. Note was taken of the average amount of alcohol consumed at a sitting and of the number of sittings in the previous 7 days. This was categorised into beer, wine and spirits, and converted into units of alcohol on the basis of half pint of beer, 1 glass of wine and a single measure of spirits being equivalent to one unit of alcohol (7.9 g absolute alcohol).

The Establishment Department of the Home Office keeps detailed "Sickness Absence Records" of Executive Officers, including documentation of whether the leave was certified or uncertified. This information was extracted over the years 1982–1986 in terms of both spells and days of certified and uncertified leave. It was noted that there was a change of policy in 1982 regarding uncertified leave which allowed the first 7 days of any spell of absence to be self-certified. Sickness absence data for the year 1979–82 were already available from the previous study.

Occupational attitudes were measured using validated self-administered scales measuring attitudes to the current job and to the work ethic (Nicholson & Payne, 1979; Warr et al., 1979). The concepts examined were work involvement, intrinsic job motivation, higher order need strength, perceived job characteristics, job satisfaction and job attachment.

Respondents were asked to report the number of occasions on which they consulted their GPs over the last 12 months prior to the interview. Permission was obtained from the respondent to allow venepuncture for blood samples to determine mean corpuscular volume, alkaline phosphatase, aspartate transaminase and gamma glutamyl transpeptidase. The use of these tests as markers for alcohol intake is well documented (see Wu, Chanarin, & Leri, 1974; Skude & Wadstein, 1977; Papoz et al., 1981; Bennitt et al., 1982).

Findings

Alcohol Consumption and Demographic Variables

Although men had been substantially heavier drinkers than women in 1980 ($F = 3.692$, $p = 0.05$), in 1986 the difference in distribution of alcohol consumption between the sexes was not statistically significant ($F = 1.820$, $p = 0.18$). Table 10.1 shows the change in various parameters of alcohol consumption between 1980 and 1987 for both sexes looking at the 75 patients currently followed up. The overall mean of alcohol consumption in the two sexes remained largely unchanged between 1980 and 1987.

It can be seen that the percentage of men who are abstinent in the last 7 days rose slightly, while the percentage of abstinent women fell slightly. The proportion of men drinking over 15 units per week has fallen from one-half to one-third, and the proportion of women drinking over 15 units has fallen from 16.7% to 12.5%. However, the proportion of men drinking over 30 units per week has only fallen marginally, from 18% to 16%, and the proportion of women drinking over 30 units has remained the same.

In 1980, the average reported alcohol consumption in the last 7 days amongst the married was 16 units for men and 8 units for women; amongst the singles, it was 24 units for men and 12 units for women; amongst the divorced, it was 76 units for men (there were no divorced women in 1980); amongst the separated, it was 28 units for men and 44 units for women; and amongst the cohabiting, it was 32 units for men and 11 units for women. In 1987, the average reported alcohol consumption in the last 7 days amongst the married was 11 for men and 10 for women; amongst the singles, it was 25 for men and 8 for women; amongst the divorced, it was 25 for men and 2 for women; amongst the separated, it was 19 for men and 25 for women; and amongst the cohabiting, it was 12 for men and 11 for women. The relationship between alcohol consumption and educational qualifications in 1980 was as follows: alcohol consumption was significantly greater in women with a university degree (mean consumption 13.65 units, S.D. = 17.07) than in women with

Table 10.1. Alcohol consumption by gender, 1980 and 1987. Consumption in last week. (SDs in parentheses).

	Mean alcohol Consumption	% Abstinent in last week	% Drinking > 15 units	% Drinking > 30 units
1980:				
Male	18.5 units	17.6	54.9	17.6
	(16.6)	(9.0)	(28.0)	(9.0)
Female	10.9 units	16.7	16.7	6.3
	(14.5)	(4.0)	(4.0)	(2.0)
1987:				
Male	17.6 units	19.6	37.0	15.9
	(25.1)	(10.0)	(19.0)	(8.0)
Female	10.3 units	12.5	12.5	8.3
	(11.3)	(3.0)	(3.0)	(2.0)

Table 10.2. Relationship between weekly alcohol consumption and minor psychiatric morbidity.

Alcohol Consumption (units/week)	Men				Women			
	0	1–4	15–29	30+	0	1–14	15–29	30+
a) 1980								
Number in each range	9.0	14.0	18.0	10.0	4.0	16.0	2.0	2.0
(%)	17.6	27.5	35.3	19.6	16.7	66.7	8.3	8.3
GHQ score	5.0	3.6	2.8	3.8	9.6	4.6	4.0	5.5
(SD)	5.4	3.65	2.8	4.8	9.7	5.2	1.4	2.1
CIS score	15.0	13.1	8.6	9.1	17.0	12.3	12.0	7.5
(SD)	12.1	10.7	7.6	8.7	19.1	11.6	9.9	10.6
b) 1986								
Number in each range	10.0	22.0	9.0	10.0	3.0	18.0	1.0	2.0(%)
	19.6	43.1	17.7	19.6	12.5	75.0	4.2	9.0
GHQ score	1.8	2.8	5.1	4.4	5.7	6.9	2.0	11.06
(SD)	3.5	4.1	6.4	5.3	5.5	7.2	0	9.2
CIS score	5.9	7.6	8.2	10.8	18.0	15.4	5.0	28.0
(SD)	6.3	6.9	6.9	6.9	8.1	14.9	19.9	12.7

just "A"-level school examinations (mean consumption 9.40 units, S.D. = 9.41). The reverse was true for men, where mean consumption for men with a university degree was 18.87 units (S.D. = 14.86) and for those with only "A" levels was 24.5 units (S.D. = 25.74). By 1987, there was less difference between women with a university degree (mean consumption 10.97 units S.D. = 11.30) and women

with just "A" levels (mean consumption 9.75 units, S.D. = 12.52). However, the difference in alcohol consumption had widened between men with and without a university education. Mean consumption for men with a university degree had fallen to 13.75 units (S.D. = 14.33), while mean consumption of men with only "A" levels had remained at 24.21 units (S.D. = 30.42). In 1980, all those sampled were ex-

Table 10.3. Prediction of high and low alcohol consumption in 1986 using discriminant analysis (variables measured in 1986).

Variable	Discriminant funct. coeff.	Changes in Rao's V	P of change
Women			
Housing	0.953	8.462	0.004
Hypnotics	−0.928	9.700	0.002
Irritability	−1.554	8.430	0.004
Marriage (SSSI)	1.270	4.250	0.039
Somatic symptoms	1.471	4.928	0.026
Depression	−1.593	8.185	0.004
Fatigue	1.690	22.766	0.000
Job characteristics	0.593	26.721	0.000
Social life	0.628	23.899	0.000

Centroids of groups:
<10 units alcohol/week: 1.712
>10 units alcohol/week: −2.854
Total % of groups correctly classified: 95.83%

	Discriminant funct. coeff.	Changes in Rao's V	P of change
Men			
Housing	−1.002	6.640	0.010
Marital status	0.538	3.910	0.048
Occupation	0.556	3.255	0.071

Centroids of groups:
<30 units alcohol/week: 0.257
>30 units alcohol/week: −1.053
Total % of groups correctly classified: 76.47%

ecutive officers. By 1986, some had been promoted to higher executive officers and senior executive office level. It is of interest to note that the quantity of alcohol consumption in the week prior to interview is associated with occupational status in 1986—but in opposite directions for each sex: men's alcohol consumption decreased with promotion, while women's alcohol consumption increased.

Alcohol Consumption and Psychiatric Morbidity

Table 10.2 presents the relationships between reported alcohol consumption with overall minor psychiatric morbidity in 1980 and 1986. In 1980, abstainers have relatively high GHQ and CIS scores. In 1986, the picture is rather different in that, in general, GHQ and CIS score rise in both men and women with increasing alcohol consumption. The cross-sectional relationship of alcohol consumption with psychiatric caseness was not significant in the subcohort of 75, either in 1980 or 1986.

Alcohol Consumption and Sickness Absence

To examine the relationship of sickness absence to alcohol consumption over the period 1980 to 1986, the summed sickness absence was compared between those who consumed low quantities of alcohol in 1980 and 1986, and secondly with those who drank higher quantities at either time. In women, a cut-off point of 10 units of alcohol/week was used, while in men 30 units of alcohol/week was used. For both sexes, those drinking over those arbitrary thresholds of alcohol consumption took substantially more duration and frequency of sickness absence over the 7 years than those drinking below the threshold in both 1980 and 1986.

Factors Predicting Alcohol Consumption

In order to see what combination of social, demographic and psychological factors in 1986 might predict alcohol consumption in 1986, the following variables were chosen for discriminant analysis: sex, marital status, oc-cupational status, job attitudes, items from the *Social Stress and Supports Interview*, in-dividual symptom score and the total weighted score from the *Clinical Interview Schedule*. A cut-off point of 30 units of alco-hol/week was used to divide male subjects into high and low intake groups, and 10 units of alcohol/week for female subjects. Analyses resulted in a correct prediction of alcohol-in-take groups in 95.8% of female subjects and 76.5% male subjects. (see Table 10.3).

The significant variables in men were all social, mainly social stress and support in housing, marital status and occupation. By contrast, in women, psychological variables and perceived job characteristics were also important as well as social status and sup-port.

To see whether these variables also had a predictive value prospectively, a similar dis-criminant analysis was performed using the values obtained from the variables in 1980. On this occasion, to predict alcohol consump-tion in 1986, alcohol intake in 1980 was also included as a predictor. (see Table 10.4).

In women, such an analysis was able cor-rectly to identify 95.8% of subjects; using the psychological variables of depression, anxiety and excessive concern with bodily functions, the social variable of marital stress and sup-port, the occupational variable of intrinsic job motivation, and quantity of alcohol consumed in 1980. For men, such an analysis was able correctly to classify 94.1% of subjects, using the psychological variables of depression, anxiety, lack of concentration and consump-tion of hypnotics, together with the overall CIS score; the demographic variable of job identification, perceived job characteristics and job satisfaction, and most importantly, the quantity of alcohol consumed in 1980.

Table 10.4. Prediction of high and low alcohol consumption in 1986 using discriminant analysis (variables measured in 1980).

Variable	Discriminant funct. coeff.	Changes in Rao's V	P of change
Women			
Depression	1.594	6.823	0.009
Units alcohol; 1980	0.432	9.449	0.002
Obsessions,compulsions	−1.454	6.117	0.031
Marriage (SSSI)	1.936	6.127	0.013
Anxiety	1.153	7.514	0.006
Hypochondriasis	0.640	10.187	0.001
Job motivation	−0.442	4.496	0.034
Centroids of groups:			
<10 units alcohol/week: −1.159			
>10 units alcohol/week: 1.932			
Total % of groups correctly classified: 95.83%			
Men			
Units alcohol; 1980	1.224	9.963	0.001
Hypnotics	−1.261	5.740	0.017
Severity score; CIS	0.927	5.960	0.015
Anxiety	−1.088	6.318	0.012
Job identification	−0.805	9.322	0.002
Job characteristics	1.134	28.907	0.000
Marital status	−0.249	4.501	0.033
Job satisfaction	−0.453	5.894	0.015
Poor concentration	0.371	4.842	0.027
Depression	0.428	5.752	0.016
Centroids of groups:			
<30 units alcohol/week: −0.646			
>30 units alcohol/week: 2.648			
Total % of groups correctly classified: 94.12%			

Alcohol Consumption and Blood Tests

Measurement of liver enzymes and mean corpuscular volume gave abnormal results in only 9 subjects in the 1986 sample. These indices are on the whole more likely to be indicators of alcohol intake in a population of very heavy drinkers, and it is not surprising that only 9 abnormal results were found. It is interesting to note however that the gamma GT is said to be the most sensitive of the tests, but in our study, the MCVs showed a greater degree of abnormality. It seems that where such tests are abnormal, they are generally linked to high alcohol consumption. However, such tests are late indicators, and many subjects were drinking over safe limits with normal blood indices, as one might expect.

Stability of Alcohol Consumption

In order to examine how stable drinking patterns were over time, the units of alcohol consumed in the index week was compared in 1980 and 1986. For women, exactly one-third remained the same, one-third increased their consumption and one-third decreased it; while for men, 37.5% remained the same, 23% increased their consumption and 39.5% decreased their consumption.

Comments

In discussing the results the limitations of sample size and method must be kept in mind. While this longitudinal study of 75 male and female executive officers can provide interesting findings about patterns of drinking and their occupational consequences, only further research can determine whether any of the findings may be generalised to other cohorts of working men and women.

- The *overall mean level of alcohol consumption* in the two sexes remained largely unchanged between 1980 and 1987. This contrasts with the OPCS survey, which shows young women drinking rather more than between 1978 and 1987, with young men drinking rather less. In an occupational survey in Detroit of adults employed in a

wide range of occupations, 92% of men and 89% of women had taken a drink in the last year (Parker, 1983). This was substantially in excess of the population frequencies of 74% for men and 60% for women at that time. Also, a survey of university students (Anderson, 1982) showed that 85% of men and 80% of women had taken alcohol in the 4 days prior to the interview. These figures are similar to those found in this employed cohort in 1980 where 90% of men and 82% of women had taken a drink in the week prior to interview. However, in the follow-up subsample of 75 in 1986 the percentages are 80% and 88%, respectively.

- The fall in the number of men between 1980 and 1986 who had *taken a drink in the previous week* may be partly related to their increase in age and partly to the increased proportions who had become married. Such a hypothesis has been supported by a community study in Boston. (Parker et al., 1980). However, it is worrying to note that the same had not happened for women; instead, the proportion of women who had taken a drink in the previous week had increased. This may reflect the widespread change to an increased pattern of alcohol consumption in women (RCPsych., 1986).

- There was no association between *marital status* and alcohol consumption in females; however, single men drank about twice as much as married men. This relationship was also found in the community study in Boston, which found that married men drank significantly less than single men (Parker, 1980). But in contrast to the present study, that survey also found a similar relationship in women, though it was not significant.

- Those women who were *promoted to higher grades* (Higher Executive Officer and Senior Executive Officer) had a higher alcohol consumption than those women who had not been promoted. Promotion had no effect on alcohol consumption in men. Parker (1983) similarly found that female managers and administrators had increased rates of nondependent problem drinking compared to labour and service workers, but the reverse was true for men.

- Parker (1980), noted that there appears to be a direct relationship between alcohol consumption and *educational status* in women that does not apply to men, namely, that the better educated women drank more than the less well educated. In the Home Office Executive Officers surveyed in 1980, a finding similar to the Boston community study by Parker was noted (Jenkins, 1986). However, in the 1986 survey of the surviving cohort of Executive Officers, this relationship had changed. Men without a university degree drank more than those with a degree, but in women the quantity of alcohol drunk in the previous week was similar in both groups. It is possible to speculate that for women, the increase in alcohol consumption noted in women in recent years swamped the earlier differential effect of educational status, while for men public health warnings about heavy alcohol consumption may be reaching the better educated first. It is not clear why women are not responding to the same public health messages.

- When alcohol intake is compared with *caseness* as defined in the *Clinical Interview Schedule*, there is a trend for higher levels of alcohol consumption to be found in the cases but this difference is not significant. Difference between the sexes become apparent, however, when alcohol consumption in the earlier study is compared with the current levels of alcohol consumption, using a *longitudinal view of caseness*. In men, noncases in 1986 have a slightly decreased alcohol consumption, while cases have a markedly increased alcohol consumption. Such a relationship does not hold for women. This suggests that psychological state plays a larger role in the alcohol consumption of the men. However, this is contrary to the finding in the 1980 Home Office study and in other surveys in which it has been suggested that men drink more for social reasons than to relieve symptoms (Orford et al., 1974; Knupfer, 1964). It may be that men in general drink more for social reasons than women, but also that male cases tend to gradually increase their intake. It is interesting to note that Ross et al. (1988) looked at sex differences in the

prevalence of psychiatric disorders in patients with alcohol and drug problems who presented at an addiction research clinic and found no sex differences in psychopathology. It is clear that the relationship between chronic drinking and psychiatric morbidity has yet to be fully understood.

- Studies of alcohol and *sickness absence* usually investigate occupations known to have a high overall intake of alcohol (Hore, 1981; Rathod, 1975). Hore found that alcoholics lost 22 more working days per year than did their colleagues. Civil servants do not have a particularly high overall intake of alcohol (OPCS, 1986) compared to other professions, but even in the present study sickness absence (summed over the 7 years prior to interview) is substantially greater in those drinking over the arbitrary thresholds of 10 units for women and 30 units for men a week, on either or both interview occasions in 1980 and 1986, than in those drinking less than those thresholds. Certified absence is affected as much as uncertified absence,, and duration as much as frequency. *The relative risk of absence for those drinking more than 10 units a day is 2.4 for men and 1.6 for women.* It is worth noting that none of the diagnoses on the sickness absence certificates included overt alcohol problems!

- The unique feature of this study of alcohol consumption and sickness absence is that measurement of sickness absence is not based on self-report, but on accurate data collected routinely by the Civil Service and includes both certified and uncertified absence. Studies which attempt to ascribe a spell of absence to a particular cause (e.g. Casswell et al., 1988) ignore the well substantiated multi-factorial social, physical, psychological and cultural causation of absence (Johns & Nicholson, 1982). Furthermore, it is likely that alcohol consumption, by affecting general physical health, social relationships and social skills, will lead to an increase in absence for these reasons, and they would constitute an important element of alcohol attributable absence.

- The implications of the data on *changing consumption over the 6 years* are that, first, there is substantial stability in the system:

one-third or more remain unchanged. If their drinking has measurable harmful consequences, then there is a public health argument for early intervention to reduce consumption. Second, a substantial proportion escalate their consumption (one-third in women and one-fourth in men), which underlines the need for better educational strategies as well as early interventions and repeated screening of those who have a safe level of consumption at earlier interview. Third, the good news is that one-third of women and nearly two-fifths of men actually *decreased* their consumption over the 6 years, possibly as an effect of maturation and the acquisition of stable relationships.

- The study suggests that *even moderate drinking carries public health consequences.* The study also indicates that although there is consistency in people's drinking habits, and in fact two-thirds of the sample had altered their consumption. Therefore, it would seem that there are *great gains to be made by intervening early in a person's drinking career,* so that drinking consumption is reduced to a low level, and that to do this may avoid years of excess morbidity and sickness absence. Besides alcohol education programmes in the work-place, which are slowly becoming more common place in Britain (at least in the larger industries), there is scope for a general practitioner led initiative, using opportunistic screening, to advise young people about the risks of alcohol consumption and to offer support and advice on reducing consumption.

Implications for Public Health and Prevention Policies

Following the Second World War, emphasis was primarily placed in Europe on those individuals who were heavily addicted to alcohol, hospital admission and treatment being offered. In the 1960s and 1970s, these therapeutic activities were widened into the community to include the development of therapeutic hostels and counselling centres. However, disillusionment with the efficacy of this type of intervention directed at extremely heavy drinkers, together with a growing awareness of the fact that alcohol misuse affects a far larger segment of the population (e.g. Kamerow, 1979) encouraged the development of health education about alcohol, control policies regarding alcohol consumption, and intervention at a much earlier stage in an individual's drinking career (Hore, 1988).

The rationale of these activities, all designed to reduce alcohol consumption, rests on the observations that the distribution of alcohol consumption is strongly skewed with no sharp line of division between alcoholics and normal drinkers, and that the drinking population seems to move in concert up and down the consumption scale when change occurs (e.g. Skog, 1988). Thus, increasing overall consumption is typically associated with an increasing prevalence of heavy drinking, so that, logically, a reduction in overall consumption should result in a decreasing prevalence of heavy drinking.

Some European countries, particularly in Scandinavia, have attempted to emphasise the role of adult education to reduce drinking to safe levels. In the UK, three Royal Colleges have recently issued guidelines on safe limits of consumption. Education about alcohol in schools has a long history in the United States, but Grant (1983) concluded that while studies have shown a relationship between exposure to drug education and frequency of drug use (e.g. tobacco and marijuana), they have yet to show convincing evidence of a relation between alcohol education and drinking patterns. It is possible for knowledge to increase without behaviour being changed. Pittman (1980) suggested that family and peer attitudes toward alcohol use had more of an effect than attitudes taught in school.

Furthermore, educational messages do not necessarily reach all sectors of the population with equal impact. In Sweden, alcohol sales actually decreased between 1976 and 1981, and this was reflected in Stockholm county where detailed surveys have shown that, although the decrease in sales and consumption was followed by a general decrease in alcohol-related problems, the decreases were far from uniform across social groups. Differentials between blue-collar and white-collar workers in alcohol-related diseases appear to have widened, and the authors argue for a further reduction in alcohol consumption with additional measures to reach all social groups (Romelsjo & Diderichsen, 1989).

Grant (1983) has argued that alcohol education in schools must be rethought if it is to be effective. At present, programmes focus on the consequential damage of excessive consumption, a lesson that is already quite well internalised by most of the young people to whom these programmes are being directed. They already know that drunk people crash their cars and that alcoholics die of liver cirrhosis, but they perceive these effects as irrelevant to their own lives. More to the point would be an educational approach that could deal with the potent influence of parents, peers and the media upon their present and future drinking. There is some evidence that alcohol education provided by age-peers is more effective.

Control policies have attempted to restrict the availability of alcohol by increasing its price, restricting the drinking age, reducing access to alcohol and restricting advertising. Harrison (1986) has reviewed the political difficulties in the UK which bedevil attempts to obtain a coordinated government alcohol policy to cope with the conflicting interests between the Treasury, the Department of Trade and Industry, the Minister of Agriculture and the Department of Health. Since 1987, the Ministerial Group on Alcohol Misuse brings together Ministers of 12 government departments to tackle these difficulties (Ministerial Group on Alcohol Misuse, 1988). A recent American editorial confessed that constructing a comprehensive coordinated national policy is not easy (Healey 1986) and referred to the underlying tension between economic interests and public health concerns, and the ambivalence in our society about alcohol and those who use or abuse it.

It has been argued that excessive price increases on alcohol would price alcohol as a commodity out of the reach of many people, the vast majority of whom may not be harmed by alcohol, and thus a discriminatory measure would have been introduced (Grant & Ritson, 1983). However, if even low-moderate drinking has measurable harmful consequences, as suggested in the study of civil servants, then the strategy of reducing alcohol consumption in the whole population ceases to raise such an ethical dilemma.

The World Health Organisation, in evaluating the progress of its strategy of *Health For All 2000,* recently reported that several countries in the Eastern Mediterranean have banned the import, sale and consumption of alcoholic beverages (WHO, 1987).

Reduction of advertising may be expected to have limited value on its own. Waterson (1983) of the Brewers Association pointed out that per capita consumption in Eastern European countries, where advertising does not exist, has risen over the past 30 years at the same rate as in Western Europe.

The most recent encouraging development has been the increasing emphasis on, and demonstrable effectiveness of, early intervention. Kristenson et al. (1988) and Chick et al. (1988) have demonstrated that minimal intervention can affect drinking patterns. The World Health Organisation is currently considering the role of the primary-care physician in early intervention (WHO, 1984, 1985; Standing Medical Advisory Committee, 1989). Wallace et al. (1988) reported a randomised controlled trial of general practitioner intervention in patients with excessive alcohol consumption (taken as 35 units or more for men, 21 units or more for women). All the GPs received a training session with the use of a specially recorded video programme to illustrate the intervention. Patients were given advice and information about how to reduce consumption, and they were also given a drinking diary. At the end of a year, very substantial reductions in consumption were achieved in the treatment group compared with the controls, and the authors argue that general practitioners and other members of the primary health care team should therefore be encouraged to include counselling about alcohol consumption in their preventive activities.

References

Beary, M., D., Merry, J. (1986). The rise in alcoholism in women in fertile age (Letter). *British Journal of Addition, 81,* 142.

Bernadt, M. W., Mumford, M., Taylor, C., Smith, B., & Murray, R. M. (1982). Comparison of questionnaire and laboratory tests in the detection of excessive drinking and alcoholism. *Lancet, i,* 325–328.

Bruun, K. et al. (1975). Alcohol control polices in public health perspective Kirjapaino, Helsinki. Quoted in P. Davies & D. Walsh (Eds.), *Alcohol problems and alcohol control in Europe, 1983.* London: Croom Helm.

Casswell, S., Gilmore, L., & Ashton, T. (1988). Estimating alcohol-related absenteeism in New Zealand. *British Journal of Addiction, 83,* 677–682.

Chick, J., Lloyd, G., & Crombie, E. (1985). Counselling drinkers in medical wards: A controlled study. *British Journal 290,* 965. (Civil Service Commission, 1979. Annual Report 1978. Civil Service Commission, Basingstoke.)

Crofton, J. (1987). Extent and costs of alcohol problems in employment: A review of British data. *Alcohol and alcoholism, 22,* 321—325.

DHSS (1981). *Drinking sensibly.* A discussion document prepared by the Health Departments of Great Britain and Northern Ireland. London: HMSO.

Dunne, F. (1988). Are women more easily damaged by alcohol than men? *British Journal of Addiction, 83,* 1135–1136.

Godfrey, C., Hardman, G., & Maynard (1986). Data note–2. Measuring UK alcohol and tobacco consumption. *British Journal of Addiction, 81,* 287–293.

Goldberg, D. P. (1970). *Detecting psychiatric illness by questionnaire.* Maudsley Monograph, 21. Oxford: Oxford University Press.

Goldberg, D., Cooper, B., Eastwood, M., Kedward, H. B., & Shepherd, M. (1970). A standardised psychiatric interview for use in community surveys. *British Journal of Preventive and Social Medicine, 24,* 18–23.

Goldberg, D. (1978). *Manual of the General Health Questionnaire.* Windsor: National Foundation for Educational Research.

Grant, M. & Ritson, B. (1983). *Alcohol, the prevention debate.* London: Croom Helm.

Grant, M. (1983). Alcohol education: Does it really affect drinking problems. In P. Golding (Ed.), *Alcoholism. Analysis of a world wide problem.* Lancaster: MTP Press.

Harrison, L. (1981). Is a coordinated prevention policy really feasible. *Alcohol and Alcoholism, 21,* 5–7.

Hore, B. D. (1981). Alcohol and work. *British Journal on Alcohol and Alcoholism, 17(2),* 72–79.

Healey, J. M. (1986). Reducing the destructive impact of alcohol: The search for acceptable strategies continues. *American Journal of Public Health, 76,* 749—750.

Hore, B. D. (1988). Society's response to alcohol consumption and problem development. *Alcohol and Alcoholism, 23,* 253—257.

Jenkins, R. (1983). *Epidemiological observations of minor psychiatric morbidity.* M.D. Thesis, Cambridge University.

Jenkins, R. (1985a). Sex differences in minor psychiatric morbidity in employed men and women. *Psychological Medicine* (Monograph Supplement No. 7).

Jenkins, R. (1985b). Minor Psychiatric morbidity in employed young men and women and its contribution to sickness absence. *British Journal of Industrial Medicine, 42,* 147–154.

Jenkins, R. (1985c). Minor psychiatric morbidity and labour turnover. *British Journal of Industrial Medicine, 42,* 534–539.

Jenkins, R. (1986). Sex differences in alcohol consumption and its associated morbidity in young civil servants. *British Journal of Addiction, 81,* 525–535.

Johns, G., & Nicholson, N. (1982). The meanings of absence: New strategies for theory and research. In B. M. Staw & L. L. Cummings (Eds.), *Research in organisational behaviour.* Greenwich, CT: JAI Press.

Johnson, P., Armor, D. J., Blich, S., & Stambul, H. (1977). *U.S. drinking practices: Time trends, social correlates and sex roles.* (Working note prepared for the National Institute on Alcohol and Alcoholism, Santa Monica, California; and quoted in D.A. Parker et al., 1980, ibid.)

Kamerow, D. B., Pincus, H. A., & Macdonald, D. I. (1986). Alcohol abuse, other drug abuse and mental disorders in medical Practice. *Journal of the American Medical Association, 255,* 2054—2057.

Knupfer, G., & Room, R. (1964). Age, sex and social class as factors in amount of drinking in a metropolitan community. *Social Problems, 12,* 224–240.

Kreitman, N. (1986). Alcohol consumption and the preventative paradox. *British Journal of Addiction, 81,* 353–363.

Kreitman, N. (1986). Alcohol consumption and the preventive paradox. *British Journal of Addiction, 81,* 353—363.

Kristenson, H., Ohlin., Hutten-Nosslin, M. B., Trell, E., & Hood, B. (1983). Identification and intervention of heavy drinking in middle aged men: Results and follow-up of 24–60 months of long term study with randomised controls. *Alcoholism, Clinical and Experimental Research, 1,* 203—209.

Lederman, S. (1956). *Alcool, alcoolisme, alcoolisation.* Paris: Institut d'Etudes Demographiques.

Leland, J. (1982). Gender, drinking and alcohol abuse. In I. Al-issa (Ed.), *Gender and psychopathology.* London: Academic Press.

Litman, G. K. (1986). Women and alcohol problems: Finding the next questions. *British Journal of Addiction, 81,* 601–603.

Maynard, A., Hardman, G. & Whelan, A. (1987). Date Note—9. Measuring the social costs of addictive substances. *British Journal of Addiction, 82,* 701—706.

McDonnell, R., & Maynard, A. (1985). The costs of alcohol misuse. *British Journal of Addiction, 80,* 27–35.

Ministerial Group on Alcohol Misuse (1988). *Ministerial Group on Alcohol Misuse: First Annual Report 1987—88.* London: HMSO.

Office of Health Economics (1988). *Compendium of Health Statistics.* London: OHE.

Office of Population Censuses and Surveys (1986). *General Household Survey 1984.* London: HMSO.

Office of Population Censuses and Surveys (1988). *Drinking in England and Wales in 1987.* London: HMSO.

Orford, J., Waller, S., & Peto, J. (1974). Drinking behaviour and attitudes and their correlates among university students in England. *Quarterly Journal of Studies on Alcoholism, 35,* 1316–1374.

Papoz, L., Warrant, J. M., Pequinot, G., Eschwege, E., Cluade, J. R., & Schwart, D. (1981). Alcohol consumption in a healthy population. Relationship to gamma-glutamyl transferase activity and mean corpuscular volume. *Journal of the American Medical Association, 245*(17), 1748–1751.

Parker, D. A., Kaelber, C., Harford, T. C., & Brody, J. A. (1983). Alcohol problems among employed men and women in Metropolitan Detroit. *Journal of Studies on Alcohol, 44,* 1026–1039.

Parker, D. A., Kaelber, C., Harford, T. C., & Brody, J. A. (1983). Alcohol problems among employed men and women in Metropolitan Detroit. *Journal of Studies on alcohol, 44,* 1026–1039.

Parker, D. L., Shultz, J. M., Gertz, L., Berkelman, R., & Remington, P. L. (1987). The Social and economic costs of alcohol abuse in Minnesota, 1983. *American Journal of Public Health, 77,* 982–986.

Pittman, D. (1980). *Primary prevention of alcohol abuse and alcoholism: An evaluation of the control of consumption policy.* St. Louis: Social Science Institute, Washington University.

Popham, R., Schmidt, W., & de Lint, J. (1976). The effects of legal restraint on drinking. In B. Kissin & H. Begleiter (Eds.), *The biology of alcoholism,* Vol 4. London: Plenum.

Popham, R., Schmidt, W., & de Lint, J. (1978). The prevention of hazardous drinking: Implications of research on the effects of government control measures. In J. A. Ewing & B. A. Rowse (Eds.), *Drink-ing.* Chicago: Nelson Hall.

Romelsjo, A., & Diderichsen, F. (1989). Changes in alcohol-related inpatient care in Stockholm county in relation to socio-economic status during a period of decline in alcohol consumption. *American Journal of Public Health, 79,* 52—56.

Ross, H., Glaser, F., & Stiasny, S. (1988). Sex differences in the prevalence of psychiatric disorders in patients with alcohol and drug problems. *British Journal of Addiction, 83,*1179–1192.

Rathod, N. H. (1975). Alcoholism in industry. Notes on alcohol and alcoholism. In S. Carunana (Ed.) (2nd. ed., pp. 65–83). Medical Council on Alcoholism.

Royal College of Psychiatrists (1986). *Alcohol: Our favourite drug. New report of a special committee of the Royal College of Psychiatrists.* London: Tavistock.

Shaw, S. J. (1980). *Women and alcohol.* Camberwell Council on Alcoholism. London: Tavistock.

Skog, O. (1988). Interpreting trends in alcohol consumption and alcohol related damage. *Alcohol and Alcoholism, 23,* 193—302.

Skude, G., & Wadstein, J. (1979). Amylase, hepatic enzymes and bilirubin in serum of chronic alcoholics. *Acta medica scandinavica, 201,* 53–58.

Standing Medical Advisory Committee (1989). *Drinking problems: A challenge for every doctor.* London: Department of Health.

Tether, P., & Robinson, D. (1986). *Preventing alcohol problems—A guide to local action* (p. 151). London: Tavistock.

Warr, P., Cook, J., & Wall, T. (1979). Scales for the management of some work attitudes and aspects of psychological well-being. *Journal of Occupational Psychology, 52,* 129–148.

Waterson, M. J. (1983). The prevention debate. In M. Grant & B. Ritson (Eds.), *Alcohol* (pp. 108—113). London: Croom Helm.

World Health Organization (1984). *Guidelines for investigating alcohol problems and developing appropriate responses.* Geneva: WHO.

World Health Organization (1985). *Alcohol policies.* Geneva: WHO.

World Health Organization (1986). *Working party on alcohol problems.* Geneva: WHO.

World Health Organization (1986). *Working paper on alcohol.* Geneva: WHO.

World Health Organization (1987). *Evaluation of the strategy for health for all by the year 2000.* (Seventh report on the world health situation, Vol. 1, Global review.) Geneva: WHO.

Wu, A., Chanarin, I., & Levi, A. J. (1974). The macrocytosis of chronic alcoholism. *Lancet, i,* 829–831.

Section IV
Prevention and Early Detection

Prevention, and particularly primary prevention, has recently been the subject of several books and articles (Barter & Talbott, 1986; Felner et al., 1983; Marlowe & Weinberg, 1985) which suggest that its long-heralded promise is soon to be fulfilled. It is notable, however, that the claims made by the contributors to this section are considerably more modest as befits the rigorous evaluations that they report.

Effective prevention rests on a clear grasp of the causes of disorder and on effective and practical means of either altering the causes or, failing that, of reducing an individual's vulnerability to them. Prevention must therefore be preceded by detailed epidemiology to ascertain causes ever more precisely. This tactical work is the basis of four of the chapters in this section, by Kolvin et al., Platt et al., Zimmerman-Tansella and Siciliani, and Blanz and Schmidt. Each of these groups of workers focussed on a set of aetiological factors that were particularly likely to be associated with disorder.

Issy Kolvin and colleagues report a study of children living in a deprived part of Newcastle who were studied at the age of 6 and again at the age of 8. Between these ages half of the families received a form of preventive intervention called play-group therapy. The longitudinal design enabled the investigators to study not merely the correlates of childhood disorders, but also the factors that are related to change over time.

Stephen Platt and colleagues report a follow-up of work on poor housing, employment, income and civil status in women living with children in public housing. Previous work (e.g. Brown, in this volume) has shown that this combination of factors is likely to be associated with a high risk of affective disorder, and Platt et al used the GHQ as a measure of this. The GHQ is a sensitive index of distress associated with psychiatric disorder and tends, if anything, to result in the over-inclusion of borderline cases as Ormel et al. discuss in this section.

Christa Zimmerman-Tansella and Orazio Siciliani similarly chose factors that had been shown to be associated with vulnerability to disorder in previous work and examined that subset of life events—social problems—that might be particularly expected to be related to disorder, but also to be buffered by the particular vulnerability concept—social support—on which they focussed. Distress was measured by means of the GHQ as in the Platt et al. study.

Finally, B. Blanz and Martin Schmidt considered a comprehensive range of both environmental and developmental factors, previously reported to be associated with child and adolescent disorder.

All these studies were sizeable. Kolvin et al. intensively studied 170 children and their families on two occasions. Platt et al.'s sample included 823 women, Zimmerman-Tansella 227 men and older boys as well as 224 women and older girls, and Blanz et al. examined 399 at the age of 8 and 356 of them again at the age of 13. All of them have statistically significant findings to report, and each concludes by narrowing down the aetiologically significant factors to those which are particularly associated with increased risk. However, in the latter three studies, the amount of the variance of the GHQ score accounted for by these factors is unexpectedly small: 9.6% in the case of Platt et al., 4% for men and 9% for women in the case of Zimmerman-Tansella and Siciliani, and 18%–19% for Blanz et al.

This sort of effect size indicates either that the concept of distress is far too heterogeneous, or that social psychiatry is still a long way from a precise delineation of aetiology. This situation may occur even if some cases of a disorder are always caused by some particular factor whilst other cases are caused by other factors. It is not therefore necessarily a contraindication to prevention, as long as the relative risk of disorder being caused by a particular factor is substantial. Relative risks of depression and anxiety are reported by Zimmerman-Tansella and Siciliani to be three for marital problems in men, and less than three for other social problems in men and for all social problems in women, i.e. at the very borderline of a sufficiently powerful association to show a benefit from intervention.

These three studies thus each indicate caution in the field of primary prevention in psychiatry, although the simplicity of the remedy for poor housing targeted by Platt et al. might suggest that this would be a good candidate for prevention even though it accounts for so little of the variance, especially as poor housing is also associated with respiratory disease in children. Other useful conclusions can be drawn from them. Blanz et al., for example, provide strong evidence that current stress is a more potent cause of disorder than past stress, providing backing for targeting interventions at current social circumstances rather than at the personality consequences of past circumstances. The studies also achieve what good epidemiological studies often do: they throw up further questions. Why, for example, do Italian men benefit more from a confiding relationship than women? And why are developmental problems associated with later disorder in boys, but not in girls? Can this be explained by the contribution of autistic boys, or is it because the male organism is more perilously balanced?

The study reported by Kolvin et al. suggests that changes in behaviour in young school children are, as one might expect, heavily influenced by deprivations in the child's environment. However, more important than the deprivation itself is the mother's resilience in the face of family and environmental deprivation; that is, how well she copes with her life circumstances, combined with the quality of involvement, stimulation of her children and the thought she gives to her child-rearing practices. The effects of deprivation may be mitigated by the techniques that the mother employs in coping with family problems, her involvement with her children and her approached to child rearing. These must be seen as crucial protective factors in the face of family adversity. The authors argue that if preventive programmes are to be effective, they must take account of the environmental factors that are such potent determinants of altered behaviour, which they have documented in their study.

The two other papers in this section are concerned with issues related to secondary prevention. Like the papers considered initially, they do not report the effects of secondary prevention programmes, but examine case detection in close detail. No secondary prevention programme can be successful without accurate detection, and in Europe, with its well-developed primary medical care system, the most important agent of case detection is the general practitioner. Both Hans Ormel and colleagues and Brian Cooper and Horst Bickel, the authors of the two papers, therefore concentrate on case ascertainment by general practitioners.

The results of Cooper's study are reassuring. General practitioners seem to be improving their detection of early dementia especially, a process that can be helped by relatively simple means such as brief rating scales. General practitioner recognition rates of unspecified psychiatric disorder are much lower. In the study reported by Ormel et al. in this section, general practitioners recognized only about half of their patients who were at level 5 or more on the PSE/ID system. The most severe illnesses (severe depression and mania) were always recognized. By contrast, only 35% of the anxiety states were recognized.

Recognition increased the likelihood of patients being prescribed a psychotropic or given psychotherapy, and this finding persisted when the greater severity of recognized disorders was controlled for in a post hoc analysis. Recognized patients had a better outcome, but Ormel et al. are doubtful that increasing recognition by general practitioners would improve outcome further. Their scepticism is not based on their own data, but negative findings in the literature. Obviously such an important point needs, as the authors say, more investigation.

Prevention is not being ignored by the social psychiatrist, but neither primary nor secondary prevention seem likely to make much impact on the prevalence of psychiatric disorder for some time to come. Tertiary prevention, the prevention of chronicity, seems likely to continue to be the most effective way of reducing the need for service. Few programmes can claim to have been evaluated as comprehensively as the Finnish National Projects on Schizophrenia and Long-Stay Patients, which are described in detail in this section, by Yrjo Alanen and his colleagues. This is an opportunity to read about impressive work only rarely published in English concerning the illness that still provides psychiatrists with their greatest challenge.

References

Barter, J. T., & Talbott, S. W. (Eds.) (1986). *Primary prevention in psychiatry: State of the art.* Washington, DC: American Psychiatric Press.

Felner, R. D., Jason, L. A., Moritsugu, J. N., & Farber, S. S. (Eds.) (1983). *Preventive psychiatry: Theory, research and practice.* New York: Pergamon.

Marlowe, H., & Weinberg, R. B. (Eds.) (1985). *Is mental illness preventable? Pros & cons* (special issue of *Journal of Primary Prevention*). New York: Human Sciences Press.

Chapter 11

Factors in Prevention in Inner-City Deprivation

I. Kolvin, G. Charles, R. Nicholson, M. Fleeting & T. Fundudis

Deprivation, particularly its troublesome extent and its transmission, has been the focus of epidemiological research in Newcastle over the last three decades (Miller et al., 1960, 1985; Kolvin et al., 1983a, 1983b, 1988). However, that was "head count" research; in this paper, we address ourselves to the topics of intervention and prevention.

The classic approach to prevention has been based upon the work of Caplan (1964). Phrases such as "Cure is costly—prevention is priceless" have been coined. The most influential ideas, developed in the 1960s and 1970s, stated that primary preventive activities are important because they attempt to prevent the development of subsequent disorder by attacking its presumed origins, and by simultaneously promoting psychological adjustment (Sandford, 1965). In Newcastle, there has been particular interest in early secondary preventive activities that try to identify those children who are considered to be at grave risk of developing abnormally, and to prevent dysfunction from becoming severe or overt (Kolvin et al., 1981).

It could be argued that early prevention is likely to be more cost-effective than attempting intervention when the effects of deprivation have become deeply ingrained. This would be true only if the methods of prevention proved to be inexpensive and brief. Similarly, any screening programme would need to be equally expeditious and inexpensive. One also needs to ensure that the preventive programme does not have adverse consequences. It is essential that such preventive endeavours be evaluated before attempting to obtain political commitment to such investment. Finally, there are questions concerning the targeting of the resources: should they be aimed at the children at risk, at their families, or at their social environment?

Prevention programmes have to transcend an examination of the effects of preventive intervention as such, by studying the ways in which the adverse effects of deprivation are mitigated or mediated. What are the mechanisms and the processes that influence changes in behaviour of children? Factors that need to be taken into consideration include, first, the prevention programme itself and, second, a range of "primary prevention" factors, including the characteristics of the social and family environment. Previous and current work has led us to focus on some home or family factors that represent either deprivation (Kolvin et al., 1989) or those processes that may underpin or mediate the effects of deprivation (Charles et al., 1989). The third type of factor to be considered concerns the schools: such factors comprise

- intake factors, representing those characteristics of the school catchment area;

- the impact of the quality of organisation and academic programme of the school environment (Rutter et al. 1979);

- the social characteristics and climate of the school (Moos, 1978; Kolvin et al., 1981).

Aims of the Study

The main intention of the current project was to identify and focus on infant schools in deprived inner-city areas and to evaluate the impact of play group therapy (PGT) upon children living in deprived homes. Inevitably, any seriously deprived group includes a high proportion of children who are maladjusted or at risk of becoming maladjusted. The purpose was to compare a treated group with a control group of deprived children not receiving this form of help. If effective, the specifics of PGT could be taught to practicing professionals from a range of disciplines and this could be linked with supervised training.

Another aim of our study, with specific reference to deprivation, has been to study changes in behaviour over time of children in the inner city and to study those factors that are possibly related to the extent and direction of change. We particularly wished to ascertain whether, and to what extent, the child was influenced by the two principal environments—home and school—and whether intervention played a part in affecting the extent and/or the direction of change in behaviour.

In addition, we were concerned with identifying the mechanisms and processes which influence change in behaviour. In the family, we monitored deprivation and also examined the potential mitigating effects of mother's self-esteem, of mother's good coping skills, of evidence of mother being overwhelmed by her adverse life experiences, and the levels of maternal care and stimulation given to the child. In the school, we considered whether there may be "catchment area" differences between schools, and whether between-school differences of change in behaviour could be attributed to catchment area effects.

Method

Behavioural Change

Following our previous research (Kolvin et al., 1981), we used a formula to calculate change in behaviour from the baseline assessment to 12 months later (short term) and 24 months later (longer term). The change index ranges from major deterioration through no change to major improvement. This formula was applied to four aspects of behaviour, namely, neurotic behaviour, antisocial behaviour, hyperactive behaviour and overall disturbance.

Deprivation

Again, following previous Newcastle research (Kolvin et al., 1983 a, 1983b, 1988, 1989), six items of environmental deprivation were defined, with each family being given a score of

0 or 1 for the absence or presence of each. Finally, a composite deprivation index was obtained by summing the scores for the following six items (Kolvin et al., 1989):

1) family dependence on social welfare;

2) poor parental health;

3) marital disruption;

4) poor physical care of the child or home;

5) poor quality of mothering;

6) parental educational disadvantage.

Parental Resilience

The degree to which the family coped with, or were overwhelmed by, their life experiences was operationalised and piloted earlier in the research; this will be reported in detail elsewhere (Charles et al., 1989). In brief, the method consisted of assessing the extent to which families did not adequately identify any problems, understand them, or deal with them adaptively: the themes covered the five main areas of unemployment, finances, marital tensions, family health and child management. Those personal qualities that are associated with family resilience on the one hand, or a sense of being overwhelmed on the other, are the subject of a separate analysis (Charles et al., 1989).

Mother's Learned Helplessness

We were also impressed by Seligman's notion of learned helplessness (Seligman, 1975, 1976). We operationalised this by focusing on three themes: first, the sense that the individual feels that her life direction is beyond her power to control and is in the hands of someone else (*powerlessness*); second, that there is an inevitable determination of her destiny (*fatalism*); and finally, that the individual feels trapped by her life circumstances (*entrapment*). On the basis of the above, we developed an index of learned helplessness, which too was subject to preliminary piloting (Charles et al., 1989).

Mother's Self-Esteem

Self-esteem was measured according to the *Culture-Free Self-Esteem Inventory* devised and standardised by Battle (Battle, 1981). It is a self-report measure of the individual's personal and social self-perception.

The Home Inventory

We used the *Home Observation for Measurement of the Environment* (HOME). This is an instrument with several subscales designed to assess the quantity and quality of psychosocial stimulation and learning opportunities provided for the child within the home (Bradley & Caldwell, 1989). This instrument allowed us to obtain a picture of the nature of the family environment, mother's involvement with the child and evidence of play stimulation.

Family Dysfunction

Measures of family dysfunction as represented by cohesion as well as measures of child-management and child-rearing techniques as represented by indices of punishment, supervision, deprivation or privileges and reasoning were used (Kolvin et al., 1981).

Life Events

Recent life events were studied covering the previous 12-month period. The data were collected and examined using themes from the Life Events Inventory described elsewhere (Goodyer, Kolvin & Gatzanis, 1987).

The Measures of Behaviour

The children in the study were assessed on the Conners (1969) and Rutter (1967) teacher scales on three main occasions:

1) at *baseline* before any child was involved in preventive activity;

2) again at *1 year* after the start of the study;

3) at *2 years* after the start of the study.

In addition, the parents were interviewed about their children's behaviour at the baseline, at 1 and at 2 years after the start of the study, using the *Newcastle Behaviour and Temperament Scales* (Kolvin et al., 1975; Garside et al., 1975).

The Children and the Schools

About 170 children and their families were studied. They all attended seven inner-city primary schools in a deprived area of Central Newcastle. In order to limit the effect of just starting school, at the beginning of the study the children were in their second year of infant school, i.e. they had all completed one full year of infant school and were aged 6 years and some months. Once they were entered in the study, the children were followed up until they reached age 8 and some months. By this time, many children had moved on from infant to junior school. All the schools within the study area were included.

The Economic Climate

The study was undertaken at a time when there were very high levels of unemployment throughout the country. Within our study area, levels of up to 36% male unemployment were recorded in the 1981 census by the OPCS, as cited in City Profiles (City of Newcastle upon Tyne, 1983). However, at the start of the study period in 1985, we found that the main breadwinner was unemployed in over 60% of our inner-city families.

Findings

School Differences

The average change in behaviour of the children in the different schools was examined. Substantial between-school differences were identified which could result from intake factors, differences in school organisation and style of education as well as the social climate of the school. However, as the children were randomly allocated within schools to treatment (preventive activities) or control groups, such school differences are unlikely to influence the treatment programme substantially or differentially.

The Effects of Treatment

Assessment of the effects of treatment proved complex. Children were allocated to "treatment" or "no-treatment" programmes. However, the data still had to be analysed according to the extent to which the children completed the therapy programme and also the extent of deprivation to which they had been exposed. Furthermore, over the period of intervention, there had been industrial action within schools and the effects of this in relation to the therapeutic programme and subsequent stages of data collection are being studied. Fuller details will be reported in subsequent publications.

Home and Family Factors

We are therefore left with the attempt to estimate the importance of home and family factors in relation to changes in behaviour over time. For simplicity of presentation, we start by merely correlating the environmental indices with changes in behaviour in the short term and longer term. The findings are expressed in terms of significance of correlation rather than magnitude at the 5%, 1% and 0.1% levels.

Correlation of Change in Behaviour and Family Deprivation

We correlated the seven measures of family deprivation with short-term and long-term changes in neurotic, conduct-disordered and hyperactive behaviour, as well as overall measures of behavioural change. The composite *deprivation index* representing severity of deprivation usually correlated highly significantly ($p<0.01$ on three occasions) or very highly significantly ($p<0.001$ on two occasions) with behavioural change; the exception consisted of change in neurotic behaviour in the short term. However, this global picture obscures different patterns according to the type of deprivation (Tables 11.1 and 11.2).

1) *Parental ill-health* seems to have significant associations only in the short term, probably reflecting the transient nature of much ill health.

2) The family *dependence on social welfare* is mainly associated with long-term behavioural changes. This probably reflects the more chronic nature of social dependence.

Table 11.1. Correlation of environmental influences and change in behaviour: Short-term effects.

	Neurotic	Conduct	Hyperactive
Social welfare dependence	–	–	–
Poor parental health	**	**	–
Marital breakdown	–	–	*
Poor physical care	–	–	*
Poor mothering	–	*	–
Educational disadvantage	–	–	*
Severity of deprivation	–	***	**

Significance of correlations: * = $p<0.05$, ** = $p<0.01$, *** = $p<0.001$

Table 11.2. Correlation of environmental influences and change in behaviour: Long-term effects

	Neurotic	Conduct	Hyperactive
Social welfare dependence	**	***	**
Poor parental health	–	–	–
Marital breakdown	–	**	*
Poor physical care	–	**	*
Poor mothering	–	*	–
Educational disadvantage	**	–	**
Severity of deprivation	**	***	**

Significance of correlations: * = $p<0.05$, ** = $p<0.01$, *** = $p<0.001$

Table 11.3. Correlation of environmental influences and change in behaviour

	Neurotic ST	Neurotic LT	Conduct ST	Conduct LT	Hyperactive ST	Hyperactive LT
Play environs	–	–	–	–	–	–
Mother/child involvement	–	–	**	*	*	*
Daily stimulation	–	–	**	***	***	***

Significance of correlations: * = p<0.05, ** = p<0.01, *** = p<0.001

3) *Marital dysfunction* seems only to have a relationship with change in conduct disorder and hyperactivity.

4) *Poor physical care of the child* and *poor mothering* tend to have few strong associations but poor physical care is the more prominent. However, as described below, other measures of poor mothering provide a better picture.

5) *Parental educational disadvantage,* unlike parental health, tends to be associated mainly with long-term changes, suggesting that its influences are not transient.

The Influence of Home Environment Factors

The influence of the home environment, as reflected in the availability of a safe play environment, the level of maternal involvement with the child and the availability of daily stimulation for the child, are considered in this section. The findings demonstrate that the mere presence of toys bears little relationship to change in behaviour. Far more important is evidence of *mother's involvement,* but especially her *stimulation of the child.* There are very significant associations with changes in antisocial behaviour and hyperactivity, but not with neurotic behaviour. These findings reinforce hypotheses about the importance of mothering qualities as central mediators of behavioural change (Table 11.3).

The Effect of Maternal Resilience and Self-Esteem

The association between maternal resilience and maternal self esteem, and the degree and direction of behaviour change, was examined. Especially important are findings in relation to the sense of resilience and sense of being overwhelmed. For simplicity's sake, we only provide data on the latter. Five of the six correlations with change in behaviour proved to be very highly significant. This level of association with change in behaviour is superior to that found with the composite deprivation index, which suggests that how families respond to or cope with deprivation is likely to represent an important operative mechanism by which deprivation brings about its effects. Another mechanism may be a feeling of learned helplessness which, on balance, appears to have an association with behaviour change equal to that of the composite deprivation index itself; this is equally true of mother's sense of self-esteem (Table 11.4).

Table 11.4. Correlation of environmental influences and change in behaviour.

A Resilience

	Neurotic ST	Neurotic LT	Conduct ST	Conduct LT	Hyperactive ST	Hyperactive LT
Overwhelmed	***	***	*	***	***	***
Learned helplessness	**	**	**	**	**	**
Self-esteem	*	***	**	*	***	**

Significance of correlations: * = p<0.05, ** = p<0.01, *** = < 0.001

Other Family Factors

Other family factors, such as family cohesion, were also examined but did not give any better association with change in behaviour than did marital disruption.

Recent Life Events

Recent life events that were judged to have a negative impact and a disappointing minor association with behaviour change in the long term.

Child-Rearing Techniques

Finally, family child-rearing techniques were examined. Although at this age parental supervision had only a marginal association (and hence was excluded from the Table), firm management or discipline had a significant association with improvement in conduct-disordered behaviour and hyperactivity, thus suggesting that "firmness" helped to control these behaviours. Deprivation of privileges had less strong associations and appeared to link with improvement in the short term rather than long term—it appeared also to influence neurotic behaviour. However, reasoning with children seemed to have the strongest associations but, again, mainly in relation to conduct-disordered behaviour and hyperactivity (Table 11.5).

Environmental "Explanatory" Variables (Independent Variables) and Change in Behaviour

It is crucial to try to estimate the relative contributions of different environmental experiences in relation to changes in behaviour. For these purposes, two-way analyses of variance were undertaken in an attempt to explore the contribution of prevention on the one hand, and a series of nine environmental experiences on the other. It was found that preventive intervention seldom had an inde-

Table 11.6. Independent effects of explanatory variables over and above deprivation index: 2-way ANOVA

	Change in conduct	Change in hyperactivity
Explanatory Variables (Analysis A)		
Deprivation index	*	–
Resilience	*	**
(Analysis B)		
Deprivation	**	–
Overwhelmed	–	*
(Analysis C)		
Deprivation Index	**	–
Helplessness	–	*
(Analysis D)		
Deprivation Index	**	–
Self Esteem	–	–
(Analysis E		
Deprivation index	**	–
Reasoning	*	–
(Analysis F)		
Deprivation index	**	–
Maternal Stimulation	–	**

Significant effects: * at 5% level, ** at 1% level
Analyses were undertaken on polar groups.

Table 11.5. Correlation of environmental influences and change in behaviour.

B Child Management	Neurotic			Conduct			Hyperactive	
	ST	LT		ST	LT		ST	LT
Firmness or punishment	–	–		***	***		**	*
Deprivation of privileges	–	**		**	–		*	–
Reasoning	*	–		***	***		***	**

Significance of correlations: * = p<0.05, ** = p<0.01, *** = p0.001

pendent significant effect, whereas environmental explanatory variables commonly had significant effects. The results, suggesting that prevention does not contribute substantially to change, must be seen as tentative in view of the technical problems reported.

The next step was an attempt to ascertain which of the environmental variables studied had effects over and above that of deprivation (see Table 11.6). For these purposes, we concentrated on resilience, being overwhelmed, learned helplessness, mother's self-esteem, mother's level of reasoning with the child and mother's stimulation of the child.

The deprivation index had a significant effect in only two of the six analyses in relation to change in neurotic behaviour. (Because these were both at the 5% level, they have not been listed, in all six of changes in conduct-disordered behaviour, but never in the case of change in hyperactive behaviour.) The indices of coping, of a sense of being overwhelmed and of learned helplessness had independent effects either in relation to changes in conduct-disordered behaviour or in hyperactivity. However, in the case of learned helplessness, there are complex interactions that are not easy to interpret. Maternal stimulation also had a highly significant effect in relation to hyperactivity. Although with regard to other changes, self-esteem did not have any independent effects, mother's reasoning with the child had a significant effect in relation to changes in conduct behaviour.

Multiple regression analysis provides a picture of the best predictors (within the same prediction set) of change in the different types of behaviour that were studied. For these purposes, only changes by the 2-year follow-up were used as dependent variables. Table 11.7 provides a summary of the significant predictors. The independent variables were poor coping, overwhelmed, extent of stimulation by mother, parental punishment (firmness), reasoning with child and extent of family deprivation. The commonest significant predictors were the measures of being overwhelmed by, or coping with, adverse life experiences and firmness in the management of the child: the deprivation index only once proved a significant predictor. The only other important predictor was the extent to which the mother stimulated her children.

Table 11.7. Multiple regression analysis of significant predictors of change in behaviour over 24-month period (samples same as in Table 11.6).

Change in Neurotic Behaviour	
Overwhelmed	***
Firmness	***
Change in Conduct Disordered Behaviour	
Reasoning	***
Deprivation index	***
Firmness	***
Change in Hyperactive Behaviour	
Maternal stimulation	***
Overwhelmed	***
Coping	***
Change in Psychosomatic Behaviour	
Overwhelmed	***
Coping	***
Overall Change in Behaviour	
Overwhelmed	***
Firmness	***

All the above predictors were significant at the $p < 0.001$ level.

Discussion and Conclusions

Our findings suggest that any changes in behaviour in infant school children are profoundly influenced by the children's environment. The greater the severity or extent of deprivation, the less positive the change, and vice versa. This implies that the more chronic the deprivational factors, the stronger are the associations with lack of improvement or even deterioration of behaviour in the long term. Most of the discrete deprivations studied were linked in one or other way in the short or long term with changes in conduct-disordered behaviour and/or hyperactivity, but less frequently with neurotic behaviour. However, dependence on social welfare, poor parental health and educational disadvantage did correlate with change in neurotic behaviour. These findings suggest that the politicians' attitude toward social policy may be more important in introducing innovative social and economic measures as a primary preventive tool than any secondary preventive measures by the psychologist or sociologist.

Nevertheless, family deprivation does not necessarily imply that a particular mother's involvement with her child will be poor, nor that there will be poor stimulation of the child, nor that mother will necessarily use "negative" child-rearing or management techniques. Furthermore, it does not imply that they will be resistant to intervention even if such adverse factors are present.

Hence, it is important to attempt to ascertain the *relative contribution* of the environmental influences on changes in behaviour. However, this is not a straightforward matter, as some of these explanatory factors are likely to be at least moderately correlated with each other (multicolinearity). If we allow ourselves to ignore these intercorrelations, we can draw some tentative conclusions.

It would seem that, more important than the deprivation itself, is the *mother's resilience in the face of family and environmental deprivation*, that is, how well she copes with her life circumstances, combined with the quality of involvement, stimulation of her children and the thought she gives to her child-rearing practices. While there may well be some fluctuations in the parents' coping in the face of persistent deprivation—and we need to take this into consideration—unfortunately we only collected information on parents' coping and sense of being overwhelmed, at one point in time. Nevertheless, these measures proved to be quite powerful predictors of behavioural change. This suggests that such fluctuations were not considerable, or at least that family styles do not change substantially over fairly short periods.

In summary, the findings from analysis of variance provide some clues as to the processes and mechanisms by which adverse family experiences bring about their effects. They suggest that the effects of deprivation may be mitigated by the techniques that the mother employs in coping with family problems, her involvement with her children and her approached to child rearing. These must be seen as crucial *protective factors* in the face of family adversity.

The findings from multiple regression analysis reveal that different combinations of predictors emerge as significant in relation to the different types of behavioural changes. It is notable that either maternal resilience or not being overwhelmed by deprivation—or both—are characteristic of all the explanatory variables that proved significant in every analysis, with the exception of change in conduct-disordered behaviour. In these latter cir-

cumstances, the good predictors are reduced degrees of deprivation, which is a circumstance that is likely to be beyond the family's control, and both reasoning with children and dealing firmly with transgressions. In the case of change in neurotic behaviour, the good predictors are not being overwhelmed by life adversity, and dealing firmly with children. The good predictors of change with hyperactive behaviour consist of good maternal stimulation combined with good resilience (coping) and not being overwhelmed by life adversity.

Psychosomatic behaviour has significant predictors similar to those of neurotic behaviour. It is to be noted that it is only change in conduct-disordered behaviour that has so different a pattern of predictors of change— and this is surprising, as conduct-disordered behaviour and hyperactive behaviour are often thought to be similar, if not overlapping, disorders.

As the environmental factors seem to be such powerful influences of behaviour of children in deprived families, if prevention programmes are to be successful in bringing about more permanent changes in behaviour in infant school children, they will have to take such factors into consideration. They will have to act directly on the children, but also influence parental response to environmental experiences. In addition, they will have to give thought to how social case workers can help families to improve parenting and problem-solving skills and also the coping mechanisms they employ in relation to adversity. The schools themselves cannot be ignored— considerable between-school differences have been noted in relation to improvement in child behaviour over time. This suggests that ways need to be sought of optimising school environment as a contribution to mitigating the effects of family deprivation.

Acknowledgements

Acknowledgements to our colleagues Mrs B. Kay, Mrs F. Nicol, Mrs V. Bell, Mrs S. Lyne, Mrs L. Barrett, and Miss L. Jeffrey. Also to the schools and parents of Central West Newcastle and also Miss L. Fellowes for secretarial help. The research was supported by grants from the Mental Health Foundation and the Health Promotion Trust.

References

Battle, J. (1981). *Culture-Free Self-Esteem Inventories for Children and Adults, Manual.* Seattle: Special Child Publications.

Bradley, R., & Caldwell, B. (1980). Home environment, cognitive development and IQ among males and females. *Child Development, 51,* 1140–1148.

Caplan, G. (1964). *Principles of preventive psychiatry.* London: Tavistock.

Charles, G., Nicholson, R., Maier, E., & Kolvin, I. (1989). *An ethnographic study of the factors associated with resilience in deprived families.* In preparation.

Conners, C. K. (1969). A teacher rating scale for use in drug studies with children. *American Journal of Psychiatry, 126,* 884–888.

Garside, R. F., Birch, H., Scott, D. McI., Chambers, S., Kolvin, I., Tweddle, E. G., & Barber, L. M. (1975). Dimensions of temperament in infant school children. *Journal of Child Psychology and Psychiatry, 16,* 219–231.

Goodyer, I. M., Kolvin, I., & Gatzanis, S. R. M. (1987). The impact of recent undesirable life events on psychiatric disorders in childhood and adolescence. *British Journal of Psychiatry, 151,* 179–184.

Kolvin, I., Wolff, S., Barber, L. M., Tweddle, E. G., Garside, R. F., Scott, D. McI., & Chambers, S. (1975). Dimensions of behaviour in infant school children. *British Journal of Psychiatry, 126,* 114–126.

Kolvin, I., Garside, R. F., Nicol, A. R., Macmillan, A., Wolstenholme, F., Leitch, I. M. (1981). *Help starts here: The maladjusted child in the ordinary school.* London & New York: Tavistock.

Kolvin, I., Miller, F. J. W., Garside, R. F., & Gatzanis, S. R. M. (1983a). One thousand families over three generations: Method and some preliminary findings. In N. Madge (Ed.), *Families at risk.* London: Heinemann.

Kolvin, I., Miller, F. J. W., Fleeting, M., & Kolvin, P. A. (1988). Social and parenting factors affecting criminal-offence rates. Findings from the Newcastle Thousand Family Study (1947–1980). *British Journal of Psychiatry, 152,* 80–90.

Kolvin, I., Miller, F. J. W., Garside, R. F., Wolstenholme, F., & Gatzanis, S. R. M. (1983b). A longitudinal study of deprivation: Life cycle changes in one generation—implications for the next generation. In H. Schmidt & H. Remschmidt (Eds.), *Epidemiological approaches in child psychiatry II.* Stuttgart, New York: G. Thieme.

Kolvin, I., Miller, F. J. W., Scott, D. McI., Gatzanis, S. R. M., & Fleeting, M. (1989). *Continuities of deprivation?* London: Gower Publishing.

Miller, F. J. W., Court, S. D. M., Walton, W. S., & Knox, E. G. (1960). *Growing up in Newcastle upon Tyne.* London: Oxford University Press.

Miller, F. J. W., Kolvin, I., & Fellis, H. (1985). Becoming deprived: A cross-generation study based on the Newcastle upon Tyne 1000-Family Study. In A. R. Nicol (Ed.), *Longitudinal studies in child psychology and psychiatry .* Chichester: Wiley.

Moos, R. H. (1978). A typology of junior high and high school classrooms. *American Educational Research Journal, 15,* 53–66.

Newcastle (1983). *Newcastle upon Tyne "City Profiles."* Results from the 1981 census. Newcastle: Policy Services Department, City of Newcastle upon Tyne.

OPCS (1981). *Small area statistics.* London: HMSO.

Rutter, M. (1967). A children's behaviour questionnaire for completion by teachers. *Journal of Child Psychology and Psychiatry, 8,* 1–11.

Rutter, M., Maughan, B., Mortimore, P., & Ouston, J. (1979). *Fifteen thousand hours.* London: Open Books.

Sandford, N. (1965). The prevention of mental illness. In B. Wolman (Ed.), *Handbook of clinical psychology.* New York: McGraw-Hill.

Seligman, M. E. P. (1975). *Helplessness: On depression, development and death.* San Francisco: W. H. Freeman.

Seligman, M. E. P. (1976). Depression and learned helplessness. In H. M. Van Praag (Ed.), *Research in neuroses.* Utrecht: Bohn, Schellema and Holkema.

Chapter 12

The Mental Health of Women with Children Living in Deprived Areas of Great Britain: The Role of Living Conditions, Poverty and Unemployment

Stephen Platt, Claudia Martin & Sonja Hunt

After a brief review of the literature on social inequalities and mental health, we present the findings of a study assessing the influence of adverse living conditions, poverty and unemployment on the psychological well-being of women with children from economically deprived neighbourhoods in three British cities.

Inequalities in Health

Ill-health, disease and premature mortality have always been unevenly distributed in the British population. Recent evidence suggests that social class differences in morbidity and mortality may even be increasing (Whitehead, 1987). In their review of possible explanations for these inequalities in health, Townsend and Davidson (1982) concluded that differences in material conditions and living standards between sections of the population were the major aetiological factors. However, many of the correlates of physical morbidity are similar to those associated with psychological distress and affective disorder, namely, poor housing, unemployment and poverty.

Gender, Social Class and Mental Health

Regardless of whether the study samples comprise patients being treated by a psychiatrist or "cases" identified in random community populations, women have approximately twice the rate of affective disorder compared to men (Wing & Hailey, 1972; Varheit et al., 1973; Gove & Tudor, 1973; Weissman & Klerman, 1977; Bebbington, et al., 1981). In general practice populations, women are also more likely to be prescribed psychotropic medication (Cooperstock, 1978).

An association between low social class and psychological disturbance has been demonstrated in a large number of community studies (Dohrenwend & Dohrenwend, 1969; Comstock & Hesling, 1976; Hunt et al., 1985). This social class difference is also apparent when the index of mental ill health is psychiatric consultation or admission. Kangesu (1984), for example, found that admission rates to one psychiatric hospital were six times higher in the two most deprived electoral wards within the hospital's catchment area than in the more affluent wards.

Most studies find the highest illness rates among working-class women. Thus, Brown and Harris (1978) showed that in the 3-month period before the interview, 23% of working class women met the criteria for psychiatric "caseness" compared to only 6% of middle-class women. Of particular relevance is the finding that this social class difference was only apparent for women with children. A study in Edinburgh found that working-class women had significantly higher rates of depression on all three alternative diagnostic systems used (Surtees et al., 1983). However, not all studies confirm these social class differences in the prevalence of depression among women. Bebbington et al. (1981) report case rates of 11.1% and 17.5% for middle- and working-class women, respectively, a nonsignificant difference. This apparently discrepant result may be accounted for, at least in part, by differences in sampling and the classification of women's occupations.

The Social Aetiology of Depression

Life Events

Threatening or unpleasant life events have been shown to play a crucial role in the development of depression (Brown et al., 1975; Costello, 1982). Differential exposure to stressful life events also appears to explain, in part, gender and social class differences in the prevalence of depression (Brown et al., 1975). Brown and Harris (1978) found that although working-class women experienced a greater number of severe life events overall, the differences in life event experience between them and middle-class women were limited to four particular domains—housing, their partner's job, finance and marriage. Working-class women, moreover, appeared to be particularly vulnerable in that they were more likely to break down after a crisis event. This, in turn, was found to be related to the quality of their emotional relationships, the number of young children in the home and whether the woman was in paid employment outside the home. Low social class is more associated with various indices of material deprivation, such as poorer housing, unemployment and low income. Life events are often the end result or focus of long-term difficulties or problems rather than discrete occurrences, and it is these difficulties that are, perhaps, the significant factors.

Employment and Nonemployment

That the social class differences in Brown and Harris' (1978) study were limited to women with children suggests that aspects of motherhood may be particularly stressful for working-class women. Bebbington et al. (1981), however, argue that it is the exclusion of many women with children from the paid work-force which underpins the link between motherhood and depression. That is, it is not aspects of motherhood per se, but the consequences of that role for many women.

Unemployment and its sequelae have been associated with both poor mental and physical health. Indeed, analysis of unemployment and mortality rates in the OPCS Longitudinal Study found that suicide was among the main causes of an increased mortality rate among the unemployed (Moser et al., 1984). Other studies have linked parasuicide and suicide with unemployment in both men and women (Hawton et al., 1988; Platt & Kreitman, 1985; Platt, 1984, 1986). Although there is now considerable evidence to demonstrate the negative effects of unemployment on mental health (Warr, 1984), most studies have concentrated on men and, with some exceptions, have not considered the somewhat different position of women with respect to employment outside the home.

A recent study of women with children did not, however, find a striking effect for paid employment on their mental well-being (Parry, 1986). This contrasts with an earlier study, in Edinburgh, which did observe an association between psychiatric disorder in women and employment status (Surtees et al., 1983). The benefits of employment outside the home for women—for example, money, variety, temporal structure, social contacts and personal identity (Warr, 1984)—may only be of importance when social, financial and psychological needs are not met within the domestic role (Warr & Parry, 1982). Thus, the particular vulnerability of working-class women with children and without paid employment may be related to their possibly more segregated gender roles, fewer opportunities to make contact with family and friends because of their location on peripheral isolated estates combined with transport problems (Hunt, 1989), and the generally greater adversity they face in the course of their daily lives. However, financial strain, an obvious concomitant of nonemployment for those with no other or only minimal financial support (for example, single mothers or those whose partners are also either unemployed or on a low wage), is strongly associated with psychological distress (Warr, 1984). Financial difficulty was found to be a major factor associated with the development of depression in pregnancy (Martin et al., 1989).

Housing Conditions

The rapid extension of the public housing sector in the post-war years led to a great increase in both inappropriate and inadequate housing. Families with young children were often placed in blocks of flats on isolated estates with few facilities for the children or their mothers. Although slum clearance was, and still is, badly needed, the mass movement into new insensitively planned housing estates frequently resulted in the disruption of existing communities and the dislocation of family networks (Freeman, 1982). A number of studies have shown that aspects of housing and living conditions are related to poor mental health and psychiatric illness. In the 1950s, one study found there to be higher rates of "neurosis" and psychiatric admission among adults living in high-rise flats compared with those living in traditional houses on the same estate (Martin et al., 1957). The evidence suggested that these differences were unlikely to be due to factors such as stress associated with the move to the estate, but rather were related to housing type. A later study also observed links between psychiatric consultation and residence in a high-rise dwelling (Fanning, 1967).

Although a recent study of council house residents in Newcastle also found that living in high-rise flats was associated with raised levels of distress, the main effect on mental health was area of residence (Byrne et al., 1986). The researchers found that those living in the worst neighbourhoods—for example, those classed as "difficult to let"—had the poorest psychological health. Similarly, a comparison of two deprived estates in Belfast found that children and adults living on one of the estates (Divis) reported more psychological distress (Blackman et al., 1989). While the two estates were both economically "deprived," the housing and the facilities on the control estate (Twinbrook) were regarded locally as considerably better than those on Divis. The authors argue that the health differences between the two estates are an ". . . extreme manifestation of a wider problem of ill health in low income, 'mass housing' areas." Inevitably, housing conditions, housing type and area of residence are inter-related. There is, however, a lack of data on the specific effects of conditions within the home upon residents' physical and mental health. Moreover, poor housing is just one aspect of material deprivation and often exists within a complex of social adversity. The present study explores in some detail how these different factors interrelate and assesses their combined and independent influence on women's psychological well-being.

Background to the Present Study

In 1986 we carried out a preliminary study of a random sample of council-owned residences in a deprived area of Edinburgh. In the course of a structured interview, a profile of the physical and mental health of all adults and children was obtained. Emotional symptoms ("nerves," "headache") were significantly more prevalent among children in damp houses (especially where mould was also found), while the emotional reaction scores on the Nottingham Health Profile were significantly raised among adult respondents in damp houses (Martin et al., 1987). These findings suggested a relationship between damp/mouldy housing and mental health not previously reported in the literature. However, the number of households in the study was rather small, thus preventing a full analysis of the role of other socio-economic influences on mental health. Accordingly, funds were sought and obtained to carry out a larger-scale more detailed investigation. Once again our major objective was to assess the health impact of living in damp and mouldy dwellings. (For a summary of major findings which focuses upon adverse living conditions, see Platt et al., 1989.) On this occasion, however, we were also concerned to document the impact of other socio-economic factors on health status. To that end we ensured that the sample size was sufficiently large, and that a valid and reliable measure of psychological distress was included in the research protocol. In this chapter, we report findings concerning the relationship between adverse housing conditions, low income, nonemployment and mental health among 823 women with children living in local authority housing estates.

Method

Subjects

The study was conducted during the period February to April 1988 in Edinburgh, Glasgow and London. Within each city, discrete geographical areas of public housing were identified in which

1) families with young children predominated;

2) the prevalence of damp housing was thought to be in the range of 25–50% of total dwellings;

3) socio-economic status was likely to be fairly homogeneous;

4) housing types and building structures, including any renovations, could be clearly specified.

Only households with at least one child aged under 16 years were eligible for inclusion in the study. The intention was to achieve a sample of 500 eligible households in Edinburgh, the same in Glasgow and a sample of 200 in London. Depending on the total number of dwellings in the area, a random sample of addresses was drawn.

Surveys

The *Health Survey* was a revised version of that used by Martin et al. (1987). In the course of a structured interview, the respondent (wherever possible the female householder) was asked to complete the 30-item version of the *General Health Questionnaire* (GHQ) (Goldberg, 1972) and was also administered a series of checklists concerning her own and her children's symptomatic health status during the past two weeks. In addition, detailed information was sought on background characteristics of the household, housing conditions and facilities, and other health-related behaviours. The *house-conditions survey* was conducted by two surveyors who assessed the presence and severity of dampness and mould growth in the dwelling. Surveyors and health survey interviewers were blind to each other's findings.

Analysis

The standard 0/0/1/1 system was used to score the GHQ. Two dependent variables were derived from these data: a total score (range 0–30), computed by adding the scores of individual items, which served as a continuous measure of psychological distress; and a categorical indicator of possible psychiatric caseness (scoring 5 or more; a score of less than 5 was taken to signify probable noncaseness). Since total GHQ scores were abnormally distributed and widely dispersed about the mean, they were transformed to base-10 logarithms. Significance levels given in this paper relate to the transformed data, but for ease of exposition original values are provided. (It should be noted that significance levels were virtually identical for original and transformed data.)

The main independent variables used in the present analysis consisted of a subjective assessment of damp or mould in the dwelling ("no"/"yes"), the respondent's economic position ("not employed"/"employed") and net weekly household income per person (under £ 18/£ 18–28/over £ 28). Additional independent variables included the respondent's civil state ("not married"/"married"), paid employment in the household ("nobody employed"/"somebody employed"), overcrowding (>1.5 person per room) and highest social class of any household member ("manual"/ "nonmanual"). It was predicted that poorer mental health would be associated with adverse housing conditions, unemployment/ economic inactivity, low income, living without a partner, overcrowding and manual social class.

Univariate analyses of the relationship between each independent variable and dependent variables were carried out by means of t-tests and one-way analyses of variance (transformed GHQ score) or the chi-square test (GHQ caseness). Subsequently, multivariate analyses were performed: where the response variable was binary/categorical, logistic linear regression analysis was used (Baker & Nelder, 1978); for metric response variables, we employed analysis of variance (SPSS Inc., 1983).

Results

Response Rates

Of 1220 households with children eligible for inclusion in the study, a health interview was secured in 891 (73.0%); the refusal rate was 12.8% and the noncontact rate 14.2%. In 840 households the respondent was a woman. All subsequent analyses are based on the 823 women who received a health interview and also completed the GHQ.

Characteristics of the Sample

The sociodemographic features of the sample are summarised in Table 12.1. The typical respondent was married or cohabiting with one or two children aged under 12 years of age, and had been living at the same address for at least three years (mean = 5.7 years, s.d. 5.1). One in six respondents reported living in overcrowded circumstances, while nearly three-quarters claimed that the dwelling was damp and/or subject to visible mould growth.

Table 12.1. Characteristics of the sample (maximum N = 823; percentages based on actual N available).

	No.	%
Married/cohabiting	823	61.6
1 or 2 children only	823	77.4
Oldest child aged <12	823	71.2
Same address >3 years	810	66.4
Overcrowded conditions	823	17.7
Dampness or mould	823	71.1
"Manual" social class	673	69.9
Not in paid employment	821	73.1
No one employed in household	823	53.1
Weekly disposable income <£ 80	786	48.7

About a quarter of the respondents were in paid employment; the majority (70%) were economically inactive ("housewives"), and only 3% considered themselves to be unemployed. In over half the households, there was nobody in paid employment (i.e. the sole source of income was state benefits). In about half the households the net disposable weekly income was under £ 80 per week.

Tables 12.2. Correlates of GHQ caseness (Scoring 5+).

	% cases	Significance
Total Sample	43.1	–
Civil state		
Married (n = 576)	36.7 ⎫ 37.3	χ^2 = 20.2; 5df
Cohabiting (n = 60)	41.7 ⎭	p<0.002 (all categories)
Single (n = 125)	52.0 ⎫	
Separated (n = 107)	50.5 ⎬ 52.5	χ^2 = 17.9; 1df
Divorced (n = 71)	57.7 ⎪	p<0.001 (married,
Widowed (n = 13)	46.2 ⎭	cohab vs. others)
Economic position		
Employed (n = 219)	32.0	χ^2 = 16.7; 2df, p<0.001 (all categories)
Economically inactive (n = 576)	46.9 ⎫ 47.3	χ^2 = 14.9; 1df
Unemployed (n = 26)	57.7 ⎭	p<0.001 (employed vs. others)
Employment in household		
Nobody employed (n = 437)	49.7	χ^2 = 15.6; 1df
Somebody employed (n = 386)	35.8	p<0.001
Reported damp or mould in household		
No (n = 238)	30.7	χ^2 = 20.5; 1df
Yes (n = 585)	48.2	p<0.001
Net Weekly Household Income per Person		
Under £ 18 (n = 218)	50.0	χ^2 = 8.4; 2df
£ 18–£ 28 (n = 291)	44.0	p<0.02
Over £ 28 (n = 265)	37.0	

At least two-thirds of respondents for whom information was available could be classified as belonging to a manual social class. However, it should be noted that social class data on 150 households (18.2%) were missing. Compared to households for which it was possible to assign a social class rating, these unclassified households were significantly more likely to contain an unsupported woman who was not in paid employment and who lived on a very low level of income. If this unclassified group is assigned to the manual category, then manual households constitute 74.8% of the sample.

Correlates of GHQ Caseness

Significant correlates of GHQ caseness are presented in Table 12.2. Overall 43.1% of the sample achieved a score of 5 or more on the GHQ. In respect of civil state, the lowest proportion of cases was found among the married (36.7%), the highest among the divorced (57.7%). The significant difference between the various civil states mainly reflected a clear division between those living with and without a steady partner: the percentage of cases was 37.3% and 52.5%, respectively. Economic position was significantly associated with GHQ caseness, with the fewest cases among the employed and the most among the unemployed. When employment in the household was considered, a significantly higher proportion of respondents in households living solely on state benefits score five or more on the GHQ, compared to those living in a household dependent (at least in part) on income obtained from employment. Caseness was also negatively associated with income level, whether defined as an amount per person in the household (as shown in Table 12.2) or as an overall amount per household. Finally, a greater proportion of respondents in households reported to be suffering from damp or mould growth were likely to be psychiatric cases compared to those living in dry dwellings.

There was no evidence of significant variation in GHQ caseness by household size (number of adults, number of children), age of oldest child, overcrowding or area of residence (Glasgow/Edinburgh/London). Among those

given a social class rating, there was no difference in the proportions of cases in non-manual and manual occupation households. However, there were significantly more cases in households without a class rating (54.0%) than in households with a class rating (40.7%) ($\chi^2 = 8.29$, 1 d.f., p = 0.004).

A multivariate logistic regression analysis was undertaken in order to assess the relationship between housing conditions, respondent's economic position, respondent's civil state and household income on GHQ caseness. Civil state was included because of the strong association with the dependent variable revealed in the univariate analysis. Social class could not be included because of the frequency of missing data (see above). Respondent's rather than household economic position was chosen on the basis of preliminary multivariate analyses showing that it was more powerfully associated with the dependent variable. Because of missing data on one or more of the four independent variables, the N for this analysis was reduced to 773. The proportions of included and excluded cases reaching GHQ caseness were compared. The difference was small (43% versus 40%, respectively) and did not reach statistical significance.

Starting with a saturated model, we examined serially the unique contribution of each interaction (controlling for other interactions at the same and higher levels) and each main effect (controlling for all interactions and other main effects). The three-way interaction between income, economic position and civil state was of borderline significance (scaled deviance = 5.9, 2 d.f., p<.10), and the two-way interaction between economic position and civil state was significant (scaled deviance = 6.3, 2 d.f., p<.05). The effects of economic position (scaled deviance = 9.7, 1 d.f., p<.01), civil state (scaled deviance = 13.7, 1 d.f., p<.001) and housing conditions (scaled deviance = 21.8, 1 d.f., p<.001) reached statistical significance, while that of income level did not (scaled deviance = 0.4, 2 d.f., NS). The results of fitting various models is shown in Table 12.3. The "best" (i.e. most parsimonious) model is number 3, which requires only the main effects of housing conditions, civil state and economic position (scaled deviance = 21.3, 20 d.f., NS). The introduction of

Table 12.3. Logistic regression analysis: the influence of housing conditions, respondent's economic position, respondent's civil state and household income on GHQ caseness (n = 773).

Model fitted	Scaled deviance	df	p	Reduction in deviance	df	p
Constant	72.7	23	<0.001			
1. Housing conditions	53.0	22	<0.001	19.7	1	<0.001
2. Housing conditions + civil state			compared to model 1:			
	34.1	21	<0.05	18.9	1	<0.001
3. Housing conditions + civil state			compared to model 2:			
+ economic position	21.3	20	<0.5	12.8	1	<0.001
4. Housing + civil state + economic			compared to model 3:			
position + income	20.9	18	<0.3	0.4	2	<0.99
+ (economic position × income × civil state)			compared to model 3:			
5. Housing + civil state + economic position						
	6.1	11	<0.9	15.2	9	<0.1
6. Housing + civil state + economic position						
+ (income × civil state)			compared to model 3:			
	13.9	16	<0.7	7.4	4	<0.20

Thus, best fitting model is No.3.

Table 12.4. Correlates of GHQ score (statistical tests carried out on transformed data: see text).

	Mean (SD)	Significance
Total sample (N = 823)	6.39 (7.71)	–
Civil state		
Married (n = 447)	5.40 (7.73) ⌐ 5.42	F = 5.99; df 5,817
Cohabiting (n = 60)	5.55 (7.24) └ (7.24)	p <0.001 (all categories)
Single (n = 125)	7.74 (8.10) ⌐	
Separated (n = 107)	7.24 (7.62) │ 7.95	T = 5.20; df 821
Divorced (n = 71)	9.15 (8.64) │ (8.19)	p <0.001 (married,
Widowed (n = 13)	9.15 (10.9) └	cohab vs. others)
Economic position		
Employed (n = 219)	4.50 (6.47)	F = 11.72; df 2,818
Economically inactive (n = 576)	7.02 (7.97) ⌐ 7.10	p<0.001 (all categories)
Unemployed (n = 26)	8.88 (8.81) └ (8.01)	T = 4.57; df 819
		p <0.001 (employed vs. others)
Employment in household		
Nobody employed (n = 437)	7.39 (7.99)	T = 4.66; df 821
Somebody employed (n = 386)	5.26 (7.23)	p<0.001
Reported damp or mould in household		
No (n = 238)	4.33 (6.54)	T = 5.75; df 821
Yes (n = 585)	7.23 (7.99)	p<0.001
Net weekly household income per person		
Under £ 18 (n = 218)	7.38 (7.92)	F = 5.64; df 2,771
£ 18–£ 28 (n = 291)	6.63 (7.86)	p<0.005
Over £ 28 (n = 265)	5.64 (7.57)	

the previously noted two-way (model 5) and three-way (model 6) interactions did not significantly reduce the scaled deviance.

Correlates of GHQ Score

Significant correlates of GHQ score are presented in Table 12.4. The findings are entirely compatible with those reported in respect of GHQ caseness (see Table 12.2). Applying the Scheffe test ($\alpha = 0.05$), the civil state categories which were significantly different from each other were the married and the divorced; the employed differed significantly from both the unemployed and the economically inactive; and the lowest and highest income groups differed significantly from each other. Once again, GHQ score was unrelated to household size, age of oldest child, overcrowding and area of residence. Among those given a social class rating GHQ score was similar in the two occupational groups. However, women in households without a class rating had a significantly higher mean score (8.5, s.d. 8.7) than women in classified households (5.9, s.d. 7.4) (T = 3.26, 821 d.f., p = 0.001).

Housing conditions, respondent's economic position, respondent's civil state and household income were entered into a four-way analysis of variance, with the transformed GHQ score as the dependent variable. The N for this analysis was only 773, due to missing data on one or more of the independent variables. Although the GHQ score among the included cases was somewhat higher (mean = 7.73, s.d. 6.51) than among the excluded cases (mean = 4.58, s.d. 5.90), the difference did not reach statistical significance (T = 1.37, 821 d.f., p<0.2).

Table 12.5 provides a summary of the main findings. After controlling for each of the other main effects, housing conditions ($\beta = .21$), respondent's economic position ($\beta = .13$) and respondent's civil state ($\beta = .16$) were significantly related to GHQ score; household income, however, was not ($\beta = .03$). Although the term for all two-way interactions did not reach statistical significance, two results are worth noting. The interaction between economic position and household income was of borderline significance (p = .069), while the interaction between civil state and household income was significant (p = .048). These interactions are displayed graphically in Figures 12.1 and 12.2, respectively. Figure 12.1 shows that among respondents who are not in paid employment, GHQ score is unrelated to the level of household income. Among those with employment, however, the GHQ score is inversely related to the level of income (the lower the income, the greater the degree of psychological distress). Figure 12.2 shows that in the low-income group GHQ score is unrelated to the presence of a partner,

Table 12.5. Analysis of variance: influence of housing conditions, respondent's economic position, civil state & household income on GHQ score (N = 773).

Source of variation	F	Significance of F	β*
Main effects	15.58	0.000	
Housing conditions	36.21	0.000	0.21
Economic position	11.84	0.001	0.13
Civil state	19.48	0.000	0.16
Household income	0.32	0.729	0.03
Two-way interactions	1.62	0.106	
Economic position × Income	2.69	0.069	
Civil state × Income	3.04	0.048	
Three-way interactions	0.75	0.631	
Four-way interaction	0.23	0.793	
Explained	4.27	0.000	

Multiple R = 0.303; R^2 = 0.092
(Interactions with p>0.10 have been omitted)

*Standardised partial regression coefficient

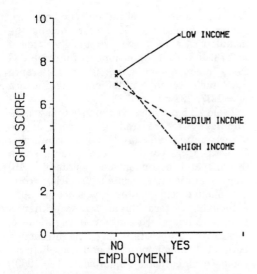

Figure 12.1. GHQ score—interaction between respondent's economic position and household income level.

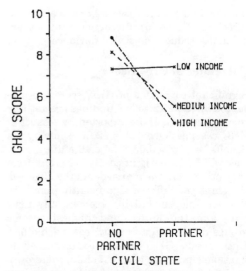

Figure 12.2. GHQ score—interaction between respondent's civil state and house income level.

whereas in the medium- and high-income groups, GHQ score is higher (more psychological distress) among women with no partner. (It should be stressed here that the labels applied to the income groups denote subdivisions of the sample, and do not refer to absolute levels of income; overall, as we have seen, this was an extremely low-income sample.) The model explained 9.6% of the variance of the GHQ score.

Discussion

In this chapter we have examined the relationship between socio-economic factors, housing conditions and mental health in a nonrepresentative sample of women resident in Edinburgh, Glasgow and London. As predicted, there was a greater likelihood of psychiatric caseness and more psychological distress among women residing in damp and mouldy dwellings; subsisting on extremely low incomes; being unemployed or outside the labour market; living in a household where nobody was in employment; and bringing up children without the support of a partner. The failure to find an association between GHQ score/caseness and household social class can probably be explained by the homogeneity of

the sample and the bias in the missing data. However, it is questionable whether any social class scheme based solely on occupation is relevant to a sample in which over half the households are living on state benefits. Contrary to expectation, overcrowding was not associated with GHQ score/caseness.

The relative importance or contribution of housing conditions, civil state, economic position and household income in explaining the variation in GHQ score/caseness was explored in two multivariate analyses. These produced fairly consistent results. Housing conditions, civil state and economic position were each related to the dependent variables after controlling for the effects of other independent variables. There was some evidence that household income interacted with economic position: in middle- and high-income groups having a paid job was associated with better mental health, whereas in the low-income group the relationship was reversed. This result suggests that role problems (strain, conflict, overload) arising out of the enactment of two major sets of duties (in the household and at work outside the home) are more likely to arise when the remuneration for paid employment is poor; multiple roles may be protective when employment is decently rewarded. Household income also interacted with civil state: in middle- and high-income groups having a steady partner was associated with better mental health; in the low-income group, there was no relationship at all between civil state and GHQ score. The frequently noted protective effect of marriage would appear to operate only when basic financial needs are adequately met. At the margins of poverty, marriage offers no protection at all against the impact of daily experience upon mental health.

Since data reported in this paper are derived from a cross-sectional survey of a nonrepresentative sample, it would be unsound to assume that the discovered association between social variables and mental health is causal. The two main types of bias that may invalidate the assumption of a causal link are respondent bias and selection bias. Respondent bias would be present if subjects who were not employed or who lived in adverse housing conditions or who were managing on low incomes tended to exaggerate the extent of their mental ill-health (i.e. score higher on the GHQ) compared to those who were employed, lived in dry dwellings or had higher disposable incomes. We offer two types of indirect evidence against the likelihood of such a social undesirability response set. First, we can show (albeit on the basis of self-reported data) that a significantly higher proportion of GHQ cases went to see their general practitioner about health problems during the two weeks prior to interview (40.5%) compared to non-cases (21.1%; χ^2 = 32.4, 1 d.f., p<0.001). Second, although we have to rely on respondent's truthfulness when informing interviewers about household income, economic activity and even civil state, objective data on housing conditions were gathered by trained surveyors for 597 of the households. In 69% of these (416/597), respondents and surveyors agreed about the presence or absence of damp and mould. In the remaining 31% of discrepant cases, differences between respondents and expert assessments were evenly balanced. Overall the level of agreement was significantly high (κ = 0.26, p<.001). Thus, we can point to some validating evidence for both the dependent variable (mental health) and the independent variable (housing conditions) which is most likely to be subject to bias. We conclude that the grounds for dismissing the

study findings on the basis of respondent bias are somewhat weak.

The other possible source of error is that of selection bias. Poor mental health may exist prior to, rather than be a consequence of, adverse socioeconomic and sociodemographic circumstances. There is no evidence from this study to support such a bias in respect of housing conditions (Platt et al., 1989). The reasonably firm conclusion from a vast literature is that the causal link goes from unemployment to financial strain and poor mental health, and not vice versa (Warr, 1984).

Given the nature of the sample, it would also be unwise to generalise the findings to other populations. However, the surprising feature of this study is the ability of the socioeconomic variables to act as discriminators in relation to the GHQ, despite the fact that the respondents were a fairly homogeneous and extreme group. It could plausibly be argued that a similar study conducted with a more heterogeneous respondent sample would produce even more striking evidence of a link between socioeconomic factors and psychological distress.

Public Health Implications

While mental ill health is experienced by individual people, the factors largely associated with feelings of depression, anxiety or distress are not individual but social. Poor housing conditions, unemployment, financial problems, isolation and lack of supporting agencies and networks are all implicated in mental health such that whole communities because of their social structure and location are vulnerable. Most people experiencing psychological distress do not consult their GP, and when they do, problems are inevitably treated as if located within the individual rather than being seen as a reflection of a social "disease." Parkes (1979) suggests that, because most of the causal factors leading to or precipitating mental ill-health are social circumstances which impinge on vulnerable sections of the community,

> . . . it is therefore reasonable to suppose that the increased focusing of psychiatric resources in the community will begin to make it possible for psy-

chiatrists to work with other community agents to develop preventive intervention programmes. (p. 50)

However, crisis intervention and post-event support, although desirable, require the identification of those individuals most "at risk." How this could be achieved on anything other than a fairly small and localised scale is problematic. Moreover, by focusing on only specific events, the individualising of stress-related problems may be perpetuated.

An alternative strategy is to develop services that are locally based and, therefore, accessible to whole communities and to which people can refer themselves. Some examples of local initiatives within a medical or quasi-medical setting which attempt to provide community-based care that goes beyond, and may prevent, the need for formal psychiatric treatment are given in RUHBC (1989). Typically, they attempt to address mental health problems in the context of the life experiences and

material conditions of particular populations. They acknowledge that the antecedents of mental ill health are largely social and that the "treatments" should therefore incorporate a significant social component. Mental health initiatives like these, however, cannot hope to effect the major societal changes which are necessary to reduce health inequalities, for example, in relation to the high rates of mental distress and depression among women. The primary prevention of mental ill health, by providing an adequate social security safety net for those outside the labour force, by ensuring that all housing (public and private) meets certain minimum tolerable standards, by guaranteeing full employment opportunities for those who wish to work outside the home, by generally reducing inequalities (social, economic, geographic), lies firmly in the hands of government.

References

Baker, R. J., & Nelder, J. A. (1978). *The GLIM system manual, release 3.* Oxford: Numerical Algorithms Group.

Bebbington, P., Hurry, J., Tennant, C., Sturt, E., & Wing, J. K. (1981). Epidemiology of mental disorders in Camberwell. *Psychological Medicine, 11,* 561–579.

Blackman, P., Evason, E., Melaugh, M., & Woods, R. (1989). Housing and health: A case study of two areas in West Belfast. *Journal of Social Policy, 18,* 1–26.

Brown, G. W., & Harris, T. O. (1978). *Social origins of depression: A study of psychiatric disorder in women.* London: Tavistock.

Brown, G. W., Ni Bhrolchain, M., & Harris, T. O. (1975). Social class and psychiatric disturbance among women in an urban population. *Sociology, 9,* 225–254.

Byrne, D. S., Harrison, S. P., Keithley, J., & McCarthy, P. (1986). *Housing and health: The relationship between housing conditions and the health of council tenants.* Aldershot, Hants: Gower.

Comstock, G. W., & Hesling, J. K. (1976). Symptoms of depression in two communities. *Psychological Medicine, 6,* 551–563.

Cooperstock, R. (1978). Sex differences in psychotropic drug use. *Social Science and Medicine, 12,* 179–186.

Costello, C. G. (1982). Social factors associated with depression: A retrospective community study. *Psychological Medicine, 12,* 329–339.

Dohrenwend, B. P., & Dohrenwend, B. S. (1969).

Social status and psychological disorder: A causal inquiry. New York: Wiley.

Fanning, D. M. (1967). Families in flats. *British Medical Journal, 4,* 382–386.

Freeman, H. L. (1982). Housing. In H. L. Freeman (Ed.), *Mental health and the environment* (pp. 197–225). London: Churchill Livingstone.

Goldberg, D. P. (1972). *The detection of psychiatric illness by questionnaire.* London: Oxford University Press.

Gove, W. R., & Tudor, J. F. (1973). Adult sex roles and mental illness. *American Journal of Sociology, 78,* 812–835.

Hawton, K., Fagg, J., & Simkin, S. (1988). Female unemployment and attempted suicide. *British Journal of Psychiatry, 152,* 632–637.

Hunt, S. M., McEwen, J., & McKenna, S. P. (1985). Social inequalities and perceived health. *Effective Health Care, 2,* 151–160.

Hunt, S. M. (1989). The public health implications of private cars. In C. J. Martin & D. V. McQueen (Eds), *Readings for a new public health.* Edinburgh: Edinburgh University Press.

Kangesu, E. (1984). *Springfield Hospital Admission Survey.* London: Camberwell Health Authority.

Martin, C. J., Platt, S. D., & Hunt, S. M. (1987). Housing conditions and ill health. *British Medical Journal, 294,* 1125–1127.

Martin, C. J., Brown, G. W., Goldberg, D. P., & Brockington, I. F. (1989). Psychosocial stress and puerperal depression. *Journal of Affective Disorders, 16,* 283–293.

Martin, F. M., Brotherston, J. H. F., & Chave, S. P. W. (1957). The incidence of neurosis in a new housing estate. *British Journal of Preventive and Social Medicine, 11,* 196–202.

Moser, K. A., Fox, A. J., & Jones, D. R. (1984). Unemployment and mortality in the OPCS Longitudinal Study. *The Lancet, ii,* 1324–1329.

Parkes, C. M. (1979). The use of community care in prevention. In M. Meacher (Ed.), *New methods of mental health care* (pp. 49–68). Oxford: Pergamon.

Parry, G. (1986). Paid employment, life events and social support and mental health in working class mothers. *Journal of Health and Social Behaviour, 27,* 193–208.

Platt, S. (1984). Unemployment and suicidal behaviour: A review of the literature. *Social Science and Medicine, 19,* 93–115.

Platt, S. (1986). Parasuicide and unemployment. *British Journal of Psychiatry, 149,* 401–405.

Platt, S., & Kreitman, N. (1985). Parasuicide and unemployment among men in Edinburgh, 1968–1982. *Psychological Medicine, 15,* 113–123.

Platt, S., Martin, C., & Hunt, S. (1989). Damp housing, mould growth and symptomatic health status. *British Medical Journal, 298,* 1673–1678.

Research Unit in Health and Behavioural Change (RUHBC) (1989). *Changing the public health.* Chichester: Wiley.

SPSS Inc. (1983). *SPSS-X users guide.* New York: McGraw-Hill.

Surtees, P. G., Dean, C., Ingham, J. G., Kreitman, N. B., Miller, P. McC., & Sashidharan, S. P. (1983). Psychiatric disorder in women from an Edinburgh community: Associations with demographic factors. *British Journal of Psychiatry, 142,* 238–246.

Townsend, P., & Davidson, N. (1982). *Inequalities in health: The Black report.* Harmondsworth: Penguin.

Varheit, G., Holzer, C., & Schwab, J. (1973). An analysis of social class and racial differences in depressive symptom aetiology: A community study. *Journal of Health and Social Behaviour, 4,* 921–929.

Warr, P. B. (1984). Job loss, unemployment and psychological well-being. In V. L. Allen & E. van de Vliert (Eds.), *Role transitions* (pp. 31–45). London: Plenum.

Warr, P. B., & Parry, G. (1982). Paid employment and women's psychological well-being. *Psychological Bulletin, 91,* 498–516.

Weissman, M. M., & Klerman, G. L. (1977). Sex differences and the epidemiology of depression. *Archives of General Psychiatry, 34,* 98–112.

Whitehead, M. (1987). *The health divide.* London: Health Education Council.

Wing, J. K., & Hailey, A. M. (Eds.) (1972). *Evaluating a community psychiatric service.* London: Oxford University Press.

Chapter 13

Social Problems, Social Support and Emotional Distress in the Community

Christa Zimmermann-Tansella & Orazio Siciliani

Whilst psychiatric patients frequently have both social problems and psychopathology (Paykel et al., 1971; Paykel, 1973; Huxley & Goldberg, 1975; Weissman et al., 1978), the relationship between social problems and the onset and course of psychological disorders in the community is complicated by mediating interactions between social context, past and present experiences, and personality variables that determine the individual's vulnerability to adversities.

Despite this complexity, a considerable body of data on minor psychological disorders in the community accumulated in the last few decades has confirmed the validity of several findings on the relationship between social problems, social support and emotional distress. In the context of the present study, the following findings and conclusions are of particular relevance:

- As far as social problems and emotional distress are concerned, in community samples there are large proportions of subjects who may have one problem in the absence of the other, despite the significant correlation between the two (Weissman et al., 1978; Dohrenwend et al., 1981, 1983; Hurry & Sturt, 1981; Casey et al., 1985). Social difficulties increase the likelihood of becoming a psychiatric patient independently of the severity of symptoms, so that when subjects with similar level of symptomatology are compared, those with social problems are more likely to contact psychiatric services (Hurry & Sturt, 1981). Social problems are therefore an important risk factor on their own.

- No gender differences have been found either in the number or types of social problems (Hurry et al., 1983; Corney & Clare,

1985), though men who are emotionally distressed have more social difficulties than similarly distressed women (Hurry et al., 1983). This suggests different stress thresholds or differences in the type of stressors experienced by men and women (Cohen & Wills, 1985).

- As far as social support and emotional distress are concerned, most community studies show that in particular the availability of a close confiding relationship has beneficial effects on mental health, either by exerting direct effects or by an interactional effect with adversities (Thoits, 1982; Broadhead et al., 1983; Barrera & Ainlay, 1983; Wethington & Kessler, 1986). These positive effects are reported to be of greater benefit to women than to men (Miller & Ingham, 1976; Henderson et al., 1981; Waring, 1985, Cohen & Wills 1985), although there are recent studies in which the availability of a close confiding relationship has been shown to be unrelated to psychological adjustment in women (Surtees, 1984; McLennan & Omodei, 1988) or related only to that of men (McLennan & Omodei, 1988). This last finding on men confirmed McLennan's and Omodei's hypothesis that a close confiding relationship might have more salience for men than for women, who compared with men have more extensive networks of facilitative relationships and therefore a wider range of support resources in adverse situations.

- While adversity in most studies has been defined in terms of recent stressful life events, the relation between ongoing chronic strains or "major difficulties" (Brown & Harris, 1978) as presented by social problem and the quality of social support is less well documented (Kessler & McLeod, 1985). Social support seems to buffer chronic adversities when it is at least roughly matched with the needs elicited by particular types of social problems (Ullah et al., 1985). The quality of a close confiding relationship therefore may be of different relevance for particular social problems and if support needs differ for men and women, a close confiding relationship may have another impact in relation to social problems and emotional distress in men compared with women.

The aims of the present crosssectional study were

1) to provide descriptive information on the distribution of social problems in relation to social support and emotional distress in a representative sample of an Italian community;

2) to investigate the extent to which some of the findings reported in the literature on the relationship between social problems, social support and emotional distress could be replicated in an Italian setting.

In consideration of the documented sex differences regarding social support and mental health, the data were analysed separately for males and females.

Method

Sample and Procedures

Subjects were 227 males and 224 females, aged 14 and above, who had been sampled from the 1986 register of residents in District 4 of the City of Verona and had agreed to participate. During 1987, they were interviewed at home by trained interviewers using semi-structured schedules of questionnaires and interviews (Siciliani et al., 1988) in the context of a study of mental health and social conditions in South Verona.

Variables

Emotional distress was assessed with the Italian version of the 30-item *General Health Questionnaire* (GHQ-30) (Goldberg, 1972), which has been tested in Italy in two general

practice settings (Fontanesi et al., 1985; Bellantuono et al., 1987) and in a community setting (Lattanzi et al., 1988) and found to have satisfactory reliability and validity coefficients. In this study a respondent was defined as emotionally distressed by the conventional cut-off point 4/5, which in Lattanzi's study gave the best result in terms of the balance between sensitivity and specificity.

Social problems were measured with the *Social Problem Questionnaire* (SPQ) identifying current social problems and derived from the *Social Maladjustment Scale* (Corney & Clare, 1985). The questionnaire contains 33 items concerning ten problem domains such as housing, work, finance, social activities. Each item is rated on a four-point scale, ranging from satisfactory adjustment (0) to very poor adjustment (3). A SPQ total score was derived from the total number of current social problems, counting only those items rated 2 or greater as indicating social problems. Subjects with a total score of 1 or greater were classified as having social problems.

Social support was assessed by a semistructured interview covering several quantitative and qualitative aspects of the social network and support system. For the present study, the measure of the quality of relationship with confidants was used as developed by Brown and Harris (1978) and adapted by Ingham et al. (1986). Four categories were obtained:

1) a close confiding relationship with husband or partner,

2) a similar relationship with some other person seen at least weekly,

3) a confidant seen less than weekly, and

4) no confiding relationship.

Respondents falling into categories 3 or 4 were classified as having poor confiding relationships.

Statistics

The associations between variables were tested by χ^2 test and Spearman's rank correlation test. To analyse the combined effects of social problems and social support on emotional distress, the χ^2 test for trends was applied.

Results

Sample Characteristics

Demographic Variables

The mean age was 40.6 (±17.6) for men and 44.8 (±18.6) for women. Most men (58%) and women (59%) were married. Compared with women (18%), only few men (3.5%) were widowed, separated or divorced, while more men (38%) than women (23%) were single. The majority of both sexes belonged to the manual occupational class (62% of men and 64% of women).

Table 13.1. Social problem domains in a male and female community sample (%).

SPQ problem domains	Men	Women
1. Living, housing	16 (7)	11 (4.9)
2. Work	29 (12.7)	23 (10.2)
3. Financial	23 (10)	24 (10.7)
4. Social relations	29 (12.7)	21 (9.3)
5. Relatives	20 (8.8)	22 (9.8)
6. Marriage	15 (6.6)	24 (10.7)
7. Family	5 (2.2)	10 (4.4)
8. Legal	1 (0.4)	0
9. Living alone	4 (1.8)	2 (0.9)
10. Other problems	7 (3)	4 (1.8)

Emotional Distress and Social Problems

More women (41%) than men (25%) had a GHQ score of 5 or greater ($\chi^2 = 13.7$, df = 1, p<0.001). Social problems were reported by 40% of the men and 35% of the women, with no difference between the sexes in the distribution over the various problem domains

Table 13.2. Quality of confiding relationships of men and women in the community (%).

Quality of confiding relationship	Men	Women
N	227	224
Close relationship with partner (1)	141 (62.1)	139 (62.1)
Close relationship with another person (2)	40 (17.6)	43 (19.2)
Confidant seen less than weekly (3)	1 (0.4)	5 (2.2)
No confiding relationship (4)	45 (19.8)	37 (16.5)

(Table 13.1). Considering only men and women with GHQ scores of five and greater, men have about twice as many social problems as women (means of 1.4 and 0.9; t = 2.04, df = 147, p<0.04), although there was no difference in their mean GHQ score (9.16 and 9.28 for men and women, respectively).

Quality of Confiding Relationships

As may be seen in Table 13.2, 20% of men and 16% of women were without a confiding relationship. The quality of confiding relationship was independent of marital status: both married and other subjects had similar proportions of subjects with poor confiding relationships (categories 3 and 4), which were for men 19.7% and 21%, and for women 19.5% and 17.6%, respectively.

Social Problems and Emotional Distress

Table 13.3 shows that there is considerable overlap of similar size in both sexes of social

Table 13.3. Emotional distress and social problems in men and women in the community (%).

N	Men 227	Women 224	χ^2 df = 1
Emotionally distressed	21 (9.3)	47 (20.9)	10.2**
With social problems	53 (23.3)	34 (15.2)	4.3*
Emotionally distressed and with social problems	35 (15.4)	45 (20.1)	NS
Without emotional distress and without social problems	117 (51.5)	98 (43.8)	NS

*p<0.05, **p<0.001

Table 13.4. The proportions of subjects with emotional distress associated with social problems and social support.

	N	GHQ>5 (%)	χ^2, df = 1
Men			
With social problems	88	35 (40)	
Without social problems	139	21 (15)	16.3*
Good social support	181	42 (23)	
Poor social support	46	14 (30)	NS
Women			
With social problems	79	45 (57)	
Without social problems	145	47 (32)	11.7*
Good social support	182	76 (42)	
Poor social support	42	16 (38)	NS

*p<0.001

problems and emotional distress. Emotional distress without associated social problems is more frequent in women, while social problems without associated emotional distress are more frequent in men. The association between social problems and emotional distress is highly significant (Table 13.4): men and women with social problems are more often distressed than those without social problems. There is also a linear relation between the number of social problems and the GHQ total score. The rank correlation coefficients were .21 and .27 (p<0.01) for men and women, respectively.

When examining the single problem domains, in men six problem domains were associated significantly with a GHQ score of 5 and above. The strongest association emerged for marriage problems (χ^2 = 13, df = 1, p<0.001), with 66% of men with marriage problems being also emotionally distressed compared with 21% of the men without such problems. The next strongest association regarded financial problems (χ^2 = 12.26) followed by housing problems (χ^2 = 7.6), social relationship problems (χ^2 = 6.17), work problems (χ^2 = 4.1) and problems with relatives (χ^2 = 3.8).

The only problem domain to be associated with emotional distress in terms of a GHQ score of 5 and above in women regarded social relationship problems, where 86.7% of the women with such problems were emotionally distressed compared with 37% of those without (χ^2 = 16.85, df = 1, p<0.001).

Social Support and Emotional Distress

As can be seen in Table 13.4, subjects with good confiding relationships and subjects with poor confiding relationships do not differ significantly in the proportion of subjects with emotional distress. The low correlation coefficients (ρ) between quality of confiding relationships and the GHQ total score, which were .05 for men and .04 for women, confirm this lack of association.

Interaction Effect Between Social Problems and Social Support on Emotional Distress

In Table 13.5 it can be seen that among men without social problems those with poor social support are about twice as often emotionally distressed as those with good social support. This difference, however, does not reach significance. Among women without social problems the opposite trend is observed: those with good social support have about twice the proportion of subjects with emotional distress compared with those with poor social support, but also this difference does not reach significance. No difference in the proportion of emotionally distressed is observed between subjects with good and subjects with poor support, who report social problems.

The correlation coefficients (ρ) between the number of social problems and the quality of confiding relationship, although significant for both sexes, were of modest size (.16 and

Table 13.5. The proportions of subjects with emotional distress associated with social support in men and women without social problems and with social problems.

| | Without social problems | | With social problems | |
	N	GHQ>5 (%)	N	GHQ>5 (%)
Men				
Good social support	120	17 (14)	29	10 (35)
Poor social support	17	4 (24)	61	25 (41)
χ^2, df = 1		NS		NS
Women				
Good social support	126	44 (35)	56	32 (57)
Poor social support	19	3 (16)	23	13 (56)
χ^2, df = 1		NS		NS

.24 for men and women, respectively). This association is confirmed also when dichotomising the two variables (χ^2 = 7.67 and 5.29, df = 1, for men and women, respectively). This contamination of the two measures, as could have been expected, is mainly due to personal relationship problems: in men these were problems with relatives and marriage problems that were significantly associated with a poor confiding relationship (χ^2 = 7.67 and 5.29, df = 1, respectively). In women, only marriage problems were associated with poor confiding relationship (χ^2 = 7.74).

For the χ^2 trend analysis, the four cells resulting from the combination of social problems and quality of confiding relationship (Table 13.5) were ranged from the least favourable situation of social problems and poor confiding relationship (SPQ+,SS–) to the most favourable situation of absence of social problems and good confiding relationship (SPQ–,SS+). Figure 13.1 shows that for men the probability of being emotionally distressed decreases proportionally from the

least favourable situation (41%) to the most favourable (14%), while in women no such consistent pattern could be detected, the decrease in the proportion of emotionally distressed being due only to the absence of social problems. In fact the non-linear trend was significant for women only (χ^2 = 7.34, df = 2, p<059).

Discussion

The principal findings of our study may be conveniently discussed under three headings: comparison of the Italian sample with other community samples; social problems in relation to emotional distress and confidant quality in relationship to emotional distress. We shall also discuss some possible implications of these findings for preventive strategies and service organisation.

Figure 13.1. The proportions of subjects with emotional distress according to combined measures of social problems (SPQ) and social support (SS).

SPQ+ = presence of social problems

SPQ– = no social problems

SS+ = good social suupport

SS– = poor social support

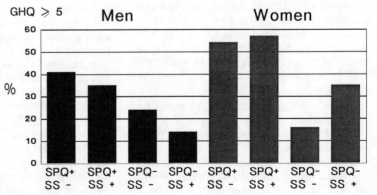

Comparison With the Findings of Other Community Studies

Examining the frequency distributions of the three measures taken into consideration, marked similarities with community samples of other countries emerged. Emotional distress, defined by the conventional GHQ-30 cut-off score 4/5, was significantly more frequent in women than in men. This is consistent with most findings on sex differences in minor psychiatric morbidity in general populations (Briscoe, 1982; Jenkins, 1985). About two-thirds of men and women reported no major social problems; similar proportions, using the same measure, were found by Corney and Clare (1985) in a random sample from the doctors list. Also, the social problem profile of Italian subjects showed no sex difference and was again similar to that reported by Corney and Clare.

About 80% of men and women reported a good confiding relationship, which corresponds closely to the percentages obtained with the same measure for female residents in Camberwell (Brown & Harris, 1978) and in Edinburgh (Ingham et al., 1986).

Social Problems and Emotional Distress

The strong overlap between social problems and emotional distress is of interest. The overlap could be an artifact, because emotionally distressed people might report more social dissatisfactions. This is not likely to have occurred, because if this was so they should have been dissatisfied also with the quality of their confiding relationship, which was not the case.

The strength of the association between number of social problems and GHQ-30 total score can be expressed as the amount of shared variance, which was only 4% for men and 7% for women, but is not too distant from the 10% reported generally for stressful life events and emotional distress (Henderson, 1988). An alternative expression is the relative risk. Men and women with at least one social problem had a relative risk of 2.5 and 1.7, respectively, to be also emotionally distressed. Research has shown that this combination of social problems and emotional distress is closely related to the possibility of

becoming a psychiatric patient. It is therefore of practical interest to know which types of problems are associated with emotional distress. In men, a wide range of problems ranging from material dissatisfactions to relationship problems were significantly associated with emotional distress, marriage problems having the highest relative risk of 3. In contrast, in women only social relationship problems were associated with emotional distress, with a relative risk of 2.3, which suggests that there might be some weakness in social skills associated with emotional distress.

In agreement with the observations of Hurry et al. (1983), our findings based upon this Italian sample of males indicated that males with emotional distress tended to report more social problems than women with similar levels of distress. This suggests that, in men, the alleviation of social problems might be a more important therapeutic intervention than for women.

Close Confiding Relationships and Emotional Distress

For both sexes the quality of the confiding relationship was unrelated to emotional distress in correlational terms as well as in terms of χ^2 tests after dichotomisation of the two variables, nor was the quality of confiding relationship shown to have any mediating effect on the relationship between social problems and emotional distress when examining the relevant partitioned χ^2 interactions. However, when the two variables—social problems and quality of confiding relationship— are combined, the linear trend in men suggests that a good confiding relationship reduces slightly the risk of emotional distress in the presence (of about 6%) and in the absence (of about 10%) of social difficulties. No mitigating contribution of good confiding relationship was detected for women.

There are several interpretations of these findings. Quality of a close confiding relationship is a functional measure of perceived availability of confidant support, which has been repeatedly demonstrated to favour the finding of interactive buffering effects but not of main effects, which are more likely to be evidenced when the support measure reflects the availability of a larger social support network (Cohen & Wills, 1985). Recently, however, it has been shown that perceived availability of a close confidant has protective effects only when it coincides with the perceived adequacy of the confidant support (Henderson & Brown, 1988).

Another possibility is that the availability of a close confidant did not match the support needs elicited by the reported social problems. This seems to be the case particularly in women, where only social relationship problems were associated with emotional distress. This is in agreement with McLennan and Omodei (1988), i.e. for women support from a wider social network might be more important for mental health than a confiding relationship. In men, marriage problems had the strongest association with emotional distress, which would explain the weak mitigating effect of a good confiding relationship that, however, might be supposed to be irrelevant to support needs provoked for example by material or work dissatisfactions. Associational analysis of the single-problem domains might have been more useful than of the dichotomous composite score of social problems, but it would have required larger number of subjects of samples with higher social morbidity.

In synthesis, the presence of social problems reported by Italian community residents was significantly related to emotional distress. In particular, these were marriage problems in men and social relationship problems in women, suggesting different support needs. The quality of confiding relationship had no protective effects on emotional distress, either in the absence or in the presence of social problems, although there was some contamination between the measures of social problems and quality of confiding relationship. A modest mitigating effect of good confiding relationship emerged for men when the two variables were combined.

Some Implications for Preventive Strategies and Service Organisations

Before arriving at possible practical consequences of these findings, we should bear in mind that indications that derive from cross-sectional population studies cannot have immediate practical relevance for psychiatric services operating in the community. At best

they help to set the general framework of these services and to orientate the type of responses to the demands made on them.

None of the interviewed residents with emotional distress had contacted the psychiatric agencies of the area during the year of the interview, and evidently none of them perceived him/herself as in need of professional help. Therefore, the referral to psychiatric agencies would be an arbitrary decision as long as we do not know the natural evolution of emotional distress in the community. It seems very important instead that social agencies and general practitioners in the community learn which social or relationship problems are associated with increased risks of emotional distress. Our findings confirm, therefore, the need to increment the collaboration and exchange of information between psychiatric services and those services that, according to the schema of Goldberg and Huxley (1980), "filter" the emotional distress upriver: social agencies with regard to social problems not yet perceived as a source of emotional distress and primary-care services.

Given these premises, our findings suggest that emotional distress has different origins in men and women and, if necessary, requires different treatment strategies. While emotional distress in men seems to be contingent on conflictual (marriage) situations and social problems of various kinds, emotional distress in women can be less easily traced back to specific problems. The finding that emotional distress in women is unrelated to the quality of confiding relationship but related to dissatisfactions with extended social relationships would suggest, as Henderson et al. (1981) have pointed out, the presence of longstanding personality problems. Therefore, the following intervention strategies may be proposed:

- To be *helped by social agencies with financial and work problems* is important not only because of the solution of a social problem, but also because the risk of emotional distress, which in men is significantly associated with these problems, can be prevented or reduced.

- *Conjoint partner or marriage counselling* aimed at improving a poor quality of confiding relationship would be another helpful strategy to reduce the risk of emotional distress in men. The same type of intervention for emotional distressed women seems insufficient to counterbalance the effects of extended social relationship problems.

- An *individual-centered psychotherapeutic approach* appears to be a more adequate intervention for emotionally distressed women than the promotion of an extended social support system, also because in our cultural (Italian) context the manifestation of emotional distress by women tends to activate spontaneously a great number of supportive persons among relatives, friends and acquaintances.

Longitudinal studies are necessary to understand the impact of these cultural peculiarities on the outcome of emotional distress episodes in the community.

Acknowledgements

This study was supported by the Regione Veneto, Ricerca Sanitaria Finalizzata, Contract No. 176.03.88 to Professor O. Siciliani. The authors thank Dr. Paul Surtees (Edinburgh), who read an earlier draft of the manuscript and gave helpful suggestions.

References

Barrera, M., & Ainley, S. L. (1983). The structure of social support: A conceptional and empirical analysis. *Journal of Community Psychology, 11,* 33–143.

Bellantuono, C., Fiorio, R., Zanotelli, R., & Tansella, M. (19??). Psychiatric screening in general practice in Italy. A validity study of the GHQ. *Social Psychiatry, 22,* 113–117.

Briscoe, M. (1982). Sex differences in psychological well being. *Psychological Medicine, Monograph, Suppl. 1,* 1–46.

Broadhead W. E., Kaplan, B. H., James, S. A., Wagner, E. H., Schoenbeck, V. J., Grimson, R., Heyden, S., Tiblin, G., & Gehlback, S. H. (1983). The epidemiological evidence for a relationship between social support and health. *American Journal of Epidemiology, 5,* 521–537.

Brown, G.W., & Harris, T. O. (1978). *Social origins of depression. A study of psychiatric disorder in women.* London: Tavistock.

Casey, P. R., Tyrer, P. J., & Platt, S. (1985). The relationship between social functioning and psychiatric symptomatology in primary care. *Social Psychiatry, 20,* 5–9.

Cohen, S., & Wills, J. A. (1985). Stress, social support and the buffering hypothesis. *Psychological Bulletin, 98,* 310–357.

Corney, R.G., & Clare, A. W. (1985). The construction, development and testing of a self-report questionnaire to identify social problems. *Psychological Medicine, 15,* 637–649.

Dohrenwend, B. S., Cook, D., & Dohrenwend, B. P. (1981). Measurement of social functioning in community populations. In J. K. Wing, P. Bebbington, & L. N. Robins (Eds), *What is a case? The problem of definition in psychiatric community surveys* (pp. 183–201). London: Grant McIntyre.

Dohrenwend, B. S., Dohrenwend, B. P., Link, B., & Levav, I. (1983). Social functioning in psychiatric patients in the general population. *Archives of General Psychiatry, 40,* 1174–1182.

Fontanesi, F., Gobetti, C., Zimmermann-Tansella, C., & Tansella, M. (1985). Validation of the Italian version of the GHQ in a general practice setting. *Psychological Medicine, 15,* 411–415.

Goldberg, D. P. (1972). *The detection of psychiatric illness by questionnaire.* London: Oxford University Press.

Goldberg, D. P., & Huxley, P. (1980). *Mental illness in the community. The pathway to psychiatric care.* London: Tavistock.

Henderson, S., & Brown, G. B. (1988). Social support: The hypothesis and the evidence. In A. S. Henderson, & G. B. Brown (Eds.), *Handbook of social psychiatry.* London: Blackwell.

Henderson, S., Byrne, D. G., & Duncan-Jones, P. (1981). *Neurosis and the social environment.* New York: Academic Press.

Hurry, J., & Sturt, E. (1981). Social performance in a population sample: Relation to psychiatric symptoms. In T. K. Wing, P. Bebbington, & L. N. Robins (Eds.), *What is a case? The problem of definition in psychiatric community surveys* (pp. 202–213). London: Grant-McIntyre.

Hurry, J., Sturt, E., Bebbington, P., & Tennant, C. (1983). Sociodemographic associations with social disablement in a community sample. *Social Psychiatry, 18,* 113–121.

Huxley, P., & Goldberg, D. P. (1985). Social versus clinical predictions in minor psychiatric disorder. *Psychological Medicine, 15,* 96–100.

Ingham, J. G., Kreitman, N. B., Miller, Mc. C., Sashidharan, S. P., & Surtees, P. G. (1986). Self esteem, vulnerability and psychiatric disorder in the community. *British Journal of Psychiatry, 148,* 375–385.

Jenkins, R. (1985). Sex differences in minor psychiatric morbidity. *Psychological Medicine, Suppl. 7,* 1–53.

Kedward, H. B. (1969). The outcome of neurotic illness in the community. *Social Psychiatry, 4,* 1–4.

Kessler, R. C., & McLeod, J. (1985). Social support

and psychological distress in community surveys. In S. Cohen, & S. L. Syme (Eds.), *Social support and health* (15–46). New York: Academic Press.

Lattanzi, M., Galvan, U., Rizzetto, A., Gavioli, I., & Zimmermann-Tansella, C. (1988). Estimating psychiatric morbidity in the community. Standardisation of the Italian version of the GHQ and CIS. *Social Psychiatry, 23,* 267–272.

McLennon, J., & Omodei, M. M. (1988). Psychological adjustment, close personal relationships and personality. *British Journal of Medical Psychology, 61,* 285–290.

Miller, P., & Ingham, J. (1976). Friends, confidants and symptoms. *Social Psychiatry, 11,* 51–58.

Paykel, E. S. (1973). Social adjustment and depression. A longitudinal study. *Archives of General Psychiatry, 28,* 659–663.

Paykel, E. S., Weissman, M., Prusoff, B. A., & Tonks, C. M. (1971). Dimensions of social adjustment in depressed women. *Journal of Nervous and Mental Disease, 152,* 158–172.

Siciliani, O., Donini, S., Turrina, C., & Zimmermann-Tansella, C. (1988). *A community survey on mental health in South-Verona.* (Research report). Ver-

ona: Istituto di Psichiatria, Universita di Verona.

Surtees, P. (1984). Kith, kin and psychiatric health: A Scottish survey. *Social Psychiatry, 19,* 63–67.

Thoits, P. A. (1982). Conceptual, methodological and theoretical problems in studying social support as a buffer against life stress. *Journal of Health and Social Behavior, 23,* 145–159.

Ullah, P., Banks, M., & Warr, P. (1985). Social support, social pressures and psychological distress during unemployment. *Psychological Medicine, 15,* 283–295.

Waring, E. M. (1985). Measurement of intimacy: Conceptual and methodological issues of studying close relationships. *Psychological Medicine, 15,* 9–14.

Weissman, M., Prusoff, B. A., Thompson, W. D., Harding, P. S., & Myers, J. K. (1978). Social adjustment by self-report in a community sample and in psychiatric outpatients. *Journal of Nervous and Mental Disease, 166,* 317–326.

Wethington, E., & Kessler, R. (1986). Perceived support, received support and adjustment to stressful life events. *Journal of Health and Social Behaviour, 27,* 78–89.

Chapter 14

The Importance of Early and Current Risk Factors for the Development of Psychiatric Disorder in Childhood and Adolescence

B. Blanz, M. H. Schmidt, G. Esser & C. von Busch

Several risk factors are considered to be of importance in the development of psychiatric disorder in children and adolescents: abnormal karyotype, male sex, physical illness, low intelligence, learning disabilities, temperament, adverse conditions during early childhood, life events and chronic psychosocial stress (Detzner & Schmidt, 1988; Minde, 1988) have all been implicated, although the significance of each of their interactions and their relation to developmental phase is only partially known.

A child's development and experiential background is mainly influenced by the early human environment, particularly the interaction between mother and child (Papousek, 1977; Papousek & Papousek, 1975, 1977; Schaffer, 1977). Deficits or conflict, for example, as a result of having a psychiatrically ill mother or because of conditions of extreme deprivation, can lead to abnormal development and psychiatric disorder.

Current psychosocial stress has also been shown to be pathological. According to Rutter (1978a; Rutter & Quinton, 1977) the factors of the *Family Adversity Index* (FAI) increase the risk for children's and adolescents' psychiatric disorder. The factors of the FAI are: father an unskilled worker, an overcrowded family (more than 1.5 persons per room), severe marital discord or an incomplete family, a depressive or neurotic mother, a delinquent father, and one or more children in the family in care. These findings have been replicated (Richman, 1977; Voll et al., 1982; McGee et al., 1984, 1985; Barron & Earls, 1984; Blanz et al., 1989).

The originators of the deprivation theory, Bowlby (1946, 1951), Goldfarb (1943, 1944/

1945, 1946, 1947) and Spitz (1945, 1946, 1954) overestimated the importance of adverse conditions of early childhood development. Early social and emotional deprivation, especially inadequate or inconsistent child care, apparently leads to less serious consequences than postulated by the scientists cited above. For instance, in a follow-up study by Ernst and Luckner (1985), children who once had been severely deprived had normal intelligence, average performance at school and did not show more antisocial behaviour than controls.

The incidence of psychiatric disorder was twice as high as in normal controls, but much better correlated with current psychosocial stress than with early childhood developmental conditions and behaviour. Tizard and Rees (1974, 1975), Dunn (1976), and Bohman and Sigvardsson (1979) report similar results.

Nevertheless, early stress may carry a risk for future development—and may be cumulative. Rutter has shown (1978b) that a single stay in hospital has no impact on social behaviour in later childhood and adolescence, whereas several stays in hospital correlated well with increased risk for psychiatric disorder. (This may, however, have been attributable to the underlying physical illness.)

The present study documents the impact of early childhood stress on the development of children and adolescents and compares it with the influence of current psychosocial stress.

Method

The results reported later on stem from a longitudinal study of psychiatric disorder and cerebral dysfunction in children and adolescents. In the course of the study, 399 8-year-old children drawn from a field sample were thoroughly investigated. Of these, 356 (89%) participated in a follow-up study at the age of 13.

The main purpose of the investigation was to determine the prevalence rate and course of psychiatric disorder (Esser & Schmidt, 1986, 1987a) and of so-called minimal cerebral dysfunction in childhood (MCD; Esser & Schmidt, 1987b; Schmidt et al., 1987).

A comprehensive array of instruments was employed initially and at follow-up. These included structured parent interviews, neurological, neuropsychological and neurophysiological examinations as well as tests of specific skills and abilities.

Expert rating of disorder was made after a 2-hour parent interview. In the second stage of the study, case definition was further supported by an additional adolescent interview carried out with the 13-year-olds. Interviews were conducted by child psychiatrists or experienced clinical psychologists, and afterwards they made diagnoses and severity ratings. Severity of psychiatric disorder was judged on a 4-point scale, with

0 = no psychiatric disorder,
1 = mild or uncertain psychiatric disorder,
2 = moderate psychiatric disorder,
3 = severe psychiatric disorder.

In some of the analyses reported below, severity ratings were dichotomized, yielding two groups of children with (scores 2 or 3) and without (0 or 1) psychiatric disorder. Early potential risks were thoroughly retrospectively investigated in the interviews with the parents of the 8-year-olds. Actual psychosocial stress was assessed from interviews of both the 8- and the 13-year-olds' parents. Early risks were defined as occurring during the first 6 years of life. A distinction was made between environmental and child-related risks.

Environmental risk factors included attitude toward pregnancy and marital status at childbirth, stays in hospital, forced toilet training and changes in caregiver (see Table 14.1). Since stays in hospital lead to separation from the primary caregivers, they were also assigned to the group of environmental risk factors and not to the group of child-related risk factors.

Child-related risk factors included CNS lesions, developmental delays and early behavioral disturbances (see Table 14.2).

An overall score was computed by adding up the environmental and child-related items with the presence of each individual item receiving a score of 1. Final results were obtained by applying Spearman Rank and Pearson Correlations as well as analyses of variance adjusted for unequal cell frequencies according to the general linear model (MANOVA, SPSS-X).

Results

Environmental and Child-Related Early Risks

Frequencies of environmental and child-related early risks are shown on Tables 14.1 and 14.2. There was little correlation between risk factors ($r = .09$ for the environmental risks, $r = .04$ for the child-related risks).

Table 14.1. Environmental early risks (N = 399).

	n	%
Unplanned pregnancy	168	42.1
Pregnancy experienced stressfully	109	27.3
Age of child's mother at birth < 18	39	9.8
Unmarried mother	40	10.0
Stay in hospital >42 days	57	14.3
Stay in hospital at age 1–2 years	99	24.8
Stay in hospital, age 1–2 years >28 days	51	12.8
Toilet training begun <9 months old	99	24.8
Continence during daytime <13 months	34	8.5
Continence during night <13 months	31	7.8
Day care	16	4.0
Mother employed >11 months	67	16.8
Person of reference not (grand)parents	72	18.0
Stay at a health resort	47	11.8

Table 14.2. Child-related early risks (N = 399).

	n	%
Meningitis	11	2.8
Epilepsy	3	0.8
Brain injury	21	5.3
Overreaction to vaccination	13	3.3
First words >23 months	64	16.0
Continence during daytime >36 months	24	6.0
Continence during nighttime >42 months	33	8.3
1st admission to kindergarten >4 years	35	8.8
Exemption from primary school	65	16.3
Kindergarten:		
Acclimatisation >3 months	38	9.5
Separation anxiety	47	11.8
Frequent quarrels with other children	31	7.8
Withdrawal or fear	43	10.8
Disturbs children's group	23	5.8
"Other problems"	49	12.3
Frequent injuries	46	11.5

Early Risks and Psychiatric Disorder in Children and Adolescents

The correlation between early risks and psychiatric disorder (severity grade 2 + 3) at the age of 8 is shown in Figure 14.1. The rate for psychiatric disorder increases considerably with increasing number of risks (environmental risks r = .28, child-related risks r = .28,

p<0.001).

In adolescents we found essentially the same results with slightly weaker effects (Figure 14.2: environmental risks r = .25, p<0.001, child-related risks = .24, p<0.001). The number of risks was also correlated with the number of symptoms.

Interaction Between Environmental and Child-Related Early Risks

Figure 14.3 shows the interaction between environmental and child-related risks from a two-factor analysis of variance. Both types of early risks were entered as independent variables, with the dependent variable being severity of psychiatric disorder. (The overall scores of environmental and child-related risks were dichotomized for all analyses of variance. Cut-off-point for environmental risks was: >5, n = 42; and for child-related risks: >3, n = 44). Besides the two main effects (p<0.001 in either case) there is an interaction effect (p<0.05).

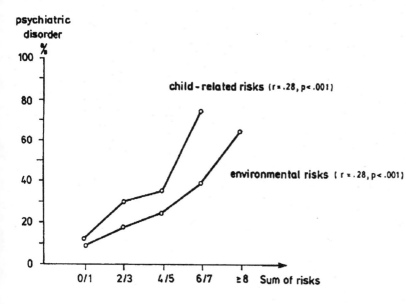

Figure 14.1. Child psychiatric disorder: Environmental and child-related early risks (8 years, n = 399).

Figure 14.2. Child psychiatric disorder: Environmental and child-related early risks (13 years, n=356).

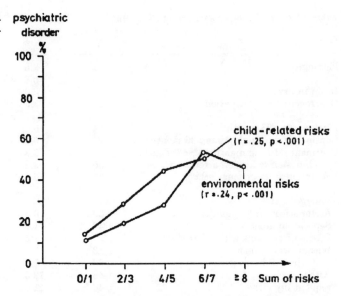

The Influence of Gender

The prevalence rate of psychiatric disorder in childhood and adolescence is widely known to be much higher in boys than in girls (e.g. Minde, 1988). One possible explanation is a gender-specific vulnerability to the risk factors discussed above.

A two-factor analysis of variance was computed as shown in Figure 14.4. The independ-

ent variables are sex and early environmental risks while severity of psychiatric disorder is the dependent variable. Both main effects are highly significant (p<0.001), and there is no significant interactional effect. Environmental stress enhances the risk for psychiatric disorder regardless of gender, i.e. both boys and girls are influenced negatively by environmental stress, but girls show a generally lower morbidity independent of these risks.

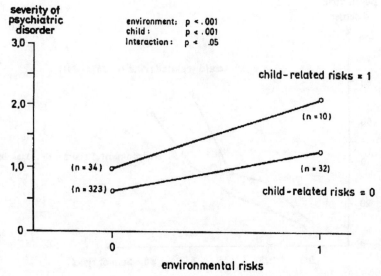

Figure 14.3. Interaction of child-related and environmental risks (8 years, n=399).

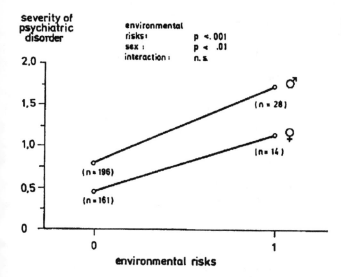

Figure 14.4. Interaction of sex and environmental risks (8 years, n=399).

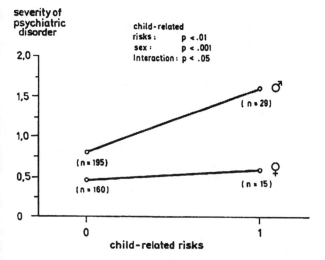

Figure 14.5. Interaction of sex and child-related risks (8 years, n=399).

A significant effect of child-related risks was only found in boys (see Figure 14.5).

The Importance of Early Risks Versus Current Psychosocial Stress

Ernst and Luckner (1985, p. 144) succeeded in demonstrating that "psychiatric disorders correlate better with psychosocial stress than with environmental factors and behaviour in early childhood." We tested this hypothesis on our data. Actual psychosocial stress was measured by means of the FAI by Rutter and Quinton's (1977) method.

As shown in Figure 14.6, current psychosocial stress represents a considerable risk for psychiatric disorder in children and adolescents. The rate for psychiatric disorder increases in children (r = .39, p<0.001) as well as in adolescents (r = .31; p<0.001) with increased current psychosocial stress.

In order to compare early and current psychosocial risks, overall scores were dichotomized (cut-off point: environment <5, child <3, FAI<1) and introduced as independent variables within a two-factor analysis of variance with severity of psychiatric disorder as the dependent variable. There were signifi-

Figure 14.6. Psychiatric disorder and acute adverse conditions in children and adolescents (n=356).

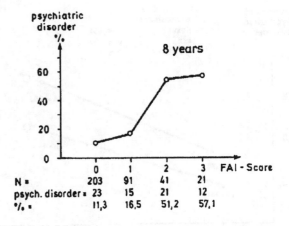

	0	1	2	3	
N =	203	91	41	21	
psych. disorder =	23	15	21	12	
% =		11,3	16,5	51,2	57,1

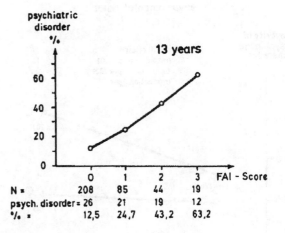

	0	1	2	3	
N =	208	85	44	19	
psych. disorder =	26	21	19	12	
% =		12,5	24,7	43,2	63,2

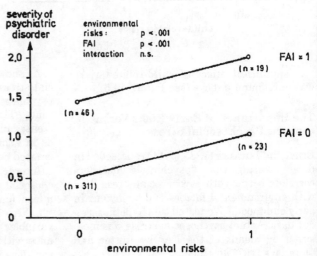

Figure 14.7. The meaning of adverse conditions in early and later childhood. I: early environmental risks and FAI (8 years, n=399).

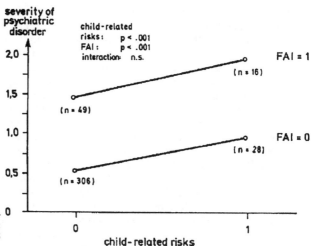

Figure 14.8. The meaning of adverse conditions in early and later childhood. II: early child-related risks and FAI (8 years, n=399).

Table 14.3. The variance explained by early and current adverse conditions.

Adverse Conditions	8 years Variance explained		13 years Variance explained
Early	4.4%		4.9%
Common variance	5.6%	Common variance	3.7%
Acute	8.9%		9.2%
Total	18.9%		17.8%

cant main effects for both groups of early risks as well as for the current psychosocial stress, but no significant interaction effect (Figures 14.7 and 14.8). These results indicate that early risk factors increase the probability for the later development of psychiatric disorder irrespective of later psychosocial stress.

The proportion of the variance "explained" by both early and current stress factors is shown in Table 14.3. Current psychosocial stress accounts for twice as much of the variance as early stress in both 8-year-olds and 13-year-olds. Early and current risk factors taken together account for a similar proportion of variance in both age groups, 19% in the 8-year-olds and 18% in the 13-year-olds.

Discussion

Although halo effects cannot be completely excluded in data collected retrospectively, they are probably weak in the present data set, since the environmental and child-related risks show low intercorrelations. There is a significant interaction between environmental and child-related adverse conditions, so each of them increases the risk for psychiatric disorder—and both do so cumulatively (a point discussed above). This cumulative effect has repeatedly been described in the literature (Rutter & Quinton, 1977; Voll et al., 1982; Rutter, 1985a; Blanz et al., 1989). It means those children who are exposed to several adverse conditions are especially at risk.

Environmental stress in early childhood increases the risk for psychiatric disorder to the same extent in boys and girls. This finding would contradict the theories about sex-related vulnerability as an explanation for the much higher incidence of several psychiatric disorders in boys (Minde, 1988, p. 177). Nor was there a difference between the effects of current psychosocial stress in 8-year-old boys and girls (Blanz et al., 1989). In early adolescence, however, girls seem to be less affected by current psychosocial stress than boys. A possible explanation could be that girls at that age are relatively more mature physically and psychologically than boys. This indicates a sex-independent but maturity-related phase—specific vulnerability to environmental stress as described by Rutter (1978b).

Unlike environmental risk, child-related risk has a gender-related effect: girls, but not boys, with child-related adverse conditions have no increased risk for psychiatric disorder. Perhaps girls are better able to compensate for these adverse conditions.

Early and current psychosocial risk factors were found to have independent effects. Schepank (1987) also found that early risk factors and later "life events" exert only an additive effect.

The overall contribution of early and current psychosocial risks to the explained variance is rather modest (18%–19%) but similar to the 12%–24% found by Ernst and Luckner (1985). West and Farrington (1973) and Tower and Esch (1974) reported similar findings.

Though our results can only be generalized with caution as the data on early risks were collected retrospectively, they do support Luckner's (1985) findings that child and adolescent psychiatric disorders are determined to a much larger extent by current psychosocial stress than by early risks. These findings contradict the hypothesis that adverse conditions in early childhood critically and irreversibly influence further development during childhood and adolescence (see above).

In fact, other studies show that positive changes within the familial environment, even when taking place in adulthood, can neutralize the effects of marked early risks. (Quinton & Rutter, 1984; Rutter, 1985b). This opens up an optimistic vista for prevention, since interventions during later childhood and adolescence may be effective.

Children who experience several adverse conditions are particularly at risk and require particular attention. Since the willingness of the families in question to seek psychiatric support does not increase in proportion to the number of risk factors (Blanz et al., 1989), active measures are needed: social services, for instance, may need to refer children at risk for early diagnostic assessment and intervention (Schmidt, 1984). Once the parents of these children have decided to seek psychiatric help, they should be encouraged to collaborate, and help should be provided for adverse family conditions. This can be done by encouraging a psychologically disordered parent to seek treatment or by giving advice in the case of contrafamilial conflict. In particularly severe cases, a temporary admission to a foster home can be a helpful preventive measure by interrupting destructive family processes.

Of course, the limited explained variance by both early and current stress means that other factors must be considered. Genetic, organic and peer group influences as well as life events need also to be taken into account for prevention to be effective.

References

Barron, A. P., & Earls, F. (1984). The relation of temperament and social factors to behaviour problems in three-year-old children. *J. Child Psychol. Psychiat., 23*, 23–33.

Blanz, B., Schmidt, M. H., & Esser, G. (1989). Familial adversities and child psychiatric disorder. *J. Child Psychol. Psychiat.* (in preparation).

Bohman, M., & Sigvardsson, S. (1979). Long-term effects of early institutional care: A prospective longitudinal study. *J. Child Psychol. Psychiat., 20*, 111.

Bowlby, J. (1946). *Forty-four juvenile thieves: Their characters and home life.* Balliere: Tindall & Cox.

Bowlby, J. (1951). *Maternal care and mental health.* Geneva: World Health Organization.

Detzner, M., &. Schmidt, M. H. (1988). Epidemiolo-

gische Methoden. In H. Remschmidt & M. H.Schmidt (Eds.), *Kinder- und Jugendpsychiatrie in Klinik u. Praxis, Bd. I* (p. 320). Stuttgart, New York: Thieme.

Dunn, J. (1976). How far do early differences in mother child relations affect later development. In B. G. Bateson &. R. A. Hinde (Eds.), *Growing points in ethology.* Cambridge: Cambridge University Press.

Esser, G., & Schmidt, M. H. (1986). Epidemiologie und Verlauf kinderpsychiatrischer Störungen im Längsschnitt von acht bis dreizehn Jahren. In M. H. Schmidt & S. Droehmann (Eds.), *Langzeitverlauf kinder- und jugendpsychiatrischer Erkrankungen.* Stuttgart: Enke.

Esser, G., & Schmidt, M. H. (1987a). Epidemiologie

und Verlauf kinderpsychiatrischer Stoerungen im Schulalter: Ergebnisse einer Längsschnittstudie. *Nervenheilkunde, 6,* 27–35.

Esser, G., & Schmidt, M. H. (1987b). *Minimale Cerebrale Dysfunktion—Leerformel oder Syndrom?* Stuttgart: Enke.

Esser, G., Blanz, B., Laucht, M., & Geisel, B. (1989). *Mannheimer Elterninterview.* Weinheim: Beltz.

Ernst, C., & v. Luckner N. (1985). *Stellt die Frühkindheit die Weichen?* Stuttgart: Enke.

Goldfarb, W. (1943). Infant rearing and problem behavior. *Am. J. Orthopsychiatry, 13,* 249–265.

Goldfarb, W. (1944). The effects of early institutional care on adolescent personality. *Am J. Orthopsychiatry, 14,* 441–447.

Goldfarb, W. (1945/1946). Effects of psychological deprivation in infancy and subsequent stimulation. *Am J. Psychiatry, 102,* 18–33.

Goldfarb, W. (1947). Variations in adolescent adjustment of institutionally raised children. *Am J. Orthopsychiatry, 17,* 449–457.

Kalverboer, A. F. (1988). Interaktionsstörungen: Anmerkungen zur Ätiologie u. Pathogenese. In H. Remschmidt & M. H. Schmidt (Eds.), *Kinder- und Jugendpsychiatrie in Klinik u. Praxis: Bd. I* (pp. 202). Stuttgart, New York: Thieme.

McGee, R., Silva, P. A., & Williams, S. (1984). Perinatal, neurological, environmental and developmental characteristics of seven year-old children with stable behaviour problems. *J. Child Psychol. Psychiat.,* 573–86.

McGee, R., Williams, S., Bradshaw, J., Chapel, J. L. Robins, A., & Silva, P. A. (1985). The Rutter scale for completion by teachers: Factor structure and relationships with cognitive abilities and family adversity for a sample of New Zealand children. *J. Child Psychol. Psychiat., 26,* 727–39.

Minde, K. (1988). Somatische, psychische, psychosoziale u. soziokulturelle Einflüsse. In H. Remschmidt & M. H. Schmidt (Eds.), *Kinder- und Jugendpsychiatrie in Klinik und Praxis: Bd. I* (p. 172). Stuttgart, New York: Thieme.

Papousek, H. (1977). Entwicklung der Lernfähigkeit im Säuglingsalter. In G. Nissen (Ed.), *Intelligenz, Lernen und Lernstörungen.* Berlin: Springer-Verlag.

Papousek, H., & Papousek, M. (1975). Cognitive aspects of preverbal social interaction between human infants and adults. In N. O'Connor (Ed.), *The parent-infant interaction.* Amsterdam: Elsevier.

Papousek, H., & Papousek, M. (1977). Die Entwicklung kognitiver Funktionen im Säuglingsalter. *Der Kinderarzt, 8,* 1187.

Power, M. J., & Ash, P. M. (1974). Delinquency and the family. *Br. J. Soc. Work, 4,* 13–38.

Quinton, D., & Rutter, M. (1984). Parenting behaviour of mothers raised "in care." In A. R. Nicol (Ed.), *Longitudinal studies in child psychology and psychiatry: Practical lessons from research experience.* Chichester: Wiley.

Richman, N. (1977). Short-term outcome of behavior problems in three year old children. In P. J.

Graham (Ed.), *Epidemiological approaches in child psychiatry.* London: Academic Press.

Rutter, M. (1978a). Family, area and school influences in the genesis of conduct disorders. In L. Hersov, M. Berger & D. Shaffer (Eds.), *Aggression and antisocial behaviour in childhood and adolescence* (pp. 95–113). Oxford: Pergamon Press.

Rutter, M. (1978b). Early sources of security and competence. In J. S. Bruner & A. Garton (Eds.), *Human growth and development.* Oxford: Carendon Press.

Rutter, M. (1985a). Resilience in the face of adversity: Protective factors and resistance to psychiatric disorder. *Brit. J. Psychiat., 147,* 598.

Rutter, M. (1985b). Family and school influences on behavioural development. *J. Child Psychol. Psychiat., 26*(3), 349–368.

Rutter, M., & Quinton, D. (1977). Psychiatric disorder: Ecological factors and concepts of causation. In M. McGurk (Ed.), *Ecological factors in human development.* Amsterdam: North-Holland.

Schaffer, H. R. (Ed.) (1977). *Studies in mother-infant interaction.* London: Academic Press.

Schepank, H. (1987). *Psychogene Erkrankungen in der Stadtbevölkerung: Eine epidemiologische tiefenpsychologische Feldstudie in Mannheim.* Berlin: Springer-Verlag.

Schmidt, M. H. (1984). Hirnfunktionsstörungen als Risikofaktoren für die seelische Gesundheit. In G. A. Rudolf & R. Toelle (Eds.), *Prävention in der Psychiatrie.* Berlin, Heidelberg, New York, Tokyo: Springer.

Schmidt, M. H., Esser, G., Allehoff, W., Geisel, B., Laucht, M., & Woerner, W. (1987). Evaluating the significance of minimal brain dysfunction: Results of an epidemiological study. *J. Child Psychol. Psychiat., 28,* 803–821.

Spitz, R. A. (1945). Hospitalism. *Psychoanal. Study Child, 1,* 53–74.

Spitz, R. A. (1946). Hospitalism: A follow-up report. *Psychoanal. Study Child, 2,* 113–17.

Spitz, R. A. (1954). *Die ersten Objektbeziehungen. Direkte Beobachtungen an Säuglingen während des ersten Lebensjahres.* Stuttgart: Klett.

Tizard, B., & Rees, J. (1974). A comparison of the effects of adoption, restoration to the natural mother and continued institutionalisation on the cognitive development of 4 year old children. *Child Develop, 45,* 92.

Tizard, B., & Rees, J. (1975). The effect of early institutional rearing on the behaviour problems and affectional relationships of 4 year old children, *J. Child Psychol. Psychiat., 16,* 61.

Voll, R., Allehoff, W. H., Esser, G., Poustka, F., & Schmidt, M. H. (1982). Widrige familiäre und soziale Bedingungen und psychiatrische Auffälligkeit bei Achtjährigen. *Z. Kinder- u. Jugendpsychiatrie, 10,* 100–109.

West, D. J., & Farrington, D. P. (1973). *Who becomes delinquent?* London: Heinemann.

Chapter 15

The Extent of Nonrecognition of Mental Health Problems in Primary Care and its Effects on Management and Outcome

J. Ormel, M. W. J. Koeter, W. van den Brink & G. van de Willige

Primary care providers come into contact with and treat the bulk of mental health problems (MHPs) in the community (Shepherd et al., 1966; Goldberg & Huxley, 1980; Williams et al., 1986; Blacker & Clare, 1987; Hoeper et al., 1979; Ormel & Giel, 1983; Shapiro et al., 1985). However, there is wide variation among general practitioners (GPs) in their detection rate of MHPs, and a substantial proportion of these problems are not recognised (Blacker & Clare, 1987; Marks et al., 1979; Hankin & Oktay, 1979). As treatment of psychiatric conditions become increasingly effective, nonrecognition might deprive a large group of patients from appropriate treatment of their MHPs. A pivotal issue is, therefore, whether recognition matters in terms of mental health outcome, GP and patient satisfaction, and costs.

Several authors have tried to improve the recognition of MHPs by simply providing information from a screening questionnaire to the clinician (Johnstone & Goldberg, 1976; Zung et al., 1983; Rand et al., 1988; Hoeper et al., 1984; Shapiro et al., 1987). Unfortunately, findings are contradictory, and both positive and negative results can be attributed to various methodological problems (see Ormel & Giel, 1989).

In this chapter, we focus on the extent of nonrecognition of MHPs in primary care and its consequences for management and outcome. In the first part, we present a selective review of studies that deal with the prevalence of conspicuous (recognised) and hidden (nonrecognised) MHPs in primary-care settings, and hence with the extent of nonrecognition. In the second part, we present some findings from our study on recognition of MHPs in primary care. Special attention will be paid to the effects of nonrecognition on management and outcome. In the third part, we discuss our findings and the consequences for secondary prevention and future research.

The Extent of Nonrecognition: A Selected Review with Special Emphasis on Studies Using the GHQ

A considerable number of studies have been published that deal with the prevalence of MHPs in primary-care settings in terms of both standardised assessment procedures (self-report questionnaires and/or [semi-] structured psychiatric interviews) and GP's caseness ratings (e.g. Barrett et al., 1988; Von Korff et al., 1987; Hoeper et al., 1979; Goldberg & Bridges, 1987;). As screening questionnaires, different versions of the *General Health Questionnaire* (GHQ) and the *Symptom Checklist* (SCL) have typically been used. The most frequently used (semi)structured interviews are the *Diagnostic Interview Schedule* (DIS), the *Schedule for Affective Disorders and Schizophrenia* (SADS), the *Clinical Interview Schedule* (CIS) and the *Present State Examination* (PSE). Detailed information on how physicians were instructed to rate the mental health status of their patients is rarely provided.

Despite considerable differences in reported

The research reported in this paper was supported by grant £ 900-556-002 from the Foundation for Medical and Health Research (MEDIGON) and by grant £ 28-1209 from the Prevention Fund.

Table 15.1. Summary of data from studies using the GHQ and GP ratings;

Study	Country	No. of particip. physicians	No. of patients	Prob prevalence % GHQ+	Conspicuous morbidity % GP+
Boardman (1987)	UK	18	920	43	21
Chancellor et al. (1977)	Australia	18	1301	52	14
Goldberg & Bridges (1987)	UK	15	590*	46	28
Goldberg et al. (1976)	UK	1 practice	365	30	36
Hoeper et al. (1979)	USA	n.r.	1072	21	n.r.
Hoeper et al. (1984)	USA	14	1452	28	16
Korff et al. (1987)	USA	45	1242	39	33
Marks et al. (1979)	UK	91	4098	40	31
Rand et al. (1988)	USA	32	520	45	17
Skuse & Williams (1984)	UK	1	272	39	24
Schein (1977)	USA	27	4086	40	18

*only new episodes of any illness; n.r.: not reported

Despite considerable differences in reported prevalences of MHPs, there is strong empirical evidence for the following conclusions:

1) Many GP attenders report substantial psychological distress on self-report screens. Table 15.1 summarises the studies that used the GHQ. The frequency of high-scorers ranges from 21% to 52%, suggesting that on the average nearly 40% of consecutive GP attenders show substantial psychological distress.

2) The prevalence of any psychiatric disorders in terms of DSM-III, RDC or PSE-Catego/ICD is generally lower and varies around 25% for series of consecutive patients. However, there is substantial variation in rates found for specific diagnostic categories. The differences are probably largely related to differences in assessment instruments, differences in classification systems and differences in target populations. Most studies agree that disorders of the depressive type constitute the majority of the MHPs found in consulting primary-care patients. For instance, two American studies with a similar two-stage design and similar assessment instruments (Von Korff et al., 1987; Hoeper et al., 1979), found nearly the same prevalence rate for major depressive disorder, 5.0 and 5.8, respectively. Recently, howver, Goldberg and Bridges (1985) reported almost equal incidence estimates for generalised anxiety disorder and depressive disorders in a sample of 380 *new* illness episodes.

3) There is considerable variation in the prevalence of "emotional disorder" or "psychiatric illnesses" according to GP caseness ratings. Table 15.1 shows rates ranging from 14% to 36%. Differences in prevalence rates between different GPs within one study are also large (Goldberg & Huxley, 1980). In a Dutch study in eight family practices serving 16,863 people, the proportion of patients consulting for mental distress ranged from 9% to 21% across practices, with a mean of 14% (Lamberts & Hartman, 1982).

4) Between 40% and 70% of the GP patients with an anxiety or depressive disorder are not assigned a (specific) psychiatric diagnosis by their GP (Blacker & Clare, 1987; Goldberg & Huxley, 1980; Marks et al., 1979; Hankin & Oktay, 1979; Skuse & Williams, 1984; Casey et al., 1984; Von Korff et al., 1987; Johnstone & Goldberg, 1976; Shapiro et al.,1987; Zung et al., 1983; Hoeper et al., 1979).

However, one should be cautious in interpreting these findings as a solid estimate of the extent of nonrecognition by GPs, because:

1) the fact that a GP did not assign a psychiatric label to a patient does not always indicate that the GP was completely unaware of the psychological distress of the patient;

2) there is no generally accepted definition of what constitutes a psychiatric case in primary-care settings; and

3) there are difficulties in the definition and

measurement of nonrecognition (Clare, 1982; Goldberg, 1982; Vaillant & Schnurr, 1988; Giel et al., 1989).

When no diagnosis is recorded, we cannot tell—unless specifically asked for—whether the GP diagnosed a disorder but did not record it, or recognised psychological distress that did not meet her/his criteria for a (specific) psychiatric disorder, or did not even recognise the psychological nature or background of the patient's complaints. Shapiro et al. (1987) and Jencks (1985) showed that mental health interventions (typically psychotropic drugs) are provided to patients without a record being made of a psychiatric diagnosis, emotional distress or social problem.

In order to standardise the measurement of (non)recognition specific forms that have to be filled in by the physician for each patient encounter have increasingly been used. Apart from (specific) psychiatric disorders, the presence of psychological distress or social problems can be recorded. The applicability of these forms has resulted in higher estimates of the sensitivity of GPs in recognising MHPs. For instance, Von Korff et al. (1987) reported that 69% of the patients with GHQ scores of 10 or above, and 73% of the patients with DIS depressive and anxiety disorders (phobias excluded), were classified by their GP as having an emotional problem.

In their study on patients presenting with new illness episodes, Goldberg and Bridges estimated GP's sensitivity to be 49% and 52% against the diagnostic systems of DSM-III and PSE-ID-CATEGO, respectively. Blacker and Thomas (1988) reported in their study of depression in primary care that, using a forced-choice technique in which a diagnostic form was completed for each patient encounter, GPs recognised 85% of the major depressed, 58% of the minor RDC depressions and 83% of the dysthymics.

The Effects of Recognition on Management and Outcome: A Naturalistic Study

Method

Data collection took place during september 1985 to May 1987 in a Northern province of

the Netherlands (for a complete description of the study design see Wilmink, 1989).

Case Definitions

Three different definitions of caseness were used in this study:

1) *GP case definition (GP+/GP-):* On the basis of all information available to the GP at the time of the index consult, GPs assessed patient's complaints and symptoms as belonging to one or more of 4 categories: (1) physical ailment or illness; (2) specific psychiatric disorder; (3) physical or psychological complaints due to psychosocial problems or stress; (4) other (e.g. comes for certificate for insurance company). Patients with complaints belonging to category 2 or 3 were defined as GP cases and denoted as the GP+ group; other patients were denoted as the GP- group.

2) *GHQ case definition (GHQ+/GHQ-):* The *General Health Questionnaire* (GHQ) (Goldberg, 1972; Goldberg, 1978) is a screening questionnaire designed to identify persons likely to have a MHP characterised by subjective distress. The instrument has been extensively tested in various cultures and linguistic groups including the Netherlands (Henderson et al., 1981; Chan & Chan, 1983; Hodiamont et al., 1987; Ormel et al., 1989). We used the 30-item version with the conventional cutpoint of 5 to establish GHQ caseness status (GHQ+ versus GHQ-). The time frame covered the past 4 weeks.

3) *PSE case definition (PSE+/PSE-):* The *Present State Examination* (PSE) is a well-known and reliable standardised semi-structured psychiatric interview that probes the presence of psychiatric symptoms during the 4 weeks preceding the interview (Wing et al., 1974). PSE data were used to construct two measures: PSE total score (PSE-TOT) and PSE Index of Definition (PSE-ID, Wing & Sturt, 1978). PSE-TOT is a simple sumscore that takes into account the total number and severity of PSE symptoms. The PSE-ID, a weighted sumscore that also takes the specificity of the symptoms into account, indicates the probability of the presence of a specific psy-

chiatric disorder. The PSE-ID ranges from 1 to 8. Two cut-off scores, ID4+ and ID5+ are used to indicate caseness (Brink et al., 1989). In addition, ID5+ cases receive a tentative ICD-8 diagnosis. Given the nature of their construction and their strong correlation (r = .80) both PSE-TOT and PSE-ID can be taken as a severity index for existing psychopathology.

Sampling and Data Collection

Sampling and data collection were interdependent and will be described together. We used a three-stage sampling procedure presented as a flow chart in Figure 15.1. Outcome studies in primary-care settings are often plagued by the fact that the history of the MHP is not taken into account. This makes the interpretation of the findings difficult since outcome of a MHP may be influenced by the history of the problem (i.e. chronicity) as well as by its management. In our study, we controlled for this factor by restricting our sample to patients who did not suffer from MHPs according to their GP during the 12 months preceding their enrolment visit.

- Stage I: Sampling of GPs. In order to obtain a representative sample of GPs with regard to their basic attitude toward family medicine, a stratified sample of 25 GPs was drawn from the total population of GPs in the city of Groningen (175,000) and surrounding villages (for details, see Wilmink et al., 1989).

- Stage II: First stage sampling of patients. Each GP recruited all patients, aged 16–65, who came for consultation (index consult) on any of 10 prespecified days (N = 2237). These days were divided over 4 weeks in a systematic manner, in order to avoid day bias. During this index consult, the GP filled out a standard form about the patient and handed out the GHQ to be filled out and mailed back to the research department. The GHQ was returned to us by 1954 patients (response rate 89%). Nonresponders did not differ from responders with respect to presence of a MHP as assessed by the GP and age, but males were more often nonresponders than females (13% vs 9%). In this paper, we present data

only on those patients who had *no* MHP diagnosed by their GP during the 12 months *preceding* the index consult. Of all patients who returned the GHQ, 1450 (73%) met this criterion and are denoted "new" patients.

- Stage III: Second stage sampling of patients. The "new" patients could be cross-classified into 4 groups according to their GP (GP+/GP-) and GHQ (GHQ+/GHQ-) caseness status. These groups were used for the next sampling stage. As can been seen from the sampling proportions, all GP+ patients were included in the study. The other groups comprise random samples. Altogether, 260 "new" patients agreed to participate in the first interview of the study. They were contacted within 2 weeks after their index consult. At that time (T1) the *Present State Examination* (PSE) and the *Groningen Social Disability Schedule* (GSDS) were administered.

PSE's were conducted by clinical psychologists and physicians, who had a three week full time training and ample opportunity to get used to the interview in a pilot study. Every PSE interview was discussed with one of the psychiatrists involved in the study. In addition, booster sessions were held every fortnight. Reliability was good (Wilmink, 1989). It should be noted that both the GHQ and PSE do not cover all DSM-III axis I diagnoses.

To assess social disability, the *Groningen Social Disability Schedule* (GSDS), a standardised semistructured interview, was used (Wiersma et al., in press) based on social role theory. We used the shortened version covering the areas of self-care, family role, social role and professional role. Interviewer-observer reliability appeared to be good; weighted kappa's ranged from .63 to .93.

PSE and GSDS interviews were repeated approximately 14 months after the initial interviews (T2). Attrition rate during follow-up was 3%. In addition, the GPs recorded management details for each patient on every visit. This included information about the prescription of drugs, referrals and whether some sort of psychotherapy was provided. GPs were blind as to the PSE and GHQ caseness status of their patients.

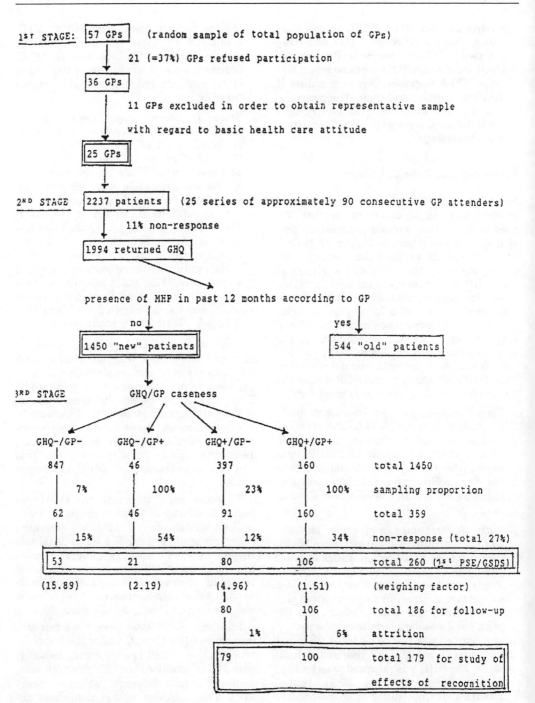

1ˢᵀ STAGE: | 57 GPs | (random sample of total population of GPs)

          21 (=37%) GPs refused participation

| 36 GPs |

          11 GPs excluded in order to obtain representative sample
          with regard to basic health care attitude

| 25 GPs |

2ᴺᴰ STAGE | 2237 patients | (25 series of approximately 90 consecutive GP attenders)

          11% non-response

| 1994 returned GHQ |

          presence of MHP in past 12 months according to GP

          no   yes

| 1450 "new" patients | | 544 "old" patients |

3ᴿᴰ STAGE   GHQ/GP caseness

GHQ-/GP-   GHQ-/GP+   GHQ+/GP-   GHQ+/GP+

847   46   397   160   total 1450

    7%   100%   23%   100%   sampling proportion

62   46   91   160   total 359

    15%   54%   12%   34%   non-response (total 27%)

53   21   80   106   total 260 (1ˢᵗ PSE/GSDS)

(15.89)   (2.19)   (4.96)   (1.51)   (weighing factor)

                            80   106   total 186 for follow-up

                                1%   6%   attrition

                            79   100   total 179 for study of
                                                     effects of recognition

Figure 15.1. GP and patient selection.

Analysis

Various subgroups of patients are presented in this paper in order to address the different research questions. All 1450 "new" patients are included when GP's recognition is evaluated against the GHQ case definition. However, when the PSE is used as a case criterion, data on recognition are available only for the 260 patients who received the PSE and GSDS at T1.

The description of the relationships between recognition, and management and outcome is examined by a comparison of "recognised" and "unrecognised" cases. Here we define caseness according to the GHQ, i.e. all GHQ+ are defined as cases. Thus, "recognised" cases are GHQ+ cases who are also identified as cases by the GPs (GHQ+/GP+ group: N = 106); "unrecognised" cases are GHQ+ cases who were not identified as cases

by the GPs (GHQ+/GP- group; N = 80). Due to attrition (3%), only 179 (186–7) GHQ+ patients participated in the follow-up study.

Finally, specific psychiatric diagnoses (CATEGO/ICD-8) are available only for patients with a PSE-ID5+ (N = 63).

Results

Recognition of Mental Health Problems.

In Table 15-2 the GPs' case definition is evaluated against the GHQ, PSE ID4+, and PSE ID5+. Data for tables 2B and 2C were available only for the 260 patients who took the initial interview. In order to make these figures comparable to those of the GP versus the GHQ, we weighted back to the cross-sectional sample by using appropriate sampling proportions.

It is apparent that the case definition applied by the GPs is more restrictive than that of the GHQ (14% GP+ vs. 38% GHQ+). Differences in rates for GP caseness (GP+) versus PSE-ID4+ and ID5+ caseness are much smaller (14% vs. 20% and 11%, respectively). Nevertheless, sensitivity figures indicate that GPs missed approximately half of the PSE cases. The specificity of .91 and .92 suggest that nearly all non-PSE cases were correctly diagnosed as noncases by the GPs.

Table 15.3 presents GPs' recognition of PSE-ID5+ cases according to CATEGO/ICD-8 diagnostic categories. Recognition of MHPs clearly varies by diagnostic category and severity, as is apparent from the last column.

In addition to recognition of MHPs, we also examined GPs' ability to correctly diagnose cases.

Table 15.2. Agreement on mental health status of "new" patients between GP and GHQ and PSE-ID. Entries denote percentages.

A. GP versus GHQ. All "new" patients

	GP+	GP-	total	Misclas. rate	.31
GHQ 5+	11.0	27.4	38.4	Sensitivity	.29
GHQ 4-	3.2	58.4	61.6	Specificity	.95
total	14.2	85.8	100% (1450)		

B. GP versus PSE-ID 4+. Results obtained by weighing

	GP+	GP-	total	Misclas. rate	.18
ID 4+	8.0	11.7	19.7	Sensitivity	.41
ID 3-	6.2	74.1	80.3	Specificity	.92
total	14.2	85.8	100%		

C. GP versus PSE-ID 5+. Results obtained by weighing

	GP+	GP-	total	Misclas. rate	.13
ID 5+	5.9	4.6	10.5	Sensitivity	.56
ID 4-	8.3	81.2	89.5	Specificity	.91
total	14.2	85.8	100%		

Table 15.3. Estimated diagnostic distribution of PSE-ID 5+ cases and recognition rates for "new" patients (N = 1450).

Diagnostic category of CATEGO/ICD-8	point-prevalence per 1000	% recognised by GPs
300.0 anxiety state	17.9	35%
300.2 phobia	31.0	44%
300.4 neurotic depression	44.8	62%
296.2 severe depression	10.3	100%
296.1 mania	1.4	100%

Table 15.4. Relationship between recognition and management (N = 179).

Management (type of intervention)	% who received treatment in		Odds ratio (95% C.I.)	Adjusted* odds ratio (95% C.I.)
	recognised group (n = 100) (GP+/GHQ+)	unrecognised group (n = 79) (GP-/GHQ+)		
psychotropic drugs	47%	15%	4.5 (2.3–9.2)	2.8 (1.3–35.5)
psychotherapy	24%	3%	12.2 (2.7–54.8)	11.4 (2.4–54.1)
referral to MH spec.	17%	6%	3.0 (1.1–8.8)	1.8 (0.6–5.7)
any MH treatment	63%	20%	6.7 (3.3–13.5)	4.6 (2.1–9.8)
ref. to non-MH spec.	22%	18%	1.3 (0.6–2.8)	1.1 (0.5–2.5)

*OR adjusted for initial severity (PSE-ID)

Again we used CATEGO/ICD-8 diagnostic categories as the criterion. Even though GPs recognised more than 50% of the cases with ID5+, only 21% of the recognised cases received a specific psychiatric diagnosis from the GP. Furthermore, diagnostic agreement between GPs and CATEGO/ICD-8 was poor.

Recognition and Management

Table 15.4 presents results concerning the relationship between recognition and various indices of management during the follow-up period. These include administering psychotropic drugs, one or more psychotherapeutic sessions with the GP, referral to mental health (MH) specialist and referral to a somatic specialist. In addition, a summary measure was used, indicating whether any of the three mental health interventions was provided.

The first two columns of Table 15.4 indicate the percentage of patients in the recognised and unrecognised group, respectively, who received the various kinds of interventions. The third column presents the same results in terms of the odds ratio (OR). (An odds ratio denotes the ratio of the odds of a particular intervention among the recognised patients to the odds of that intervention among the non-recognised. Put more simply, the OR of 4.5 given for psychotropic drugs in Table 15.4 means that the recognised patients were four and a half times more likely to receive drugs than those whose disorders were not recognised.)

GPs' recognition seems to have implications for management. Being recognised results in a more than four-fold chance of a prescription for psychotropic drugs and a twelve-fold chance of a psychotherapeutic session with the GP. It also implies a three-fold chance of being referred to a mental health specialist, but no increased change of referral to (any) somatic specialist. This indicates that recognition is related to treatments which are specifically directed to the management of MHPs. The table also demonstrates that the majority of recognised cases are not referred to mental health specialists. They are treated by their GPs with psychotropic drugs or—less often—short-term psychotherapy.

The relationship between recognition and management is potentially confounded by symptom severity. We assume that patients with more severe psychopathology are more readily recognised by their GPs than less severe patients. On the other hand, they may receive more treatment regardless of whether they are recognised or not. Thus GPs may more readily treat these patients even when they have not explicitly labelled them as cases. In order to account for this possibility, we controlled for initial severity as measured by PSE-ID level at T1. The results are presented in terms of adjusted ORs (Table 15.4, column 4). It is apparent that the relationship between recognition and management can only be partly attributed to initial symptom severity.

A rather peculiar finding was that some nonrecognised cases received MH treatment during the follow up period. This finding is likely to be the result of delayed recognition of a MHP already present at the index consult or to recognition of a MHP that emerged during follow-up.

Table 15.5. Recognition and outcome in terms of psychopathology and social disability for "New" GHQ+ patients.

	Psychopathology		Social dysfunctioning
	PSE-ID	PSE-TOT	GSDS-TOT
GP nonrecognised (N = 79)			
Mean initial score , T₁	2.76	5.73	0.77
Mean follow-up score,T₂	2.63	5.10	0.57
Difference	0.13	0.63	0.20
Percent improved	33%	46%	24%
GP recognised (N = 100)			
Mean initial score, T₁	4.15	11.90	1.45
Mean follow-up score,T₂	2.70	6.04	0.71
Difference	1.45*	5.86*	0.74*
Percent improved	75%	81%	56%

*p<0.05—indicating significant improvement

Recognition and Outcome

Outcome has been defined as improvement versus nonimprovement in terms of PSE-ID level over the 14-month follow-up period. Table 15.5 presents mean initial and follow-up levels of psychopathology and social dysfunction, as well as percentages of improved patients for both recognised and unrecognised new GHQ+ patients.

The ratio of the odds for improvement of the recognised group to the odds for the unrecognised group was 6.03 (95% confidence interval 3.14–11.59). Thus, *being recognised results in a six-fold greater chance of improvement compared to being unrecognised.* However, the role of symptom severity as a potential confounder of the relationship between recognition and management has to be considered. Obviously, patients with more severe psychopathology have more room for improvement compared to those with less severe psychopathology. Since the former are more heavily represented in the recognised group (see Table 15.5), severity may account for some of the relationship between recognition and outcome. But when symptom severity (in terms of PSE-ID level) was controlled for, the effect of recognition on outcome remained substan-

tial (odds ratio = 4.11, 95% confidence interval 2.05–8.21).

We also examined the effects of recognition on social dysfunctioning defined as improvement versus nonimprovement in terms of GSDS total score. The odds ratio for improvement, comparing the recognised to the unrecognised group, was 4.93 (confidence interval 2.51–9.69). After controlling for initial level of social dysfunctioning, the effect of recognition on outcome in terms of social functioning remained significant and substantial (odds ratio = 3.06, confidence interval 1.52–6.16).

Thus, recognition seems to matter for outcome in terms of both psychopathology and social functioning.

Management and Outcome

So far the results showed recognition to be related to both management and outcome of MHPs. The next question is whether the relationship between recognition and outcome is mediated by treatment. To test this hypothesis, we examined the relationship between the various indices of management and outcome. The results are presented in Table 15.6.

The overall picture that emerges from this table is a rather weak or nonsignificant relationship between mental health treatment and outcome.

Table 15.6. Relationship between management and outcome.

	Outcome (Odds ratio; 95% conf. interval)	
Management (type of treatment by GP)	Psychopathology	Social dysfunctioning
Psychotropic drugs	2.37 (1.23–4.53)	1.41 (0.75–2.66)
Psychotherapy	1.90 (0.78–4.63)	1.77 (0.77–4.08)
Referral to MH specialist	0.74 (0.30–1.82)	1.46 (0.60–3.57)
Any MH treatment	2.43 (1.32–4.51)	2.01 (1.08–3.74)

Recognition, Management and Outcome

Finally, the relationship between recognition, management and outcome has been studied by entering all three components into one logistic regression model. In this model, the dependent variable was outcome either in terms of PSE or social functioning, and management was defined as any kind of mental health treatment.

Two logistic regression models predicting outcome were compared. In the first model, recognition was the only predictor of outcome; in the second, both recognition and "any kind of treatment" were entered into the equation. As indicated in the previous section, the odds ratio in the first model was 5.48 for outcome in terms of psychopathology and 4.04 for outcome in terms of social functioning. In the second model, the odds ratios were 4.94 (95% confidence interval 2.4–10.11) and 3.74 (95% confidence interval 1.85–7.67) for outcome in terms of psychopathology and social functioning, respectively. Adjusted odds ratios proved to be very similar to unadjusted odds ratios. In addition, the likelihood ratio test revealed a significant effect of GP recognition on outcome over and above the effect of any treatment on outcome (psychopathology $\chi^2 = 21.90$, df = 1, p<0.001; social functioning $\chi^2 = 14.13$, df = 1, p<0.001). These findings suggest the existence of an important path between recognition and outcome, which is not mediated by management. We deal with this finding in more detail in the discussion below.

Discussion

Some findings of our study require further discussion. First, the effect of recognition on outcome was only mediated to a small extent by the MH treatment. This is not surprising given the fact that MH treatments were only weakly related to outcome (see Table 15.6). These weak or absent relations should be interpreted carefully. Although they may indicate the ineffectiveness of treatment, they may also be interpreted as the result of a feedback process; that is, the amount of MH treatment during the follow-up period may not only depend on recognition of the problem by the GP and the initial severity of the dis-

order, but also on the success of treatment. It is possible that the less effective GPs are in their interventions with a particular patient, the greater the range of treatments that they will provide. This alternative hypothesis is supported by the observation that drug therapy, the typical GP treatment for mental health problems, is significantly related to better outcome, whereas less common—second-stage—interventions like psychotherapy or referral to a MH specialist, are not. Referrals often take place when the GP's own interventions—drugs or simple counselling—are unsuccessful.

Additional explanations for the relatively small intermediary role of MH treatments might be that recognition itself has beneficial effects and the possibility that recognition elicits interventions (by the GP or network members) which are not covered by our management measures.

Our results might suggest that notification of existing MHPs to GPs will have a positive effect on management and outcome. In fact, Johnstone and Goldberg (1976) demonstrated that unrecognised GHQ cases about whom the GP had been informed had a better prognosis than unrecognised GHQ cases about whom the GP was not informed. However, Hoeper et al. (1984) and Shapiro et al. (1987) reported that providing GHQ scores to the GP at the time of the enrollment visit had only limited impact on GP's assessment of MHPs and subsequent treatment. We assume that the only GP involved in the Johnstone and Goldberg study had a better training in managing MHPs than the GPs in the other studies. In our opinion, these conflicting findings show that notification is not identical with (spontaneous) recognition and that notification will have a positive impact on management and outcome only when GPs are trained in handling this information and MH interventions. Therefore, experiments that seek to establish the benefits of improved detection of MHP by GPs should use MH training of the GPs as an additional experimental variable.

Finally, it should be stressed that the findings reported here should be tested in a randomised design in which an experimental intervention succeeds in altering GP recognition. Because of its nonexperimental character, the present naturalistic study can only demonstrate associations, not causal effects.

Summary

This chapter addresses the issues of recognition and labeling of mental health problems (MHPs) by general practitioners (GPs), and the effects of recognition on management and outcome. In *part I,* we selectively reviewed the existing literature on the extent of nonrecognition of MHPs by GPs. Most studies showed that a considerable fraction of consecutive series of primary-care patients with psychological distress as indicated by a high score on a self-report questionnaire and patients with a psychiatric disorder according to DSM-III, RDC, or PSE-Catego/ICD are not recognised as such by their GP. It was also stated that these findings should be interpreted cautiously, because serious doubts can be raised as to the validity of the definitions and measurements of "recognition of MHPs" in these studies. The application of standardised procedures for the assessment of MHP-recognition and emphasis on the process of recognition were advocated. Recent studies showed that this leads to lower estimates of the nonrecognised fractions of MHPs and consequently to higher estimates of the GP's sensitivity to MHPs.

In *part II,* we presented the results of our naturalistic study on the effects of nonrecognition of MHPs on management and outcome in terms of psychological distress. Nearly 2000 attenders of 25 GPs were screened with the GHQ, and a stratified sample of 260 patients was examined twice using the *Present State Examination* (PSE) and the *Groningen Social Disability Schedule* (GSDS). Patients who had an MHP in the 12 months preceding the enrollment visit were excluded.

Prevalence rates of MHPs according to the GHQ, GP and PSE were 38%, 14% and 11%, respectively. GPs missed half of the PSE cases and typically assigned nonspecific diagnoses to recognised cases. Depressions were more readily recognised than anxiety disorders and detection rates for severe disorders were higher than those for less severe disorders. Similar observations have been made by others (Goldberg & Huxley, 1980; Hoeper et al., 1979; Skuse & Williams, 1984; Casey et al., 1984; Goldberg et al., 1987; Von Korff et al., 1987).

Recognition had a substantial effect on management and outcome. Recognised as compared to nonrecognised cases were more likely to receive MH interventions from their GP (OR = 6.7) and had better outcomes in terms of both psychopathology (OR = 6.0) and social functioning (OR = 4.9), even after controlling for initial severity.

Finally, it should be noted that we do not yet advocate large-scale screening programmes for MHPs in primary-care settings, but only have stressed the importance of improvement of detection and diagnosis. To date, no convincing evidence documenting the benefits of screening in terms of patient outcome and costs is available to justify screening for MHPs (Campbell, 1987). However, new experiments that take into account the training aspects may soon force us to reassess this opinion. In any case, our findings demonstrate the desirability of more sophisticated screening experiments.

References

Barrett, J. E., Barrett, J. A., Oxman, T. E., & Gerber, P. D. (1988). The prevalence of psychiatric disorders in a primary care practice. *Arch. Gen. Practice, 45,* 1100–1119.

Blacker, C. V. R., & Clare, W. (1987). Depressive disorder in primary care. *Brit. J. of Psychiatry, 150,* 737–751.

Boardman, A. P. (1987). The General Health Questionnaire and the detection of emotional disorder: A replicated study. *British Journal of Psychiatry, 151,* 373–381.

Brink, W., Koeter, M. W. J., Ormel, J., Dykstra, W., Giel, R., Stooff, C., & Wohlfart, T. (1989). Psychiatric diagnosis in an outpatient population. A comparative study of PSE Catego and DSM-III. *Archives of General Psychiatry, 46,* 369–372.

Campbell, T. L. (1987). An opposing view. *The Journal of Family Practice, 5,* 184–187.

Casey, P. R., Dillon, S., & Tyrer, P. J. (1984). The diagnostic status of patients with conspicuous psychiatric morbidity in primary care. *Psychol. Med., 14,* 673–683.

Chan, D. W., & Chan T. S. C. (1983). Reliability, validity and the structure of the General Health Questionnaire in a Chinese context. *Psychol. Med., 13,* 363–371.

Clare, A. W. (1982). Problems of psychiatric classification in general practice. In A. W. Clare & M. Lader (Eds.), *Psychiatry and general practice.* London: Academic Press.

Giel, R., Koeter, M. W. H., & Ormel, J. (1989). *Detection and referral of primary-care patients with mental health problems: The second and third filter in the pathway to psychiatric care.* Chapter in this book.

Goldberg, D. (1978). *Manual of the General Health Questionnaire.* Slough: National Foundation for Education Research.

Goldberg, D. (1982). The concept of a psychiatric "case" in general practice. *Soc. Psychiatry, 17,* 61–65.

Goldberg, D. P. (1972). *The detection of psychiatric illness by questionnaire.* London: Oxford University Press.

Goldberg, D. P., Bridges, K., Duncan-Jones, P., & Grayson, D. (1987). Dimensions of neuroses seen in primary-care settings. *Psychol. Med., 17,* 461–470.

Goldberg, D., & Bridges, K. (1987). Screening for psychiatric illness in general practice: The general practitioner versus the screening questionnaire. *J. of the Royal College of General Practitioners, 37,* 15–18.

Goldberg, D., & Huxley, P. (1980). *Mental illness in the community, the pathway to psychiatric care.* London, New York: Tavistock.

Goldberg, D., & Sharp, M. E. (1979). Detection and assessment of emotional disorders in a primary-care setting. *Int. J. Ment. Health, 8,* 30–48.

Hankin, J. R., & Oktay, J. S. (1979). *Mental disorder and primary medical care: An analytic review of the literature 1979.* Washington, DC: Department of Health and Human Services, publication number (ADM) 78–661, National Institute of Mental Health Series D5.

Henderson, S., Byrne, D. G., & Duncan-Jones, P. (1981). *Neurosis and the social environment.* New York: Academic Press.

Hodiamont, P., Peer, N., & Syben, N. (1986). Epidemiological aspects of psychiatric disorder in a Dutch health area. *Psychol. Med., 17,* 495–505.

Hoeper, E. W., Nycz, G. R., Cleary, P. D., Regier, D. A., & Goldberg, I. D. (1979). Estimated prevalence of RDC mental disorder in primary medical care. *Int. J. Ment. Health, 8,* 6–15.

Hoeper, E. W., Nycz, L. G., Kessler, J. D., Burke, J. D., & Pierce, W. E. (1984). The usefulness of screening for mental illness. *The Lancet, i,* 33–35.

Jencks, S. F. (1985). Recognition of mental distress and diagnosis of mental disorder in primary care. *JAMA, 253*(13), 1903–1907.

Johnstone, A, & Goldberg, D. (1976). Psychiatric screening in general practice. Controlled trial. *The Lancet, 20,* 605–609.

Lamberts, H., & Hartman, B. (1982). Psychische en sociale problemen in de huisartspraktijk. 1. Gegevens over het prbleemgedrag en het monitoring project. *Huisarts en Wetenschap, 25,* 333–342.

Marks, J. N., Goldberg, D. P., & Hillier, V. F. (1979). Determinants of the ability of general practitioners to defect psychiatric illness. *Psychol. Med., 9,* 337–353.

Ormel, J., & Giel, R. (1983). Omvang, beloop en behandeling van psychische stoornissen in de praktijk van de huisarts. (Prevalence, course and treatment of psychiatric disorders in primary care settings). *Tijdschrift voor Psychiatrie, 25,* 668–710.

Ormel, J., Koeter, M. W. J., Brink, W., & Giel, R. (1989). Concurrent validity of GHQ and PSE as measures of change. *Psychological Medicine, 19,* 1007–1013.

Rand, E. H., L. W., Badger, & Coggings, D. R. (1988). Toward a resolution of contradictions: Utility of feedback from the GHQ. *Gen. Hosp. Psychiat., 10*(3), 189–196.

Shapiro, S., German, P. S., Skinner, E. A., von Korff, M., Turner, R. W., Klein, L. E., Teitelbaum, M. L., Kramer, M., Burke, J. D., & Burns, B. J. (1987). An experiment to change detection and management of mental morbidity in primary care. *Med. Care, 25,* 327–339.

Shapiro, S., Skinner, E. A., Kramer, M., et al. (1985). Measuring need for mental health services in a general population. *Med. Care, 3,* 1033–1043.

Shepherd, M., Cooper, B., Brown, A. C., & Kalton, G. W. (1966). *Psychiatric illness in general practice.* London: Oxford University Press.

Skuse, D., & Williams, P.(1984). Screening for psychiatric disorder in general practice. *Psychological Medicine, 14,* 365–377.

Vaillant, G. E., & Schnurr, P. (1988). What is a case? A 45-year study of psychiatric impairment within a college sample selected for mental health. *Arch. Gen. Psychiatry, 45,* 313–376.

Von Korff, M., Shapiro, S., Burke, J. D., Teitlebaum, M., Skinner, E. A., German, P., Turner, R. W., Klein, L., & Burns, B. (1987). Anxiety and depression in a primary care clinic: Comparison of DIS, GHQ and practitioner assessments. *Arch. Gen. Psychiatry, 44,* 152–156.

Wiersma, D., de Jong, A. , & Ormel, J. (1989). The Groningen social disability schedule. *Int. J. of Rehabilitation.* (in press)

Williams, P., Tarnopolsky, A., Hand, D., & Shepherd, M. (1986). Minor psychiatric morbidity and general practice consultations: The West London Survey. *Psychological Medicine, 9,* 1–37.

Wilmink, F. W. (1989). *Detection of mental health problems by Dutch GPs.* Ph.D. thesis, Dept. of Social Psychiatry. University of Groningen.

Wilmink, F. W., & Snijders, T. A. B. (1989). Polytomous logistic regression of the General Health Questionnaire and the Present State Examination. *Psychological Medicine, 19,* 755–764.

Wilmink, F. W., Ormel, J., Giel, R., Krol, B., Lindeboom, E. G., v. d. Meer, K., & Soeterman, J. H. (in press). General practitioners characteristics and the assessment of psychiatric illness. *J. of Psychiatric Research*.

Wing, J. K., Cooper, J., & Sartorius, N. (1974). *The measurement and classification of psychiatric symptoms*. Cambridge: Cambridge University Press.

Wing, J. K., & Sturt, E. (1978). *The PSE-ID-CATEGO system: A supplementary manual*. London: Institute of Psychiatry (mimeo).

Zung, L. S., Magill, M., Moore, J. T., et al. (1983). Recognition and treatment of depression in a family medicine practice. *J. Clin. Psychiatry, 44*(3).

Chapter 16

Early Detection of Dementia in the Primary-Care Setting

Brian Cooper and Horst Bickel

The main argument for promoting early detection of disease is that it permits medical treatment and management to commence at an early stage, when the prognosis is likely to be most favourable. In the case of late-life dementia, there is as yet no evidence for the efficacy of early treatment. Nonetheless, diagnosis at this stage can be valuable for a number of other reasons. It allows the natural history of the condition to be studied, including the time sequence and spread of both neuropathological and psychological changes. It may be useful in differentiating between clinical syndromes before they converge upon a common pathway, and in identifying their different provoking agents. It helps the clinician to plan case management and, if indicated, to discuss this with family caregivers. Finally, it can provide a baseline for testing new therapeutic advances. The scope for early detection and diagnosis of dementia in the elderly population should therefore be explored, even though there are no grounds for prescriptive screening (Cooper & Bickel, 1984).

General practice represents an important focal point for such endeavours. Old people with dementing disorders tend to be referred to specialists, if at all, only when the condition is advanced, whereas in general practice the earlier stages are seen every day. While the expense of setting up neuropsychiatric assessment centres on the requisite scale would be prohibitive, the development of diagnostic methods and tools in the primary-care setting may result in procedures at once much less costly and more effective in terms of case yield (Eastwood & Corbin, 1981). Screening programmes that involve admission to, or attendance at, a specialist clinic are unlikely to evoke such a good response as when the investigation is carried out by family doctors and their team. Moreover, the need for continuing surveillance must be borne in mind. Because the risk of cognitive decline increases with age, screening to be effective must either be repeated at intervals, or else incorporated into the practice routine, so that early detection becomes, in effect, an integral part of the doctor-patient contact.

Approaches to Early Detection in Community and General Practice Studies

Over the past two decades, a number of experimental projects have been reported in which geriatric screening has been conducted in general practice and outpatient settings. These projects have paid little attention to cognitive impairment, though it is known to be a leading cause of disability in old age. Thus, the *Boston Vulnerability Index* contains a single item on cognition ("Could you please tell me what year it is?"), while other, similar question batteries fail to include even one (Taylor & Ford, 1987). This is perhaps understandable in that cognitive assessment would double the time required and, unlike the other aspects of geriatric screening, would involve putting the respondent in a test situation. Nevertheless, the problem is too important to be ignored in this way.

The investigator's dream of a quick screening test for dementia that dispenses with the need to ask awkward questions may in the future be realised by the emergence of biological markers. It has been postulated that dementia of Alzheimer type is the neuropsychiatric manifestation of a generalised systemic disease, with alterations in cells other than neurons, for example, in red-blood cells and platelets (Small & Greenberg, 1988). As yet, however, no such marker has been identified that could be utilised under field-study conditions—and whose use in unselected samples of the elderly population would be justifiable. For the present, we must continue to rely upon "psychological" methods that are focused on the assessment of cognitive function. Here, as elsewhere in psychiatry, such screening methods are based on two main types of approach. One consists in the application of simple tests of cognitive function, such as the so-called "dementia scales," or short, clinically oriented interview procedures. The other relies upon the use of key informants, among whom the general practitioner occupies a special place because of the unique combination of professional training and personal knowledge of the patient. Each of these approaches are considered briefly below.

Dementia Scales and Short Interviews

A large number of "dementia scales," stemming originally from "bedside" diagnostic techniques, have been developed, and some of these, such as the *Mental Status Questionnaire* (Kahn et al., 1960) and the *Mini Mental State Examination* (Folstein et al., 1975) have found world-wide use as research tools. Since most are short question batteries, designed to be administered in a few minutes, it is not surprising that their specificity for dementia is low. However, by using high cut-off scores, they can be made to serve as useful detectors of hitherto undeclared cases. In the Baltimore ECA survey, for example, the *Mini Mental State* with a cut-point of 23 exhibited a sensitivity of 100% and a positive predictive value of 26.4% (Folstein et al., 1985). In this population, the number of persons to be interviewed in more detail could be reduced by two-thirds, without missing any significant number of severe or moderately severe cases.

The detection of previously undeclared cases is, of course, by no means the same as that of early cognitive decline. On this latter topic, information is still scarce; indeed, "mild dementia" is such an ill-defined entity that it is very difficult to gauge the sensitivity of different screening tests to its presence. Find-

ings of field studies in Baltimore (Folstein et al., 1985), Hobart (Kay et al., 1985) and elsewhere suggest that the cut-off points on scales such as the *Mini Mental State* and *Mental Status Questionnaire* would probably have to be set so high for this purpose that they would yield unacceptably large numbers of "false positives" in the elderly population. A study in southern California, by Pfeffer and others (1981), in which expert diagnostic assessment by neurologists provided the standard of validity, pointed to the same general conclusion.

The use of interview procedures that are lengthy and call for skilled diagnostic judgments would obviously be a highly uneconomic method of screening unselected population samples. If the interview can be pared down to its bare essentials and so structured that it can be administered by lay persons, it may serve as a screening instrument. This is in effect what Copeland and his co-workers have done in their Liverpool survey of psychogeriatric illness (Copeland et al., 1986).

The community version of the *Geriatric Mental Status Schedule*, GMS-A, is a short, structured interview that can be administered in about 15 minutes, on average. As responses are analysed by the computer diagnostic programme "AGECAT," no diagnostic judgment is required on the interviewer's part. The interview schedule includes some items that test cognition, and the computer programme allocates each respondent to one of six levels of probability for organic mental impairment.

The Liverpool study is of particular interest in that it has a prospective longitudinal design. The method, customary in cross-sectional studies, of checking the current validity of a screening test against an interview diagnosis based on clinical classification, is of limited use for early detection, since evidence of cognitive decline must be assessed before a firm diagnosis can be made on the basis of ICD or DSM criteria. The issue of prediction of new onset cases thus becomes crucial.

A sample of 1,070 elderly persons, drawn from the lists of local general practitioners, was interviewed with the aid of the GMS-A schedule (Copeland et al., 1986). Subsamples of high and low scorers, comprising in all a

167

Table 16.1. Incidence rates per 1,000 for dementia, according to cognitive-scale scores at first interview (N = 420).

Age group (years)	Community sample (N = 313)		Institutional residents (N = 107)	
	Cognition normal: 0–3 (n = 283)	Mildly impaired: 4+ (n = 30)	Cognition normal: 0–3 (N = 54)	Mildly impaired: 4+ (N = 53)
65–79	10.1 ± 2.8	32.0 ± 22.3	13.0 ± 12.9	–*
80+	27.4 ± 7.5	74.8 ± 29.2	48.5 ± 19.3	197.2 ± 41.6
65+	14.7 ± 2.9	55.8 ± 19.2	34.8 ± 12.9	147.7 ± 32.1

*No new cases in this subgroup, which had only 30.6 person-years at risk.

group of 126 persons, were re-examined after a mean interval of 75 weeks, and at this stage diagnostic assessments were made by psychiatrists. Of 12 persons diagnosed as cases of dementia, nine had been rated as probably organically impaired at the initial screening, on the basis of the "AGECAT" algorithm. Of a total of 28 persons originally picked out as "subclinical" cases, three were found at follow-up to have a definite dementing illness. Although the numbers involved were small and the period of follow-up varied widely, these early findings are quite promising.

Data from a recent study of old people in Mannheim also indicate a useful potential for the prediction of new cases of dementia. Here, a sample of 343 elderly community residents was followed up for eight years, and a sample of 176 old people in long-term institutional care, drawn from the same background population, for six years (Cooper & Bickel, 1989; Bickel & Cooper, 1989). The mental health status was assessed initially by means of a German version of the *Clinical Interview Schedule* (Goldberg et al., 1970), adapted for use with the elderly (Cooper & Schwarz, 1982).

At follow-up, the psychiatric interview was repeated on all respondents who were still alive. Contact was also made with relatives or former caregivers of those who had died, and information obtained on the mental health status and the events preceding death. Mental deterioration was accepted as evidence of a dementing condition only if it had become apparent at least 6 months before the person's demise, and was rated for severity according to the "staging criteria" of Hughes et al.

(1982). A diagnostic appraisal of each new case of dementia during the follow-up period was made on the basis of all available information.

The mean annual incidence rate for dementia of clinical severity, in the total population aged over 65 years, was estimated at 15.4 per 1,000 (Cooper & Bickel, 1989). This level of incidence is in agreement with the findings of other field studies, most of which have also reported annual rates of 1–2% for this age range. It stands in sharp contrast to corresponding case-register data on the "treatment incidence" of dementia, which is of the order of only 2–4 per 1,000, or about one-fifth of the total incidence.

The psychiatric interview included a short cognitive scale of 14 items, similar in form and content to most such instruments. Responses are scored 0, 1 or 2 points each, so that the total (unweighted) error scale ranges from 0 (normal cognitive functioning) to 28 (inability to answer any of the questions even approximately). The scale was not intended for the early detection of cognitive decline, but simply as an exploratory help for the interviewing psychiatrist in making his diagnostic assessment. In the event, however, it proved the most useful part of the interview for predicting mental deterioration. This can be demonstrated by excluding from the survey samples all those individuals given a diagnosis of organic mental disorder at the first interview, and considering only the remainder.

The presence of minor cognitive deficits at the first interview, as expressed in terms of the error score on the simple scale used at that time, was the best single predictor found for dementia. A score of 4 or more points on this scale, indicating minor memory lapses, vague, imprecise responses to questions or some difficulty in recalling details of past events, though in the absence of any definite disability in everyday life, was found to raise the probability of onset of dementia in the following period by nearly 250% in the community sample and by over 300% in the institutional sample. The predictive effect of this score was so pronounced that, once it had been partialled out in a multivariate analysis, age above 65 years ceased to have a significant influence on the risk of dementia.

The cumulative incidence of dementia during the follow-up period was computed separately for the groups with and without initial mild cognitive deficits, using the Cox proportional hazards regression model (Allgulander & Fisher, 1984). Once the effect of age was held constant, the risk of dementia was consistently higher for the group with a raised error score, being more than double that for the comparison group. The cumulative incidence for the latter group lagged, in effect, 2 to 3 years behind that for the former. This

time-lag appears to represent the approximate time-span over which the probability of onset of a dementing disorder can be predicted with a useful degree of accuracy (Cooper & Bickel, 1989). In other words, to gain the maximum benefit from such a simple screening procedure, it would have to be repeated after about this length of interval.

Despite such clear-cut differences, high mortality in the at-risk group makes the predictive value of the test difficult to quantify. In Figure 16.1, cumulative incidence curves are plotted separately for the groups with and without initial deficits ("demented among survivors"). It can be seen that the group with cognitive deficits has a consistently higher cumulative incidence, rising to 30%, as against only 4% in the other group. However, the former group also has a much higher mortality rate than the latter, which is at least partly because of its higher mean age. The cumulative incidence of dementia among survivors therefore gives an underestimate of the test's predictive power. For this reason, curves are also given in Figure 16.1 for the combined cumulative risk of dementia onset

Figure 16.1. Cumulative probabilities of dementia and death during 3-year follow-up period, according to cognitive status at initial screening.

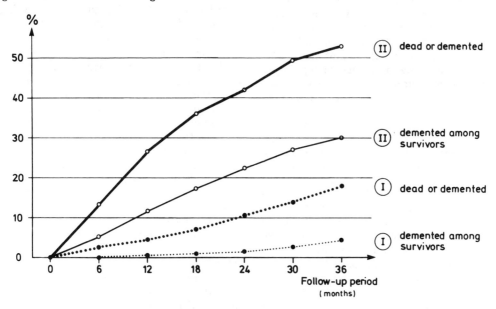

I = no cognitive impairment initially

II = mild cognitive impairment initially

or death over the first 3 years of follow-up ("dead or demented"). This measure of risk can be seen to rise over 3 years to 53% in the group with cognitive deficits, compared with just under 18% in the comparison group. However, such a composite measure of risk is itself problematic.

The fact that predictions can be made with some success over a 3-year interval, by means of a crude, unvalidated screening test, suggests that it should become possible in the future, by developing more refined and accurate techniques, to identify a high proportion of cases of primary degenerative dementia in the early stages.

Role of the General Practitioner in Early Detection

How good are general practitioners at detecting cognitive decline in their elderly patients? A study by Williamson and others (1964) in Edinburgh has been widely cited in this context, as showing that the great majority of cases go unrecognised. Of 48 cases identified by the research team in a sample of elderly patients, only seven were apparently known to their family doctors: A finding which points to gross underdiagnosis of the condition. These data, however, should be interpreted cautiously, since the proportion of patients reported to be dementing was unusually high, and it thus seems probable that the practitioners' case recognition was being judged against a false standard. It is also possible that diagnostic standards have improved in the past 25 years.

A recent study in Cambridge provided some evidence that this has occurred. O'Connor and others (1988) examined persons aged over 75 years who were on the registered patient lists of six practices in that city. The practitioners were asked to rate the patients, independently of the research team, as definitely not demented, possibly demented or definitely demented. They correctly identified 48 of 96 patients found to be mildly demented, 52 of 85 found to be moderately demented, and 21 out of 27 found to be severely demented. Thus, they detected 58% of all cases (121/208) and 65% of cases of moderate or severe dementia (73/112). Significantly, they were more often aware of dementia in those patients who had

consulted frequently in the previous year.

The Cambridge findings can be compared with preliminary data from a current research project in Mannheim, which also has as one aim an assessment of early detection of dementia by general practitioners. Here, the sampling frame in each practice is comprised of all patients aged over 65 years who consult general practitioners, or who are visited at home by them, during a 4-week period. The practitioner is supplied with brief guidelines for rating the cognitive status of the patient and allocating him or her to one of four categories: cognitively normal; mildly forgetful without disability; mildly demented; moderately or severely demented. A subsample of the patients in each practice, stratified according to the doctor's rating of cognitive status, is drawn by the research team, contacted with the practitioner's help and asked to accept a home interview by a member of the research team. In the course of home interview, the cognitive status and probability of a dementing illness are assessed, using an augmented form of the *Hierarchic Dementia Scale* of Cole and Dastoor (1987), and a provisional diagnosis is allocated, if appropriate, on the basis of the "CAMDEX" diagnostic criteria (Roth et al., 1986). Table 16.2 gives the distribution of consulting patients, according to the practitioners' ratings of cognitive status, in the first eight practices.

The proportion of elderly patients rated as moderately or severely demented, 5.6%, is closely similar to that estimated from the earlier prevalence survey of old people in Mannheim, suggesting that elderly patients consulting in general practice are not a high-risk group in this respect. More striking, however, are the high proportions of patients rated as suffering from mild dementia (16.9%) or forgetfulness (39.8%), and the fact that less than 40% are categorised as free from any cognitive impairment. While some variation was found between individual practices, the proportion of elderly patients rated fully unimpaired was above 50% for men in only one practice, and for women in none.

The practitioners' ratings can be compared with those of the research team for the subsample of 145 patients so far interviewed in these practices (Table 16.3). When this is done, it appears that the practitioners, so far

Table 16.2. General practitioners' ratings of cognitive status of elderly consulting patients in 8 Mannheim practices, by age and sex (N = 1,513).

Cognitive status	Men		Women		Both sexes	
	65–74	75+	65–74	75	65–74	75+
Normal; no impairment	61.6	25.7	55.4	21.2	57.5	22.4
Mild memory deficits	33.5	42.7	36.6	43.2	35.6	43.1
Mild dementia	4.9	25.2	7.3	24.9	6.5	25.0
Moderate to severe dementia	–	6.4	0.7	10.7	0.4	9.5
Total	100.0	100.0	100.0	100.0	100.0	100.0
n =	224	234	437	618	661	852

from underdiagnosing cognitive impairment in their elderly patients, actually tend to over-diagnose it. They correctly identified 50 out of 52 cases with dementia of clinical severity, and 31 out of 32 cases of mild cognitive deficit. Indeed, the accuracy of their assessments varied remarkably little with the degree of severity of impairment.

In Table 16.4, the performance of the Cambridge and that of the Mannheim practitioners as screening agents are compared. These data indicate that in general the Mannheim doctors appeared to be functioning significantly better in this respect. However, here again the research findings must be in-terpreted cautiously, because of important differences in design and method between the two research projects. Perhaps the most important difference is that the Mannheim study focuses on consulting, not on registered patients. It has to do so, since strictly speaking there is no patient registration in the West German system of care; if the patient fails to hand in the prepaid health insurance voucher each quarter, the doctor-patient contract automatically terminates. In fact, most elderly patients remain with the same doctors for long periods. The practical issue, however, is that the Mannheim doctors made their ratings at face-to-face contact with each patient,

Table 16.3. General practitioners' ratings of cognitive status, compared with research interview assessments (N = 145).

Research interview assessment (CAMDEX criteria)	General practitioners' ratings			
	Normal	Only mild memory deficits	Mild dementia	Moderate to severe dementia
Normal; no impairment	33	26	2	–
Mild memory deficits only	1	11	20	–
Mild dementia	–	2	9	4
Moderate to severe dementia	–	–	9	28
Total	34	39	40	32

Table 16.4. Accuracy of general practitioners in assessing cognitive status of elderly patients in two research projects.

Research interview assessment (CAMDEX criteria)	Mannheim GPs' ratings			Cambridge GPs' ratings*		
	Not demented (incl. minimal deficits)	Mild to severe dementia	Total	Not demented	Possibly or definitely demented	Total
Not demented	71	22	93	185	51	236
Mild to severe dementia	2	50	52	87	121	208
Total	73	72	145	272	172	444

*Source: O'Connor et al. (1988)

Sensitivity	96.2	58.2
Specificity	76.3	78.4
Positive predictive value	69.4	70.3
Negative predictive value	97.3	68.0

the Cambridge doctors from their recollections of each patient and their clinical notes. Furthermore, the Mannheim practitioners were provided with a one-page rating key, which gives brief guidelines for allocating each patient to a cognitive-status category, whereas those in Cambridge were simply asked to decide whether each patient was definitely not demented, possibly demented or definitely demented. The use of simple guidelines seems to be of considerable help to the practitioner in achieving accuracy of clinical rating.

A third, possibly relevant difference lies in the fact that the Cambridge doctors were in group practice, whereas those in Mannheim, as is still usual in West Germany, were all working single-handedly. This may mean that the Mannheim doctors tend to have a closer personal knowledge of the elderly patients who consult them. However, further information would be required before reaching a conclusion on this question. The fact that the Cambridge study was restricted to patients aged 75 or over may also have had an influence, since it is particularly among patients in the highest age groups that difficulties of diagnostic assessment, above all with respect to mild dementia, are likely to arise.

Finally, the method of selecting practices may have played a part. In Mannheim, where it is planned to include in all some 20 practitioners in the current study, the first eight are probably above average both in their readiness to participate and with respect to their interest in the problems of elderly patients. It is thus entirely possible that the level of case detection may decline somewhat as the study proceeds and other practices are incorporated.

A finding that calls for some explanation is the tendency of the Mannheim doctors to overdiagnose and, in consequence, to manifest a lower specificity as screening agents than their Cambridge colleagues. The 22 patients who proved to be "false positives" included a high proportion with sensory or physical impairment. It thus seems plausible that the practitioners were influenced by knowledge of these patients' disabilities in activities of daily living to underestimate their level of mental functioning.

Early Detection and the Staging of Dementia

How much can approaches of this kind contribute to the early detection of progressive dementing disorders? While a firm answer to this question must await the findings of prospective longitudinal studies, some useful hints may be provided by data already available from cross-sectional studies. Thus, by establishing which specific impairments of cognitive and related neuropsychological functions are manifested by elderly persons with mild, moderate and severe dementia, it may be possible to decide if the resulting profiles correspond to the stages of a progressive

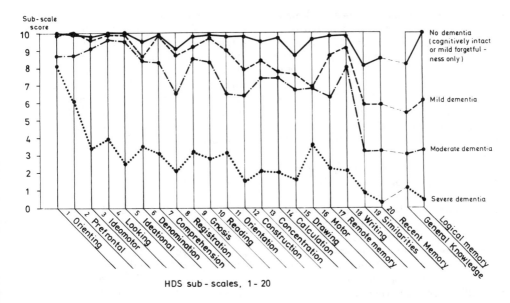

Figure 16.2. Mean subscale scores on augmented *Hierarchic Dementia Scale,* according to degree of dementia (CAMDEX severity criteria).

dementing illness, as differentiated by Reisberg et al. (1982), Hughes et al. (1982) and other workers.

In Figure 16.2, profiles of neuropsychological functioning, based on the 22 subscales of the augmented *Hierarchic Dementia Scale* (Cole & Dastoor, 1987), are compared for the patients investigated in Mannheim, divided into four groups according to the "CAMDEX" criteria of clinical severity. All the ratings included here are based entirely on testing the old people concerned, and exclude other information obtained at interview, such as ratings of everyday disability or evidence of behavioural disturbance reported by relatives. The profiles are clearly differentiated and correspond to a pattern of progressive mental deterioration which commences in the areas of abstract thinking, short-term memory and recall; thence spreads to affect cognitive performance more generally and finally attacks psychomotor functions. Since a progression of this kind is entirely consistent with what is known from clinical research about the staging of dementia, it is a tenable working hypothesis that at least a proportion of the patients classed as cases of mild cognitive impairment are actually in the early

stages of progressive dementing illness and will become dependent on care within the next year or two.

Discussion

The data presented here support the view that early detection of dementia is now feasible in a high proportion of cases, by quite simple techniques. Preliminary findings in Mannheim as well as those of the Cambridge project (O'Connor et al., 1988) point to general practice as a potentially important setting for case detection, and eventually for secondary or tertiary preventive measures.

It would appear that many general practitioners are now much better at recognising dementia and cognitive decline in their elderly patients than has been widely supposed. Possibly their abilities in this respect have improved a good deal over the past quarter century, as one effect of a growth in awareness of the importance of geriatric medicine for the family doctor.

Which strategies of screening and case finding should be adopted remains an open question, awaiting further research. Undoubtedly most practitioners would require some kind of systematic help. Short question batteries such as the *Mental Status Questionnaire* could serve this purpose, but a danger exists that their routine use would be delegated to practice nurses and receptionists; that they would be applied too mechanically and that they would distress or alienate some patients. Moreover, the problem of continuing surveillance could not easily be resolved by this means.

The approach preferred in Mannheim— that of supplying the practitioner with simple practical guidelines for rating the old person's cognitive status—could overcome these objections, but requires active participation and a degree of personal engagement on the doctor's part. Its application on a large scale and over prolonged periods has still to be tried out. A complementary strategy of potential importance calls for the involvement of practice-at-tached community nurses in the assessment of old people's mental status and disabilities, on the basis of home visits (Harwin, 1973).

Each of these methods must be carefully evaluated. If their application, singly or in combination, proves effective in the early detection of dementia, it will represent a first step towards resolving what seems destined to be one of the major public-health problems of the decades ahead.

Acknowledgement

The study of dementia in Mannheim general practice patients is supported by a grant from the Federal Ministry of Science and Technology. We are grateful to our co-workers, Dr. M. Arneburg, Dr. H. Sandholzer, Martina Schäufele, and Dr. A. Zintl-Wiegand, for their cooperation and help in the research project.

References

Allgulander, C., Fisher, L. B. 1986). Survival analysis (or time-to-an-event analysis) and the Cox regression model: Methods for longitudinal psychiatric research. *Acta Psychiatrica Scandinavica, 74,* 529–535.

Bickel, H., & Cooper, B. (1989). Incidence of dementing illness among persons aged over 65 years in an urban population. In B. Cooper & T. Helgason (Eds.), *Epidemiology and the prevention of mental disorder* (pp. 59–76). London: Routledge.

Cole, M., & Dastoor, D. (1987). A new hierarchic approach to the measurement of dementia. *Psychosomatics, 28,* 298–304.

Cooper, B., & Bickel, H. (1984). Population screening and the early detection of dementing disorders in old age: A review. *Psychological Medicine, 14,* 81–95.

Cooper, B., & Bickel, H. (1989). Prävalenz und Inzidenz von Demenzerkrankungen in der Altenbevölkerung. Ergebnisse einer poulationsbezogenen Laengsschnittstudie in Mannheim. *Der Nervenarzt, 60,* 472–482.

Cooper, B., & Morgan, H. G. (1973). *Epidemiological psychiatry.* Springfield, IL: C.C. Thomas.

Cooper, B., & Schwarz, R. (1982). Psychiatric case-identification in an elderly urban population. *Social Psychiatry, 17,* 43–52.

Copeland, J. R. M., McWilliams, C., & Dewey, M. E. (1986). The early recognition of dementia in the elderly: A preliminary communication about a longitudinal study using the GMS-AGECAT package (community version). *International Journal of Geriatric Psychiatry, 1,* 63–70.

Eastwood, M. R., & Corbin, S. (1981). Investigation of suspect dementia. *Lancet, i,* 1261.

Folstein, M. E., & Folstein, S. E. (1975). Mini Mental State. A practical method for grading the cognitive state of patients for the clinician. *Journal of Psychiatric Research, 12,* 189–195.

Folstein, M., Anthony, J. C., Parhad, I. et al.(1985). The meaning of cognitive impairment in the elderly. *Journal of the American Geriatric Society, 33,* 228–235.

Goldberg, D. P., Cooper, B., Eastwood, M. R. et al. (1970). A standardised psychiatric interview for use in community surveys. *British Journal of Preventive and Social Medicine, 24,* 18–23.

Harwin, B. (1973). Psychiatric morbidity among the physically impaired elderly in the community: A preliminary report. In J. K. Wing & H. Häfner (Eds.), *Roots of evaluation* (pp. 269–278). London: Oxford University Press.

Hughes, C. P., Berg, L., Danziger, W. L. et al. (1982). A clinical scale for the staging of dementia. *British Journal of Psychiatry, 140,* 566–572.

Kahn, R. L., Goldfarb, A. I., Pollack, M. et al. (1960). Brief objective measures for the determination of mental status in the aged. *American Journal of Psychiatry, 117,* 326–328.

Kay, D. W. K., Henderson, A. S., Scott, R. et al. (1985). Dementia and depression among the elderly living in the Hobart community: Effect of diagnostic criteria on prevalence rates. *Psychological Medicine, 15,* 771–788.

O'Connor, D. W., Pollitt, P. A., Hyde, J. B. et al. (1988). Do general practitioners miss dementia in elderly patients? *British Medical Journal, 297,* 1107–1110.

Pfeffer, R. I., Kurosaki, T. T., Harrah, C. H. et al. (1981). A survey diagnostic tool for senile dementia. *American Journal of Epidemiology, 114,* 515–527.

Reisberg, B., Ferris, S. H., De Leon, M. J., & Crook, T. (1982). The Global Deterioration Scale for assessment of primary degenerative dementia. *American Journal of Psychiatry, 139,* 1136–1139.

Roth, M., Tym, E., Mountjoy, C. Q. et al. (1986). CAMDEX: A standardised instrument for the diagnosis of mental disorder in the elderly, with special reference to the early detection of dementia. *British Journal of Psychiatry, 149,* 698–709.

Small, G. W., & Greenberg, D. A. (1988). Biologic markers, genetics and Alzheimer's disease. *Archives of General Psychiatry, 45,* 945–947.

Taylor, R. C., & Ford, G. G. (1987). Functional geriatric screening: A critical review of current developments. In R. C. Taylor & E. G. Buckley (Eds.), *Preventive care of the elderly: A review of current developments* (Occasional Paper 35). London: Royal College of General Practitioners.

Williamson, J., Stokoe, I. H., Gray, S. et al. (1964). Old people at home: Their unreported needs. *Lancet, i,* 1117–1120.

Chapter 17
Tertiary Prevention: Treatment and Rehabilitation of Schizophrenic Patients— Results of the Finnish National Programme

Yrjö O. Alanen, Raimo K. R. Salokangas, Markku Ojanen, Viljo Räkköläinen & Kari Pylkkänen

Schizophrenia is certainly the most disregarded of the major public health issues. In Finland, for example, the hospital expenses attributable to schizophrenia rose to more than 12% of all hospital expenditure in 1985. Moreover, treatment costs are estimated to be only one-third of the real economic losses caused by mental disorders. The contribution of other expenses, especially those caused by the absence from work due to the long duration of the illness, amounts to 65% of the total cost to the community (Vinni, 1983).

Schizophrenia was the reason for about 11% of disability pensions granted to Finns of working age, with the percentage rising to 24% for the 16–44 age group. The total cost of schizophrenia is therefore comparable to that of cancer (Keith, 1987).

There are different reasons for the disregard of the schizophrenia problem. We can note the old prejudices against mental illness, combined with the surprisingly persistent, if ungrounded, belief that there is no real cure for schizophrenia. This goes hand in hand with the stigma commonly experienced by individuals prone to psychosis, whose ability to influence public opinion is markedly less than that of other medical patients, such as heart-disease patients.

Need for an Integrated Approach to Schizophrenia

One of the causes hampering the progress of secondary and tertiary prevention of schizophrenia is the lack of consensus about the nature of the illness among researchers and mental health staff. Aetiological hypotheses emphasising biomedical or psychological aspects, or the significance of the family and other interpersonal networks, all have their own supporters, who often restrict themselves, inappropriately, to their own limited field of research.

The causes of schizophrenia are still unknown. We are probably dealing with a multifactorial syndrome with different causes having different weight in different individuals. It is most probable that biological, psychological and social factors all contribute to the aetiology and course of schizophrenia. Particular attention is now being given to the phases of puberty and adolescence and their typical problems along with the earlier stages of development.

Although several models of treatment could be based on these different approaches (cf. e.g. Alanen, 1985), in practice hardly anybody wishes to deny that neuroleptic medication, confidential long-term individual relationships, family-supportive measures and social rehabilitation all contribute to the treatment of schizophrenic patients.

Because of the heterogeneity of schizophrenic conditions, the therapeutic needs of each patient—and his or her immediate environment—must be considered in detail, determining which therapeutic measures are indicated and how they can best be implemented and mutually combined.

The same is true of the choice of psychotherapeutic treatments. The experiences obtained in Turku (Alanen et al., 1986, 1988b) clearly suggested that the effects of a global psychotherapeutic approach on the patients' prognosis are favourable compared with more limited psychotherapy. By global approach we here mean a therapeutic approach that is at the same time integrated and individually planned, striving to meet the needs of each patient (e.g., whether family therapy or individual therapy or a combination thereof) in a case-specific manner.

Neuroleptic treatment should also be integrated as part of a more comprehensive therapeutic approach. In our opinion, the most suitable dose of neuroleptic medication is the minimum amount that suffices to bring the patient's ability of contact and communication to a level optimal for his status. These drugs alleviate the symptoms of the acute phase and, according to numerous investigations (cf. Davis et al., 1982), reduce the liability to relapse. Our own findings indicate that protracted high-dose treatment may have adverse psychosocial effects (Alanen et al., 1986). Psychopharmacological researchers (e.g. Donaldson et al., 1983) now propose that the customary doses should be cut down because of the risk of tardive dyskinesia.

Few question the importance of a family-centered psychiatric approach both in the beginning and during the later phases of treatment. The importance is even greater when the emphasis of psychiatric activities is transferred from hospital to the community.

Administration of Tertiary Prevention

The treatment and rehabilitation of schizophrenic patients are responsibilities of the public health care system. The reasons for this include the frequently serious nature of the illness, the long duration of the treatment and, especially, the variability of the challenges posed by treatment and rehabilitation. Most patients require both inpatient and outpatient care, particularly during the early stages of their illness. It is therefore necessary that the health care system function flexibly, and that the staff of different units are capable of mutual cooperation.

Treatment resources are best concentrated at the level of secondary, specialised health care, but close cooperation between the pri-

mary and secondary health care systems is also needed. The role of primary care is particularly important at the early stages of treatment when psychosis can be detected early on and the first, influential contacts with patients and their families are being made. Primary health care also has an important role during the later stages of treatment, when the responsibility for the treatment and rehabilitation of discharged long-term patients is divided between the primary and secondary health care systems. We must ensure liaison and a consequent functional integration between these two organisations. In the countries or areas in which secondary psychiatric health care is undeveloped, the role of primary services in the treatment of schizophrenia is particularly conspicuous.

Another sector cooperating with psychiatric health care is the social welfare system, which is needed for the financial and social support of the patients (sickness allowance, pensions, lodging services, domestic help, etc.). Cooperation is also necessary with vocational guidance and employment officers. Counselling and guidance in decisions concerning work and studying, trials of work, courses and sheltered work are important aspects of tertiary prevention in this field.

Preventive measures should also reach beyond the official organisations. Good working conditions should be ensured for voluntary health care associations and especially organisations of patients and their relatives. It is important to maintain cooperation between these organisations and the official administration. As Wing (1986) points out, the patients' relatives are in fact the most essential agents of primary care and should therefore be supported in many different ways both within the health care system (home nursing) and outside it.

The follow-up findings of the *WHO International Pilot Study of Schizophrenia* (WHO, 1973, 1979) indicated that both the psychosocial and the clinical prognosis of schizophrenia are clearly better in the developing than in the developed world. The reason postulated for this is the greater cohesion of the supportive extended kinship networks in the developing countries (Mosher & Keith, 1979; British Medical Journal, 1980), as well as the generally less complicated social systems, which make the return to work and other activities easier for the patients.

Waxler (1979), who studied schizophrenia in Sri Lanka, particularly underlined the significance of cultural beliefs and the lack of social labelling as factors influencing the prognosis. Without commenting on these hypotheses any further, we can justifiably point out that as the separateness and loneliness of people is increasing in our societies, so mental health workers have every reason to fight against this development by supporting existing communal groups and networks and by creating new human environments in place of those already lost. Psychotherapeutic schizophrenia research has indicated the critical position of symbiotic needs and their relevant satisfaction in the lives of schizophrenic individuals as well as their enhanced tendency to feel anxiety upon separation (e.g. Searles, 1965; Burnham et al., 1969).

Problems of the Health Care System

Until the 1950s, the central goal of psychiatric health care in the treatment of schizophrenia was to build hospitals. In Finland, for example, a large program of building mental hospitals understood to be custodial places without any special need to discharge patients was undertaken in the late 1950s and early 1960s. These new hospital beds replaced a system of low standard nursing homes and provided a better institutional milieu for the chronically ill patients. This building programme doubled the number of psychiatric beds, bringing it up to about 4 per thousand of our 5 million population.

A new era began in the 1960s. The advent of neuroleptic medication and the development of outpatient care resulted in a new, socially progressive ideology to bring the patients out of the hospital, providing them alternative modes of treatment and therapeutic milieus outside hospitals. In the United States, this trend was notably promoted by the Community Mental Health Centers Act passed by the Kennedy administration in 1963. In Britain and the Netherlands, such innovators as Early (1960), Freudenberg (Wing, 1960) and Speijer (1961) developed re-

habilitation for return to work by setting up sheltered workshops and industrial therapy organisations. Later development of deinstitutionalising and rehabilitative activities has been described, for example, by Wing and Brown (1970), Bennett (1978), Talbott (1984) and Anttinen (1985, 1989; cf. Figure 17.1).

Many of the European countries also began gradually to develop a sectorised psychiatric organisation whose goals were to minimise the barrier between the hospital and the community, and to strive toward an integrated administration based on catchment area responsibility. An early initiative was also made in Finland to develop a network of psychiatric outpatient care pivoting on outpatient centers, which are separate from hospitals, but belong to the same district administration. Presently, there are 250 decentralised centers of this kind in Finland.

In the 1970s, and especially in the 1980s, the reorganisation of the psychiatric health care system has met with problems and resistance in many countries, which have notably restricted the possibilities of developing outpatient care and associated alternative modes of treatment (e.g. Stein & Test, 1978) and rehabilitation in the public health sector. While the goal of the innovators was to achieve deinstitutionalisation to improve the patients' life quality and, we can even say, to improve their human rights, governments with conservative social-political ideologies felt it to be, first and foremost, an easy way to save tax-payers' money. There are alarming reports from the United States especially of previous mental hospital patients being left to their own devices, a marginal group in a hard-nosed society (e.g. Borus, 1981; Freedman, 1989).

Leading social psychiatrists in many countries have therefore been fully entitled to claim that the resources liberated by decreasing pressure on the hospitals should still be used for the treatment of the patients, although the focus of treatment is now different. The information from Italy, where the 1978 Mental Health Act was the most radical in the world as regards deinstitutionalisation, has been contradictory, suggesting that there are marked regional differences in the enforcement of the law and the experiences obtained from the innovations. Good and flex-

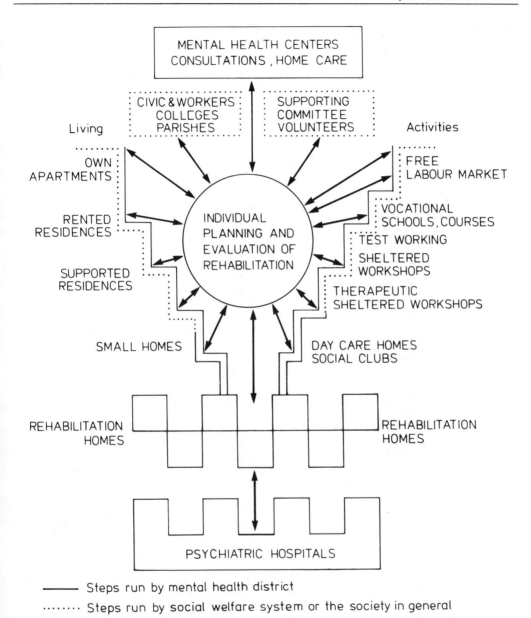

Figure 17.1. An integrated rehabilitation model for long-term psychiatric patients (after Anttinen, 1989).

ible cooperation between mental health serv-ices and other health and social services as well as a systematic collection of data about the activities of the service occur in some areas (Pirella, 1989), but not in others.

The Nordic countries have so far avoided the most acute effects of such social-political disputes. In Finland, the 1980s signified con-siderable progress in psychiatric health care. An indication of this is the National Schizo-phrenia Programme, whose structure and re-sults will be reported below.

The National Schizophrenia Programme in Finland

In Finland, the local authorities are responsible for providing health care including the mental health services. The central government shares the financial responsibility for the service by subsidising approximately 50% of the costs. After the Second World War, the country was divided into Mental Health Districts that are run by local administrative units and provide both outpatient and inpatient mental health services.

At the end of the 1970s, psychiatric public health activities continued to be quite hospital-centered in Finland. The number of all psychiatric beds was still one of the highest in the world: 4.0 per 1000 inhabitants. 10,000 of these beds—that is, about 50%—were occupied by schizophrenic patients, and three-quarters of these patients had been in the hospital continuously for over a year.

The situation did not change during the decade despite the efforts to improve staff resources in psychiatric outpatient care: the treatment system was stagnating.

In 1981, the National Board of Health launched a state-wide project in cooperation with the Association of Mental Hospitals and the Finnish Hospital League, in order to promote the research of schizophrenia and to improve the treatment and rehabilitation of patients suffering from this disorder. A national project organisation was established, and the National Programme thus initiated was a central tool in the general health policy aiming at a reorganisation of all psychiatric treatment by developing a community-based system with an emphasis on outpatient care.[*]

The more specific aim of the National Programme was to cut down the number of both new and old long-stay schizophrenic patients in hospitals by half during the 10-year period from 1981 to 1991. It was assumed that the methods for achieving this would be developed by the year 1987. The summary report of the programme was published in Finland in 1988 and will be published in English in 1989 (National Board of Health in Finland, 1989).

There were two main aims:

1) to research the existing system of care and its effects;

2) to encourage the inclusion of innovative experiments in the projects in order to improve therapeutic activities and to develop the system of psychiatric care.

Each Mental Health District in the country was asked to participate and to nominate contact persons for the programme, and workshops for them were organised. An annual follow-up including all the districts was arranged, with a special effort to demonstrate the changes in the numbers of new and old long-term schizophrenic patients as well as in the use of psychiatric beds in general, and developments in the provision of outpatient services.

Two extensive action research projects were carried out. One aimed at modifying the treatment of new schizophrenic patients (the NSP project[**]), the other at an improvement of the rehabilitative activities provided for long-term schizophrenic hospital patients (the LSP-project[***]).

In addition to this, the districts were encouraged to initiate developmental projects of their own, supervised by the national project organisation. We also established special expert groups to advise on prevention and primary health care. In the latter part of our programme, a special project was established in one district to find models for innovation within the framework of an integrated district-wide setting.

Sixteen of the 22 Mental Health Districts in Finland participated actively in the projects. During the years 1981–1988, 15 reports were published by the project organisation in Finnish. Two of the main reports of the programme have been translated into English (National Board of Health in Finland, 1987, 1989).

---

[*]   Project leader: Prof. Yrjö O. Alanen; leader of Task Force Committee: Dr. Kari Pylkkänen.
[**]   Research leader: Prof. Raimo K. R. Salokangas; leader of the developmental activities: Dr. Viljo Räkköläinen.
[***] Leader: Professor Markku Ojanen.

Research Findings

Incidence and Prevalence of Schizophrenia

The incidence of schizophrenia as estimated by new schizophrenic patients contacting psychiatric care for the first time in their life in 1983–1984 was found in the NSP to be 16–19 per 100,000 annually (Salokangas et al., 1987). The patients were diagnosed according to the DSM-III criteria (schizophrenic disorder, schizophreniform psychosis and schizoaffective psychosis). No regional differences worth mentioning were found in the incidence of new cases between six districts in various parts of the country.

If the patient's stay in hospital for the first time lasted for more than 1 continuous year (as shown by censuses carried out at the end of two consecutive years), he was defined as *a new long-stay case*. A patient staying continuously for more than 2 years in hospital was defined as *an old long-stay case*. The survey covered the whole country.

The findings indicated that there were great regional differences in the chronicity of schizophrenia. Both the annual incidence of new longstay patients and the prevalence of old long-stay patients varied as much as fourfold regionally in 1982. The mean annual incidence of new long-stay schizophrenics was as high as 8.7 per 100,000 at the beginning of the project.

We considered two explanations for the combination of regional differences in chronicity with no differences in incidence (Alanen et al., 1988a):

1) A high prevalence of long-stay in-patients was clearly associated with a large number of hospital beds within the district (especially with a high number of inactive hospital beds outside the main hospital of the district).

2) The prevalence of chronic hospital schizophrenics tended to be higher in the socioeconomically inferior areas of eastern and northern Finland as compared with the more well-to-do areas in southern and southwestern Finland.

These differences were not explained by the number of psychiatric staff. The findings were regarded as an indication of the need to improve the psychosocial skills of the staff as well as the availability of alternative psychiatric services.

The New Schizophrenia Project (NSP)

The aims of the NSP project were defined as follows:

1) to estimate the annual incidence of new schizophrenic patients in Finland;

2) to develop new treatment practices emphasising a psychotherapeutic and family-centered orientation;

3) to evaluate these treatments and their effect on patient outcome;

4) to make suggestions for public health policy about the treatment of schizophrenia.

Six mental health districts from various parts of the country were included in the study, covering a population of approximately 1.1 million. The conditions of life in these districts represented quite well the total population of the country (Salokangas et al., 1987).

The developmental activities of this action research project included:

1) commitment of the districts to carrying out the project,

2) establishment of a project organisation in the districts, with the members participating in national workshops,

3) workshops arranged for the local project organisations in the districts,

4) support given to developmental activities in the districts through supervision and consultation,

5) planning of structured questionnaires that, apart from collecting data, should stimulate the psychotherapeutic and family-centered orientation of the treatment.

Data were collected on all new schizophrenic patients between 15 and 44 years of age (N = 227) and their families, who sought psychiatric care between 1 March 1983 and 29 February 1984. Follow-up studies including both the patients and their families were carried out 12 and 24 months after the admission, and a 5-year follow-up has just proceeded to its final stage. These investigations were carried out by the teams involved in the treatment, and the follow-up also included a revision of the treatment plans.

The therapeutic approach stimulated by the NSP project was mainly based on the "need-specific approach" earlier developed in Turku (Alanen & al., 1986, 1988b) and included the following goals:

1) Treatment should be coordinated and correspond to case-specific needs.

2) The treatment should be psychotherapeutic in a broad sense and family-centered in orientation (based on a psychodynamic frame of reference).

3) There should be an initial family-centered intervention with both the patient and the persons close to him present.

4) Treatment should be, as much as possible, carried out within the framework of the outpatient system.

5) Large doses of maintenance neuroleptic drugs should be avoided.

6) Rehabilitation needs should be clarified and taken into account from the beginning.

The initial family-centered intervention was carried out in 70% of the cases in the six districts included in the study. Our experience was that initial family-centered interventions clearly diminished the regression and individual labelling of many patients and aided considerably the diagnostic planning of the treatment. During the follow-up period, 60% of the patients had individual psychotherapy and 40% had received family therapy on a regular basis, for at least a short time. 95% of the patients received neuroleptic drugs, but only 63% of them were on neuroleptic medication at the end of the follow-up period.

A notable finding was that 70% of the schizophrenic patients had—even when first admitted for treatment—needs for rehabilitative measures, at least in a broad sense. The percentage of patients of this kind was greatest in the eastern district of North Carelia (87%), while only 50% of the patients in the Turku district in the southwestern part of the country displayed such needs.

At the end of the 2-year follow-up period, the percentage of patients with psychotic

symptoms had diminished to 50%. According to the *Swedish Comprehensive Psychopathological Rating Scale* (CPRS, Jacobson et al., 1978), the number of subjects having symptoms compatible with the DSM-III criteria of schizophrenia declined from the initial 90% to 30% by the end of the follow-up (Figure 17.2). The number of patients with neurotic and depressive symptoms changed less. At the end of the follow-up period they numbered 32% and 58%, respectively (Salokangas et al., 1988).

Figure 17.2. Clinical state (no psychotic symptoms) and social state (in work or studying; on disability pension; unemployed; in work the entire preceding year) of the NSP patients at the time of admission, at 1-year follow-up (n=226), and at 2-year follow-up (n=219).

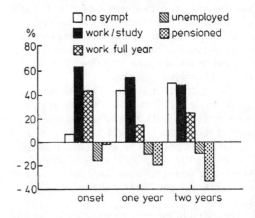

At the beginning of the follow-up, 63% of our patients were working at home or outside the home or were studying. At the end of the follow-up the corresponding number was 48%. One-third of the patients had been granted a pension because of their illness.

The clinical prognosis of the patients was thus relatively good. The social prognosis, however, was worse. An increase of patients without manifest psychotic symptoms with a simultaneous decrease of the amount of patients active in the working life is a trend conspicuous in Finland also found in other recent follow-up investigations (Kuusi, 1986), compared with earlier prognostic estimates (Achte et al., 1980; Salokangas, 1978). The employment situation during the 1970s is one possible explanation. However, because of benefits, the economic dependency of many patients had diminished during the second follow-up year.

At the end of the second follow-up year, the main treatment setting of our patients was the mental health outpatient centre, which took care of 51% of all the cases. Almost 18% no longer needed treatment, and only 9.1% were hospitalised. The amount of hospital treatment still varied considerably between different districts: the mean was 86 days per patient (24% of the time) during the first follow-up year and 30 days (8% of the time) during the second follow-up year.

Multivariate analyses applying the theory of log-linear models (Bishop et al., 1975) indicated that the psychosocial factors explained the prognosis of the patients better than clinical factors. The most important individual predictor was the team's assessment of the patient's grip on life goals and forms of satisfaction (Salokangas et al., 1989). The other important predictors include employment and the duration of symptoms before the beginning of treatment. Of the treatment variables, there was a significant trend for the combination of initial family-centered intervention and psychotherapy to be associated with a good grip on life ($p<0.01$) and with gainful employment at the end of the follow-up period ($p<0.05$) even when the background factors most significantly explaining these prognostic factors had been kept constant.

These findings strongly support a health policy emphasising early treatment and careful consideration of the psychosocial state of the patient. We also considered the preliminary experiences of the initial family-centered interventions to be promising enough to be recommended for adoption in the treatment of every schizophrenic patient.

The Long-Term Schizophrenia Project (LSP)

Eight districts participated in the LSP project. The aims of the LSP project included:

- *Support for the Foundation of New Treatment and Rehabilitation Alternatives*

Here the main model followed was the integrated, step-wise *Sopimusvuori Model*

founded by Erik E. Anttinen and his co-workers in Tampere in 1970 (Anttinen, 1985, 1989) and especially designed for the rehabilitation of long-term psychiatric hospital patients (see Figure 17.1 for a plan of the model).

At the time of the foundation of the Sopimusvuori Association, Finnish legislation did not provide all necessary activities within the public mental health system. The programme was therefore launched as a private health care plan, although in close cooperation with the public system and designed to complement its services. The *Sopimusvuori Model* has, as a result of the Schizophrenia Programme, since been adopted throughout the Finnish mental health system.

Anttinen emphasises that rehabilitation should be seen as an integrated process which aims at improving several aspects of the patient's quality of life (psychological status, social skills, occupational capabilities, physical condition). The patient's own health resources are of marked importance, and they can be stimulated by accepting the patient, as often as possible and on an equal basis, in the planning and decision-making concerning his or her own rehabilitation.

- *Implementation of the Concept of Planned Treatment Programs in the Daily Practice of Rehabilitation and Improvement of the Atmosphere of the Care*

Apart from the *Sopimusvuori Model*, which emphasises the importance of a milieu for stimulating the growth of interpersonal relationships, other models based on learning theory (exemplified by Paul & Lentz, 1977) were also tested. The contents of the programmes applied in different units could thus vary, but every programme was to have a clear structure and aim at normality of behaviour and environment. A clear structure signifies explicit individual and group plans and active participation in the programme. The daily and weekly activities were to form a coherent whole where the major parts supported each other.

- *Study of the Attitudes of Both the General Public and the Mental Health Personnel Toward Long-Term Hospitalised Psychiatric Patients*

The effects of the LSP project were evaluated

Table 17.1. The 4-year follow-up results of 137 chronic schizophrenic patients in major psychosocial variables: The means (and standard deviations) on initial and follow-up measures.

	1983	1987	
1. Symptoms (patient)	78.1	80.5	103
	(19.8)	(15.9)	
2. Symptoms (staff)	71.2	73.9	92
	(14.8)	(13.1)	
3. Symptoms (interv.)	72.1	77.6*	103
	(23.2)	(13.9)	
4. Social skills (staff)	51.3	54.2	92
	(13.4)	(12.8)	
5. Social skills (test)	46.0	55.2**	54
	(16.5)	(19.3)	
6. Psychic health (staff)	66.1	64.9	132
	(14.1)	(15.8)	
7. Psychic health (patient)	66.0	66.2	133
	(17.5)	(16.6)	

*$p<0.05$,, **$p<0.01$, paired t-test

Notes: The figures in the table are transformed to go from 0 to 100. The maximum positive value is in all variables 100 and the minimum negative 0. A value of 50 is the mean scale value. The high values are always positive and low negative. The value of patient symptoms of 1983 (78.1) can be interpreted so that the mean of patient symptoms was 78% of the maximum *positive* value. The most negative ratings were in social skills.
Description of variables:
1) Made for the LSP study. The total sum of 18 symptoms. Each symptom had 5-step scale from "not at all" to "a lot."
2) From Overall et al. (1972). The total sum consists of 18 symptoms that are rated with a 7-step scale.
3) BPRS, Overall & Gorham (1962).
4) Made for LSP. The total sum consists of 22 social skills that were rated with a 7-step scale from "very poor skills" to "very good skills."
5) Made for LSP. The test consists of 80 questions concerning everyday social skills. Both knowledge and actual skills are measured. Because of the length of the test, it could be given twice only to 54 patients.
6) A graphic or visual analogue rating scale devised to LSP. The highest level of psychic health (100) was "no symptoms, normal behavior" and the lowest (0) "very serious symptoms, continuous depression or psychosis, needs constant care and control."
7) A similar graphic scale as above (6) given to patients described in ordinary language.
The internal consistency reliabilities (variables 1–5) were between .84 and .95. The graphic scales correlate well (over .60) with summated variables of symptoms.

at two levels: First, a 4-year follow-up from 1983 to 1987 was carried out on 137 chronic schizophrenic patients from 20 different treatment or rehabilitation units in eight mental health districts. Initially, 57% of these patients were in hospitals and 43% in community care. The patients had stayed for an average of 12 years in mental hospitals. The mean GAS (Endicott et al., 1976) was 4.2. Most patients were evaluated eight times with a large battery of tests and rating scales. Second, the rehabilitation unit atmosphere and patients' behaviour were evaluated at follow-up by both the staff members and the patients with rating scales. Thirteen units from eight districts participated in this part of the study.

It was found (Ojanen, 1988) that, during the 4 years, 58% of the follow-up sample of 137 patients moved at last one step upwards on the scale based on the rehabilitation ladder. Some 24% remained at the same step as in the beginning, and 18% went down in the ladder. Of those in hospital, 54% moved into the community (25% of all patients into the highest ladder). The changes in the major variables during the 4-year follow-up period were small (Table 17.1) with the exception of the ratings of symptoms by local interviewers and the results of the social skills questionnaire.

Some well-organised, highly structured units of the LSP or units working in close association with the project functioned very well. These units succeeded in placing their patients into the community and achieved statistically significant changes in the patients, too.

The changes in the staff ratings of the unit atmosphere were favourable (Table 17.2). The largest changes took place in working experience, organisational leadership, unit structure, evaluation of unit results and organisational behavior. Thus, favorable changes were seen during the project both in the unit and in the whole organisation (usually a hospital). In the average patient behavior ratings no significant differences were seen.

These findings clearly indicate the importance of structured unit program planning. The favorable possibilities of rehabilitating many long-term patients outside hospitals reported by the Sopimusvuori follow-ups (Anttinen, 1985, 1989; Anttinen & Ojanen, 1984)

Table 17.2. The changes in unit atmosphere and behavior in 13 LSP units from 1983 to 1987: The means (and standard deviations) of initial and final staff ratings in 10 dimensions.

	1983	1987
1. Work satisfaction	70.6	73.3
	(10.0)	(7.5)
2. Unit results evaluation	65.7	71.2*
	(11.1)	(4.5)
3. Work experience	56.5	69.5**
	(5.0)	(8.1)
4. Organisational behavior	44.4	50.3*
	(13.2)	(13.8)
5. Work atmosphere	66.0	71.5
	(17.3)	(10.6)
6. Unit structure	54.3	59.8*
	(6.9)	(5.2)
7. Therapeutic community	61.9	67.6
	(11.9)	(7.7)
8. Patient behavior	52.9	58.1
	(17.3)	(10.0)
9. Organisational leadership	54.4	60.6*
	(15.0)	(13.7)
10. Unit leadership	68.2	74.7
	(12.8)	(7.7)

*$p<0.05$, **$p<0.01$, paired t-test

Notes: All variables are from a test called *The Finnish Rating Scale of Treatment Communities*. The first two variables are continuous graphic or visual analogue rating scales. The highest level (described as 100) means that work is rated as very satisfactory or that unit results correspond very well with the stated aims of the unit. The lowest value (0) means that the working conditions are very unsatisfactory or aims are not obtained at all.
The last eight variables are sums of six to ten items. Each item had seven alternatives. As an example, the seventh variable measures the application of Jonesian type of therapeutic community principles. The median internal consistency reliability of these eight variables was .80.
The variables were transformed so that the maximum positive value is in all variables 100 and the minimum negative 0. A value of 50 is the mean scale value. At least 2/3 of staff members rated their units.

were confirmed. The most distinct individual factor predisposing to a better social prognosis was a change in the everyday skills and coping abilities rather than in factors related to symptoms of the illness.

Table 17.3. The National Schizophrenia Programme. The whole country: Evaluation of development; 1982–1986.

Indicator	1982	1986	Change %
Overall use of psychiatric beds per 1000 (census 31.12.)	3.48	2.65	-24.1
Number of old long-stay schizophrenic patients (>2 yrs in hospital)	5.687	4.419	-22.3
Number of new long-stay schizophrenic patients (1 yr, <2 yrs in hospital)	406	348	-14.3

Impact on National Development

Table 17.3 summarises developments between 1982 and 1986 throughout the country. Within the same period, the number of lodgings provided by the Mental Health Districts increased by 50%, rising to 0.3 per thousand per population. This was one of the preconditions for the success of the often long-lasting rehabilitation activities started in the hospital setting.

The 10-year goals of the programme were still far from being achieved in 1986. Even so, the change that had taken place in the overall use of psychiatric beds during four years appears quite considerable. The rehabilitation of older long-stay patients to outpatient care was more successful than the reduction of long-stay treatment of new schizophrenic patients. This was, at least partly, explained by the finding that the average time between the first admission and the first long-stay period was 7 years; the results of our NSP project thus cannot be seen very quickly.

The national programme clearly had a stimulating effect on development. We found it rewarding to experience the atmosphere of genuine enthusiasm that was aroused among the staff in several districts and served to improve the self-esteem of our entire psychiatric community.

Conclusions

Our project results lead us to the following conclusions:

1) The treatment of schizophrenic patients should be coordinated and according to case-specific needs.

2) We must improve the social situation of schizophrenic patients—psychosocial factors influence their prognosis more than clinical factors.

3) We must encourage earlier admission for treatment.

4) An initial family- (or network-) centered intervention is a good way to start the treatment and to diagnose therapeutic needs. This succeeds best when it is made by a team with family-therapy training.

5) We can diminish the dosage of neuroleptic drugs by promoting psychotherapy and family-centered activities

6) Good results of rehabilitation are related to the structure of programmes, a stimulating climate in the units, and the stepwise rehabilitation organisation developed in the districts.

7) The rehabilitation of long-term hospitalised patients into the community is economically less expensive than hospital treatment but should necessarily be combined with the establishment of alternative services.

8) Committed leadership and qualitative resources hold the key position.

One of the central recommendations of the project to improve the quality of care was to establish multi-professional acute psychosis teams, which were to take care of the interactionally oriented initial intervention and follow-up of the new cases. Similarly, the establishment of rehabilitation teams to develop and integrate the activities included in the tertiary prevention of schizophrenia was recommended by the National Programme (National Board of Health in Finland, 1987, 1989).

References

Achté, K., Lönnqvist, J., Piirtola, O., & Niskanen, P. (1980). Verlauf und Prognose schizophrener Psychosen in Helsinki. In G. W. Schimmelpenning (Ed.), *Psychiatrische Verlaufsforschung. Methoden und Ergebnisse*. Bern: Huber.

Alanen, Y. O. (1985). Family therapy as part of the treatment of schizophrenia. In T. Helgason (Ed.), *The long-term treatment of functional psychoses*. Cambridge: Cambridge University Press.

Alanen, Y. O., Räkköläinen, V., Laakso, J., Rasimus, R., & Kaljonen, A. (1986). *Towards need-specific treatment of schizophrenic psychoses*. Heidelberg: Springer-Verlag.

Alanen, Y. O., Pylkkänen, K., & Kokkola, A. (1988). The Finnish national programme for the treatment and rehabilitation of schizophrenic patients. *International Hospital Federation, Official Yearbook 1988*, 103–109.

Alanen, Y. O., Lehtinen, K., & Räkköläinen, V. (1988b). *Need-specific treatment of new schizophrenic patients. Further experiences in the Turku project*. Paper presented at IX International Symposium on the Psychotherapy of Schizophrenia, Torino. To be published in congress proceedings.

Anttinen, E. E. (1985). Chronicity and hospitalisation: Can the vicious circle be broken? In T. Helgason (Ed.), *The long-term treatment of functional psychoses*. Cambridge: Cambridge University Press.

Anttinen, E. E. (1989). Integrated model of rehabilitation for schizophrenic patients. In *Lectures and reports*. WPA Regional symposium. Granada.

Anttinen, E. E., & Ojanen, M. (1984). *Sopimusvuoren terapeuttiset yhteisöt*. Tampere: Lege Artis.

Bennett, D. (1978). Social forms of psychiatric treatment. In J. K. Wing (Ed.), *Schizophrenia, towards a new synthesis*. London: Academic Press.

Bishop, Y. M. M., Frenberg, F. E., & Hollan, P. W. (1975). *Discrete multivariate analysis: Theory and practice*. Cambridge, MA: MIT Press.

Borus, J. F. (1981). Deinstitutionalization of the chronically mentally ill. *New England J. Med., 305*, 339–342.

British Medical Journal (1980). 2 Feb: Schizophrenia in different cultures (Editorial).

Burnham, D. L., Gladstone, A. I., & Gibson, R. W. (1969). *Schizophrenia and need-fear dilemma*. New York: Internat. Universities Press.

Davis, J. M., Janicek, P., Chang, S., & Klerman, K. (1982). Recent advances in the pharmacologic treatment of the schizophrenic disorders. In *Psychiatry 1982, Annual Review*. Washington, DC: The American Psychiatric Association.

Donaldson, S. R., Gelenberg, A. J., & Baldessarini, R. J. (1983). The pharmacological treatment of schizophrenia: A progress report. *Schizophrenia Bull., 9*, 502–527.

Early, D. C. (1960). The industrial therapy organisation (Bristol). *Lancet, 2*, 754–757.

Endicott, J., Spitzer, R. L., Fleiss, J. L., & Cohen, J. (1976). The global assessment scale. A procedure for measuring overall severity of psychiatric disturbance. *Arch. Gen. Psychiatry, 33,* 766–771.

Freedman, A. M. (1989). U.S. community mental health: Myths and reality. In *Lectures and reports.* WPA Regional symposium. Granada.

Jacobson, L., von Knorring, L., Matsson, B., Perris, C., Edenius, B., Kettner, B., Magnusson, K.-E., & Willemoes, P. (1978). The comprehensive psychopathological rating scale—CPRS—in patients with schizophrenic syndromes. *Acta Psychiat. Scand., Suppl 271,* 39–44.

Keith, S. J. (1987). Personal communication.

Kuusi, K. (1986). *Prognosis of schizophrenic psychoses in Helsinki 1975–1983.* (Finnish, with English summary.) Helsinki: Monographs of Psychiatria Fennica, No 13.

Mosher, L. R., & Keith, S. J. (1979). Research on the psychosocial treatment of schizophrenia: A summary report. *Am. J. Psychiatry, 136,* 623–631.

National Board of Health in Finland (1987). *Treatment and rehabilitation of schizophrenic patients: The treatment model.* (Report No 103. Finnish, to be published in English as a Supplement to *Nordisk Psykiatrisk Tidsskrift* 1990 by Alanen et al.)

National Board of Health in Finland (1989). *The Finnish Schizophrenia Programme: The summary report.* To be published in the Research Report Series of the National Board of Health.

Ojanen, M. (1988). *Rehabilitation of schizophrenic long-term patients: The follow-up results of the LSP project.* (Finnish with English summary. Reports of *Psychiatria Fennica* No. 82.)

Overall, J. E., & Gorham, D. R. (1962). The brief psychiatric rating scale. *Psychol. Rep., 10,* 799.

Overall, J. E., Henry, B. W., & Markett, J. R. (1972). Validity of an empirically derived phenomenological typology. *J. of Psychiat. Res., 9,* 87–99.

Paul, G. L., & Lentz, R. J. (1977). *Psychosocial treatment of chronic mental patients: Milieu vs. social-learning programs.* Cambridge, MA: Harvard University Press.

Pirella, A. (1989). Ten years of deinstitutionalisation in Italy. In *Lectures and reports.* WPA Regional symposium. Granada.

Räkköläinen, V., Salokangas, R. K. R., & Lehtinen, P. (1979). Protective constructions in the course of psychosis: A follow-up study. In C. Muller (Ed.). *Psychotherapy of schizophrenia.* Amsterdam: Excerpta Medica.

Salokangas, R. K. R. (1978). Psychosocial prognosis in schizophrenia. *Ann. Univ. Turkuensis, Ser. D, 9.*

Salokangas, R. K. R., Stengård, E., Räkköläinen, V., Helle, I., & Kaljonen, A. (1987). *New schizophrenic patients and their families.* (Finnish, with English summary. Helsinki: Reports of *Psychiatria Fennica* No. 78.)

Salokangas, R. K. R., Räkköläinen, V., Stengård, E., & Kaljonen, A. (1988). *Treatment and outcome of new schizophrenic patients: A two-year follow-up.* (Finnish, with English summary. Helsinki: Reports of *Psychiatria Fennica* No. 81.)

Salokangas, R. K. R., Räkköläinen, V., & Alanen, Y. O. (1989). Maintenance of grip on life and goals of life: A valuable criterion for evaluating outcome in schizophrenia. *Acta Psychiatr. Scand., 80,* 187–193.

Searles, H. F. (1965). *Collected papers on schizophrenia and related subjects.* New York: Internat. Univ. Press.

Speijer, N. (1961). *The mentally handicapped in the sheltered workshops.* Hague: Ministry of Social Affairs and Public Health.

Stein, L. I., & Test, M. A. (1978). *Alternatives to mental hospital treatment.* New York: Plenum.

Talbott, J. A. (Ed.) (1984). *The chronic mental patient five years later.* Orlando, FL: Grune & Stratton.

Vinni, K. (1983). The cost of mental disorders to the community. *Finnish. Social Review, 1,* 23–24.

Waxler, N. E. (1979). Is outcome for schizophrenia better in non-industrial societies? *J. Nerv. Ment. Dis., 167,* 144–192.

Wing, J. K. (1960). A pilot experiment of long hospitalised male schizophrenic patients. *Brit. J. Prev. Soc. Med., 14,* 173–180.

Wing, J. K. (1988). Coping with schizophrenia at home. In C. N. Stefanis & A.D. Rabavilas (Eds.), *Schizophrenia: Recent biosocial developments.* New York: Human Sciences Press.

Wing, J. K., & Brown, G. W. (1970). *Institutionalism and schizophrenia. A comparative study of three mental hospitals 1960–1968.* Cambridge: Cambridge Univ Press.

World Health Organization (1973). *The international pilot study of schizophrenia.* Geneva: WHO.

World Health Organization (1979). *Schizophrenia: An international follow-up study.* Chichester: Wiley.

Section V

The Organization of Services

*I*n their chapter in this section, Horst Dilling and W. Bolstorff consider the German nineteenth century debate between Griesinger and Roller about the relative value of community and institutional care of psychiatric disorder. This debate has been repeated, and is still being repeated, in many other European countries and in the United States. Which side wins will dictate the development of the public health services for the mentally ill for a decade or more—until the debate is re-opened by a new generation. It therefore makes more than historical sense for Dilling and Bolstorff to open their chapter with an account of it and, indeed, for it to be the point of departure for this introduction.

Griesinger was, as in other respects, ahead of his time in championing community care, and for social psychiatrists it is almost impossible to disagree with him. Although the institution may be able to provide a healthy environment, and even a psychologically satisfactory one, social psychiatrists recognize that that is not enough to ensure healthy psychological development. A reasonably normal social environment is also required—something institutions cannot provide.

It is, therefore, no surprise that none of the authors of chapters in this section advocates an end to the current emphasis on community care in all the psychiatric services of the developed world. On the other hand, none of them is unaware of the potential for abuse and neglect inherent in community care, which so often seems to the health service administrator to promise a better service for less money. This neglect is particularly likely to affect groups with little economic or social status: the elderly, the chronically mentally ill and those with schizophrenia.

Each of these groups has a particular chapter devoted to them in this section. John Wing's chapter on planning psychiatric services concentrates on the needs of the chronically ill or disabled in particular. He adumbrates three "fundamental public health principles":

- that health and social authorities have a responsibility for the public health of a defined population;

- that a full range of services should be provided; and

- that they should be integrated, with easy movement between them.

Achieving these aims relies heavily on the work of social psychiatrists. Not only must the distribution, course and causes of disease be investigated, but so must be the means by which disease can be identified in its earliest stages, and—the features of specific relevance to this section—social psychiatrists must provide information about the needs of specific populations and the extent to which they are being met.

Epidemiology has been less successful in these last two areas, but with the development of standardized methods of diagnosis and comprehensive data-bases on service use in different localities and different countries, advances are now being made, as Wing points out. One of the immediate, striking results of comparisons between different services is that the amount of service needed varies considerably between areas much more than any variation in the incidence of disease. The variation is closely related to the level of social support or social integration in the area, and Wing advocates marital status and a composite index of social advantage as measures that a planner could use.

As Griesinger recognized, community care principally means care by relatives or close friends. Its success therefore depends on the availability and functioning of families and social networks. These factors will also determine how many and what kind of services will be needed in a particular area. Medical factors will also influence service provision—Wing gives the examples of neurological impairment in mentally ill people and aloofness in the mentally handicapped—but social psychiatrists may have given too much attention to these at the expense of examining social support in more detail.

The elderly are, like the chronically mentally ill, a group at a particular disadvantage. Anthony Mann and his colleagues, in a very detailed account of services for the elderly mentally ill in one particular area of London, demonstrate the use of both medical and social indices of need for service. The picture that emerges is that somatic symptoms do predict use of the general practitioner, but the presence of dementia does not, and although the presence of depression does predict general practice attendance, it is a weak relationship and does not often lead to the prescription of specific treatment by the general practitioner. The presence of depression or dementia has little influence on the provision of other services: what does predict this are whether or not a person is living alone and the extent to which their activity is limited. Mann et al.'s findings are a cause of some concern, in that services were so little influenced by diagnosis, but they reinforce the importance of social factors in influencing the course of disorder and the needs for treatment.

In a provocative article in this section, Berthold Gersons argues that services would be better if they were provided by mental health specialists, to whom general practitioners should more often refer. He considers the low referral rate to be the result of competition between general practitioners and secondary mental health care providers, and he would like to see it increased. He also takes the view that general practitioners are refractory to training in the detection of psychiatric disorder, a view with which our own experience (Gask et al., 1988) forces us to disagree. The Dutch situation, based as it is on a traditionally large mental illness sector, is obviously different from the British one. Gersons' chapter is important because it focusses attention

on the relationship between the general practitioner and the specialist services, which is always an area of potential difficulty in community care. It does not, however, consider the social factors that may influence a general practitioner referral to a specialist, although, as already noted, these may be the major determinants of help-seeking in the first place.

Specialist treatment agencies, on the other hand, are beginning to recognize the need for partnership with the existing social supports of the patients referred to them and two chapters specifically address this. Tom Burns discusses a novel service in which home assessment and follow-up replaces hospital attendance, and Dilling and Bolstorff discuss the development of psycho-educational workshops in Lübeck and the relatives' support groups to which they led. Neither of these innovations have had full evaluations, but both provide suggestions of an improvement in outcome and in relatives' satisfaction.

The principles of crisis intervention, home assessment, and family support have been known for a considerable time and even evaluated, notably in Denver (Polak & Kirby, 1976). They have been gradually adopted in other services, but much more slowly in Europe than in the United States. They are a feasible alternative to hospital-based care and have an immense appeal, both to the general public, for whom the institution is often an object of fear or stigma, and to the health administrator, whose budget can be relieved of the heavy economic demands of large hospital units. The cost of community care is not less than hospital care, it is simply spread more widely. Once the community begins to count it, history shows that a reaction to deinstitutionalization can be expected.

Hospitals provide a synthetic social network that encroaches on and may engulf any of the patient's pre-existing networks. If these latter networks are therapeutic or potentially so, then hospital admission may be destructive. If they are nonfunctioning or even harmful, then admission is likely to be constructive. The extent of social adaptation is, therefore, as Wing documents in his chapter, a crucial determinant of what type of service a person needs. Many doctors intuitively understand this. The low rates of determination of psychiatric disorder described by Gersons and Mann et al. in their chapters are possibly the result of the use by general practitioners of such a social criterion of illness: certainly in Mann et al.'s study, depression and dementia were more likely to be recognized when they were coupled with social impairments.

Terms like social adaptation or social support are so vague that their use as a principle in the organization of services seems equally ill-defined. Such terms were not devised to assist those responsible for the organisation of services, and it is perhaps hardly surprising that they have not proved equal to the task. Clinical psychiatrists intuitively recognise that social factors are of great importance in deciding whether treatment of a given episode of psychotic illness would be better undertaken in hospital or at home, but they have been reluctant to devote the same amount of effort to systematic descriptions of such factors as they have to the measurement of details of psychopathology.

In the typical evaluation of community care versus institutional care, patients with a wide range of social characteristics are randomly assigned to two conditions, with the ultimate aim of showing which kind of approach has the best overall characteristics. However, there is ample evidence that hospital and home treatment of psychiatric disorder are not opposed but complementary. A breakthrough in the organization of psychiatric services would be made if the next generation of evaluative studies were to recognize this, and to be directed to determining which types of treatment best suit which patients rather than making a case for one type of service being better than another for unselected patients. If these studies were also to discover *measures of social need that were sensitive to the effects of treatment*, then considerable progress would be made in the direction of meeting one of the public health challenges that Holland draws psychiatrists' attention to in the first chapter of this volume: that of making the medical treatment as effective in reducing the disability of chronic psychosis as it has been in the reduction of the impact of heart disease.

References

Gask, L., Goldberg, D., Lesser, A. L., & Millar, T. (1988). Improving the psychiatric skills of the general practice trainee: An evaluation of a group training course. *Medical Education, 22*, 132–138.

Polak, P. R., & Kirby, M. W. (1976). A model to replace psychiatric hospitals. *Journal of Nervous and Mental Disease, 162*, 13–22.

Chapter 18

From Hospital to Community— A Self-Help Organisation Developed by Family Members of Schizophrenic Patients

H. Dilling & W. Bolstorff

The importance of family life-style and inter-action for the course of schizophrenia has been acknowledged since the early 1970s. In 1962, Brown et al. and in 1976 Vaughn and Leff indicated that a high score of expressed emotion in families favoured a relapse compared to families with a low index of EE. The importance of family interaction for relapse of schizophrenics was confirmed by Angermeyer (1984c) in West Germany. In the 1980s research findings on the whole stimulated interest in family interaction, which before had been neglected in many instances (Hubschmid, 1985).

Though family therapy has been carried out for many years (Kaufmann, 1969), interest in family help for psychotic patients dates back even further, into the last century. In the 1860s and 1870s, this subject was strenuously discussed in Germany. On the one side was the famous German psychiatrist Griesinger, who wanted psychiatric departments in the general hospital and family care outside the hospital (Griesinger, 1865), and on the other side were many directors of the mental hospitals like Roller (1874) and others who fought for inpatient care far from the cities—and far from the families of the patient. The same struggle was repeated in the early 1930s when again a movement of socially oriented psychiatrists tried to promote different types of family care (Bufe, 1939). But these efforts were wiped out by the destruction of German psychiatry in the murder of about 100,000 patients during the "Third Reich." After the war, mental hospitals again came to be used as before. The old hospital-centered system was restored, and no need for psychiatric reforms was felt.

Thus, in Germany, the reform movement started later than in other countries. The landmark was the so called "Enquête Report" of an expert commission in 1975 with recommendations for a reform of psychiatric care (Bericht, 1975). In November 1988 another report and recommendations followed. This time the situation of the families burdened with psychiatric patients was represented in particular (Empfehlungen, 1988).

The first manifestation of schizophrenic illness is followed by many cognitive and emotional difficulties for the patient and the patient's family. This means that, especially in the initial stage, there is need for information and therapeutic intervention in the family. The psychiatrist is expected to give specific information about the disease, which often is refused by the doctor or given inadequately because of a contrasting position to the family, fear of personal involvement or lack of time.

Often family members, especially parents and spouses, feel helpless as guilt and hidden aggression burden their relationship with the patient. In this respect, concepts like the "schizophrenogenic mother," by no means proven, have done harm to the families.

Help in this desperate situation may offered from different sides. Apart from psychoanalytical or educational family therapy together with the patient (Hogarty et al., 1986; Smith & Birchwood, 1987), new possibilities have been developed to support the relatives. Katschnig and Konieczna (1984b) distinguished between the dominance of experts and the dominance of family members in different types of groups: on the one hand, family therapy and patient-centered family member groups with strong influence of professional therapists, and on the other hand family member groups with or without experts, which are dominated by the relatives of the patients.

The tendency to form self-help groups is characterized by typical dynamics, as described by a number of authors. In most instances—at least in Germany—the starting point is in the institution, and the self-help movement in the community is the last step in the development (Angermeyer, 1984b; Hubschmied, 1985). Thus, the experiences described in this chapter are quite typical of self-help schemes induced by experts, and constitute a necessary aspect of the psychiatric reform in our country (Bolstorff, 1988). Although Angermeyer (1984b) described an early approach to this subject in 1968, in Germany general interest in this subject arose later compared to England, France, Italy or the United States. In these countries the reform of services predominantly meant dehospitalisation, and self-help organisations of family members accompanied the reform, since families were much more confronted with their ill members.

At the Lübeck psychiatric department, we started to work with relatives in 1980. We initially offered open groups to family members of schizophrenics, but this attempt was not successful, since no group situation with continuous contacts developed. We therefore continued with closed groups of 10–12 family members, mostly parents, but also spouses and siblings. These groups started at a fixed date and were designed to end after eight weekly sessions. We invited families of all schizophrenic patients admitted to our wards. Initially, our closed groups were guided by one or two psychiatrists, but later it appeared to us that the needs of the relatives called for participation of other professionals as well. At present, the groups are run by our clinic-nurse and a social worker. A psychiatrist assists only at some occasions when medical information is the main topic of the session.

The aims of our groups can be described as follows:

- information about the *disorder and its therapy*;

- information about *social help and financial*

questions (these are important items in our country since one-fifth of the cost for chronic psychiatric patients is paid for by the patient and the family, which of course means an additional burden);

- the chance to *talk about the present problems* to an understanding and empathic audience;

- the *exchange of experiences* between the members of the group;

- learning to reflect not only the problems of the patient but also their *own needs,* which have usually been suppressed: not only the well-being of the patient matters, but also that of the family member defined as healthy!

Thus, the group is often considered as a place to take a breather: there is an identity of in-group feeling derived from common suffering as contrasted with the outer world.

After the scheduled eight meetings, some of our groups decided to continue and did so. Yet there was also a need to contact members of other groups to discuss questions they had in common. For this reason, we arranged a meeting for the participants of our former 10 to 12 groups covering a period of 4 years. This meeting in 1987 was attended by about 50 former participants. It was impressive to listen to the experiences of the family members: social isolation, violence and attacks by the patients, discrimination by the social environment and financial hardships. A special problem was the lack of expert medical help especially at night and on weekends. Even if the emergency department of the hospital was able to contact the mental illness service connected with it during the weekend, this was not an acceptable solution. Most of the families wanted contact with psychiatrists who routinely treat the patients, and yet they do not offer an emergency service. Another urgent problem is the lack of professional occupation outside the home. As a result of the discussion, we proposed a self-help-organisation that should try to promote the demands so urgently felt.

Following this meeting, a core group of members started to build up an association of family members and friends of psychiatric patients outside the hospital in the community,

Table 18.1. Number of self-help groups in the Federal Republic of Germany in relation to the number of inhabitants.

State	Inhabitants (in millions)	No. of groups	Group per inhabitants (in thousands)
Berlin	1.9	10	185
Hamburg	1.6	16	101
Lower Saxony	7.2	28	259
Schleswig-Holstein	2.6	20	131
Hesse	5.6	37	150
North Rhein-Westfalia	16.8	79	213
Rheinland-Palatinate	3.6	8	454
Saarland	1.1	4	263
Baden-Württemberg	9.2	36	257
Bavaria	11.0	42	261
Bremen	0.7	1	677
Federal Republic of Germany	61.3	281	218

which rapidly spread over the whole state of Schleswig-Holstein. Now, 2 years later, 20 groups of family members are established, working in all parts of the state.

Their aims are the promotion of community psychiatry and acquisition of equal status for psychiatric patients vis-à-vis other medical patients. This can be achieved by further development of community psychiatry with adequate services, and is expected to reduce discrimination at the same time. To reach this goal, the next task is informing the general public, e.g. through the press and other mass media and by contacts to politicians. As it is difficult for the patients themselves to forward their own interests in public, family members have to form a pressure group.

The day-to-day work is done by offering telephone services to all relatives in need of help and by special office hours, for instance, in the local building of the health insurance organization. Regular groups are offered as open in-groups consisting only of relatives. Another type are information groups with invited professionals from different institutions.

It is a demonstration of the present necessity that such an organization could have been built up in such a short period of time:

an administration, a group organisation, an information service and a lobby for psychiatric patients.

The "Angehörigenverband" is connected with comparable associations in the Federal Republic which founded a central national association some years ago. Compared to 1982, when Angermeyer (1984b) reported not even 20 self-help groups in the entire Federal Republic, an investigation in January 1989 showed 281 groups in existence in our country—quite a progress!

However, on average, each group still has a "catchment area" of more than 200,000 inhabitants (see Table 18.1). This is certainly not enough groups yet, but the movement is still growing.

In this paper, we have described the increasing impact of the work of organized family members of schizophrenics in Germany. This development should be regarded by professionals as an important addition to our somewhat stagnant psychiatric reform, and it should be seen as an essential part of community psychiatry. One would hope that in time many unsolved public health problems concerning psychiatric prevention and rehabilitation may be approached more effectively.

References

Angermeyer, M. C.(1984a). Der theorie-graue Star im Auge des Psychiaters—Zur Rezeption der Wissensstände der Familienforschung in der Sozialpsychiatrie. In M. C. Angermeyer & A. Finzen (Eds.), *Die Angehörigengruppe* (pp. 17–24). Stuttgart: Enke.

Angermeyer, M. C. (1984b). Seit kurzem auf dem Weg zur Selbsthilfe: Angehörigeninitiativen in der Bundesrepublik Deutschland. In M. C. Angermeyer & A. Finzen (Eds.), *Die Angehörigengruppe* (pp. 70–76). Stuttgart: Enke.

Angermeyer, M. C. (1984c). Zusammenhänge zwischen der familialen Umwelt und dem Verlauf psychischer Krankheit—Ein Argument für die Gruppenarbeit mit Angehörigen. In M. C. Angermeyer & A. Finzen (Eds.), *Die Angehörigengruppe* (pp. 79–99). Stuttgart: Enke.

Bericht über die Lage der Psychiatrie in der Bundesrepublik Deutschland (1975). Bonn: Deutscher Bundestag. Drucksache 7/4200 und 4201.

Bolstorff, W. (1988). Arbeit mit Angehörigen schizophren erkrankter Patienten. *Schleswig-Holsteinisches Ärzteblatt, 9,* 552–54.

Brown, G. W., Monck, E. M., Carstairs, G. M., & Wing, J. K. (1962). The influence of family life on the course of schizophrenic illness. *British Journal of Preventive and Soc. Med., 16,* 55–68.

Buchkremer, L., & Lewandowski, L. (1987). Therapeutische Angehörigenarbeit bei schizophrenen Patienten: Rationales, Konzept und praktische Anleitung. *Psychiat. Praxis, 14,* 73–77.

Bufe, E. (1939). *Die Familienpflege Kranksinniger.* Halle a.S.: Carl Marhold.

Empfehlungen der Expertenkommission der Bundesregierung zur Reform der Versorgung im psychiatrischen und psychotherapeutisch / psychosomatischen Bereich auf der Grundlage des Modellprogramms Psychiatrie der Bundesregierung (1988). Aktion Psychisch Kranke (Ed.). Bonn: Bundesminister für Jugend, Familie, Frauen und Gesundheit.

Falloon, I. R. H., McGill, C. W., Boyd, J. L., & Pederson, J. (1987). Family management in the prevention of morbidity of schizophrenia: Social outcome of a two-year longitudinal study. *Psychological Medicine, 17,* 59–66.

Griesinger, W. (1865). Über die familiale Ver-

pflegung. *Allgemeine Zeitschrift für Psychiatrie und psychiatrisch-gerichtliche Medizin, 22,* 390.

Hell, D. (1988). Angehörigenarbeit und Schizophrenieverlauf. *Der Nervenarzt, 59,* 66–72.

Hogarty, G. E., Anderson, C. M., Reiss, D. J., Kornblith, S. J., Greenwald, D. P., Javna, C. D., & Madonia, M. J. (1986). Family psychoeducation, social skills training, and maintenance chemotherapy in the aftercare treatment of schizophrenia. *Archives of General Psychiatry, 43,* 633–642.

Hubschmid, T. (1985). Von der Familientherapie zur Angehörigenarbeit oder vom therapeutischen zum präventiv-rehabilitativen Paradigma in der Schizophreniebehandlung. *Fortschr. Neurol. Psychiat., 53,* 117–122.

Katschnig, H., & Konieczna, T. (1984a). Angehörigenprobleme im Spiegel von Selbsterfahrungsgruppen. In M. C. Angermeyer & A. Finzen (Eds.), *Die Angehörigengruppe* (pp. 100–109). Stuttgart: Enke.

Katschnig, H., & Konieczna, T. (1984b). Typen der Angehörigenarbeit in der Psychiatrie. *Psychiat. Prax., 11,* 137–142.

Kaufmann, L. (1969). Die Handhabung der Beziehung zwischen Familie, Patient und Klinik. *Z. Psychother. Med. Psychol., 19,* 221–229.

Leff, J., Kuipers, L., Berkowitz, R., Eberlein-Vries, R., & Sturgeon, D. (1982). A controlled trial of social intervention in the families of schizophrenic patients. *Brit. J. Psychiat., 141,* 121–134.

Masz, E. (1989). *Die Angehörigenbewegung in der Bundesrepublik Deutschland.* Lübeck: unpublished manuscript.

Roller, C. F. W. (1874). *Psychiatrische Zeitfragen aus dem Gebiet der Irrenfürsorge.* Berlin: Georg Reimer.

Schindler, R. (1976). Bifokale Familientherapie. In H. E. Richter et al. (Eds.), *Familie und seelische Krankheit* (pp. 216–235). Reinbek: Rowohlt.

Smith, J. V., & Birchwood, M. J. (1987). Specific and nonspecific effects of educational intervention with families living with a schizophrenic relative. *Brit. J. Psychiat., 150,* 645–652.

Vaughn, C., & Leff, J.P. (1976). The measurement of expressed emotion in families of psychiatric patients. *Br. J. Soc. Clin. Psychol., 15,* 157–165.

Chapter 19

The Evaluation of a Home-Based Treatment Approach in Acute Psychiatry

Tom Burns

There is a growing body of evidence (Stein & Test, 1980; Braun et al., 1981; Hoult, 1984,) that psychiatric services based on an approach stressing ready availability, active out-reach and comprehensive provision of psychological, nursing and medical care in noninstitutional settings is an approach acceptable to both patients and their families. Such services have been shown to result in a reduction in hospital usage without sacrificing either clinical or social recovery. Where families have been interviewed and assessed, there has been no clear evidence of any increased burden on them. The Mendota County Study (Stein & Test, 1980; Weisbrod et al., 1980), perhaps the most ambitious of all these studies, claims improved social and clinical functioning in the noninstitutional cohort achieved with only a modest increase in cost. Given the savings in cost demonstrated by Hoult (1981), Mosher (1983) has questioned why these research findings have not been translated into clinical practice.

Psychiatry has traditionally had a low public health profile. The absence of any established effective interventions for primary prevention and, indeed, scepticism that any such activities are feasible have hampered such a development. The climate in the United States has not always been so pessimistic. Caplan (1970) has emphasised the preventative potential of early intervention in psychiatric and psychological disorders. Crisis intervention theory has proposed that such early intervention is of value both in shortening the duration of suffering for patients' families and also in preventing the development of dysfunctional adaptations from the crisis. A simple example of this would be increased alcohol consumption to self-medicate anxiety symptoms during a crisis leading to an enduring alcohol dependency syndrome.

The methodological problems of effectively testing such a hypothesis are enormous. Consequently, evidence of the crucial influence of crisis intervention is lacking despite its obvious clinical relevance in a proportion of cases. Thus, the main burden of early intervention trials to date has been to examine their impact on rates of hospitalisation and the clinical and social recovery of patients, rather than to test their role in prevention.

Professional concern for the implementation of these research findings has become particularly pertinent in the light of two internationally important developments. First, there is the shift to community care and the decanting of patients from mental hospitals in the industrial West. It makes little sense to expend all this energy getting patients out of hospital and yet rely on readmission as the basis for treatment in subsequent relapses. It is essential that mental health professionals begin to adapt their practices to the changing options available to the patients. Second, there has been the recent growth of the consumer movement in mental health. The reduction in social stigma attached to mental illness has allowed families of sufferers, and in some cases the sufferers themselves (e.g. The Mental Health Patients Union in Holland and Camden Consortium in the U.K.), to form politically articulate bodies to lobby for improvements in the provision of their care. When measured, home-based care has resulted in greater consumer satisfaction than control treatments (e.g. Stein & Test, 1980; Hoult, 1981). In the U.K., the National Schizophrenia Fellowship has lobbied energetically for the expansion of CPN services.

Mosher (1983) suggests that professional opposition to enacting community care initiatives derives mainly from psychiatrists' view of themselves as hospital specialists. Active out-reach and home-based care patterns would threaten a decrease in status to that of a primary-care provider. It would also threaten to distance the psychiatrist from specialist colleagues and to undo much of the progress over the last 30 years in legitimising psychiatry as a mainstream medical activity. While there is undoubtedly substance to this suggestion, there remain other important sources of resistance expressed by psychiatrists in the U.K.

- First, there is a general concern about extrapolating from service research findings to clinical practice. The placebo effect of enthusiastic research teams is known to contribute substantially to improved outcome. The quality of mental health services is notoriously sensitive to issues of professional morale. This scepticism is confirmed by the experience of well documented, successful experimental services drifting back to the status quo when the grant has finished and the research team disperses. Concerns about the "specialness" of research experiences are further heightened by the many exclusion criteria that are often necessary to generate a homogeneous patient sample for assessment.

- Second, only one substantial controlled study (Stefansson & Cullberg, 1986) evaluating a fully comprehensive psychiatric service of the type common in North Europe has been published to date. The North American and Australian studies have described practice dealing almost exclusively with psychotic patients. Short-term and minor disorders are dealt with in private practice and insurance-based services. Comprehensive mental health care services in the U.K. need to take account of a wide range of morbidity. Demonstrated advantages in one group of patients may be outweighed by possible drawbacks in applying the same style of service to a very different type of patient. Indeed this is highlighted in the Stefansson and Cullberg study, in which the compulsory admission rates rose rather than fell after the introduction of an active community programme. It is unlikely that small sectorised

services such as exist in the U.K. (with a recommendation of one consultant led team to a population of 40,000) could operate efficiently with more than one basic model of service delivery. Also, the role of the general practitioner is central to U.K. medical practice, and nowhere is this dealt with in any of the published studies of alternatives to hospital-based care.

Notwithstanding this absence of local research literature, a number of home-based psychiatric services have developed in the U.K., for example, Dingleton (Jones, 1987) and Napsbury (Scott & Starr, 1981). These have been based on varying theoretical models. The Dingleton service in the Scottish borders is the most longstanding service, having existed in a stable form for over two decades. The hospital serves a discrete rural and semirural catchment area of 100,000. It offers all new referrals prompt (1–10 days) home assessment by a multidisciplinary team that always includes a psychiatrist, a trained member of another discipline (social work, nursing, psychology) and usually a student. There are no routine outpatient clinics. Home-based treatment is the aim where possible and is usually carried out by members of the assessing team often in close cooperation with the patient's GP. A small inpatient unit is available for patients who need 24-hour nursing care. Home treatment is usually focussed and short term, involving the family and often drawing heavily on crisis intervention theory (Caplan, 1970) for its structure. The team maintains a close working relationship with GPs by regular monthly meetings.

The author had trained in this method of working as a trainee psychiatrist and subsequently introduced a similar scheme to his suburban London sector on appointment as consultant. The service proved feasible within the resource limitations of the NHS and was popular with local GPs, trainees, students and patients. Given its modest resource requirements and durability, it seemed a suitable model of home-based treatment to evaluate for wider use within the NHS. Local colleagues declared themselves willing to take part in a randomised study, and a grant was sought and obtained from the DHSS.

The Services Studied

Three pairs of consultants agreed to take part in the study. Each pair and their teams shared responsibility for a sector between 56,000 and 84,000 (not all were full-time). Each sector was normally divided between the teams into two discrete patches but served by the same social service area office and hospital unit. For the duration of sample collection, the paired teams agreed to take any referral from within the joint sector and retain responsibility for that patient for a full year. Sectorisation of adult psychiatric services has been established for many years. Local general practitioners are used to having only one psychiatric team to refer to. All were written to in advance of the study, and none objected openly to the prospect of a small number of their patients being treated by the neighbouring team. One team in each pair undertook to provide the experimental service (referred to subsequently as CC—Community Care), the other providing the control service (subsequently referred to as SC—Standard Care).

Two sectors (Wimbledon and Mitcham) are in the London Borough of Merton. These are essentially suburban areas and are in the mid-range of social deprivation as assessed by the Jarman indices (Jarman, 1983). Wimbledon is the more affluent of the two with only a small immigrant population and its housing is mainly owner-occupied. Mitcham has a higher proportion of municipal housing including the Borough's problem estate. Local authority mental health provision in the borough is scant with no local authority staffed hostel and only one local authority day centre. The third sector, Wandsworth/North Battersea, is in the inner city with considerable deprivation and large decaying public housing estates. It has a large immigrant population and a significant transient population with high psychiatric morbidity. It is in the top 10% of social deprivation as measured by the Jarman indices. All inpatient services (other than 5 beds in an outlying hospital) are provided from Springfield Psychiatric Hospital, which is also the base for the CPN service and district psychology service to all three sectors. All the teams have input from the local authority social services and have

trainees and medical students attached whose needs have also to be considered.

The Home-Based Treatment Team (CC)

The study required of the experimental team that all new referrals be assessed in their homes (or exceptionally in GP surgeries/local authority day centres) by a psychiatrist and another trained mental health worker. The assessment was to be as soon as practicable, and the team would operate without any waiting list. They were encouraged to treat the patient at home if possible, but the study design did not preclude admission if the clinical circumstances demanded it. Close contact with GPs was encouraged, but clearly the randomisation procedure precluded the regular close working of the Dingleton model.

Two of the experimental teams had no experience of working in this manner. Monthly lunch-time meetings were arranged to discuss possible problems, and a CPN experienced in the home treatment service worked alongside these two teams for a number of weeks to model the experimental service. A period of 4 weeks operating the appointment and assessment system (to eliminate administrative hitches) preceded the randomisation.

The Study

Intake was completed in each of the three sectors before starting on the next one. All patients aged 16 to 75 referred by their GPs who had not been in contact with the psychiatric teams in the preceding 12 months were randomised. Randomisation was conducted by daily interception of all referrals—by telephone or letter. The research secretary contacted the relevant team secretaries and allocated all referrals using a random number sequence. Teams were under instructions not to initiate any response to a new referral until the research secretary had allocated them. It was agreed that, in dire emergency, a coin would be flipped, but this never proved necessary.

The SC team either sent routine outpatient appointments, admitted direct or assessed on urgent DVs as appropriate. The experimental team operated as outlined above. Direct ad-

Table 19.1. Details of the assessment programme.

Patient Measures	Intake	1/12	6/12	1 year
Social History	+			
PSE	+			+
BPRS	+	+	+	+
Clinical interview	+	+	+	+
Social functioning	+	+	+	+
Life events	+			+
Economics questionnaire	+			+
Consumer satisfaction		+	+	+
Informant Measures				
Assessment of patient's symptoms	+	+	+	+
Family burden	+	+	+	+
Assessment of patient's social functioning	+	+	+	+
Economics questionnaire	+			+
Consumer satisfaction		+	+	+

missions to hospital (e.g. compulsory and emergency patients) were randomised separately on the ward to ensure their equal distribution. Patients needed adequate English to be interviewed. There were no other social or clinical exclusion criteria. Assessments were at intake, 6 weeks, 6 months and 12 months. These assessments were by experienced clinical interviewers not involved in the patient's management. The interviews covered social and demographic data, clinical status, social disability, family burden, life events and consumer satisfaction. Their timing is shown in Table 19.1.

In addition to this series of four cross-sectional assessments, a treatment diary was kept for outpatient treatments. The extent of inpatient and day-patient care was recorded retrospectively from notes. These data are to form the basis for a comparison of costs incurred.

Early Results

Patient Flow

A total of 332 referrals were randomised over the period of 14 months. A total of 53 patients failed to show. As expected, failure to show was more common in the standard care group:

- Community Care: 12 out of 150 (8%);
- Standard Care: 41 out of 182 (22%); ($\chi^2 = 12.94$; p<0.001).

A further 53 were excluded because it was found at contact that they lived outside the catchment area or were already in active treatment. Fifty-four patients refused assessment by the research team after assessment by the clinical team. No significant differences were found in these latter rates for the two treatment groups. Of the 172 patients entered in the study, 143 continued to cooperate with further follow-up interviews. A total of 130 was assessed on four occasions. In both groups about half the patients was assessed within the first week (51% CC, 47% SC). These patients were usually referred by telephone with a request for urgent assessment. The CC patients had a much higher rate of initial assessment in the next 2 weeks. Ninety-six percent of CC patients were assessed by 3 weeks as opposed to 74% of SC patients ($\chi^2 = 16.25$, p<0.001).

Patient Characteristics

The two groups were found to be closely comparable in terms of basic sociodemographic data. Table 19.2 shows the initial PSE categories (Hoult's figures from Sydney are given alongside for comparison). The PSE discriminates between "psychotic depression" and

Table 19.2. Initial PSE categories—London/Sydney.

ICD 8 Diagnostic groups:	London		Sydney*
285.3 Paranoid Schizophrenia			
296.1 Mania	20.9%		74%
296.2 Psychotic Depression			
297.9 Paranoid Psychosis			
296.2/300.4 Psychotic or Neurotic Depression	16.6%		8%
300.4 Depressive Neurosis	25.7%		6%
		39.9%	
300.0/300.2 Other Neuroses	14.2%		
No diagnosis	22.7%		12.5%
Mean total PSE score	17		30.7

* Department of Health, New South Wales (1983). *Psychiatric hospital versus community treatment—A controlled study.* Sydney: Department of Health, New South Wales.

Table 19.3. Hospital admission rates.

	CC	SC
Study patients	n = 94	n = 76
Admitted 1st month	11 (11%)	22 (28%)
		p<0.05
Admitted overall	17 (18%)	26 (33%)
		p<0.05

Significance tested with χ^2

"neurotic depression." Where the clinical picture does not confidently identify neurotic depression, the patients are included along with the psychotic depression patients in the category "psychotic or neurotic depression," but if neurotic depression can be clearly distinguished, the patients are classified in the neuroses. The figures for individual sectors and CC and SC samples have not, as yet, been separated. A preliminary check of the patients with a diagnosis of psychosis shows a higher rate in Wandsworth (30%) than in Mitcham and Wimbledon (12.5% and 18.6%, respectively) as would be expected from the populations served.

Admission Rates

Table 19.3 shows admission rates for the first month after assessment and for the total period of the study. The admission rates are significantly lower in the CC group both for the first month after assessment (11% vs.

28%) and for the whole follow-up year (18% vs. 33%). It should be stressed that this is only a preliminary analysis and more detailed analyses of social and clinical outcome are as yet uncompleted.

Discussion

It is risky to draw conclusions from early data on such a heterogeneous group of patients and outcome data are not, as yet, analysed in any detail. Some observations can, however, be made on the broad patterns of involvement with patients who were randomised into the study. All the staff involved (including quite senior clinicians) remarked that the sheer variety of pathways by which patients found their way into psychiatric care came as a surprise to them. Similarly, the course of treatment often differed markedly from what they had expected.

The rate of patients failing to attend (22%) in the SC group is very similar to that reported nationally for psychiatric patients. The 8% rate in the CC sample is significantly less. In most of these cases, it represents a failure to confirm the appointment or a cancellation. It is the practice to ask the patient to confirm the appointment by telephone. Very few visits were made to empty homes. This rate of non-attendance is higher than that routinely experienced in the Wimbledon service, which on retrospective checking runs at about 3–4%.

Failing a home visit requires active avoidance whereas failure to attend outpatients obviously does not. Our impression was that other factors were also at work in no-show patients, although the study does not allow us to examine this in any detail. Many patients told the researchers that the psychiatric referral often came as a surprise to them, and that they rarely had had a chance to talk it through in any detail with their GP. In many cases the delay between referral and assessment in the SC group may have resulted in the patient reevaluating the situation and not attending. Nor could the GP characterise the psychiatric response with any certainty at the point of referral due to the randomisation and lack of personal familiarity with one of the teams. This may have contributed to continuing ambivalence to treatment in the patient.

Preliminary examination of diagnoses does support this with a higher proportion of the CC patients suffering from minor affective disorders, alcohol abuse, or adjustment reactions. This shift in the emphasis of disorders treated when a service improves accessibility has been reported by Stefansson and Cullberg. It is not justified to assume simply that all these disorders are self-limiting, and that professional intervention is redundant. It can be argued (e.g. Lloyd, 1989) that a modest early intervention can be successful in the course of disorders where energetic treatment of the entrenched condition is costly and often unavailing. While this shift in level of morbidity was reported by the teams, none of them considered they were seeing patients they would not normally assess and treat in standard practice. While they were seeing more of such patients, they did not consider them inappropriate referrals or the "worried well." The possible preventative effect of such interventions would warrant future research.

Bearing in mind the possible impact of this shift in sampling, the admission rates for patients shown in Table 19.3 were recalculated for both patients assessed and those who failed to attend. Admission rates were, therefore, calculated for a CC sample of 106 and an SC sample of 119. While the rates of admission still favoured the CC group both at 1 month (10% vs. 18%) and for the whole follow-up (16% vs. 22%), these differences fail to achieve significance at the 5% level. This modest reduction in admissions is particularly important, however, when it is borne in mind that no extra resources had been provided for the CC team to treat these patients in their homes. Possible increased provision was considered at great length at the outset of the study. As the model of psychiatric care becomes increasingly community oriented, then appropriate redistribution of staff (in particular nurses) from in-patient services to the community must take place. Without this

the range of options available to the CC teams is severely limited. For example, it was not possible in this study to nurse patients at home for extensive (2–3 hours) periods and certainly not possible to provide any out-of-hours service. Such a facility, strengthened by OT input, would probably have avoided admission in some cases.

The decision to proceed without resource strengthening reflects our aim to meet the needs of realistic everyday practice. Others having established the success of tailor-made services in treating patients outside of hospitals, we wished to focus on the impact on outcome of what is essentially only a shift in treatment tactics. This strategic decision carried the risk that we could end up underestimating the efficacy of the community care programme. We felt in the present state of the debate that the risk should be taken.

An important issue in such a study is the reactions of those involved. Staff attitudes have been considered of considerable importance in the success or otherwise of CC research. Apart from the author, none of the psychiatrists involved had any prior experience of, or commitment to, this way of working. Their attitudes toward the trial ranged from tolerant scepticism to mild enthusiasm. All cooperated with remarkable generosity despite the heavy burden that the study inevitably imposed. Their cooperation stemmed in some measure from them having identified the model being tested as "realistic." It was not too radical for them to consider incorporating some of its principles if it should demonstrate advantages in patient care. In particular, the nonprescriptive nature of the study was essential for obtaining cooperation. None of the teams felt that a comprehensive psychiatric service could be run without inpatient beds. They would not have been prepared to take part if admission had been proscribed.

It also needs to be recognised that successful CC teams derive considerable enthusiasm and satisfaction from the sense of creating their own style of working. After all, they relinquish the security of the tried and tested for the challenge of generating their own solutions to complex problems. Our study (despite keeping the methodological constraints to a minimum) was unable to harness this potential and undoubtedly suffers as a consequence of having imposed a model of working. This resistance to an "imposed model" was even more evident in the nonmedical disciplines. In particular, the joint assessments were seen by some as devaluing professional autonomy. The need to be available for prompt assessments was viewed by others as disruptive of important long-term work. One of the originally selected possible CC teams had a sceptical consultant who was successfully converted by the trial period, but whose team was not willing to take part. Concerns about the time-consuming nature of the work were also common initially, but were usually dispelled by the trial run.

A whole host of practical problems was highlighted by the study. Because of the study duration and design, shaping of GP expectations and behaviour could not take place. In the established service, GPs usually inform patients that they will be seen at home within the next week and obtain telephone numbers to arrange appointments. As a result the experimental teams had great difficulty in equalling the early assessments characteristic of established CC teams. The absence of a multidisciplinary base, staffed by a secretary, as a central contact point for each team proved a major problem. Such a base would hold multidisciplinary case notes, and team members could meet regularly. Such a facility emerged as an essential prerequisite for such work. The general feeling of the CC teams was that their way of working was not sustainable in the long term without such a base. The problems of adequate notekeeping under these circumstances were at times overwhelming.

None of the CC teams expressed a wish to return to standard care after the study experience. They have welcomed the end of the study, however, as a chance to review their experiences and introduce those modifications and improvements that best suit the needs of their particular team and sector. Inevitably, this will involve some form of routine outpatient review (whether as a separate OP ward round or as a dedicated time slot at the end of the IP ward round) as patients requiring multiple input are treated outside hospital. The overwhelming need for such reviews, in addition to informal consultations, has been clearly identified by a number of authorities (Wooff & Goldberg, 1988; Holloway, 1988).

Joint working and formal multidisciplinary reviewing are usually stressed by established CC teams as one of the strengths of their system and an important contribution to staff morale. The two traditional practitioners of CC (the CPN and consultant on domiciliary visits), however, have been used to this activity being isolated and unscrutinised. Scrutiny—whether by a research project or by one's colleagues—can be (and was) initially very stressful. Teams moving to this way of working need to allow time and space to get to know and trust one another.

How did the customers evaluate the two services? Consumer satisfaction data are not complete yet, but some early observations on patient and family response can be reported. Information on GP opinions is yet to be sought. On the whole, patients and their families have expressed a preference for the CC model. This is often spontaneous and has been most obvious in those patients who have had previous experience of SC. The practical convenience is often cited—our travelling to them rather than their travelling to us. The problems of getting organised to attend outpatients should not be underestimated in some of these very handicapped patients. For some, on the other hand, the teams felt that more demands could have been placed directly on the patients.

The unusualness of the CC response sometimes led patients to draw unwarranted conclusions. Many took the visit as a proof of the team's special concern for them, and this probably helped cement the therapeutic alliance. Some, on the other hand, were terrified that the speed and extent of the response implied that they were much iller than their GP was letting them know! Many stated that being on their own territory (and also avoiding the mounting anxiety from waiting around in outpatient departments) made them able to communicate their concerns more openly and fully. Families saw the visit as a sign that the whole situation (not just the patient's symptoms) was being taken seriously and welcomed it.

What were the drawbacks? Concern that the neighbours might talk was expressed. This concern may reflect the stigma of being known to have a psychiatric problem or may in some cases be worries about, say, a young housewife being regularly visited at home by a man when her husband is at work. Lack of clarity about follow-up visits was a frequent complaint. Patients needed to have just as an accurate timing of the visit as for an OP appointment. "Sometime next Tuesday morning" is simply not good enough. Despite these drawbacks, few patients or families expressed a preference for SC.

Data on family burden and costing are also incomplete and unanalysed. No obvious trends emerge and clearly the task of making sense of this data is going to be extremely complex.

Summary

It has proved possible to conduct a naturalistic experiment randomising 172 patients between standard care and a model of home-based care operating within NHS resource levels. Offering rapid home assessment and treatment has resulted in a higher contact rate with referred patients. Consequently, intervention has been possible in a higher proportion of early and milder disorders than that achieved in SC without any obvious detriment to access for the more severe and chronic patients. This early intervention may lead to healthier resolution of such crises with less recourse to self-medication with alcohol or long-term dependence on prescribed medication.

This fairly simple shift in practice appears to achieve a modest reduction in hospital admission rates and to be welcomed by the patients and their families. It is unlikely, however, to be sustainable over time without adequate investment in appropriate team bases and a strengthening of the community nursing provision.

Perhaps the most important, though unmeasurable, benefit of this study is that it has introduced both junior doctors and medical students to the reality of psychiatric patients' circumstances. Many of the decisions in psychiatric practice which lead to bafflement in students make eminent sense when the patient's whole situation can be appreciated. Working closely with other professionals, though costly, permits the development of a wider perspective on psychiatric management and gives the social dimension of patient care its proper status alongside the biological. It has helped the involved teams to confront the need to establish the same professional standards (multidisciplinary working, regular reviews, etc.) for community patients as exist for inpatients.

Acknowledgements

My thanks are due to the clinical teams led by Drs. Julie Hollyman, Richard Penrose, Nick Kitson, Barry Matthews and Christopher Jarman from Springfield Hospital, Tooting, for their generous cooperation in taking part in this study.

References

Braun, P., Kochansky, G., Shapiro, R., Greenberg, S., Gudeman, J. E., Johnson, S., & Shore, M. (1981). Overview: Deinstitutionalisation of psychiatric patients, a critical review of outcome studies. *American Journal of Psychiatry, 138,* 736–749.

Caplan, G. (1970). *The theory and practice of mental health consultation.* New York: Basic Books.

Holloway, F. (1988). Prescribing for the long-term mentally ill: A study of treatment practices. *British Journal of Psychiatry, 152,* 511–515.

Hoult, J., Reynolds, I., Powis, M. C., Weekes, P., & Briggs, J. (1981). Psychiatric hospital versus community treatment: The results of a randomised trial. *Australian and New Zealand Journal of Psychiatry, 17,* 160–167.

Jarman, B. (1983). Identification of underprivileged areas. *British Medical Journal, 286,* 1705–1709.

Jones, D. (1987). Community psychiatry in the borders. In N. Drucker (Ed.), *Creating community mental health services in Scotland.* SAMH Publications.

Lloyd, G. (1989). Early intervention for alcohol abuse. In J. H. Lacey & T. Burns (Eds.), *Psychological management of the physically ill.* London: Churchill Livingstone.

Mosher, L. R. (1983). Alternatives to psychiatric hospitalisation: Why has research failed to be translated into practice? *New England Journal of Medicine, 309,* 1579–1580.

Scott, D., & Starr, I. (1981). A twenty-four hour family-orientated psychiatric and crisis service. *Journal of Family Therapy, 3,* 177–186.

Stefansson, C. G., & Cullberg, J. (1986). Introducing community mental health services. *Acta Psychiatrica Scandinavica, 74,* 368–378.

Stein, L. I., & Test, M. A. (1980). Alternative to mental hospital treatment I: Conceptual model, treatment program, and clinical evaluation. *Archives of General Psychiatry, 37,* 392–397.

Weisbrod, B. A., Test, M. A., & Stein, L. I. (1980). Alternative to mental hospital II: Economic cost-benefit analysis. *Archives of General Psychiatry, 37,* 400–405.

Wooff, K., & Goldberg, D. P. (1988). Further observations on the practice of community care in Salford: Differences between community psychiatric nurses and mental health social workers. *British Journal of Psychiatry, 153,* 30–37.

Chapter 20

The Gospel Oak Project: The Use of Services by the Elderly with Psychiatric Disorder in the Community

Anthony Mann, Gill Livingston, Angela Hawkins,
Nori Graham & Bob Blizard

Demographic Trends in the United Kingdom Population

During the 1980s, the ageing of the population has become a matter of public and political comment, particularly with current emphases on resource management in health and social services. In 1985, 15.2% of the population were 65 years old or over, 5.1% 75 years old or over and 1.2% 85 years old or over (OPCS, 1976). Warnes (1989) recently reviewed population trends for elderly people in Great Britain, commenting that the recent novelty has been the attention given to the ageing population, rather than the ageing itself. The U.K. population has been changing in its demographic distribution since the beginning of the century as a product of increased longevity and falling birth rates. Annual death rates have fallen from over 30 to 10 per 1000, and life expectancy in the male extended from 48.5 to 71.6 years during this century. These findings are common to all European countries, though demographic ageing has not yet occurred in African or Asian countries. However, with the introduction of programmes for improvements in public health and in birth control, such changes may be expected. In the U.K., the proportions of persons over 65 are not likely to increase dramatically over the next 20 years, unless there are further falls in fertility of the population or medical advances are made that further reduce old-age mortality. During the early part of the next century, however, there is likely to be a further increase in the elderly population from the baby booms that occurred after the World War II.

Yet the stability of the elderly population until the end of the century does not imply that health and social services can be maintained at the current level. There is a hidden trend. The projections of the Office of Population Censuses and Surveys (OPCS, 1987) suggest that by 1996, the proportion of those over 85 years of age amongst the population will have increased to 1.9%—a 50% increase in 10 years of approximately 400,000 people. The increase in this particular age band, who are predominantly female, widowed and often alone, will require particular resources. Physical disability, dependency on others for day-to-day activity and dementia prevalence are all greatly increased in very old age. As is shown later in this chapter, each of these factors are associated already with greater service contact.

Health Service Use and the Elderly

Reports from the United States (Waxman et al., 1983) and West Germany (Weyerer et al., 1983) suggest that the elderly patient with a psychiatric disorder, notably depression, tends to visit the family physician regularly but underuses specialist psychiatric services. Possible reasons for this discrepancy have been suggested: missed diagnoses at the primary care level, a reluctance to refer by the physician (because accompanying physical illness seemed more important), ignorance of the opportunity on the part of the elderly patient or distance to the hospital.

In the U.K., the role of the general practitioner in the treatment and referral of elderly patients has been more systematically studied. Thirty-three percent of all elderly are stated to have seen their general practitioner in the month before the survey (General Household Survey, 1984), a proportion shown to increase with the presence of psychiatric illness to 47% (Morgan et al., 1987). Attitudes toward the general practitioner were contrasted between elderly residents in London and in New York in the U.S./U.K. Community Study, in which random samples of approximately 400 elderly residents in each city were interviewed by the same standard interview for the purpose of gaining comparable data (Gurland et al., 1983). Virtually all London residents claim to have a local doctor and go there for medical care. Two-thirds had visited in the previous year, but one-fifth reported receiving a prescription from the doctor without an interview. Londoners were confident that they could be visited at home. In contrast, more New Yorkers went to hospital for primary medical care and felt that a doctor would never visit them at home. However, no New Yorker received a prescription without interview.

Despite these reports of contact between elderly residents in the U.K. and their general practitioners, there has been some disturbing evidence that psychiatric disorders in the elderly are not being recognised or treated. Williamson (1964) reported that the general practitioner was aware of only 7 out of 48 cases of dementia discovered by a research psychiatrist investigating patients on general practitioners' lists. This startling finding, however, has been challenged recently as part of the Hughes Hall project in Cambridge (O'Connor et al., 1988). From a large-scale screening, 208 cases of elderly people in the community met the CAMDEX criteria for dementia. The general practitioner had recognised 58% of all these cases and 65% of those with severe dementia. Frequency of contact in the past year by the patient with the general practitioner strongly predicted recognition.

Williamson (1964) also implied that many cases of depression were not being recognised at the primary care level. Macdonald (1986) investigated this further. Thirty-one percent of 235 consecutive attenders of 65 and over attending a general practitioner met research criteria for depression. There was a 71% agreement between these criteria and the general practitioner's diagnosis. Four-fifths of the disagreement was due to overdiagnosis by the general practitioner, only one-fifth to missed depression—a surprising finding. However, Macdonald also reported that only 7% with moderate or severe depression were being prescribed antidepressants, and only one person from the whole series was referred for specialist psychiatric help.

Prescriptions can be used as a marker of general practitioner activity. Psychotropic drug consumption rises sharply with age. Williams (1980) surveyed 6000 community residents over 65 in London, 14% of men and 22% of women admitted to taking a psychotropic drug—antidepressant, tranquilliser or hypnotic. However, there was a low degree of association between this consumption and psychiatric morbidity as detected by screening questionnaire. This implies either that the psychiatric diagnosis was being missed or that treatment was being continued unnecessarily. Williams' finding contrasts with that by Morgan et al. (1987). In their general practice based study of elderly subjects, psychotropic medication was being received by 42% of those with psychiatric illness diagnosed by the *Symptoms of Anxiety and Depression Scale* (Bedford et al., 1976), compared to a 20% rate in the whole of their study population.

Data for the use of other arms of the health service are found in the *General Household Survey*. Eight percent of those over 65 were visited at home by a health visitor or nurse, 17% attended outpatients in the 3 months before data collection. However, these figures are not categorised by the presence or absence of psychiatric illness.

Social Service Use

That support and care of the physically and mentally disabled elderly should be at home as long as possible has been a persistent theme of government policy at least since 1977 (Callaghan, 1977). The majority of day-to-day support is provided by the family, even in the United Kingdom, where statutory social services are better organised than, for example, in the United States. In the U.S./U.K. Community Study, it was discovered that about one-third of the sample in each city were dependent on another for day-to-day living at home. Family or friends were the primary supporters of 80% of these dependent elderly residents in New York, compared to 69% of their equivalents in London. Formal (statutory) services provided the primary support for 15% of the dependants in New York, compared to 22% in London. Thus, even with the greater availability of formal support in London, this study revealed little evidence that more dependent people were being supported in the community in London, nor that large numbers of family or friends were being relieved by it (Gurland et al., 1983).

The importance of the family has been emphasised again in a survey from Wales of 1066 elderly over 70, of which 338 were found to need help for day-to-day living (Jones & Vetter, 1985), 37 of which were in residential care. Of the remainder, 267 were receiving active help from a primary carer, with only 6 reporting that no one was looking after them and 28 receiving solely social service care. Forty percent of the family carers were daughters or daughters-in-law, 26% were spouses, 79% were female. Help with household tasks was the most common activity, then with mobility and finally personal care, the intensity of help increasing with disability. However, the reasons for the disability, whether from physical or psychiatric illness was not specified in this report.

The *General Household Survey* provides data on formal service use, showing that in England and Wales 10% of the over 65 population receive a home help, 3% meals on wheels and 8% attend a day centre. The Welsh study demonstrated a relationship of these provisions to disability—17% of the disabled being visited by a home help, 20% by a community nurse and 11% visiting a day centre. The relationship of these services to the presence of psychiatric illness was shown in Nottingham by Morgan et al. (1987). Thirteen percent of those with probable psychiatric illness were visited by a community nurse, compared to 8.6% of the screened population as a whole. Twenty-five percent of those with psychiatric illness received a home help, compared to 15% in the population at large. However, even if more services are given to the psychiatrically ill, there are huge

gaps. Levin et al. (1986), from a survey of confused elderly persons and their supporters in three health districts, showed that most sufferers and their carers had been in contact with one or the other arm of the social services, but that many obvious helps to the carer were not being offered, even to those who were looking after the most severely demented and incontinent.

Pattern of Services

The published literature on service contact and the delivery to the elderly mentally ill at home is patchy and contradictory. Those with depression, despite seeking primary care contact, may not receive adequate interventions or specialist help. Those with dementia who remain at home, however, are not particularly likely to be in touch with medical services, though if they are well known to the general practitioner, they are likely to be recognised as suffering from dementia by the practitioner. Despite this, many dementia sufferers may not be receiving the full range of services to support care at home. Services may be directed to those with more obvious physical disability.

It would seem probable that there is a lack of coordination and provision, given the two administrative arms to service delivery to the elderly. Do some elderly have a multiplicity of care, others none? What is the impact of regular family contact, too, upon likelihood of receiving statutory care? Will family members activate this care, or does family support imply discrimination against delivery of service by those responsible for them in times of resource rationing? Such issues can only be addressed in a longitudinal study of an elderly population.

The Gospel Oak Study

The Gospel Oak Project was established in an electoral ward in North London to determine prevalence rates of psychiatric morbidity amongst the residents of this inner-city area as well as its natural history and the use of health and social services made by these residents. The first stage was to establish a register of all residents in this ward during 1987, to assess them at home by standard interview, while collecting other demographic and the service contact data. The first follow-up is due later this year (1989). In 1992 a new register will be established, thereby providing a cohort comparison with those in the 1987 survey.

Inner-city areas are likely to be under greatest stress, often with a higher than average percentage of elderly residents, a higher degree of social deprivation and many single-handed general practitioners. Gospel Oak was chosen as a useful site in which to study developments for the elderly over the next few years, a period in which there are likely to be major changes in the administration of health and social services together with the changing demography of the elderly population. The ward population consists of 6136 residents in approximately 3000 households. The proportion of pensioners at 16% is similar to that in the country as whole and for the rest of the Hampstead Health Authority. On several indices, this ward can be judged as having higher rates of social deprivation than the rest of England and Wales: e.g. 50% more unemployment, 50% higher rates of infant mortality. Fifteen percent of the residents live in overcrowded conditions (more than one to a room), compared to 7% in the rest of the country (Hampstead Health Authority, 1985). Data are presented from the results of the first cross-sectional survey illustrating current service contact by this inner-city elderly population with particular reference to the relationship of this contact to two manifestations of psychiatric morbidity—depression and dementia.

Method

A sampling frame of 932 residents was established by visiting all the homes in the electoral ward. 813 (87%) of the sample were interviewed by *SHORT CARE*. The remaining 13% consisted of some who refused to be interviewed, others never discovered in their homes, and others who spoke no English. Thirty-five residents of a local authority home were included in this sample.

The *SHORT CARE* (Gurland et al., 1984) is a semistructured instrument developed from *CORE CARE,* containing six indicator scales that assess organic brain syndrome, depression, subjective memory impairment, sleep disorder, somatic symptoms and activity limitation. The scales are best used as screening measures to identify problems in these areas for further assessment. Two scales, those for depression and dementia, have been further refined to become diagnostic scales, detecting probable cases of pervasive dementia or pervasive depression (Kay et al., 1985).

- *Pervasive dementia* implies a clinical state characterised by marked cognitive impairment, handicap in normal day-to-day living, and one that is likely to deteriorate over one year.

- *Pervasive depression* is a state of depression for which a psychiatrist would judge clinical intervention as necessary.

The interrater reliability, internal consistency and validity of these scales have been shown to be satisfactory. As some respondents score above cut points for both depression and dementia, a scoring method has been devised to separate these respondents into the one or the other category, according to degree of cognitive impairment obtained. While a double diagnosis is clinically possible, survey reports usually require that each respondent is not counted more than once. The *Activity Limitation Scale* score is obtained by summing points for reported limitations and various day-to-day activities, such as going out, preparing meals, housework, shopping, bathing and dressing. In addition to the interview, questions were asked concerning contacts during the last month with the general practitioner, the local hospital and the various arms of the social services and the home nursing services. Details of visitors to the home, attendance at local day centres and contact with local voluntary or church agencies were also recorded. The residents were asked for details of current medication.

Fourteen interviewers were trained in the *SHORT CARE*. During the interviewing phase, these interviewers were monitored by a training interviewer and one interview was co-rated. Two psychiatrists conducted 61% of the interviews, 35% were conducted by other psychiatrists and 4% by psychiatric nurses. All interviewers were experienced in work with the elderly. The field interviews took place in 1987.

Results

A detailed paper of the cross-sectional survey has been published elsewhere (Livingston et al., 1990). Some summary data will be presented here before data on service use.

Demographic Data

Of the interviewed sample, 9.1% consisted of females 60–64 years of age, whose data have been excluded. Of the remainder, 27% were between 65 and 69, 50% between 70 and 79, 23% more than 80; a distribution of ages containing more over 80-year-olds than the population in the U.K. as a whole. Sixty-three percent of the population were female, 41% were still married. The social class distribution of this population is suggested by the reported main life time occupations. Forty-two percent of the women had been in paid domestic work, 19% had done clerical work and 9% had served in shops—only 7% had professional or skilled work. Fifty-two percent of the men were in semiskilled and 40% in unskilled occupations. Eighty percent of the sample lived in local authority housing; 45% of the pensioners lived alone.

Prevalence Rates

Of the residents in their own homes 4.7% met the criteria for caseness on the *Dementia Diagnostic Scale*. This figure increased to 7.3% if the residents of the Part III home were included. Of the population over 65, 15.9%

were classed as depressed on the *Depression Diagnostic Scale,* a rate that increased to 18.5% if the residents of the local authority home were included. These two prevalence rates were those obtained after the 12 respondents who scored above cut points on both scales had been allocated to one or other diagnostic category. Thirty-two percent of the sample were above the cut-off point on the *Activity Limitation Scale,* implying that they reported an equivalent degree of impairment to those dependent on others in the U.S./U.K. Community Samples. An analysis of the interactions between the scales showed that activity limitation was more closely related to the presence of dementia, than to depression.

Service Contacts

Table 20.1 lists the frequency of contact with the various agencies available to an elderly resident of Gospel Oak during the month before interview. Contact rates are shown for the whole population, for those with dementia and those with depression.

It can be seen that contact with the health services and social services occurred at greater frequency for those with psychiatric morbidity, notably with the health service for the depressed and social services for those with dementia. A similar increase was not noted with the voluntary agencies.

Demographic variables (age, sex, marital status, living alone) and scores on the six indicator scales of the *SHORT CARE* were included in a multivariate analysis to determine which factors most significantly and independently related to contact with these agencies (see Table 20.2).

Table 20.1. Contacts between elderly residents, over 65 at home, and services in previous month.

Number	All 705	Depression 112	Dementia 33
Seen general practitioner	37%	48%	32%
Hospital visit	24%	39%	31%
Home nurse	9%	18%	29%
Home help	19%	3%	49%
Day centre	11%	21%	26%
Meals on Wheels and other services at home	13%	23%	34%
Voluntary agency	2%	1%	3%
Church visitor	8%	8%	9%

Table 20.2. Factors associated with contact in the last month (showing independent and significant associations p<0.02).

General Practitioner (37%)
  Depression present
  Activity limitation present
Hospital Visit (24%)
  Younger age
  Somatic symptoms present
  Activity Limitation present
Home Nurse (9%)
  Older age
  Activity limitation present
  Depression present
Day Centre (11%)
  Living alone
  Activity limitation present
  Somatic symptoms present
Home Help (19%)
  Older age
  Living alone
  Activity limitation present
Meals on wheels and other services at home (13%)
  Older age
  Living alone
  Activity limitation present
  Sleep disturbance present

Only those variables that remain independently associated with contact and at a statistical significance level of p<0.02 or less are included. It can be seen that activity limitation is a consistent predictor of contact, but the presence of dementia per se does not appear as a predictor variable. Depression was associated with contact with the general practitioner. This analysis was repeated, including a variable, "visited by family or friends during the previous week," so that the effect of being in reasonable social contact upon contact with service agencies could be examined. There was no effect upon the relationships shown in Table 20.2, except attendance at a day centre. In that case, a significant negative association emerged. Reporting visitors to the home in the past week seem to preclude contact with a day centre.

Multiplicity of Contacts

In Table 20.3, the contacts have been grouped into six types, and residents have been scored according to how many of the types, with which they report contact, a score range from 0 to 6.

Analysis was carried out to compare those elderly in contact with no services (281), with those in contact with four or five (37). The presence of somatic symptoms, activity limitation and living alone were significantly associated with being in contact with many services. Those in contact with one service were most commonly seeing the general practitioner, those with two contacts the general practitioner and the local hospital or day centre or a home help. Home nurse contact and meals on wheels were most common among those reporting three contacts in the past month.

Table 20.3. Index of service use.
Services grouped into 6 types: GP Contact, Hospital Visit, Home Nurse, Home Help, Day Centre, Meals on Wheels and other services

(Each individual scored with 0–6 contacts)

Distribution of Contacts: *Mode for each contact*
  0   (281) 40%
  1   (209) 30%   General practitioner
  2   (119) 17%   Hospital, home help, day centre
  3   (59) 8%   Meals on wheels, home visit
  4   (29) 4%
  5   (7) 1%
  6   (1) 0%

Comparison of those with 0 services (281) with those with 4, 5 or 6 (37)
          Somatic symptoms present
          Activity limitation present
          Living alone

General Practitioner Contact

The 813 residents were registered with 59 different general practitioners, only 3 residents reporting no general practitioner. The range for each general practitioner lay between 1 and 123 residents. Nine general practitioners were responsible for more than 27 residents, together being responsible for 72% of the sample.

The commonest reason for consulting the general practitioner was given as repeat prescription (26%), other common causes were for chest symptoms (13%), and blood pressure (10%). Seventy-three percent of the sample were taking some form of medication, 12% benzodiazepines, and 4.4% antidepressants.

General Practitioners and Depression

The nine general practitioners referred to above were then compared for particular reference to depression amongst their patients—and its treatment amongst those of the sample who had consulted them in the past month. The prevalence rate of depression ranged between 9% and 26% amongst the patients of the nine general practitioners; the current antidepressant prescription lay between 0% and 12% amongst the same respondents. There was no correlation between the proportion depressed and the proportion receiving antidepressants when the two sets of figures were compared. Overall, only 12% of those classified as suffering from pervasive depression were receiving antidepressants. A comparison of these depressed consulters between the nine general practitioners showed that the range of prescription of antidepressant medication for these depressed patients lay between 0% and 25%.

Discussion

As part as a comprehensive survey of an elderly population, the data on contact with local general practitioners and other services have been analysed. This population was discovered to have been in contact with the two aspects of the health service over the previous month at a rate comparable with the national figures. Social service provision, however, was at a higher rate than is reported for the country as a whole. The latter finding is both surprising and impressive, given the constraints placed upon local authorities in inner-city areas.

Pattern of Service Contact

Only one in 12 of those residents in contact with one component of a service were in contact with three or more at the same time. This finding does not suggest a great reduplication. Older age and living alone were two demographic variables that were associated with increased likelihood of such degree of contact. Disability, as shown by responses to the *Activity Limitation Scale* on the *SHORT CARE,* was closely associated with contact of all types. Having a family visiting or friends visiting during the previous week did not have impact upon these contacts, apart from making it less likely that the resident would attend a day centre. These data do not, in general, provide much support for a hypothesis that there is inverse relationship between family support and receipt of service.

Dementia and Depression

Those with dementia were in greater contact with some aspects of the social services, indeed, nearly 50% were receiving some help. This does not, however, imply that all that could be provided for these sufferers and their carers is already being provided. Only detailed follow-up in the style of the study from the the National Institute of Social Work (Levin et al., 1987) would determine this. The multivariate analysis implied that the disability of the dementia sufferers led to contact. But the diagnosis by *SHORT CARE* of pervasive depression was directly associated with greater contact with general practitioners.

The General Practitioner

Because of the particular importance of general practitioners in relationship to depression in the elderly, this contact was analysed in greater detail. It is clear that even in a small geographic area such as Gospel Oak, in which the general practices were actually sited, the elderly residents' links with primary care are widespread. Fifty-nine general practitioners were involved in their care. Such a finding must have implications for surveys that base themselves upon general practitioners' lists rather than, as with this one, on a population base. The elderly studied from practice lists cannot be assumed to be living in one immediate and geographically defined neighbourhood. Given the high base rates of clinical (or pervasive) depression in this population as well as the association of this diagnosis and contact with general practitioner, it was disappointing to find so few receiving antidepressant medication. Only 12% of the depressed amongst those consulting the nine general practitioners whose contacts were specially analysed were receiving antidepressants. The absence of correlation between prescription of this form of medica-

tion and the prevalence of depression amongst the patients consulting these nine general practitioners suggests a wide variation amongst the general practitioners. Whether this difference reflects lack of recognition, as suggested by Williamson (1964), or lack of response, as suggested by Macdonald (1987), cannot be determined from this survey.

Acknowledgements

The authors would like to acknowledge the help of the following for interviewing: Dr M. Aimer, Ms H. Allen, Dr D. Ames, Dr M. Canete, Ms Phyllis Chin, Ms Meg Copeland, Dr H. Henderson, Dr S. Ibrahimi, Dr G. Rands, Dr J. Richardson, Ms Lesley Wood.

References

Bedford, A., Foulds, G. A., Sheffield, B. F. (1976). A new personal disturbance scale. *British Journal of Social & Clinical Psychology*, 15, 387–394.

Callaghan, J. (1977). *Address for A. G. M. of Age Concern.*

Dean, L. (1983). *The mind and mood of ageing: The mental health problems of the community elderly in New York and London.* New York: Haworth Press; London: Croom Helm.

Gurland, B. J., Golden, R. R., Teresi, J. A., & Challop, J. (1984). The SHORT CARE: An efficient instrument for the assessment of depression, dementia and disability. *Journal of Gerontology*, 39(2), 166–169.

Hampstead Health Authority (1985). *Identifying needs: To have and have not.*

Jones, D. A., & Vetter, N. J. (1985). Formal and informal support received by carers of elderly dependants. *British Medical Journal*, 291, 643–645.

Kay, D. W. K., Henderson, A. S., Scott, R., Wilson, J., Rickwood, D., & Grayson, D. A.(1985). Dementia and depression among the elderly living in the Hobart community: The effect of the diagnostic criteria on the prevalence rates. *Psychological Medicine*, 15, 771–778.

Levin, E., Sinclair, I., & Gorbach, P. (1989). *Families services and confusion in old age.* Aldershot: Gower.

Livingston, G., Hawkins, A., Graham, N., Blizard, R., & Mann, A. H. (1990). The Gospel Oak Study: Prevalence rates of dementia, depression and activity limitation among elderly residents in inner

London. *Psychol. Med.*, in press.

Macdonald, A. J. D. (1986). Do general practitioners "miss" depression in elderly patients? *British Medical Journal*, 292, 1365–1367.

Morgan, K., Dallosso, H., Ebrahim, S., Arie, T., & Fentem, P. (1987). Mental health and contact with primary care services in old age. *International Journal of Geriatric Psychiatry*, 2, 223–226.

O'Connor, D. W., Pollitt, P. A., Hyde, J. B., Brook, C. P. B., Reiss, B. B., & Roth, M. (1988). Do general practitioners "miss" dementia in elderly patients? *British Medical Journal*, 297, 1107–1110.

OPCS (1984). *The General Household Survey.* London: HMSO.

OPCS (1987). *Population Projections 1985–2025.* London: HMSO.

Warnes, A. M. (1989). Elderly people in Great Britain: Variable projections and characteristics. *Care of Elderly*, 1, 7–10.

Waxman, H. M., Carner, E. A., & Blum, A. (1983). Depressive symptoms and health service utilization among the community elderly. *Journal American Geriatrics Society*, 31, 417–420.

Weyerer, S. (1983). Mental disorders among the elderly: True prevalence and use of medical service. *Arch. Gerontol. Geriat.*, 2, 11–22.

Williams, P. (1980). Prescribing antidepressants, hypnotics and tranquillisers. *Geriatric Medicine*, 10, 50–55.

Williamson, J., Stokoe, I. H., Gray, S. et al. (1964). Old people at home: Their unreported needs. *Lancet*, i, 1117–1120.

Chapter 21

The Competitive Relationship Between Mental Health Services and Family Practice: Future Implications

Berthold Gersons

Over and over again, epidemiological studies have shown a high prevalence of mental disorders in the general population. Goldberg and Huxley (1980) in the United Kingdom and more recently Von Korff et al. (1987) in the United States have concluded that the annual prevalence in the adult population is as high as 25%.

In consequence, mental disorders are prominent in general practice; in fact, they form something like 10% of all disorders, taking third place after diseases of the respiratory system and of the circulatory system (Shepherd & Wilkinson, 1988). General practice is therefore an important sector for the mental health professional, and one must assume that, by the same token, mental health services are of importance to the family physician.

Wilkinson (1989) has shown that of all referrals in general practice, only 3% concern psychiatry (this excludes referrals to social workers and psychologists). Goldberg and Huxley, among others, have called attention not only to the low referral rate, but also to the fact that one-third of psychiatrically disordered patients are not recognized as such by their general practitioner. Both of these findings raise questions about the relationship between GPs and psychiatric services.

Much energy is being devoted at present to research studies focussing on those factors responsible for the low GP referral rate (Jorgensen, 1986; Zintl-Wiegand et al., 1988; Boardman et al., 1988; Wilkinson, 1989) and to the evaluation of GP training programmes (Rutz et al. 1989). These very valuable efforts, however, are based on the assumption that the relationship between family practice and mental health services is complementary.

I would like to dwell for a moment on the forces that arise from the existing rivalry between the two health-care systems—family practice and mental health care—and on the other elements that also influence the relationship. I will call this the *competitive relationship*.

Mental Health Services

Before analyzing the relationship between mental health care and general practice, it is necessary to give a brief description of the two systems. This sketch is based primarily on the current situation in The Netherlands, although there are many similarities with developments in other European countries (WHO, 1983).

As in most other countries, there is an increasing trend in mental health toward shifting the locus of care from the hospital to the community. The number of personnel in ambulatory mental health settings has increased, and the range of ambulatory mental health services has also become more varied. All kinds of different psychotherapy schools have been successful in promoting their specific methods as part of the regular mental health services.

The differentiation of mental health disciplines has become an essential part of mental health services in which multidisciplinary team meetings have become a matter of routine (Mitchell, 1985). The medical doctor, especially the psychiatrist, is no longer automatically designated as leader of the team, and there is an ongoing debate on the issue of who is actually responsible for treatment. Even psychiatrists working in the Regional Centres for Community Mental Health (RCCMH) have different opinions regarding the issue of responsibility. Schwarz (1987), in a study of a sizeable cross-section of Dutch community psychiatrists, found that 77% were of the opinion that they were responsible for the treatment of psychotic patients, 57% for patients with depression and/or anxiety and 52% for suicidal patients.

Most ambulatory mental health services have been grouped together into *regional centers for community mental health*. In The Netherlands, these *RCCMH's* have catchment areas of between 90,000 and 700,000 inhabitants. They offer 24-hour psychiatric emergency and crisis services, psychiatric treatment and long-term care for adult and chronic psychiatric patients, psychotherapy, women's mental health services, services for children and adolescents and ambulatory psychogeriatric services. Most centers also offer preventive services. Each RCCMH employs between 50 and 150 mental health professionals.

In addition to these regional centres for community mental health, there are also a large number of outpatient psychiatric departments in general hospitals and in most mental hospitals. These departments are smaller than the RCCMHs, have less community outreach and a higher proportion of psychiatrists on their staff.

Inpatient facilities have also changed in the last 20 years. Many mental hospitals have, as a reaction to the criticism from the outside world, come to focus more on inpatient-intensive psychotherapy according to the therapeutic community model (Jones, 1968; Kernberg, 1976). Facilities for chronic patients have been brought up to date allowing room for small-scale living apartments, sometimes even outside the mental hospitals in sheltered care facilities. Day treatment and day care are becoming more and more important as alternative forms of treatment and care settings for mental patients (Schene & Gersons, 1986). Small-scale psychiatric inpatient units, together with day-hospitals, outpatient treatment and liaison services, have also been established in many district general hospitals.

The *public health consequences* of these changes are that

1) the supply of mental health services has increased in recent years,

2) the locus of care is shifting from the hospital to the community,

3) the content of the mental health "product" has partly shifted from traditional medical services to multidisciplinary psychotherapy:

4) mental health services have become much more district based.

It is likely that these four different tendencies have resulted in the recruitment of new populations of mental patients, especially of patients with mild to moderately severe disorder, and that many of these patients would have formerly sought treatment in the primary-care sector. A substantial number of psychotherapy patients in The Netherlands, for instance, approach the psychiatric services without prior consultation with their family doctors.

Family Practice

The family practice is regarded as a very valuable basic medical service in every European country. An average family practice in Holland serves a population of approximately 3,000 inhabitants, or 10,000 patients in a health care centre. General practice offers immediate medical services in both the consulting room and the home, for most moderate medical disorders. For chronic medical diseases, the GP also offers continuity of care usually in cooperation with the district public health nurse. Many family doctors also offer counselling for psychological complaints and work together with, or refer their patients to, the social workers.

Only in the last 25 years has the family medical practice become a new medical specialty, with the establishment of new chairs in the medical faculties. By becoming a member of the medical faculty, the GPs have regained lost territory against other medical specialties that have tended to overshadow the importance of family medicine in the past. The struggle is still on, however, because medical specialists are ever increasing their outpatient departments by offering new kinds of specialized treatments. Postgraduate training courses offered by medical specialists to GP's have therefore become of vital importance in restoring the balance between the volume and level of specialist treatment skills in comparison with the services offered by the family doctors.

The service implications of these changes are that

1) general practice medicine has had to *defend its territory* against specialized hospital services;

2) family practice is especially suited to the provision of *basic medical care* for moderately severe disorders;

3) family practitioners, in collaboration with district nurses and social workers, also provide *first-line psychosocial services*.

Although some of these activities complement those provided by specialized medical services, there is also the *risk of competition*.

The Relationship Between Mental Health Services and Family Practice

Many studies have shown that the level of psychosocial competence in family doctors can differ greatly (Marks, 1979; Verhaak, 1986). Some doctors are good diagnosticians of psychiatric disorders and good counsellors as well, while others have no talent for psychiatry and show little tolerance toward psychiatric patients. Postgraduate training also appears to be only partially successful. Whewell et al. (1988) reported the results of a GP training programme aimed at improving their ability to recognize emotional disturbances, in which it became evident that some GPs were "resistant" to improving their skills.

The general practitioner, viewed from the public health angle, is regarded as the gatekeeper of the total health care system. Horder (1988) speaks of the "protective shield of general practice" toward the mental health system. The GP is the first to recognize a patient's complaint as a symptom of a disease. Querido (1966) has called this the function of the first echelon.

The GP is usually the first doctor to officially recognize, or repudiate, illness and also to determine whether referral should take place to specialist services. These specialized services are called the second echelon. The "defensive" character of the first, GP echelon helps to limit the cost of health care, overburdened as it is by the high costs of specialized hospital services.

It is very difficult for a GP to limit patient access to the specialized services if the patient is eager to use these services. For instance, most heart or cancer patients prefer to be under the care of a cardiologist or an oncologist, and this preference derives from the knowledge that the specialist has particular skills to deal with the situation. This, in turn, helps to decrease the patient's feelings of fear and anxiety.

To summarize:

1) In theory, the relationship between general practice and specialized services is complementary and well-organized, in accordance with the echelon principles.

2) The GP has a key role in the process of referral to specialized services.

3) The public can put pressure on the GP when they themselves feel the need for some kind of specialized treatment.

When looking at the special relationship of the GP with the mental health care system, we must assume these three factors play an important role. The relationship is a complementary, although limited one, as many studies have already shown. There is much debate among the psychiatrists especially about the GP's skill in acting as gatekeeper for the mental health services.

Models of Primary Care/Psychiatrist Collaboration

Williams and Clare (1986) have described three models of collaboration. One is the *replacement model*, in which the psychiatrist is the patient's first contact doctor. In this model, the echelon system is no longer present. The second model is called the *increased throughput* model. Here the GP is the first contact doctor, who preferably will refer most mental patients for more specialized treatment. The third model, which enjoys increasing popularity in Great Britain, is called the *liaison-attachment* model.

In the latter, psychiatrists work partially in primary-care settings, seeing patients at the request of the GP, sometimes jointly with the GP, and giving consultation and advice in case conferences during which the GP is also present. It is known that, by 1984, 20% of British psychiatrists spent some time in general practice. Williams and Balestrieri (1989) have given some support for the expectation that this model could help to decrease the number of psychiatric admissions.

The value of the liaison model is obvious, although the description does call for added clarification. The Netherlands, as already mentioned, has separate organizations for primary and mental health care. Psychiatrists and other mental health professionals work on a less individual basis. To describe these relationships and to discuss the value of the different relationships on a more theoretical basis, I propose a slightly different kind of typology.

The first type of relationship between the GP and the psychiatrist is called the *referral relationship* and the public health aspects of this are

1) that the GP is expected to be competent in giving basic mental health care and to be able to recognize the need for specialized services when appropriate;

2) that the limited resources for mental health care are not overburdened by unnecessary referrals.

The second type of relationship is called the *counter-referral relationship,* which resembles the replacement model. In this model, it is argued that psychiatrists are the first responsible professionals for psychiatric patients, and therefore they decide which patients should be referred to the GP, within the limits of competence. This theoretical model would have the following *public health implications:*

1) The GP has only a limited responsibility for mental health care, thereby justifying his limited knowledge and skills.

2) It provides a very striking division between the mental health care system and the "somatic" health care system.

The third kind of relationship is called the *collaborative relationship,* which closely resembles the liaison model. In this relationship, there are no sharp boundaries between the two sectors. There is a shared responsibility, and the differentiation between who is treating which patient is part of an ongoing process of negotiation. Here the *public health consequences* are that

1) the high prevalence of mental disorders that cannot be solved adequately by the limited mental health care resources is taken more into consideration;

2) the potential of GP-mental health care together with social workers can be utilized at a reasonable level;

3) it gives far more possibilities for preventive efforts, early recognition and the avoidance of stigmatization.

Contradictions and Bottlenecks

We have to realize that efforts at improving the relationship between general practice and psychiatry already have a history. In the 1960s especially, the optimism resulting from new methods of treatment such as crisis intervention and psychotherapy stimulated the mental health professionals to approach their colleagues in general practice. Balint (1964) started groups for GPs enabling them to discuss their attitudes toward patients with emotional difficulties. These groups were very effective in changing the GP's attitude and also resulted in the improvement of their interviewing skills (Boer et al., 1970) although it is not known whether diagnostic skills were also improved.

Caplan (1970) favoured a different approach toward improving the GP's skills. He called his method *mental health consultation.* Here, the GP's attitude was not the consulting psychiatrist's primary concern. Case conferences provided the GP with information about diagnosis, interview strategies, treatment possibilities and referral advice. Secondary to this was the hope that the attitudes and skills of the GP would also improve.

Why did these two methods not succeed in achieving the collaborative relationship?

Both methods were based on the notion that skill in detecting psychiatric illness and in communicating empathically was necessary, and that the attitude of many GPs toward psychological problems should be improved. Such an improvement could be the result of postgraduate action. It became clear that both methods only attracted those GPs who were already favorably disposed toward mental health issues, and who were willing to profit from increased knowledge and skill. A stumbling block is that a high proportion of GPs are in fact *resistant* to most methods aimed at improving their skills, a fact that again became all too apparent in a recent, much more structured training programme described by Whewell et al.(1988).

More benefit may be achieved if, in the future, more consideration is given to differences in GP's attitudes in developing postgraduate training programmes. The industrial model of "marketing" might be helpful in constructing training programmes ranging from formal courses to Balint groups. Evaluation should focus not only on which approach is the best, but much more on the type of person for whom this approach is most suited.

The difficulties in improving the mental health skills of the GP confront us as mental health professionals with the fact that mental health problems form only a limited fraction of GP's total workload. Horder (1988), who has his eye trained to the difficulties inherent in the relationship between the GP and the psychiatrist and who is not afraid to speak about rivalry, is nonetheless very satisfied with the GP relationship with psychiatry in day-to-day practice. He points out that the GP values quick support in emergency, prompt case summaries when patients are discharged and the possibility of consultation by telephone.

There is a good deal of overlap between patients with mental problems in general practice and those seen by psychiatrists in outpatient settings. Brown et al. (1988) have shown that hospitals in particular deal with acute psychosis and personality disorders, while outpatient services—in comparison with family practice—deal with the less common neuroses and the personality disorders. However, most studies find few differences between the psychological disorders treated in primary care and in psychiatric outpatient care, with mood disorders preponderating in both settings (Berkanovic et al., 1988; Frank, 1988).

It is likely that psychiatrists see more chronic disorders. However, Wright (1988), using the GHQ, found that of the 35% of GP attenders who had a high GHQ score at either of two assessments a year apart, 19% changed from abnormal to normal in the course of the year, and 8% changed from normal to abnormal. The remaining 9% had persistently high scores, though less than half had been given a psychiatric diagnosis.

There seems to be a significant overlap in patient categories, which makes it difficult to judge which patient should be treated—and if so, by whom. Balestrieri et al. (1988) showed in a metaanalysis that treatment by specialist mental health professionals had only a 10% greater success rate compared with GP care. It is not surprising, therefore, that a number of GPs doubt the need for special training by psychiatrists or for increasing their referrals to the mental health system.

It is possible that the average GP is not only fairly satisfied with the mental health services, but is also quite satisfied with his own level of functioning. The average GP may not therefore feel much urge to change his or her routine in day-to-day practice.

Another important consideration is that a GP may not enjoy having to relinquish patients to the psychiatrist. This reluctance on the GP's part may be concealed by an apparent reluctance by the patient to be referred to a psychiatrist because of the stigma in society. It is clear that GPs are not, on the whole, disturbed by the extensive number of patients suffering from psychiatric disorders. If they also feel that they are as effective as a mental health professional, it is not surprising that an element of competition enters into the relationship between family practice and the mental health services.

When we consider how to improve the relationship between GPs and psychiatrists, it is important to realize the difference of experiences in day-to-day practice between them. It is well known that there is a difference in the mean duration of the consultation, which is usually 7 to 10 minutes in the GP practice and 30–60 minutes in the mental health services. Also psychiatrists usually see patients with solely psychiatric problems and may run the risk of overlooking the presence of somatic problems.

Conclusion

The role and skills of psychiatrists in reinforcing the effectiveness of the general practitioner and the primary-care team remains a very important but still unresolved issue (Wilkinson, 1988). Scope for an improvement is limited because neither the public nor the GP experience the present situation as bad. There is a balance of interests between the two health sectors—the general practice and the mental health system—and there are few factors that look likely to bring about any radical change in this equilibrium in the near future.

In many countries, however, direct communication between GPs and psychiatrists is improving and increasing. We anticipate that this process will be more successful in the long run in improving the quality of GP mental health care than formal training programmes. The relationship should exist on a continuing basis over a period of time and should range from telephone consultations to seeing patients together. Only when psychiatry is able to introduce much more effective treatment methods can we expect to see a new stream of referrals to psychiatry followed by a new change toward a more competitive GP/psychiatrist relationship.

References

Balestrieri, M., Williams, P., & Wilkinson, G. (1988). Specialist mental health treatment in general practice: A meta-analysis. *Psychological Medicine, 18,* 711–717.

Balint, M. (1964). *The doctor, his patient and the illness.* London: Pitman.

Berkanovic, E., Hurwicz, M., & Landsverk, J. (1988). Psychological distress and the decision to seek medical care. *Soc. Sci. Med., 27,* 1215–1221.

Boardman, A. P., Bouras, N., & Craig, T. K. J. (1988). General practitioner referrals to an ambulatory psychiatric service. The effects of establishing an ease of access service. *The International J. of Social Psychiatry, 34,* 172–183.

Boer, R. A., Jaspars, P., Van Leeuwen, P., Van Der Meer, F., Radder, J. J., & Van Schaik, C. T. (1970). An evaluation of long-term seminars in psychiatry for family physicians. *Psychiatry, 33,* 468–481.

Brown, R. M. A., Strathdee, J. R. W., Christie-Brown, J. R. W., & Robinson, P. H. (1988). A comparison of referrals to primary-care and hospital outpatient clinics. *British Journal of Psychiatry, 153,* 168–173.

Caplan, G. (1970). *The theory and practice of mental health consultation.* London: Tavistock.

Frank, R. G. (1988). Use of mental health services and the persistence of emotional distress. *Medical Care, 26,* 1203–1215.

Goldberg, D., & Huxley, P. (1980). *Mental illness in the community: The pathway to psychiatric care.* London: Tavistock.

Horder, J. (1988). Working with general practitioners. *Br. J. of Psychiatry, 153,* 513–520.

Kernberg, O. F. (1976). *Object-relations theory and clinical psychoanalysis.* New York: Jason Aronson.

Jones, M. (1968). *Social psychiatry in practice.* Baltimore, MD: Penguin Books.

Jorgensen, P. M. (1986). General practitioners' selection of patients for treatment in community psychiatric services. *Psychological Medicine, 16,* 611–619.

Marks, J., Goldberg, D. P., & Hillier, V. F. (1979). Determinants of the ability of general practitioners to detect psychiatric illness. *Psychological Medicine, 9,* 337–353.

Mitchell, A. R. K. (1985). Psychiatrists in primary health care settings. *British Journal of Psychiatry, 147,* 371–379.

Querido, A. (1966). Mental health programmes in public health planning. In H. P. David (Ed.), *International trends in mental health.* New York.

Rutz, W., Walinder, J. et al. (1989). An educational program on depressive disorders for general practitioners on Gotland: background and evaluation. *Acta Psychiatr. Scand., 79,* 19–26.

Schene, A. H., & Gersons, B. P. R. (1986). Effectiveness and application of partial hospitalization. *Acta Psychiatr. Scand., 74,* 335–340.

Schwarz, R. (1987). *The psychiatrist in the RIAGG.* Dissertation, University of Amsterdam.

Shepherd, M., & Wilkinson, G. (1988). Primary care as the middle ground for psychiatric epidemiology. *Psychological Medicine, 18,* 263–267.

Strathdee, G., & Williams, P. (1984). A survey of psychiatrists in primary care: The silent growth of a new service. *J. of the Royal College of General Practitioners, 34,* 615–618.

Verhaak, P. F. M. (1986). Interpretation and treatment of psychosocial complaints by general practitioners. In G. J. Visser et al. (Eds.), *Mental health and primary care; Dutch and Israeli experience.* Utrecht, Netherlands: Institute of Primary Health Care.

Von Korff, M., & Shapiro, S. et al. (1987). Anxiety and depression in a primary care clinic: Comparison of Diagnostic Interview Schedule, General Health Questionnaire, and practitioner assessments. *Arch. Gen. Psychiatry, 44,* 152–156.

Whewell, P. J., Gore, V. A., & Leach, C. (1988). Training general practitioners to improve their recognition of emotional disturbance in the consultation. *J. of the Royal College of General Practitioners, 38,* 259–262.

Williams, P., & Clare, A. (1981). Changing patterns of psychiatric care. *Br. Medical J., 282,* 375–377.

Wilkinson, G. (1988). I don't want to see a psychiatrist. *British Medical Journal, 297,* 1144–1145.

Wilkinson, G. (1989). Referrals from general practitioners to psychiatrists and paramedical mental health professionals. *British Journal of Psychiatry, 154,* 72–76.

Williams, P., & Balestrieri, M. (1989). Psychiatric clinics in general practice: Do they reduce admissions? *British Journal of Psychiatry, 154,* 67–71.

Williams, P., & Clare, A. (1981). Changing pattern of psychiatric care. *British Medical Journal, 282,* 375–377.

World Health Organization (1984). *First-contact mental health care.* Report on a WHO meeting. Copenhagen, EURO Reports and Studies 92.

Wright, A. F. (1988). Psychological distress: Outcome and consultation rates in one general practice. *Journal of the Royal College of Practitioners, 38,* 542–545.

Zintl-Wiegand, A., & Krumm, B. et al. (1988). Psychiatric morbidity and referral rates in general practice: Comparison of an industrial town and a rural area in West Germany. *Social Psychiatry and Epidemiology, 23,* 49–56.

Chapter 22

Planning and Evaluating Health and Social Services for People with a Long-Term Psychiatric Disorder

J. K. Wing

Social Disablement

The first aim of public health services is to prevent the development of social disablement from disease, disability and disadvantage. To the extent that primary prevention is not feasible, the chief aim is to contain impairment and any associated social disablement at the lowest level practicable in the light of current knowledge. Stamped on the other side of the same coin is the intention to help maintain an optimal quality of life, through the provision of opportunities that will enable people who remain disabled to make full use of their abilities. These fundamental, far-reaching and highly complex aims cannot be divided into types labelled "medical" and "social." Terms such as "public health" and "social psychiatry" indicate the indivisibility of our subject.

The concept of "social disablement" (Wing, 1972, 1978) is similar to, but broader than, the "disablement" of the World Health Organization (WHO, 1980), which does not contain the adjective "social" and is more exclusively medical. Rather, it comprises a set of consequences of disease, beginning with impairment (loss or abnormality of function), which may lead to disabilities (restriction of activities or failures in accomplishment), which in turn may lead to handicaps (disadvantages in interacting with or adapting to the individual's environment). Thus, any social and personal problems are considered only insofar as they stem from impairment, whereas "social disablement" allows cause and effect to operate in the opposite direction as well. In fact, there is usually an interaction.

Social disablement is central to any attempt to evaluate the extent to which the basic aims of a system of services, or of any component in a system, are achieved. For present purposes, it includes any inability to perform up to personal expectations, or to those of important others, that is associated with illness or disability. In what follows, "inability to perform" excludes "lack of wish to perform," and social disablement is considered only if associated with psychiatric disorder or, more loosely, with the problems that psychiatrists and their colleagues are asked to help solve. Examples are taken from research into the effects of moving the focus of psychiatric care from large hospitals to smaller, mostly nonhospital, alternatives.

Several components in social disablement have to be considered, each of which has its own implication for evaluating psychiatric services. In the first place, there is illness or injury, recognised by the presence of psychobiological dysfunctions; these sometimes persist as long-term impairments, such as slowness or thought disorder in schizophrenia or rapid cycling in bipolar disorder. Such impairments can be socially disabling in their own right and may be the chief cause of disablement.

In the second place, there are disadvantages that can also in themselves be socially disabling, whether they are an effect or a cause or independent of psychiatric disorder. Examples are a lack of occupational or social skills from poverty or a poor education, absence of social supports, and environmental stressors of many kinds. Inadequate or positively harmful treatment of illness or impairment as well as stigmatizing social attitudes provide examples in which there is substantial scope for cultural variation. Adverse personality factors (some of which could, of course, be regarded as primary impairments in their own right) may also be socially disadvantageous.

Each of these two types of factors causing social disablement may have an adverse effect on self-attitudes—damaging self-confidence and self-esteem, and decreasing motivation to achieve goals that are, in fact, attainable. This third element amplifies the disablement arising from the other two, and it can persist even when the others are no longer important causes.

Thus, all three types of causal factors—impairments, disadvantages and adverse self-attitudes—interact. It is notoriously difficult to disentangle their effects since social factors can cause disorder and disorder can cause disadvantage—as well as both causing a loss of morale and motivation. Nevertheless, from the point of view of secondary and tertiary prevention, it is necessary to try to do so, because different elements may need different remedies. It is therefore important to devise methods that will ensure that, in the end, all the elements are covered. That is a challenge for research.

Principles of Service Provision

In developed countries, three principles have long been accepted as fundamental to the achievement of the public health aim:

1) In addition to their role in primary prevention, health and social authorities should accept responsibility, within a given geographical area, for identifying and providing appropriate help for anyone who is socially disabled by psychiatric disorder. This help should not depend on ability to pay for it.

2) The services provided should be comprehensive and varied, including provision for short-term and long-term social and medical needs. Staff should be sufficiently skilled to administer all the forms of treatment, rehabilitation, care, support and protection that may be required.

3) Despite the variety of the service units,

they should be integrated, with easy movement and communications between them. Each unit should be guided by an operating policy that ensures full coverage of all needs in the district. Monitoring should ensure that the aims of units and the service in general are indeed being achieved.

These principles are reflexive, in the sense that each leads to the next and the third leads back to the first. Because they are based on the concept of reducing disablement and increasing quality of life, they also provide a basis for evaluation.

Principles of Evaluation

The primary aim of evaluative research is to use accumulated knowledge of the causes, characteristics and distributions of psychiatric disorders as well as of the most effective, acceptable and economic methods of treatment and care, to assess how far basic service aims are being achieved and to discover better ways of achieving them. In this respect, the aims of researchers are the same as those of planners and administrators.

Strategically, population-based evaluative studies are concerned with answering six types of questions, against a background of knowledge about population movement, risk factors and the history of local service development. The questions are all client-based. Although planners and evaluators do construct mental models of the "ideal" service, most are aware that services evolve gradually and need to be improved gradually, with plenty of time for mistakes to be corrected. This is how the questions were formulated in 1972 (Wing, 1972):

1) How many people are in contact with services that already exist? What patterns of contact do they make? What are the temporal trends?

2) What are the needs of these people and their supporters?

3) Are the services meeting these needs effectively, economically and acceptably?

4) How many other people, not in touch with services, also have needs? Are these different from those of people already in contact?

5) What new services, or modifications to existing services, would cater for the unmet needs discovered in steps 3 and 4?

6) When innovations in service provision are introduced, do they in fact help to meet unmet need efficiently, economically and acceptably?

This strategy proceeds from the known to the unknown; from the routine collection of statistical data concerning services that already exist to disability in the general population and the planning and evaluation of new services. If such a cycle of evaluation-planning-reevaluation-replanning could be pursued over a period of time in one district, it would indeed be possible to speak of rational planning.

In practice, it would be difficult to pursue such a strategy in a single geographical district, although the principle is sound. The problems have to be broken down into manageable fragments and investigated separately. As in other fields of research, if testable hypotheses are put forward and comparable techniques of investigation are used, knowledge will accumulate. It is not essential for the results of good research in one district to be implemented locally—or even implemented at all at that time. The goal is to get as close to the truth as possible and to express it in terms that are replicable elsewhere. But since the intention of evaluative research is to help planners and administrators achieve the common aim of reducing disability associated with psychiatric disorder to the lowest possible level, there is some urgency in the need to draw attention to relevant results.

Designs for Evaluation

Employed with discrimination and awareness of the advantages and limitations, a wide variety of research designs may be used, from descriptive statistics to highly sophisticated controlled trials. Walter Holland (this volume) points out that public health applications must be securely based in two kinds of knowledge; first, about the identification, distribution, causes and course of disease and disability and, second, about methods of prevention, cure and care. These are the epidemiological and clinical foundations for health services research (Patrick & Peach, 1989).

Population-Based Descriptive Statistics

Leaving aside age, sex and urban-rural location, many of the most useful census indicators of the population risk for serious psychiatric disorders (and therefore of possible need for services) can be placed into three groups: poverty, social isolation and ethnicity. Sainsbury (1955) was one of the first to show that factors indicating social isolation were more important than the more obvious indicators of poverty in predicting the rank order of suicide rates in London boroughs. The theory derives from Durkheim (1897). Of all the factors related to social isolation (which include the frequency of rooming houses, the presence of railway termini, migration into and out of the area, etc.), marital status is one of the simplest and most useful. Sainsbury found that married people with children have the lowest rates, with the unmarried, divorced and separated sequentially higher.

Stein (1957), in a study of first admission rates in east and west London boroughs, found that schizophrenia was commoner in the richer but more socially isolated West. Odegaard (1946) and Hare (1956) emphasized the importance of marital status as an index of risk; it is also correlated with admission rates for an astonishingly wide range of disorders across the whole medical spectrum.

Although it is important to check indices of social isolation separately from those of poverty (Buglass et al., 1980), the two often occur together. Poverty indices include low occupational status, unemployment, overcrowding and low ratable value of housing. Jarman (1983, 1984) compiled a measure of "underprivilege" from eight census factors as an index of demand for primary-care services. The weighted index for 192 English Health Districts ranges from +55 to −33 and has been shown to be correlated with measures of use of acute psychiatric hospitals as well (Hirsch, 1988).

Proper use of service statistics was made by the Audit Commission (1986) when they pointed to the slow progress being made toward targets set by the Government in the White Paper *Better Services for the Mentally Ill* (1975). The importance of the original figures can be questioned because they were not based on adequate research, and, in any case, estimates of need may reasonably be changed over time. Nevertheless, the Commission has pointed to areas where research is needed. Cooper (1989) has criticized the quality of much of the routine information collected at the moment, compared, for example, to that compiled by the expert staff of case registers.

A comparative exercise conducted by eight psychiatric case registers proved informative with respect to census indices and population trends (Gibbons, Jennings & Wing, 1984). The registers covered a range of areas from Oxford and Worcester (attractive districts with a rural hinterland), through medium-sized industrial cities (Cardiff, Nottingham and Southampton—all fairly close statistically to England and Wales as a whole), to Salford and Camberwell, both inner conurban areas. Population movement was most dramatically illustrated by the fact that Oxford (Jarman rank 123 out of 192) had doubled in size in 60 years, while Camberwell (Jarman rank 6) had declined to half its original number of inhabitants in the same time. Such long-term trends, indicating a differential migration between areas (possibly two-way), might well have had a cumulative effect on the picture shown by the cross-sectional indices, which did indeed differ very substantially.

The marked difference in census indices between register areas was reflected in certain measures of service use; in particular, inpatients staying for less than 1 year and also from 1 to 5 years. The very long stay (over 5 years) rates were affected by an artefact in the denominator if the population had been expanding or contracting steadily over the previous 60 years. Correcting for this eliminated a large part of such differences (Der, 1989). Age-specific admission rates for those aged 15–64 also showed higher rates for Camberwell than for Worcester. Data from the Worcester register, which covered the former County of Worcester, could be divided to compare admission rates between rural and urban areas, the former being markedly lower (Hassall, personal communication). Hirsch

and colleagues (1988) have pointed out that high admission rates are not necessarily correlated with low rates for other services. Indeed, the opposite is often the case.

It seems reasonable to hypothesize that a significant part of the variation in service use between geographical areas is due to relatively stable characteristics of the local environment, although the changes might have come about over a fairly long period of time.

A further group of historical variables to be taken into account is related to the pattern of services and their geographical distribution. Services in the areas represented in the eight register projects had developed in ways that reflected local policies and local personalities. The hospital might be placed centrally, with easy access—or remote from the population it was supposed to serve. Indeed, many of the characteristics of the services based on Mapperley, Netherne and Severalls hospitals during the 1960s reflected the interests and influence over many earlier years of their medical superintendents (Brown et al., 1966; Wing & Brown, 1970).

The implications for planners of these multiple influences are important, since "norms" derived from national, regional or even district statistics cannot be applied without modification to estimate the nature of local need. Descriptive statistics, even when of good quality, are only part of the evaluative information that planners require. The implications for evaluators are also important since they have to be aware of the limitations imposed by sampling.

A more recent edition of the interregister report, with chapters on aspects of research based on the registers, has recently been published. A chapter is devoted to the use of routinely collected service statistics (Cooper, 1989). Although these can provide useful information, there is a major difficulty in providing high-quality data. It is therefore particularly to be regretted that central financial support was withdrawn from three of the British registers, one of which (Southampton) had to close, and local support was withdrawn from the Worcester register, which has also closed. Fortunately, several British registers remain strongly in operation, and there is a movement to set up new ones throughout Europe (ten Horn et al., 1986) as their importance for accurate monitoring of trends and their provision of a background and a sampling frame for evaluative research becomes recognized.

More Complex Designs

The most rigorous designs can hardly be applied to total services, each of which is unique. Controlled experiments with random allocation are limited by practical and ethical considerations. They are well suited to treatment trials and can readily be used for service evaluation when the method of care under test is "delivered" by a member of staff who, in effect, *is* the service. An experiment to evaluate the effect of increased social stimulation for severely disabled schizophrenic patients illustrates the procedure (Wing & Freudenberg, 1961). A study of treatment of depression by community nurses compared with outpatient treatment shows the feasibility of the design in community settings (Paykel et al., 1982), as does the study by Leff and colleagues of family intervention to reduce high "emotional expression" in the relatives of schizophrenics (Leff et al., 1985).

Randomised controlled studies of service units or centres are more difficult to carry out because the "treatment" may contain several elements, some difficult to specify: several staff are involved, the amount of contact with attenders or residents may vary, and the unit is quite likely to be a pioneering one with features that are very difficult to replicate in routine practice. Moreover, people allocated at random to control units may well be exposed to care that overlaps in various ways with that of the experimental group. Feasibility is limited because of the need to obtain the consent and collaboration of many staff, some of whom may be opposed to the whole idea of random allocation.

There are, however, several examples of useful studies in this mode. One compared a course of industrial rehabilitation for moderately disabled long-stay patients with schizophrenia compared with others chosen at random who continued rehabilitation in a hospital with an excellent reputation in this field (Wing, 1960). This was followed by a comparison (without random allocation) of industrial rehabilitation for patients from two hospitals with markedly different preparatory methods (Wing, Bennett & Denham, 1964). Another example with useful results concerns the evaluation of a hospital hostel (Hyde et al., 1987).

A further example illustrates a very powerful design. It was based on a sample, drawn from the Camberwell register, of people who had formerly been diagnosed as having a psychotic illness, had been discharged from hospital more than a year previously, were aged under 55 and—although eligible for employment—were out of work. Those who agreed were allocated at random to a preparatory period in a day hospital followed if suitable by a further course in a rehabilitation workshop, while the others received no extra help. The original register sample was then followed for 2 years (Wing L. et al., 1972). This combination of an epidemiological base, a strictly controlled design and a follow-up study of the whole sample whether included in the trial or not provides a stringent test of the service under review.

Most studies of services cannot spare the resources for this degree of sophistication, but comparative surveys with a population base are still worthwhile even if they do not involve random allocation, particularly if part of a wider scheme of evaluative research. In Camberwell (South Southwark), for a time during the late 1960s and 1970s, there was a concerted effort by administrators, professionals from the health and social services, and local research workers to find and fill the gaps in provision that had resulted from the usual haphazard development, complicated in this case by the presence of one postgraduate and two undergraduate teaching hospitals. The area was covered by a psychiatric case register, and evaluative studies were made of issues of substantial relevance to service planning. The results were of particular value for people with long-term disablement, who previously had not been well catered for within the area. Camberwell was one of the first inner London areas to cease admissions to the distant "catchment" mental hospital (Wing & Hailey, 1972). Many of the conclusions were acted upon. Subsequent studies have disclosed new kinds of need and so progress continues (Brewin et al., 1988; Wing, 1982).

The Concept of Need

It is beyond the scope of this chapter to review the rich and varied literature devoted to the measurement of variables needed for the evaluation of health services. In terms of the present analysis, the factors involved can be summarized as three parts of a continuous process of identifying and meeting need (Wing, 1972, 1978):

- identification of specific problems causing social disablement;

- identification of methods (including modification of the environment) likely to solve or ameliorate these problems;

- application of the appropriate forms of help by appropriate agents working in organised service settings; outcome is measured in terms of success in solving the problems.

A potential need for some form of help is defined in terms of the presence of problems. Problems are defined on the basis of minimum standards of functioning, below which it is assumed that people should generally not fall. Whether a potential need becomes actual depends on whether a knowledgeable person (usually a professional) considers that there is a method of solving or ameliorating it that is worth trying. This decision in turn depends on background theories (not always very consciously formulated) of how various kinds of problem come about. Methods of help are usually mediated through a helper (though self-help is often an option) who works in some sort of setting—office, residential unit, day centre, hospital ward, etc. The setting may itself have social features that can be regarded as influencing the process of treatment or care. The settings, collectively, together with the staff who work in or from them, form part of a set of more or less planned and organized services.

It is possible to try to operationalize the segments of this process in order to measure need for help, need for helpers and need for a service setting. Once these specifications have been made, it is relatively simple to decide whether needs are met or unmet, i.e. in need of further intervention. Using such a scheme depends crucially upon the availability of techniques of assessment that can identify

the nature of clinical, psychological and social components in disablement (Brewin & Wing, 1988; Brewin et al., 1987, 1988; Goldberg & Warburton, 1979; Weissman, 1975; Wing, 1989, Wing et al., 1989; Wykes & Sturt, 1986, 1987) and the ability to use them to specify appropriate forms of care.

Brewin and Mangen have described the needs-assessment system we have used in Camberwell to evaluate the care and services provided for long-term day attenders. It could also be useful in clinical audit (RCP, 1989) and be used in association with techniques drawn from health economics (O'Donnell, Maynard & Wright, 1988).

Examples of the wide range of factors that have to be measured in order to carry out evaluative research are given by Leff and in the two studies described below.

Evaluating the Closure of Hospitals

In the UK at the moment, one of the key issues in planning services is the part that should be played, if any, by large hospitals. Government policy is to replace the functions of those that are not conveniently placed to serve a district population. These should then be closed. All the problems of planning and evaluation outlined above are raised by such a policy. Two examples are given to illustrate the potential opportunities for rational planning to be gained from evaluative research in this field and the possible disadvantages that might accrue if the results were ignored.

Closing a Large Hospital for the Mentally Ill

The first example of closure concerns Powick Hospital, which used to serve the County of Worcester (since amalgamated into the County of Worcester and Hereford). The process of rundown to closure at the beginning of 1989 has not been evaluated in much detail and certainly not with a rationally constructed design as in the case of Darenth Park, described below. The interest of evaluation has centred upon the new pattern of services that was put into place before Powick was

Table 22.1. Three register areas. Resident inpatients, 31 December 1981, aged 15–64. Rate per 100,000 total population.

Register area	Jarman Index	Length of stay			Total
		<1 yr	1–5 yr	5+ yr	
Salford HD	37	34	18	46	98
Southampton HD	76	36	17	21	74
WDP Worcester HD	146 ⌐	19	5	18	42
Kidderminster HD	159 ⌐				

Source: Gibbons, Jennings & Wing, 1984

Table 22.2. Three register areas. Day attenders, 31 December 1981, aged 15–64. Rate per 100,000 total population.

Register area	Day hospital		Day centre		Total
	<1 yr	1+ yr	<1 yr	1+ yr	
Salford HD	25	19	21	16	81
Southampten HD	29	15	31	23	98
WDP	16	7	28	32	83

Source: Gibbons, Jennings & Wing, 1984

Table 22.3. WDP Area. Day attenders, diagnosis and problem score, 31 December 1981.

Diagnostic Group	Problem score		Total
	0–9	10 +	
Organic disorder	7	28	35
Mental retardation	9	8	17
Schizophrenia	26	29	55
Affective psychosis	12	11	23
Neurosis	36	9	45
Total	90	85	175

Source: Wing & Bennett, 1989

closed to admissions in 1978. This is shown in Figure 22.1. It comprises: new District General hospitals in the two main towns, Worcester and Kidderminster, each with a day hospital; peripheral day hospitals, day centres; hostels and group homes; and community psychiatric and social work services. The services are as complete as experts planning about 15 years ago could make them. The final act of closure (also of a rehabilitation hospital in the area, St. Wulstan's; but that is part of a different but overlapping story) was completed by the transfer of 200 residents to further new accomodation within the community. Probably no area in the UK is as well provided for, and none has had the benefit of extra funds from central goverment on such a scale.

Since, as part of the evaluation, a cumulative psychiatric case register was provided from 1973 (Hassall, Annual Reports), good population based descriptive statistics are available which illustrate in a practical way many of the points made earlier. This, rather than the more evaluative projects (Bennett, 1989; Wing & Bennett, 1989b), will be the focus of consideration here.

First, it is necessary to consider the population trends. Worcester comes second only to Oxford among the eight English and Welsh case-register areas for the amount of increase in the population during the 60 years before the 1981 census. It is an attractive area. Second, its sociographic profile is favourable; the Jarman rank for the Worcester Health District is 146 out of 192, while that for Kidderminster is 159. Third, the association with rates per 100,000 total population of resident inpatients aged 15–64, by length of stay, shown for three register areas in Table 22.1, is as predicted. For the reasons given earlier, the over-5-year rate cannot be taken at face value, but the rates for the under-1-year and the 1–5-year groups are markedly lower in the WDP area than in Southampton or Salford.

The situation in respect of day hospital and day centre places, as shown in Table 22.2, is somewhat different. The age group is again 15–64. Attenders are divided into those who had attended for under or over 1 year. Inasmuch as day hospital places are concerned, the WDP area has smaller numbers. Day centre places (provided by the local authority Social Services Department), on the other hand, are rather more plentiful than in Southampton and substantially more so than in Salford. In fact, there are more day centre than day hospital places in the WDP area, which is the reverse of the national position (Edwards & Carter, 1979).

The reason for making these points is twofold. First, the register figures provide a check on sampling for more intensive studies. This is one of the useful characteristics of registers. In fact the main focus of the WDP research carried out by our Unit was long-term day care, and the sampling was quite good. Second, the Worcester results can be placed into context. The reason for the high provision of day centre places is probably that the "norms" put forward in the goverment White Paper *Better Services for the Mentally Ill* were actually fulfilled for both types of day care, although a mixed rural and small urban area with low indices of deprivation probably did not require provision at national average levels.

Table 22.3 shows one of the possible consequences. Out of 175 long-term day attenders aged 16–64 whose problems were assessed by a research team, 35 had severe organic disorders, mostly neurological. Most were not attending day hospitals but day centres, where there were no nursing staff, no physiotherapists and no occupational therapists. Compared with attenders who had (or had had) psychiatric disorders, this group was characterized by high problem scores and unmet needs. One reason given for their presence at day centres was positive; that mixing people with different types of disability would decrease stigma and labelling. It also seems likely, however, that the fact of spare capacity played some part.

These observations are germane to the interpretation of the results of the more intensive research studies and to comparison of the WDP services with those elsewhere in the UK. It is important to note, however, that although generalization to other areas must be made with great circumspection, one kind of comparison can probably be made with fair

confidence. The whole range of problems to be found anywhere is likely also to be discovered in the WDP area, and conclusions drawn there would certainly be of interest elsewhere. The frequency, density and visibility of severe problems would have to be taken into account as well.

Closing a Large Hospital for People with a Mental Handicap

Severe mental handicap is a subject that tends to be avoided by psychiatrists and the problems of diagnosis and treatment, particularly of that sizable group of developmental disorders associated with severe social impairment that lies within the autistic spectrum, are not well understood. Darenth Park hospital in Kent has been running down since the 1920s. When a team of research workers from our Unit, led by Lorna Wing, started studying the process in 1980, it was already down to about 900 adult residents from its peak of over 2000. Detailed results of the first half of a 10-year study have now been published (Wing L., 1989).

The evaluation was theory driven, since earlier research had indicated patterns of disability among people with a mental handicap that required different types of environment in which to provide the most effective forms of help. The most able and sociable would benefit from regimes that promoted, as far as possible, choice of occupation and leisure activities and the use of ordinary community amenities. The most profoundly physically and mentally disabled, many of them nonmobile, required physiotherapy, treatment and protection. The presence of severe social impairment would necessitate much care and supervision, from staff with expert knowledge of how to cope with stereotyped behaviour, distress at changing regimes, and difficulty in conforming to "normal" expectations of behaviour and the kinds of activity that ought to be found enjoyable. Mixing these groups might not be in the interests any of them. Those with the least severe problems would be likely to be discharged first.

Since randomization to alternative facilities was not practicable, the design chosen was

1) to make an initial survey of all residents, their treatments and their settings,

Table 22.4. Rundown of Darenth Park Hospital, first phase.

Place at follow-up	Clinical group			Total
	"Aloof"	"Passive"	"Sociable"	
Movers				
Another hospital	26	10	44	80
Hostel, etc.	8	30	161	199
Stayers				
In Darenth	182	94	338	614
Total	216	134	543	893

Excludes 125 deaths; source: L. Wing, 1989.

2) to follow up all those who were transferred to alternative accommodation (the "movers,") and

3) to match them on predetermined variables—chosen because of their relevance to the hypotheses under test—with appropriate residents who remained behind ("stayers").

Remarkably good matching was obtained, the problem of bias due to selection for transfer being largely overcome by the fact that there were far fewer movers than stayers during this first phase. As fewer matches became available, the design changed to one of self-control, since there was a long period of baseline observation before transfer. A similar design was later adopted for the work at Friern and Claybury.

Table 22.4 summarizes the results at the half-way stage. Three subgroups are differentiated: two with disorders within the autistic spectrum (those who are "aloof" and those who are "passive"), the third not "socially impaired." These terms indicate differences that are crucial for the test of hypotheses (Wing L., 1984). The table shows that nearly 300 people moved, while over 600 stayed. Of the movers, 80 were transferred to another, smaller, hospital; nearly all the rest went to a variety of hostel settings. According to hypothesis, the aloof group was least likely to move and those who did were most likely to be transferred to the other hospital. These proportions were reversed for the sociable group, while the passive group was intermediate.

Compared with their initial status, movers experienced few or no changes as indicated by measures of skills, behaviour or life style.

Privacy and use of local specialist services improved somewhat for the passive and sociable groups, but opportunities for education, occupation and leisure decreased somewhat for the sociable group. When movers were compared with matched stayers, both initial and follow-up results were virtually identical within the three groups; in other words, there was no differential change between movers and stayers.

Since then, the process of transfer has been completed and Darenth Park hospital has closed. The research project has just over 1 year to run to complete 10 years of data collection. During this second phase, unlike during the first, residents have been moved to purpose built or preferentially selected forms of accommodation rather than to whatever existing settings could be found. Moreover, the planners have had the benefit of knowing the results of the first phase. The hypotheses, however, remain the same and will undergo strict test.

Conclusions

Evaluative research is much like other research in that scientific objectives (trial and the elimination of error) and scientific designs, sampling and methodology are used to test hypotheses. It differs from some, but by no means all, research in that the services under scrutiny are operated by people who are doing their best, perhaps in difficult circumstances, to help their patients or clients. If I may be excused a personal note, I have found that this has only rarely stood in the way of agreement to have a service examined or to give fair consideration to the results. Fully controlled experiments are the exception rather than the rule, but discriminating attention to the background of descriptive statistics and to the choice of the most appropriate design and methods can overcome many of the problems. Above all, replication and the accumulation of hard fact is most likely to lead to the work being taken seriously. At a time when the traditional pattern of psychiatric services is being challenged all over Europe, there is an opportunity for research to inform planning.

References

Audit Commission (1986). *Making a reality of community care. The audit commission for local authorities in England and Wales.* London: HMSO.

Bennett, C. (1989). The Worcester Development Project. General practitioner satisfaction with a new community service. *Journal of the Royal College of General Practitioners, 39,* 106–109.

Brewin, C. R., & Wing, J. K. (1988). *The MRC needs for care assessment manual.* London: MRC Social Psychiatry Unit.

Brewin, C. R., Wing, J. K., Mangan, S., Brugha, T., & MacCarthy, B. (1987). Principles and practice of measuring needs in the long term mentally ill. The MRC needs for care assessment. *Psychological Medicine, 17,* 971–981.

Brewin, C. R., Wing, J. K., Mangan, S., Brugha, T., MacCarthy, B., & Lesage, A. (1988). Needs for care among the long term mentally ill. A report from the Camberwell High Contact Survey. *Psychological Medicine, 18,* 457–468.

Buglass, D., Duffy, K., & Kreitman, N. (1980). *A register of social and medical indices by local government area in Edinburgh and Lothian.* Edinburgh: Scottish Office Central Research Papers.

Brown, G. W., Bone, M., Dalison, B., & Wing, J. K. (1966). *Schizophrenia and social care.* London: Oxford University Press.

Cooper, J. E. (1989). Information for planning. Case registers and Körner. In J. K. Wing (Ed.), *Health services planning and research. Contributions from psychiatric case registers* (pp. 115–120). London: Gaskell.

Der, G. (1989). The effect of population changes on long stay in-patient rates. In J. K. Wing (Ed.), *Health services planning and research. Contributions from psychiatric case registers* (pp. 53–57). London: Gaskell.

Department of Health and Social Security (1975). *Better services for the mentally ill. Cmnd. 6233.* London: HMSO.

Durkheim, E. (1897). *Le suicide: Etude de sociologie.* Paris: Alcan. (Trans. Spaulding J. A. and Simpson G., 1952. London: Routledge.)

Edwards, C., & Carter, J. (1979). Day services and the mentally ill. In J. K. Wing & M. R. Olsen (Eds.), *Community care for the mentally disabled* (pp. 36–59). Oxford: Oxford University Press.

Gibbons, J., Jennings, C., & Wing, J. K. (Eds.) (1984). *Psychiatric care in 8 register areas.* Southampton: University Department of Psychiatry.

Goldberg, E. M., & Warburton, R. W. (1979). *Ends and means in social work. The development and outcome of a case review system for social workers.* London: National Institute of Social Work.

Hare, E. H. (1956). Mental illness and social conditions in Bristol. *Journal of Mental Science, 102,* 349–357.

Hassall, C. *Annual reports of the Worcester Case Register.* Birmingham: University Department of Psychiatry.

Hirsch, S. R. (Chairman) (1988). *Psychiatric beds and resources. Factors influencing bed use and service planning* (Report of a Working Party). London: Gaskell.

ten Horn, G. H., Giel, R., & Gulbinat, W. (Eds) (1986). *Psychiatric case registers in public health. A worldwide inventory 1960–1985.* Amsterdam: Elsevier.

Hyde, C., Bridges, K., Goldberg, D., Lowson, K., Sterling, C., & Farquhar, B. (1987). The evaluation of a hostel ward. A controlled study using modified cost-benefit analysis. *British Journal of Psychiatry, 151,* 805–812.

Jarman, B. (1983). Identification of underprivileged areas. *British Medical Journal, 286,* 1705–1709.

Jarman, B. (1984). Validation and distribution of scores. *British Medical Journal, 289,* 1587–1592.

Leff, J., Kuipers, L., Berkowitz, R., & Sturgeon, D. (1985). A controlled trial of social intervention in the families of schizophrenic patients. Two year follow-up. *British Journal of Psychiatry, 146,* 594–600.

Odegaard, O. (1946). Marriage and mental disease. *Journal of Mental Science, 99,* 778.

O'Donnell, O., Maynard, A., & Wright, K. (1988). *The economic evaluation of mental health care. A review* (Discussion Paper 51). York: Centre for Health Economics.

Patrick, D. L., & Peach, H. (1989). *Disablement in the Community.* Oxford: Oxford University Press.

Paykel, E. S., Mangen, S. P., Griffith, J. H., & Burns, T. P. (1982). Community psychiatric nursing for neurotic patients: A controlled trial. *British Journal of Psychiatry, 140,* 531–581.

Royal College of Physicians (1989). *Report of the working party on medical audit.* London: Author.

Sainsbury, P. (1955). *Suicide in London. An ecological study* (Maudsley Monograph No. 1). London: Chapman and Hall.

Stein, L. (1957). Social class gradient in schizophrenia. *British Journal of Preventive and Social Medicine, 11,* 181.

Weissman, M. (1975). The assessment of social adjustment by patient self report. *Archives of General Psychiatry, 32,* 357–365.

Wing, J. K. (1960). A pilot experiment on the rehabilitation of long-hospitalised male schizophrenic patients. *British Journal of Preventive and Social Medicine, 14,* 173–180.

Wing, J. K. (1972). Principles of evaluation. In J. K. Wing & A. M. Hailey (Eds.), *Evaluating a community psychiatric service. The Camberwell Register, 1964–1971* (pp. 11–40). London: Oxford University Press.

Wing, J. K. (1978). Medical and social science and medical and social care. In J. Barnes & N. Connelly (Eds.), *Social care research* (pp. 123–137). London: Bedford Square Press.

Wing, J. K. (Ed.) (1982). *Long-term community care: Experience in a London borough* (Psychological Medicine Monograph, Suppl. No. 2). Cambridge: University Press.

Wing, J. K. (1989). The measurement of social disablement. The MRC social behaviour and social role performance schedules. Social psychiatry and epidemiology. *Social Psychiatry, 24,* 173–178.

Wing, J. K., Babor, T., Brugha, T., Burke, J., Cooper, J., Giel, R., Jablensky, A., Regier, D., & Sartorius, N. (1990). SCAN: Schedules for Clinical Assessment in Neuropsychiatry. *Archives of General Psychiatry,* in press.

Wing, J.K., & Bennett, C. (Eds) (1989). *Long-term care in the Worcester Development Project* (Report on Research. Penultimate Draft). Unpublished report circulated for comment, January 1989.

Wing, J. K., Bennett, D. H., & Denham, J. (1964). *The industrial rehabilitation of long-stay schizophrenic patients. Medical Res. Council Memo, No. 42.* London: HMSO.

Wing, J. K., & Brown, G. W. (1970). *Institutionalism and schizophrenia.* London: Cambridge University Press.

Wing, J. K., & Freudenberg, R. K. (1961). The response of severely ill chronic schizophrenic patients to social stimulation. *American Journal of Psychiatry, 118,* 311–322.

Wing, J. K., & Hailey, A. M. (Eds.) (1972). *Evaluating a community psychiatric service. The Camberwell Register, 1964–1971.* London: Oxford University Press.

Wing, L. (1984). Psychoses of early childhood. In J. K. Wing & L. Wing (Eds.), *Psychoses of uncertain aetiology* (pp. 185–190). London: Cambridge University Press.

Wing, L. (1989). *Closing Darenth Park Hospital.* London: Gower.

Wing, L., Wing, J. K., Stevens, B., & Griffiths, D. (1972). An epidemiological and experimental evaluation of industrial rehabilitation of chronic psychotic patients in the community. In J. K. Wing & A. M. Hailey (Eds.), *Evaluating a community psychiatric service. The Camberwell Register, 1964–1971* (pp. 283–308). London: Oxford University Press.

World Health Organization (1980). *International classification of impairments, disabilities and handicaps.* Geneva: WHO.

Wykes, T., & Sturt, E. (1986). The measurement of social behaviour in in psychiatric patients. An assessment of the reliability and validity of the SBS schedule. *British Journal of Psychiatry, 148,* 1–11.

Wykes, T., & Sturt, E. (1987). Assessment schedules for chronic psychiatric patients. *Psychological Medicine, 17,* 485–493.

Person Index

Subject Index

OCEAN'S DEPTHS YOU
SEE FROM SURFACE
PREDICTABLE AS
THE MOON TURNS TIDES.

ANON

CLOPIXOL®

zuclopenthixol

Your broad antipsychotic

Lundbeck

FACING THE FUTURE TOGETHER

Further information is available on request from:

LUNDBECK LTD. LUNDBECK HOUSE, HASTINGS STREET, LUTON, BEDS LU1 5BE

SKIES SURRENDER TO
AN UPWARD GLANCE
RAISING HEADS
LIFTING MOODS

ANON

DEPIXOL® *Injection*
cis(Z)- flupenthixol decanoate

For the withdrawn schizophrenic

Lundbeck

FACING THE FUTURE TOGETHER

Further information is available on request from:
LUNDBECK LTD. LUNDBECK HOUSE. HASTINGS STREET, LUTON, BEDS LU1 5BE